"Stroll from your campsite directly to a sandy beach extending miles in either direction. The energy of crashing waves, the extensive coastal views, the beauty of the open ocean—these are the reasons to come here."

—*Half Moon Bay State Beach, Page 80*

"Protecting the largest stand of old-growth redwoods south of Humboldt County, Big Basin features a forest world like no other in the Bay Area."

—*Big Basin Redwoods State Park, Page 97*

"In the middle of the Bay, less than 5 miles from downtown San Francisco, Angel Island rises like a jewel. Accessible only by boat, the island offers a backpacking experience unlike any other, where vistas sweep 360 degrees around the Bay, gentle paths mingle with history, and unique rock outcrops tell unusual tales."

—*Angel Island State Park, Page 163*

"It is as it was. Rolling hills cleft by valleys, split by ridges, battered by the sea. A land of sweeping vistas, vibrant life, and dramatic geology in a protected natural world isolated from the bustle of the Bay Area."

—*The Marin Headlands, Page 169*

"Wildcat Beach is arguably the most remote stretch of accessible coastline in the entire Bay Area. Bounded to the south and north by the sheer escarpments of Double Point and Millers Point, respectively, it is flanked by cliffs of twisted geology and can only be easily accessed in one spot—Wildcat Camp."

—*Point Reyes National Seashore, Page 199*

"Undulating through open serpentine grasslands dotted with rock outcrops and fabulous spring wildflower displays, the open trail provides far-reaching views as it traverses along the upper slopes of the Alameda Creek drainage."

—*The Ohlone Trail, Page 298*

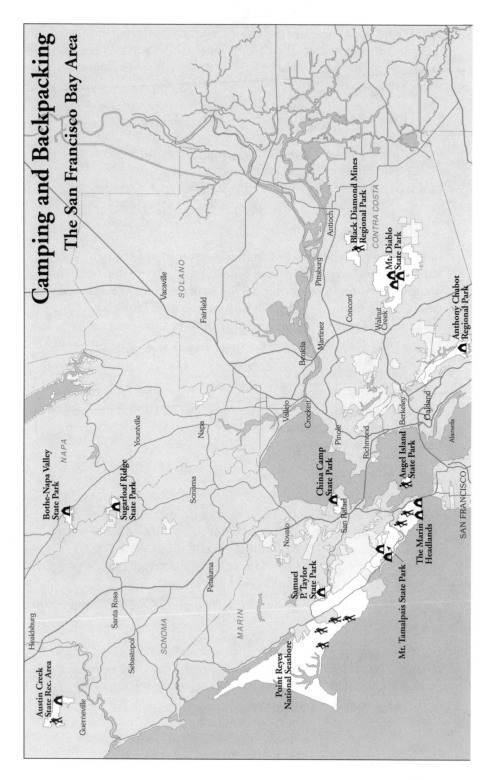

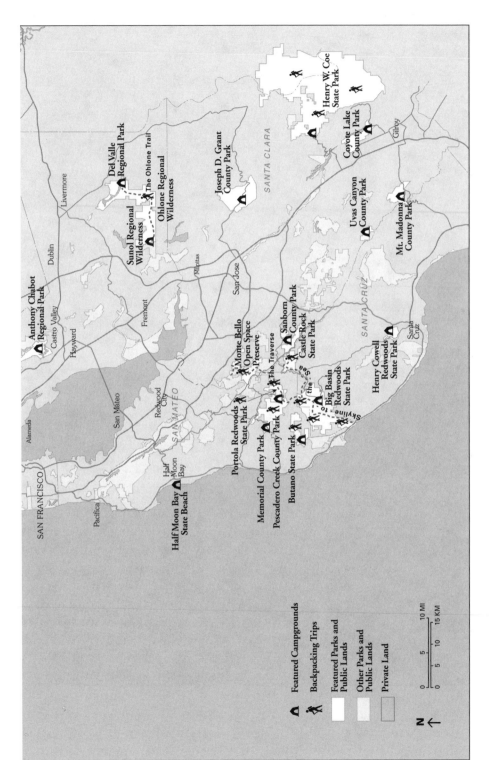

Camping &
Backpacking the
San Francisco
Bay Area

Matt Heid

 WILDERNESS PRESS · BERKELEY, CA

Camping & Backpacking the San Francisco Bay Area

1st EDITION September 2003

Copyright © 2003 by Matt Heid

Front cover photo (background) © 2003 by Jim Lundgren
Front cover photos (insets) © 2003 by Matt Heid
Back cover photos © 2003 by Matt Heid
Interior photos, except where noted, by Matt Heid
Location maps and camping section maps: Ben Pease / Pease Press
Backpacking maps: created using TOPO! Interactive Maps on CD-ROM from
   National Geographic Maps. Trails were drawn by Matt Heid.
Cover design: Larry B. Van Dyke
Book design: Scott Perry / Archetype
Book editor: Kris Kaiyala

ISBN 0-89997-295-0
UPC 7-19609-97295-2

Manufactured in the United States of America

Published by: **Wilderness Press**
            1200 5th Street
            Berkeley, CA 94710
            (800) 443-7227; FAX (510) 558-1696
            info@wildernesspress.com
            www.wildernesspress.com

Visit our website for a complete listing of our books and for ordering information.

Cover photos: *(front background)* Oak tree in Mt. Diablo State Park
                (front insets, l to r) View of the Golden Gate from Angel Island State Park,
                                The Ohlone Trail in Del Valle Regional Park,
                                California poppy
                (back) The Ohlone Wilderness
Frontispiece: Perles Beach Moment

Top left:
Oak View site,
Sunol Backpack
Area

Top right:
Divide Meadow,
Point Reyes
National
Seashore

Middle:
Mississippi Lake
campsite, Henry
Coe State Park

Bottom:
Alamere Falls,
Point Reyes
National
Seashore

Table of Contents

Trips by Theme

EPIC VIEWS

WATERFALLS

WILDFLOWERS

WILDLIFE

GOOD FOR DOGS

LAKES

CREEKS AND RIVERS

FISHING

BOATING

GEOLOGY

REDWOOD FOREST

OAK WOODLAND

LESSER-TRAVELED DESTINATIONS

ACCESSIBLE BY PUBLIC TRANSPORTATION

2-DAY BACKPACKING TRIPS

3-5 DAY BACKPACKING TRIPS

AUTHOR'S FAVORITES

Campgrounds

Backpacking Trips

Preface

Hundreds of parks, preserves, and protected open spaces infuse the San Francisco Bay Area with a world of unparalleled natural wonder. Straddling an incredible range of geographic and ecological diversity, it provides avenues for adventure in all terrains, seasons, and environments. An overnight journey only deepens the outdoor experience. With more than two dozen public campgrounds and over 20 backpacking trips accessible within a two-hour drive from any point in the Bay Area, the options for reflection and recreation are numerous and spectacular.

Managed by nearly a dozen different governing agencies, the parks of the Bay Area also present a challenging logistics puzzle. Regulations, sources of information, and reservation systems vary widely by park district. The proximity of millions of people means that advance reservations are required for many destinations. Unraveling this complicated milieu on your own can be difficult and frustrating.

This book is the answer—a comprehensive guide to every public campground and backpacking adventure in the San Francisco Bay Area. Within these pages you'll find detailed information on regulations, contact information, crowds, and reservations for every overnight destination—plus human history, natural history, trail descriptions, fun activities, maps, and lots of other good stuff. There is no better time to explore the magic of the Bay Area outdoors than right now. Have fun!

Acknowledgments

Thanks first go to the innumerable rangers and park volunteers who aided in this book's research. Thank you for being the caring stewards of our parklands. Specific thanks goes to: Gerrie Kunin, Steep Ravine; Eric Chase, Samuel P. Taylor State Park; Bill Mentzer, Mt. Tamalpais State Park; Bob Poirier, Cathy Petrick, and Margaret Badger, Marin Headlands; Patrick Robards, China Camp State Park; John Allen, Bothe-Napa Valley State Park; Fina Olson, Half Moon Bay State Beach; Sandy Jones, Sugarloaf Ridge State Park; Matthew Del Carlo, Memorial County Park; Candice Regen, Henry Cowell Redwoods State Park; Annie Morrisette, Anthony Chabot Regional Park; Ron Brichont, Joseph D. Grant County Park; Vita Lawson, Austin Creek State Recreation Area; Ken Huie, Angel Island State Park; Bob Kanagaki, Black Diamond Mines Regional Park; Dave Jones, Big Basin Redwoods State Park; Barry Breckling and Patrick Goodrich, Henry W. Coe State Park; Diny Van der Velden, Hidden Villa Hostel; Art and Sylvia Carroll, Sanborn Hostel; and Crista Francis, Point Reyes Hostel.

My deepest gratitude goes to all of you who have supported me over the years. To Gretchen, with all my love. To Heid, the greatest brother ever. To Mom, Dad, Joann, and Sid, for always being there. To Grandpa, for your kindness and love of the outdoors. To Pogen, for 4½ wonderful years at 15B. To Analise, for your boundless positive energy. To Big Tom, for your generosity and gamin' skills. To Trevor, for telling it like it is. To E, for keeping it real. To all the other coveheads: Heart and Lissen; Doug, Elizabeth, and Jasper; Marcy, Troy, and Ida; Aaron; Mike and Shannon; and Arno. And to the rest of the family crew: Marie, Marsha, Amber, and Lindsey. Thank you also to the Ela family, and Helen "Nana" Powers, for your kindness and generosity.

It has been a privilege to work with the many wonderful people of REI Berkeley. I will never forget your endless enthusiasm, support, and encouragement. Thank you Jeremy Aaron,

Brett Anderson, Polly Bolling, Brad and Rachel Bostrom, George-Anne Bowers, Joshua Brown, Sallie Chestnut, Howard Chin, Rich Davies, Ed Devine, Martin and Margaret Dickinson, Libby DiGennaro, Susan Fraimow-Wong, Rebecca Fehr, Kurt Feilke, Randy Kermode, Garry Klein, Dan Lowry, Steve Noble, Karin Reese, Migmar Sherpa, Bonnie Stich, Ruth Tretbar, Erik Vance, Chris Von Marschall, Sage Wike-Brown, and everybody else at the best REI ever!

To all the folks at Wilderness Press, thank you for making it such a great place to work. To Mike Jones, for your easy-going style, trust, and support of my adventures. To Jannie Dresser, for caring so deeply. To Jessica Lage, for our life conversations. To Box Dixon, for never-ending warehouse fun. To Teddy Hargrove, for telling it straight. To Matthew Chilcot, for your humor and insights. To Larry Van Dyke, for two great covers. To Jaan Hitt, for dealing with my computer snafus. Thank you also to Kris Kaiyala, for improving this book until the very end; and to Garth, Joe, Jessica Benner, and Laura Keresty.

And to Everybody, I say: Live for your passions and follow your dreams, for reality is only as reality seems. Best of luck to you all!

— *Matt Heid*
June 2003

READ THIS!

An important aspect of outdoor adventuring is the presence of potential dangers and risks. Even in the peaceable San Francisco Bay Area, this is true. Ensure your safety whenever you head outdoors and set out on a trail. The fact that a trail is described in this book does not mean that it will be safe for *you*. Trails vary greatly in difficulty and in the degree of conditioning and agility you need to enjoy them safely. Routes may change and trail conditions may have deteriorated since this book was published. A trail that is safe on a dry day, or that is relatively easy for a fit hiker, may be completely unsafe for a beginner or in bad weather.

Minimize your risks by becoming knowledgeable about your surroundings and knowing your limitations. Know where you are going and what variables you might encounter. Be prepared and alert. Although we don't have bears in the Bay Area anymore, and tigers are not native to North America, we still have an occasional mountain lion sighting. We also have poisonous plants, dangerous road crossings, and unfriendly or threatening individuals. Anticipate adverse weather conditions, like the late afternoon downpour that is predicted even though it seems to be a perfectly sunny day. There's no way this book can give you a full treatise on outdoor safety, but good books are available and there are classes that cover trail safety, survival techniques, and first-aid.

Tell us what you really think Something unclear, outdated, or just plain wrong in this book? Have a good suggestion for making it better? We welcome reader feedback on all of our publications. If we use your suggestion, we'll send you a free book. Please email comments to: update@wildernesspress.com

Dedicated to the Cove
and coveheads everywhere

Looking north to Antioch,
Black Diamond Mines Regional Park

How To Use This Book

For the purposes of this book, the Bay Area is divided into three geographic regions—the North Bay, Santa Cruz Mountains, and East of the Bay—and both campgrounds and backpacking trips are listed in separate sections in that regional order. The campgrounds are featured first, followed by the backpacking trips, and locator maps are included for both activities. Each campground and backpacking trip utilizes a standard format, described in greater detail below.

To prepare for your adventure, first read the chapter *Safety, Gear, and the Wilderness Ethic.* Those unfamiliar with the outdoor world of the Bay Area or unsure about where to visit should consult the chapter *Where Should I Go?* For those looking for a specific feature, the campgrounds and backpacking trips are grouped by theme after the Table of Contents. Otherwise just flip through the pages and evaluate each adventure based on the standard information provided.

CAMPGROUNDS

This book features every public campground in the Bay Area—those located on public land and managed by a government park agency. (Private campgrounds and RV parks are listed in Appendix D.) Most campgrounds allow you to drive up and park directly at your site, while a few are walk-in only and located a short distance from the parking area. Depending on the park and governing agency, most sites cost $8-16 and can accommodate a maximum of 6-10 people. Group campsites (15-100+ people) are

Oaks above a Del Valle site

available at most campgrounds (a complete list can be found in Appendix A). Each campground is described with a standard, easily understood template. Going from top to bottom, the template is divided into three parts—Campground Description, The Details, and Giving Back:

Campground Description

Title. The name of the park containing the featured campground.

Highlights. The best features of the campground and surrounding landscape. The reasons to visit.

The Campground. An overview of the campground itself. Site locations, privacy, noise, and climate are discussed in the opening paragraphs, followed by the campground's natural history—flora, fauna, geology, etc.

Crowds and Reservations. The times when the campground is likely to be full, empty, or completely reserved in advance. Contact information for reservations is provided plus details on how and when to make them. (For a general overview of Bay Area crowds and park use, see *Beating the Crowds* below.)

Trails. A discussion of the hiking and biking opportunities available in the park, plus recommendations.

Other Fun Activities. Amenities other than hiking and biking trails that are available within or very near the featured park, such as swimming pools, horseback rides, astronomical observatories, elephant seals, and historic railroads.

To Reach the Park. Concise driving directions. This book assumes you have a basic highway map of the Bay Area. Since every car's odometer is slightly different, please note that mileages may vary between those listed here and in your vehicle. If public transportation is available to the park, it will be listed. (Parks accessible by public transportation are also listed in *Trips by Theme* at the beginning of the book.)

The Details

Governing Agency. Contact information for the governing agency that manages the park, usually park district headquarters.

Park Contact Information. Provided only if contact information for the park itself differs from the governing agency. For specific questions about a park or campground, it is often better to contact the park directly.

Visitor Center. If there is one it will be mentioned here. Opening hours are included but note that schedules are subject to change.

Sites. Lists the numbers of each type of campsite available. Walk-in sites require parking the vehicle in a nearby lot and walking a short distance to the site (usually less than 100 yards). Hike/bike sites are designated for those traveling by muscle power. Handicapped-accessible sites (nearly every campground provides at least one) are wheelchair friendly and reserved for campers whose mobility is limited by a physical disability. The number of trailer and RV sites, and the maximum length permitted, will be mentioned here as well.

Costs. Overnight fees are always listed per site rather than per person. All other applicable fees will be mentioned, including any extra vehicle fees, dog fees, boat launch fees, etc. Senior discounts will be listed where applicable. Lastly, for those intrigued by the park but uninterested in staying the night, the day-use fee is included.

BEATING THE CROWDS

According to the 2000 Census, more than 7 million people live in the 10 greater Bay Area counties (Alameda, Contra Costa, Marin, Napa, San Francisco, San Mateo, Santa Clara, Santa Cruz, Solano, and Sonoma). Most of this dense collection of humanity exists around the common American schedule of busy weekdays, recreational weekends, and summer vacation. For the nearby and easily accessible parks of the Bay Area, this means that weekends are significantly—often exponentially—busier than weekdays. The crowd contrast between a weekday and weekend can be startling, with solitude one day and human torrents the next.

Summer is by far the busiest season. Most parks are busy on weekdays and absolutely packed on weekends and holidays from Memorial Day through Labor Day. Almost every campground in the Bay Area is fully reserved on weekends during this time—advance planning is essential. Weekend crowds reduce as fall fades into winter and slowly increase once again as the rainy season tapers off in spring. Expect some full weekends in popular campgrounds and backpacking destinations in April, May, and October but weekdays will be quiet everywhere from September through May. Overnight use is very slight during the magical winter months from November through March.

Park usage varies widely. Parks in Marin County are visited considerably more than those in any other region in the Bay Area due to their scenic beauty, large contiguous acreage, and easy accessibility from much of the Bay Area. Weekends are particularly manic. Parks in the Santa Cruz Mountains and East of the Bay are more lightly visited and better for finding peace and quiet. Note that a few campgrounds and trail camps are first-come, first-serve year-round—perfect for last-minute trips. These destinations, as well as those more lightly traveled, are listed in *Trips by Theme* at the beginning of the book.

Group Sites. Many campgrounds offer sites specifically for large groups. This section lists the number of group sites; their location, capacity, and costs; reservation information; and any restrictions that may apply to the type of group using the site. Note that many parks without family campgrounds offer group sites—these are listed in Appendix A: *Group Campgrounds of the Bay Area.*

Months Open/Closed. Most campgrounds remain open year-round, but a few close during the wet winter months.

Maps. The recommended maps for exploring the surrounding park. Note that a free or inexpensive ($1-2) park map is usually available at the park itself and is generally adequate for hiking and exploration.

Facilities. Unless specifically mentioned, every campground provides bathrooms, picnic tables, and potable water. This section lists any additional amenities, including hot showers, pay phones, RV facilities, and availability of firewood for purchase.

Regulations. All the nitty-gritty rules concerning fires, dogs, bikes, alcohol, and fishing, followed by the maximum number of people and vehicles per site, check-out time, maximum length of stay, and other relevant rules. The parks of the Bay Area receive considerable use and pressure from the millions who live here. Keep in mind that park regulations are designed to preserve and protect parklands for future generations. Please respect them.

Giving Back

Had an uplifting experience while camping? Interested in contributing some of your time or money to the park so that others may enjoy it as you did? This final part of the template lists at least one non-profit group (and its contact information) that works closely with the featured park through volunteer work or financial aid. Here is your chance to give something back to the natural world of the Bay Area.

BACKPACKING TRIPS

With the exception of Henry W. Coe State Park, all backpacking trips in the Bay Area require spending the night at a designated trail camp. Locations specifically designed for backcountry camping, most trail camps offer amenities

Above Gerbode Valley, Marin Headlands

like picnic tables, food lockers, pit toilets, potable water, and obvious tent sites. Most trail camps require advance reservations in order to secure a spot and a small fee is charged for their use (roughly $2-8 per person). Note that stiff fines are levied on those caught camping outside of designated areas. While stoves are allowed at all trail camps, campfires are almost always prohibited. Dogs are prohibited on nearly every backpacking trip in the Bay Area; Black Diamond Mines Regional Park is the only exception.

Most backpacking trips are described using a standard, easily understood template. Going from top to bottom, the template is divided into three parts— The Header, Hike Description, and Listings. Note that the template may vary slightly given the needs of specific parks or hikes.

The Header

Title. Usually the park containing the hike, or a commonly used name for the hike (e.g. Skyline-to-the-Sea).

Highlights. What makes the trip special, unique, and impossible to resist.

The Park(s). The specific park(s) the hiking route visits.

Distance. The total mileage of the hike. For point-to-point hikes, the one-way distance is listed.

Total Elevation Gain/Loss. The amount of climbing and descending on the hike, measured in vertical feet. It can be significantly greater than the difference between the hike's lowest and highest points.

Trip Length. This is the recommended number of days for the trip. A range of days is listed for trips requiring more than two days to complete. The lower number indicates the amount of time a fit individual can complete the trip hiking daily for long periods of time (8-12 hours). The higher number indicates the recommended amount of time for slower hikers or for those who want to hike less per day (4-8 hours) and spend more time in camp and on hiking breaks. While the total number of hours required for hiking is not included, it may be estimated using the following guidelines: A reasonably fit hiker can expect to cover 2-3 miles per hour over level ground and on gradual descents, 1-2 miles per hour on gradual climbs, and only about 1 mile—or 750-1000 feet of elevation—per hour on the steepest ascents.

Difficulty. This book utilizes a five-star rating system. Most featured trips travel obvious, well-signed trails that are seldom rough, rocky, or uneven. This makes hiking in the Bay Area considerably less challenging than other outdoor destinations and few of the hikes present significant difficulties. Most backpacking trips fall in the two-to-three-star category and are consequently suitable for anybody in decent shape. Here are the general criteria for each level:

★ *Easy.* Short and level, these hikes can be done by nearly anybody and have less than 500 feet of elevation gain.

★★   *Moderate.* Shorter hikes with approximately 500-1500 feet of total elevation gain along good, easy-to-follow trails. Suitable for any reasonably fit hiker.

★★★   *Strenuous.* Longer hikes with roughly 1000-2000 feet of elevation gain per day on more challenging trails. Good fitness required.

★★★★   *Challenging.* A very strenuous hike involving considerable and constant elevation gain and loss of 2000-3000 feet per day on well-maintained, easy-to-follow trails. The Ohlone Trail and The Traverse are the only two hikes that fall into this category.

Looking north from Del Valle Regional Park, the Ohlone Trail

★★★★★   *Epic.* An adventure with considerable and constant elevation gain and loss in remote regions on challenging trails. Route finding and bushwhacking required. Experienced wilderness users only. The excursion into Henry W. Coe State Park's Orestimba Wilderness is the only trip that falls into this category.

Best Times. The ideal season(s) to undertake the hike. Note that many of the trips can be done outside of the times listed, but weather or crowds will probably make them far less appealing.

Recommended Maps. Most hikes can be completed using only the maps in this book or those available at the trailhead, but greater safety and enjoyment come with more detailed and comprehensive maps—especially on hikes that traverse multiple parks or venture into more remote areas. The appropriate USGS 7.5-minute topographic maps are listed here, along with any other recommended reference maps.

Symbols. Used to quickly describe key attributes of the hike.

⟷   An out-and-back hike that returns to the starting trailhead by retracing its route.

◯   A loop or semi-loop that retraces little or none of its route to return to the starting trailhead.

⟶   A point-to-point hike is one that ends at a different trailhead. Two cars or a shuttle are required to return to the starting trailhead.

🚶   A hike bearing this good-for-children symbol will be short, easy, and appropriate for a first-time backpacking experience.

Hike Description

The hike description is broken down into four main sections:

Hike Overview. A general description of the hike, discussing seasonal differences, trail highlights, and whether the trail camp is accessible by bicycle and good for bikepacking.

The Trail Camps. Detailed descriptions of the trail camps, including location, natural surroundings, and facilities. Information about reservations and crowds is also included in this section, as well as regulations concerning capacity, maximum length of stay, and other restrictions.

To Reach the Trailhead. Concise driving directions to the trailhead. This book assumes you have a basic highway map of the Bay Area. Since every car's odometer is different, please note that mileages may vary between those listed here and in your vehicle. If *public transportation* is available to the park, it also will be listed here. Parks accessible by public transportation are also listed in *Trips by Theme* at the beginning of the book.

Trail Description. A detailed narrative of the hike itself. Parenthetical notations such as (3849′) indicate elevation in feet. Parenthetical notations such as (3.2/1450) are included in the text at all trail junctions and important landmarks. The first number represents the total distance traveled from the trailhead in miles, the second identifies the elevation of the location in feet.

Listings

Park Contact Information. Address, phone number, and web site for the park(s) featured on the hike. If there is a visitor center, it will be mentioned here. Opening hours are included but be aware that these are subject to change.

Giving Back. A list of non-profit groups that help support the parks through volunteer work or financial aid. Contact information is provided. Here is your chance to give something back to the natural world of the Bay Area so that others may enjoy the experience as you did.

THE MAPS IN THIS BOOK

The backpacking maps in this book were created using the California State Series TOPO! software (2000) from National Geographic Maps and may be downloaded for free at www.maps.nationalgeographic.com/topo. While the maps are designed to be sufficient for completing the featured hike, they do not show the myriad other trails that lace nearly every park in the Bay Area. Most hikers will want to purchase the Recommended Maps. Standard symbols are utilized on each map. Note that the maps are reproduced at different sizes, and that scale (indicated at the bottom) varies from map to map.

See map legends on pages 42 and 162.

Where *did* I park my car?

Safety, Gear, and the Wilderness Ethic

SAFETY

Venturing into the outdoors entails a degree of risk. Preparation, knowledge, and awareness help mitigate this risk. The following section outlines the common hazards encountered in the Bay Area outdoors and discusses how to approach them.

Wildlife Hazards

Rattlesnakes. Common throughout the eastern Bay Area, these venomous creatures like to bask on hot rocks in the sun and typically begin to emerge from winter hibernation as temperatures warm in spring. They usually flee at the first sight of people and will only attack if threatened. Be wary when hiking off-trail and don't put your hands where you can't see them when scrambling on rocky slopes. Rattlesnake bites are rarely fatal. If bitten, the goal is to reduce the rate at which the poison circulates through your body—try and remain calm, keep the bite site below the level of your heart, remove any constricting items (rings, watches, etc.) from the soon-to-be swollen extremity, and *do not* apply ice or chemical cold to the bite as this can cause further damage to the surrounding tissue. Seek medical attention as quickly as possible.

Ticks. These parasites love brushy areas and are common throughout the Bay Area, especially during the rainy season. Always perform regular body checks when hiking through tick country. If you find a tick attached to you, *do not* try to pull it out with your fingers or pinch the body; this can inject tick fluid under the skin and increase the risk of infection. Using an appropriate tool, gently pull the tick out by lifting upward from the base of the body where it is attached to the skin. Pull straight out until the tick releases and do not twist or jerk as this may break the mouth parts off under your skin. A small V cut in the side of a credit card works well for this operation.

Ticks are known for transmitting *Lyme Disease,* but only one of the 48 tick species found in California is capable of transmitting it—the diminutive western black-legged tick—and chances are low for exposure. Even if you are bitten, an infected tick must be attached for a minimum of six hours in order to transmit the disease. Caused by a spirochete, Lyme Disease can be life-threatening if not diagnosed in its early phases. Common early symptoms include fatigue, chills and fever, headache, muscle and joint pain, swollen lymph nodes, and a blotchy skin rash that clears centrally to produce a characteristic ring shape 3-30 days after exposure. If you fear that you have been exposed to Lyme Disease, consult a doctor immediately.

Giardia. Giardia lamblia is a microscopic organism occasionally found in backcountry water sources. Existing in a dormant cyst while in the water, it develops in the gastrointestinal tract upon being consumed and can cause diarrhea, excessive flatulence, foul-smelling excrement, nausea, fatigue, and abdominal cramps. While the risk of contraction is slight, the potential consequences are worth preventing. All water taken from the backcountry should be purified with a filter, a chemical treatment, or by boiling for 1-3 minutes.

Raccoons, Skunks, and Foxes. While not a threat to humans, these nocturnal varmints are a major hazard for food supplies and have learned that campgrounds and trail camps are prime locations for free meals. Never leave your food unattended and always store it somewhere safe at night. Food lockers are provided at most campgrounds and trail camps; otherwise hang it from a nearby tree. Bringing food inside the tent with you is not a good idea.

Mountain Lions. While they exist throughout most of the Bay Area, mountain lions are rarely seen and pose minimal threat. If you do happen to encounter a mountain lion acting in an aggressive manner, make yourself look as large as possible and do not run away.

Bears. Surprisingly a bear was spotted in Point Reyes in May 2003. Eliminated from the region in the 1800s by unregulated hunting, the black bear population *may* be expanding back into its former Bay Area habitat.

Plant Hazards

Poison Oak. If you learn to recognize only one plant in California, it better be this one. Poison oak grows throughout the Bay Area and is particularly abundant in oak woodland and coastal scrub environments. A low-lying shrub or bush, its glossy, oak-like leaves always grow in clusters of three and turn bright red in the fall before dropping off in the winter. Both the leaves and stems contain an oil that causes a strong allergic reaction in most people, creating a maddening and long-lived itchy rash that can spread across the body. You should wash thoroughly with soap after any exposure and clean clothing

JESSICA LAGE

that may have come in contact with the plant. Residual oil on pants is a prime rash culprit. The presence of poison oak is noted in the hike and campground descriptions.

Stinging Nettle. Common along the coast, especially on Point Reyes National Seashore, this plant causes an unpleasant stinging sensation when any part of it comes in contact with your skin. Typically 1-2 feet tall, it can be recognized by its spiny leaves and the tiny stinging hairs that cover all parts of the plant. It is mentioned in the hike description if it appears along the trail.

Physical Dangers

Hypothermia. This occurs when the body is unable to stay adequately warm and its core temperature begins to drop. It is a life-threatening condition whose initial symptoms include weakness, mental confusion, slurred speech, and uncontrollable shivering. Cold, wet weather poses the greatest hazard as wet clothes conduct heat away from the body roughly 20 times faster than dry layers. Fatigue reduces your body's ability to produce its own heat and wind poses an increased risk as it can quickly strip away warmth. In the Bay Area, the cold damp months of winter create prime hypothermic conditions.

Immediate treatment is critical and entails raising the body's core temperature as quickly as possible. Get out of the wind, take off wet clothes, drink warm beverages, eat simple energy foods, and take shelter in a warm tent or sleeping bag. *Do not* drink alcohol as this dilates the blood vessels and causes increased heat loss.

Heat Stroke. The opposite of hypothermia, this occurs when the body is unable to control its internal temperature and overheats. Usually brought on by excessive exposure to the sun and accompanying dehydration, symptoms include cramping, headache, and mental confusion. Treatment entails rapid, aggressive cooling of the body through whatever means available—cooling the head and torso is most important. Stay hydrated and have some type of sun protection for your head if you expect to travel along a hot, exposed section of trail. Parks located East of the Bay have plenty of scorching heat and shadeless terrain during the summer months, posing the region's greatest risk for heat stroke.

Sunburn. The Bay Area sun can fry you quickly, even if the sky is overcast with light fog or clouds. Always wear sunscreen of sufficiently high SPF and consider regularly wearing a hat or visor to shield your face from the sun. An SPF of 30 or more filters out virtually all of the sun's damaging rays.

The Pacific Ocean. The waters of the Pacific are frigid (temperature in the 50s year-round), swirling with strong currents, and ripping with undertows that can instantly suck the unwary out to sea. Rogue waves can always occur, sweeping the unsuspecting from seemingly safe rocks and beaches—especially during times of large swell. Unless you are confident in your abilities and knowledge of the ocean, don't tempt fate by going in the water.

Hiking Safety

Leave an Itinerary. Always tell somebody where you are hiking and when you expect to return. Friends, family, rangers, and visitor centers are all valuable resources that can save you from a backcountry disaster when you fail to reappear on time.

Know Your Limits. Don't undertake a hike that exceeds your physical fitness or outdoor abilities.

Avoid Hiking Alone. A hiking partner can provide the margin between life and death in the event of a serious backcountry mishap.

GEAR

Survival Essentials

Always have with you:

Water. Carry at least 1 liter of water (preferably 2), drink frequently, and have some means of purifying backcountry sources (chemical treatment or filter).

Fire and Light. Waterproof matches for starting an emergency fire, headlamp or flashlight in case you are still hiking after the sun goes down.

First Aid Kit. At a minimum this should include an over-the-counter painkiller/swelling reducer (ibuprofen is always good); a 2-4 inch-wide elastic (ACE) bandage for wrapping sprained ankles, knees, and other joints; and the basics for treating a bleeding wound: antibiotic ointment, sterile gauze, small bandages, medical tape, and large band-aids. Prepackaged kits are readily available at any outdoor equipment store.

Map and Compass. To find your way home. Even the simplest compass is useful.

Knife. A good knife can be invaluable in the event of a disaster. Pocket knives and all-in-one tools have many other useful features as well.

Extra Clothes and Food. Warm clothing can be critical in the event of an unexpected night out or a developing fog. A few extra energy bars can make a huge difference in morale and energy level if you are out longer than expected.

Other Good Ideas. A whistle is a powerful distress signal and can save your life if you become immobilized. Sunscreen and sunglasses protect you from blazing sun.

For Your Feet

Your feet are your most important piece of gear. Keep them happy, and you will be even more so. Appreciate them. Care for them.

Footwear. The appropriate hiking footwear provides stability and support for your feet and ankles while protecting them from the abuses of the environment. Most trails in the Bay Area present little in the way of rough or uneven terrain. While a pair of lightweight hiking boots or trail running shoes is generally adequate for most hikes, those with weak ankles may want to opt for heavier, mid-weight hiking boots. When selecting footwear, keep in mind that *the most important feature is a good fit*—your toes should not hit the front while going downhill, your heel should be locked in place inside the boot to prevent friction and blisters, and there should be minimal extra space around your foot (although you should be able to wiggle your toes freely). When lacing, leave the laces over the top of your foot (instep) loose but tie them tightly across the ankle to lock the heel down. Stability over uneven ground is enhanced by a stiffer sole and higher ankle collar—good for those with weak ankles. All-leather boots last longer, have a good deal of natural water resistance, and will mold to your feet over time. Footwear made from synthetic materials or a fabric/leather combination are lighter and cheaper, but not as durable. Some boots have Gore-Tex, a waterproof-breathable material. Be sure to break-in new boots before taking them on an extended hike—simply wear them around as much as possible beforehand.

Socks. After armpits, feet are the sweatiest part of the human body. Unfortunately, wet feet are much more prone to blisters. Good hiking socks will wick moisture away from your skin and provide padding for your feet. Avoid cotton socks at all cost as these get quickly saturated, stay wet inside your shoes, and take forever to dry. Many socks are a confusing mix of natural and synthetic fibers. *Wool* provides warmth and padding and, while it does absorb roughly 30% of its weight in water, is effective at keeping your feet dry. If regular wool makes your feet itch, try softer *merino wool,* which is obtained from the first few shearings of a sheep. *Nylon, polyester, acrylic,* and *polypropylene* (also called *olefin*) are all synthetic fibers that absorb very little water, dry quickly, and add durability. *Liner socks* are a thin pair of socks worn underneath the principal socks and are designed to more effectively wick moisture away—good for really sweaty feet.

Blister Kit. As everybody knows, blisters suck. They are almost always caused by friction from foot movement (slippage) inside the shoe. Prevent blisters by buying properly fitting footwear, taking a minimum of 1-2 weeks to break them in, and wearing appropriate socks. If the heel is slipping and blistering, try tightening the laces across the ankle to keep the heel in place. If you notice a blister or hotspot developing, stop immediately and apply adhesive padding (such as moleskin) over the problem spot. Bring a lightweight pair of scissors to easily cut the moleskin.

Outdoor Clothing

Get dressed and go! The following information is useful for staying warm and dry in camp or on the trail.

The Fabrics. Cotton is generally a lousy fabric for outdoor activity and should be avoided. It absorbs water quickly and takes a long time to dry, leaving a cold wet layer next to your skin and increasing the risk of hypothermia. Jeans are the worst. In hot, dry environments, however—such as those found east of the Bay during the summer months—cotton is useful as the water it retains helps keep you cool for longer periods of time. *Polyester* and *nylon* are two commonly used, and recommended, fibers in outdoor clothing. They dry almost instantly, wick moisture effectively, and are lighter weight than natural fibers. Fleece clothing (made from polyester) provides good insulation and will keep you warm even when wet. Synthetic materials melt quickly, however, if placed in contact with a heat source (camp stove, fire, sparks, etc.). *Wool* is a good natural fiber for hiking. Despite the fact that it retains up to 30 percent of its weight in water, it still insulates when wet.

Raingear/Windgear. There are three types available: waterproof/breathable, waterproof/non-breathable, and water-resistant. *Waterproof/breathable* shells contain Gore-Tex or an equivalent fabric and effectively keep liquid water out while still allowing water vapor (i.e., your sweat) to pass through. They keep you comfortable during heavy exertions in the rain but are generally bulky and more expensive. *Waterproof/non-breathable* shells are typically coated nylon or rubber and keep water out but hold all your sweat in. Seams must be taped for them to be completely waterproof. Although wearing these on a strenuous hike is a hot and sticky experience, they are cheap and often very lightweight. *Water-resistant* shells are typically lightweight nylon windbreakers that have been coated with a water repellent chemical. The seams will not be taped. They will often keep you dry for a short period of time but will quickly soak through in a heavy rain. All three are good in the wind. In the Bay Area, a lightweight windbreaker is all that is needed May-October when rain is a rarity but coastal and inland breezes common. During winter months, however, fully waterproof raingear is strongly recommended.

Keeping Your Head and Neck Warm. The three most important parts of the body to insulate are the torso, neck, and head. Your body will strive to keep these a constant temperature at all times. Without any insulation, the heat coursing through your neck to your brain radiates out into space and is lost. Warmth that might have been directed to your extremities is instead spent replacing the heat lost from your head. A thin balaclava or warm hat and neck gaiter are small items, weigh almost nothing, and are more effective at keeping you warm than an extra sweater.

Keeping Your Hands Warm. Hiking in cold and damp conditions (such as those found in the redwood forest) will often chill your hands unpleasantly. A lightweight pair of synthetic liner gloves will do wonders.

Backpacking Equipment

Backpack. For overnight trips, a pack with at least 3000 cubic inches is generally necessary and more than 4000 cubic inches recommended. Two types of packs are available: *external frame* and *internal frame*. *External frame* packs consist of a small pack attached to a large aluminum frame by numerous small pins. Tent, sleeping bag, and sleeping pad are usually strapped to the frame rather than stored inside the pack. These packs are cheaper, have many pockets, and offer good ventilation for the back. They also have several disadvantages. Weight is carried farther from your body, causing the pack to markedly shift if doing any kind of off-trail scrambling; they are usually less comfortable and harder to adjust for fit; and they are cumbersome for traveling, making them less versatile. *Internal frame* packs have alumi-num stiffeners inside the pack itself and usually provide two large main compartments. The lower compartment is desig-nated for your sleeping bag, while tent and sleeping pad are either strapped to the side or packed within the upper com-partment. Internal frame packs generally offer a better, more comfortable fit; ride closer to your body and are better for off-trail scrambling; and are better for use as travel luggage. How-ever, they are more expensive, have fewer pockets and less accessibility, and provide no ventilation for the back.

When shopping for a pack keep in mind that, just like footwear, the most important feature is a good fit. A properly fitting backpack allows you to carry the vast majority of weight on your hips and lower body, sparing the easily-fatigued muscles of the shoulders and back. When trying on packs, loosen the shoulder straps, position the waist belt so that the top of your hips (the bony iliac crest) is in the middle of the belt, attach and cinch the waist belt, and then tighten the shoulder straps. The waist belt should fit snugly around your hips, with no gaps. The shoulder straps should rise slightly off your shoulders before dipping back down to attach to the pack about an inch below your shoulders— no weight should be resting on the top of your shoulders and you should be able to shrug them freely. Most packs will have load stabilizer straps that attach to the pack behind your ears and lift the shoulder straps upwards, off of your shoulders. A sternum strap links the two shoulder straps together across your chest and prevents them from slipping away from your body. Keep in mind that most packs are highly adjustable—a knowledgeable employee at an outdoor equipment shop can be invaluable in helping you achieve the proper fit.

Load your pack to keep its center of gravity as close to your middle and lower back as possible. Heaviest items should go against the back, becoming progressively lighter as you go outwards and upwards. Do not place heavy items at or below the level of the hip belt—this precludes the ability to carry that weight on the lower body and is one of the main reasons internal frame packs have their sleeping bag compartments in that location.

Sleeping Bag. Nights are surprisingly cool year-round in the Bay Area. While freezing conditions are uncommon, expect nighttime temperatures in the 50s for most of the year with dips into the 40s and even 30s during the winter. For those who sleep cold, a sleeping bag rated to 20°F is recommended for all-purpose use, while those who sleep warm should find a 30-35°F bag adequate (keep in mind that manufacturer's temperature ratings are highly subjective). Down sleeping bags offer the highest warmth-to-weight ratio, are incredibly compressible, and will easily last 5-10 years without losing much of their loft. However, down loses all of its insulating ability when wet and takes forever to dry—a genuine concern during the rainy Bay Area winters. Synthetic-fill sleeping bags retain their insulating abilities even when wet and are cheaper, but the increased bulk and weight is a drawback. While Polarguard 3D and Polarguard Delta are currently the lightest weight synthetic fills, older-generation fills such as Polarguard HV or Holofil will be significantly cheaper (though heavier and bulkier). Keep in mind that synthetic-fill bags lose some of their loft and insulating ability after a few seasons of use.

Sleeping Pad. Sleeping pads offer vital comfort and insulation from the cold ground. Inflatable, foam-filled pads (such as Therm-a-Rest) are the most compact and comfortable to sleep on, but expensive and mildly time-consuming to inflate and deflate. Basic foam pads are lightweight, cheap, and virtually indestructible. Comfort makes the call.

A shady site at
Sugarloaf Ridge State Park

Tent. A lightweight, three-season tent is all that is required for most Bay Area backpacking trips. They average about 6 pounds for a two-person tent and usually feature see-through, weight-saving mesh on the tent body for ventilation and star viewing. A rain fly that extends to the ground on all sides is critical for staying dry. Leaks are typically caused by water seeping through unsealed seams and/or contact between a wet rainfly and the tent body. Seal any untaped seams that are directly exposed to the rain or to water running off the fly—pay close attention to the floor corners of the tent body. Pitch the tent as tautly as possible to keep a wet and saggy rain fly away from the tent body. While most trail camps offer good shelter from the wind, a few do not. Stability in wind is enhanced by pole intersections—the more poles and the more times they cross, the stronger the tent will be in blustery conditions. Placing a tarp between the tent floor and the ground will protect the floor from ground moisture, wear and tear, and will increase the lifespan of your tent. Most tents these days have an optional *footprint* which exactly matches the floor—a nice accessory.

Cooking Equipment. A stove is necessary if you want hot food on the trail. Two types are available. *Canister stoves* run on a butane/propane blend pressurized in a metal canister. Simply attach the stove burner to the canister, turn the knob, and light. Such stoves are simple, safe, cheap, and have an adjustable flame. However, the canisters are usually available only at outdoor equipment stores, are more expensive and hard to recycle, do not work below freezing, and heat very slowly when less than a quarter full. Their safety and simmer-ability make them a good choice for Bay Area backpacking. *Liquid fuel stoves* run on white gas contained in a self-pressurized tank or bottle. White gas is very inexpensive, burns hot, is widely available around the world, and works in extremely cold conditions. However, you must work directly with liquid fuel in order to prime the stove, adding an element of danger. They're also prone to flaring up, usually do not have an adjustable flame, and are more expensive. Liquid fuel stoves are a good choice for those interested in winter camping or international travel.

A simple 2-3 quart pot is all that is usually needed for backcountry cooking. Add a small frying pan if necessary. A black, or blackened, pot will absorb heat more quickly and increase fuel efficiency. A windscreen for the stove is helpful in breezy conditions. The only dish needed is a plate with upturned edges, which can double as a broad bowl—a Frisbee or gold pan works well. Don't forget the silverware! Lastly, an insulated mug is essential for enjoying hot drinks.

Other Good Stuff. A length of *nylon cord* is useful for hanging food, stringing clotheslines, and guying out tents. A simple *repair kit* should include needle, thread, and duct tape. A plastic *trowel* is nice for digging crapholes. *Insect repellent* will keep the bugs away. A pair of *sandals* or *running shoes* for around camp are a great relief from hiking boots. A *pen and waterproof notebook* allow you to record outdoor epiphanies on the spot. Extra *Zip-loc* or *garbage bags* always come in handy. *Compression stuff sacks* will reduce the bulk of your sleeping bag and clothes by about a third.

Fun Equipment. Make sure your *camera* is ready for outdoor abuse and keep it safe from dirt and moisture. A good protective camera bag costs much less than a new camera. Old-school, fully manual 35mm cameras are extremely durable. A polarizing filter is good for taking outdoor pictures with lots of sky and water. Shady forests are challenging to photograph when the sun is out— wait for foggy or overcast days and carry a small tripod and shutter-release cable for shooting in the low-light conditions. An *altimeter* is a fun toy for tracking your progress and identifying your location. With *binoculars* you can see more and with a *hacky sack, Frisbee,* or *cards* you can play more.

Car Camping Equipment

While most of the equipment information above is applicable to car camping, the ability to drive gear directly to the campsite allows for bringing more stuff.

Family Tents. A large (4-6+ person) tent is great for families. Note that most giant tents available are designed for sheltered, fair-weather camping only. The rain fly on such tents is typically minimal and ineffective, and the height of these tents makes them highly unstable in wind. From May through October, this is not a problem— nearly all Bay Area campgrounds are well-sheltered from wind and rain is an unlikely occurrence. During the winter months, however, look for a family tent with a to-the-ground rainfly and multiple pole intersections for increased weather protection.

Propane Stoves and Lanterns. A two-burner propane stove is great for cooking big meals. A bright lantern will illuminate the entire campsite at night. A large, refillable propane tank is cheap to fill, lasts a long time, and is much, much better for the environment. (The small, heavy propane canisters are not recyclable or refillable and go straight to the dump.)

Other Good Stuff. Bring along *firewood* for the evening campfire. Wood collecting is prohibited in all Bay Area campgrounds, and firewood (when available for purchase) is expensive. A *cooler* makes for refreshing beverages and keeps food from spoiling. *Paper plates* are easy to deal with at clean-up time. A large *water container* is nice to have in camp.

THE WILDERNESS ETHIC

In order to preserve the Bay Area outdoors for future generations, follow some simple guidelines to leave no trace of your passage:

Do Not Scar the Land. Do not cut switchbacks. Stay on the trail as much as possible. Leave rocks, plants, and other natural objects as you find them.

Camping. Camp only at established sites. Do not dig ditches around your tent. Keep your camp clean and never leave food out. Confine activities to where vegetation is absent.

Fires. Campfires, where allowed, should always be made in a fire ring. In the Bay Area, no wood collecting of any kind is allowed. Make sure the fire is completely out before leaving.

Sanitation. When Nature calls, choose a spot at least 200 feet away from trails, water sources, and campsites. Dig a cat hole six inches deep, make your deposit, and cover it with the soil you removed. Do not bury toilet paper.

Washing. To wash yourself or your dishes, carry water 200 feet away from streams or lakes. Scatter strained dishwater. Avoid the use of soap if possible, otherwise use only small amounts of biodegradable soap.

Garbage. Carry out all garbage and burn only paper. Thoroughly inspect your site for trash and spilled food before leaving.

Group Size. Keep groups small to minimize impact.

Animals. Do not feed wildlife. Observe only from a distance.

Meeting Horses on the Trail. Move off the trail on the downhill side and stand still until the animals pass by.

Noise. Be respectful of other wilderness users. Listen to the sounds of Nature.

Have a good time . . .

Foggy welcome at
Point Reyes National Seashore

Where Should I Go?

Where Should I Go?

Blessed with mild year-round weather and tremendous natural diversity, the Bay Area offers a wide variety of overnight outdoor adventures in every month of the year—but only if you know where to go. The following sections describe the geography, weather, ecosystems, and governing agencies of the Bay Area outdoors, allowing you to better choose the perfect overnight adventure. At the end, a *Season-by-Season Playbook* summarizes all the factors into a year-round cycle of Bay Area outdoor fun.

BAY AREA GEOGRAPHY

The rocks of the Bay Area have been crushed by colliding tectonic plates, sliced by massive faults, and squeezed upwards into a rumpled world of rolling hills, steep ridges, deep valleys, and an overall convoluted topography. For the purpose of this book, the region's unique geography is roughly grouped into three regions: the North Bay, Santa Cruz Mountains, and East of the Bay. A general overview of each region's geography and featured parks follows.

The North Bay includes the region found north of the Golden Gate and is characterized by rugged topography and a wild coastline. A series of high ridges and peaks geographically isolates the western coastal areas from the population centers found closer to the Bay.

Eagle's Eyrie, Sunol Backpack Area

Farther east, linear Sonoma and Napa valleys lie between mountainous ridges of volcanic rock. The region is remarkable for the large amount of easily accessible protected open space available for exploration —44% of nearby Marin County is composed of parks, preserves, and other public land.

Most of the campgrounds and all of the backpacking trips in the North Bay are found in the western regions closer to the coast, with Point Reyes National Seashore, Mt. Tamalpais, and the Marin Headlands the principal destinations. They also are some of the most popular—and crowded—parks in the Bay Area. Farther east and to the north, beyond the reach of the fog, the wine-producing regions of Napa and Sonoma valleys offer two pleasant and less-traveled state parks for camping—Bothe–Napa Valley and Sugarloaf Ridge. In between is China Camp State Park, the only campground on the shores of San Francisco Bay. Finally, the book reaches as far north as Austin Creek State Recreation Area, a more distant destination tucked in the folds of the Coast Ranges near the Russian River.

The Santa Cruz Mountains extend south from Half Moon Bay to Santa Cruz and then west to the Santa Clara Valley south of San Jose. A rugged, ridge-lined landscape deeply incised by a multitude of creeks, the geography is largely defined by the axis of long, north-west-trending Skyline Ridge. Stretching more than 50 miles from near Gilroy to Highway 92 above Half Moon Bay, it rises some 3000 feet and separates the developed Bay Area from the wild heart of these mountains. West of Skyline Ridge, a multitude of creeks and rivers tumble toward the ocean, the largest of which are (from north to south) Pescadero Creek, Waddell Creek, and the San Lorenzo River. Redwood forest characterizes most outdoor adventures in the region.

Skyline Wilderness Park

Most of the Santa Cruz Mountains and nearly all of the protected parklands in them run along the west side of Skyline Ridge. In the heart of the mountains lies a large complex of contiguous and interconnected parks centered around the Pescadero and Waddell creek drainages—Sam McDonald, Memorial, and Pescadero Creek county parks; and Portola Redwoods, Butano, Castle Rock, and Big Basin Redwoods state parks. With the exception of Butano, all of these parks either border each other or are connected via an extensive network of trails. With four drive-up campgrounds and more than 10 backcountry trail camps in this complex, opportunities for overnight adventures among the redwoods are extensive. Beyond the central Santa Cruz Mountains, overnight opportunities await east of Skyline Ridge in Monte Bello Ridge Open Space Preserve and Sanborn County Park; the Bay Area's only beachside camping awaits at Half Moon

BAY AREA GEOLOGY

A long, long time ago, the western edge of North America was in the vicinity of today's Sierra Nevada foothills. Offshore, a massive tectonic plate was being slowly driven beneath the continent. Covered by the ocean for millions of years, the tectonic plate had accumulated deep layers of sand, mud, and microscopic sea creature skeletons on its rocky underwater surface. As the plate slid beneath pre-historic California, this collection of mud, sand, skeletons, and rocks was scraped off, scrambled in a deep offshore trench, and left a confused and jumbled mix which today has risen to form most of the San Francisco Bay Area landscape.

This jumble is known as the *Franciscan Formation*. Several common rock types are associated with it and regularly appear in Bay Area campgrounds and backpacking trips. *Chert* formed from the accumulated silica-rich skeletons and is easily recognized by its obvious layering, resistance to erosion (often found in cliff faces and rock outcrops), sharp edges, and typical dark red coloration (although it can also appear a pale, translucent white or green). *Sandstone* is easily recognized by its brown color, rough surfaces, and tiny sand grains. *Shale* is hardened, compressed mud and is identified by its microscopic grains, a gray-black coloration, and its tendency to fracture in a rectangular fashion. *Greenstone,* or *pillow basalt,* comes from the deep rocks of the sea floor and is formed as molten rock is forced to the underwater surface from deep within the Earth. Also highly resistant to erosion, it appears frequently in cliffs and rocky shores and is identified by its green color on freshly broken faces, lack of layering, and by the 1-3 foot bulbous masses (the "pillows") that are often identified in exposures. *Serpentine*, California's state rock, comes from the bowels of the Earth where rocks first solidify above molten material. Scraped off and jumbled near the surface, it reacts with groundwater to form a slippery, waxy green rock.

The region west of the San Andreas Fault tells a different geologic tale. Once upon a time, after the rock scramble described above, the San Andreas Fault was born somewhere in Southern California. Land west of the fault was ripped from its moorings and moved north-ward. Formed principally of the same granite that today sits in the southern Sierra Nevada, this migrant piece of California was buried

Double Point, Point Reyes National Seashore

beneath the sea on its journey north and blanketed with mud and sand. Today it has been pushed back above the surface to form the rugged hills found west of the fault—the western Santa Cruz Mountains and Point Reyes peninsula. While loosely consolidated sandstone and mudstone still cover most of the underlying granite, the unique "salt-and-pepper" color of granitic rock does appear in places.

Bay State Beach; and the truly motivated can undertake The Traverse, a five-day backpack across the entire Santa Cruz Mountains.

Intricate Buckeye pattern, Black Diamond Mines Regional Park

East of the Bay. For the purposes of this book, this includes the ecologically similar regions found east of San Francisco Bay and the Santa Clara Valley. A multitude of north-south trending ridges compose the hilly terrain found East of the Bay, offering little in the way of level ground. In the northern area, monolithic Mt. Diablo dominates; at 3849 feet it towers over the surrounding landscape and overlooks the lower-lying Oakland/ Berkeley Hills to the west. Farther south, the land is wrinkled into the tortured Diablo Range, a series of furrowed ridges and peaks rising 3000 feet and higher.

Seven camping destination are scattered East of the Bay. Mt. Diablo State Park supports the Bay Area's highest campground (3000'); the East Bay Regional Park District provides three campgrounds near lakes and creeks; and the wilderness of the Diablo Range is brushed by campgrounds in Joseph D. Grant County Park, Henry W. Coe State Park, and Coyote Lake County Park. Backpacking trips are largely confined to two destinations in the heart of the Diablo Range—The Ohlone Trail and Henry W. Coe State Park. Both offer opportunity to explore the Bay Area's deepest backcountry on extended multi-day excursions as well as shorter, overnight trips. The only other backpacking option is Black Diamond Mines Regional Park, a place of rich history, woodlands, and wildlife in the eastern Mt. Diablo foothills.

WEATHER OF THE SAN FRANCISCO BAY AREA

The Bay Area is characterized by a Mediterranean climate. To put it simply: from November through April, it rains; from May through October, it doesn't. Snow is rare, temperatures are mild year-round, and outdoor excursions are possible in every month of the year.

Dry Season, May through October. During this period, Bay Area weather is dominated by two things: sun and fog. It seldom rains, leaving most areas to bask in hot solar rays. Temperatures become increasingly warm farther inland, with readings in the 90s not uncommon for many regions east of the Bay. Meanwhile, over the cold Pacific Ocean, fog forms. Moisture contained in warm summer air condenses over the frigid waters into a ground-hugging cloud, which is then pushed onshore by prevailing winds. Flowing inland like an airborne river, the low-lying fog is typically blocked by the high ridges of the

Santa Cruz Mountains and North Bay, but low *fog gaps*—such as the Golden Gate—will allow it to move deeper inland. The farther inland, the more likely the fog will burn off by late morning or early afternoon. Meanwhile, coastal destinations can smother under fog for days on end, with brisk onshore winds blowing from the northwest. Fog is common throughout the summer, is at its thickest in July and August, and tapers off as September fades into October.

Golden Gate vista from Angel Island

Haze, heat, and fog are common from May through August and finding an ideal outdoor destination is challenging—redwood forest is always a good option during this period. While the Indian summer months of September and October still bring bouts of fog and inland heat, they also are the months most likely to produce sunny, warm days perfect for exploring anywhere across the entire region. Conditions are extremely dry throughout this period, wildfire risk is often extreme, and campfire restrictions are often in effect. In the fall a dash of color can be seen along creeks in the yellow leaves of sycamores and big-leaf maples, heralding the return of the . . .

Rainy Season, November through April. As the winter months approach, the jet stream flows south over Northern California and brings with it winter storms born in the Gulf of Alaska. Rain drenches the Bay Area as cold fronts regularly sweep through, becoming increasingly frequent as the winter months progress. Strong winds typically blow from the south as the fronts approach and a storm can drop several inches of rain in a day's time, making for extremely wet and windy outdoor conditions. While the higher elevations (2000′+) around the Bay Area receive an occasional snow flurry in the winter months, it is a rare occurrence.

A sea of fog below Sky Camp, Point Reyes National Seashore

In a typical year, the first rogue storms arrive sometime in late October, increase in frequency during November and December, hit hardest in January and February (the wettest months), and start tapering off in March. April tends to be unpredictable and summer days (complete with coastal fog) are just as likely as cold wintry storms.

While the weather is challenging during the rainy season, these are the glory

WHAT DRIVES THE WEATHER

The Bay Area's weather patterns are determined primarily by a dominating influence known as the Pacific High. Wherever the sun most directly strikes the earth, air near the surface is warmed, loses pressure, and rises into the upper atmosphere. Closer to the chill of space, this heated column of air then cools as it moves toward the poles. As the temperature drops, the air increases in density and consequently sinks toward the surface to form a large area of high pressure.

From May through September, the sun most directly strikes the northern hemisphere, causing a large zone of high pressure to form over the North Pacific Ocean between roughly 35°N and 40°N latitude. Located at 38°N, the San Francisco Bay Area receives the effects of this Pacific High from May, when it first forms, through October, when its long-stabilized presence finally dissipates as the sun moves over the southern hemisphere. Forcing the eastward-flowing jet stream to the north, the Pacific High prevents storms brewed in the Gulf of Alaska from reaching California and creates the hot, dry days of Bay Area summer. However, it also creates conditions perfect for the development of coastal fog and wind.

Air flows from areas of high pressure to regions of low pressure. This means that winds flow from the Pacific High toward the lower pressure zones found inland. Slightly twisted in direction by the Coriolis Effect, these cool winds consequently strike Northern California's coast from the northwest for as long as the Pacific High is present. What's more, ocean surface water moves perpendicular to wind direction. This means that the warmer surface waters near land are pushed offshore by the prevailing winds, leaving a void that is filled by colder water from the ocean depths. With temperatures in the low 50s, this frigid water chills the air above it. Cold air holds less moisture than warm air, and thus upon contact with the cold ocean waters, the nicely heated summer air suddenly condenses into thick, soupy, chilly *FOG*.

In October and November, as the sun strikes the earth farther down the southern hemisphere, the Pacific High dissipates. No longer impeded by the zone of high pressure, the jet stream flows over California and brings with it the storms of winter. From November through March, these storms regularly lash the Bay Area until, once again, the sun returns north to rebuild the Pacific High.

months for outdoor adventure in the Bay Area. Warm sunny days regularly occur between storm fronts and can last for days, especially in the shoulder months of November and April. The wind and storms purge the air of smog and haze, leaving behind crystalline views. The first rains of the season pour life into the landscape and it quickly flourishes green, exploding with wildflowers from late February until May. Winter waves along the coast become large and powerful, an impressive display of Nature's power. Keep a close eye on the weather forecast and windows of sunny opportunity will always open, for now the entire Bay Area is empty and open for outdoor adventure play.

THE LIVING BAY AREA

For the sake of simplicity, the Living Bay Area is categorized in this book into five basic ecosystems that share common characteristics and flora: redwood forest, mixed-evergreen forest, oak woodland, chaparral, and coastal scrub. Bear in mind, however, that the Bay Area is a world of extraordinary ecological diversity and that much greater detail can be found in the sources recommended in Appendix E.

The ecosystems of the Bay Area are determined largely by one factor— the availability of water. Land farther inland bakes in stronger summer temperatures, reducing available moisture dramatically during the dry season. Regions closer to the coast receive more moisture from arriving storms, and the damp breath of summer fog provides for a year-round water supply. The following environments result and are presented below in order of decreasing moisture.

Redwood Forest occurs in a narrow belt close to the coast where winter rainfall is abundant (30-60″ annually) and summer fog is common. This damp and shady world is characterized by the majestic coast redwood (*Sequoia sempervirens*), a tree world-famous for its size, longevity, and beauty. In the Bay Area, redwood forest occurs throughout the western Santa Cruz Mountains and fills many of the coastal drainages of the North Bay, extending as far inland as Napa and Sonoma valleys. While the majority of redwood forest has been logged over the past 150 years, numerous old-growth stands still remain.

Redwoods on the
Skyline-to-the-Sea Trail,
Big Basin State Park

Other moisture-loving plants join the redwoods: the drooping branches, rough bark, and feathery cones of *Douglas-fir*; the large spiny leaves of *tanoak*, particularly abundant in the understory of second-growth forest; the small pointed leaves and thick bushes of *huckleberry*, which dangle edible blue/black fruit in the fall; the velvety soft leaves of *California hazel* shrubs; and the large leaves and thin branches of *big-leaf maple*, common along streams and blushing gold in the fall. Lush flora also carpets the ground: the large fronds of *sword ferns*, easily identified by the "hilt" at the base of their leaves; the huge fronds of *chain ferns,* the largest of all California ferns and found only in the wettest locations; the delicate *5-finger fern,* often found hanging off steep rock faces with more than five "fingers"; and a thick carpet of clover-like *redwood sorrel,* whose light-intolerant leaves fold up when struck by direct sunlight. Mushrooms explode from the forest floor during the wet months of winter, including two of the world's deadliest: the *death cap* and *destroying angel.* While animal life is abundant in the redwood forest, the dense foliage makes sightings rare. Clambering orange-bellied *newts* and the ubiquitous *banana slug* are the most common fauna seen.

Mixed-Evergreen Forest is similar to redwood forest and shares many of the same flora, but does not receive enough moisture to sustain the redwood trees themselves. It commonly occurs along the margins of redwood forests and the two ecosystems often gradate into each other. It is found throughout the Santa Cruz Mountains, especially in the upper elevations; bordering the redwood forest drainages of the North Bay; covering Inverness Ridge in Point Reyes National Seashore; and in scattered moist pockets throughout the Bay Area, often on cooler north-facing slopes.

　　Douglas-fir is the dominant tree of mixed-evergreen forest, accompanied by its redwood-forest constituents of huckleberry, tanoak, and big-leaf maple. These are joined by the smooth peeling bark, twisting branches, and large oval leaves of *madrone* trees; the long, thin, and fragrant leaves of *California bay* trees, often arching gracefully across the forest; the gnarled forms of evergreen *canyon* and *interior live oak,* which commonly hybridize and grow both ragged-toothed and smooth-edged leaves on the same tree; and tall deciduous *black oak* trees, which bud out red leaves in the spring, drop golden leaves in the fall, and are easily identified by the spine-tipped lobes of their large leaves.

Oak Woodland occurs where rainfall is low (15-25″ annually) and summers are hot and dry. Fog is rare and provides little, if any, moisture. Extremely common in regions east of the Bay, oak woodland occurs only intermittently in the North Bay and rarely in the Santa Cruz Mountains. As conditions become progressively drier in this environment,

Sunol Regional Wilderness

the forest transitions from a continuous, shady cover to an increasingly open landscape dotted with solitary trees in large, grassy fields (the latter is also known as *oak savannah*).

　　This ecosystem overlaps closely with the range of *gray pine,* a thin wispy pine tree with a trunk that typically splits into several main stems, has long

(8-12″) gray-green needles in bundles of three, and massive cones that often weigh in at more than three pounds. In damp locations along stream gullies, California bay and madrone are often joined by the mottled gray bole and twisting personage of *California sycamore*, characterized by huge leaves and spiny seed balls; and by the broad, brilliantly green palmate leaves of *California buckeye*, the first tree to emerge with new leaves in spring (often as early as January) and the first to drop them in summer, leaving behind large one-eyed (buckeyed) seed balls dangling on the branches. But it is the oaks that dominate.

Valley oak is the largest and most majestic of these beautiful trees, identified by its deeply lobed, 4-6″ deciduous leaves with smooth margins. The hardiest of the oaks, *blue oak* survives in conditions too hot and dry for other oaks and is increasingly common in the dry landscape farther east. Often occurring in pure stands, it is known by its barely lobed wavy leaf margins and blue-green cast in late summer and fall. Other oaks include *coast live oak,* its round, spiny, evergreen leaves curled into concave form; *Oregon oak,* with lobed leaves similar to valley oak but occurring only in scattered locations in the North Bay; and *black oak,* which typically only occurs at elevations above 2000 feet. *Spring wildflowers* are dazzling in oak woodlands—a sweeping palette of color infuses the landscape from March through May. *Wildlife* is abundant as well, and the open forest makes sightings much easier. *Deer, bobcats, wild pigs, wild turkeys,* and *hawks* are often seen, along with a wide variety of other birdlife. Unfortunately, *poison oak* is extremely common in this environment as well—be watchful!

Chaparral grows in the driest of environments, adapted to survival in conditions intolerable for any tree. Low-lying and scrubby, chaparral offers little in the way of shade for overheating hikers and makes for difficult off-trail trekking. It flourishes on the dry slopes and exposed ridges found East of the Bay, along the eastern flanks of the Santa Cruz Mountains, and in scattered eastern locations of the North Bay. Pockets of chaparral regularly appear within oak woodlands.

Shrubs of the chaparral adapt to the dry environment with small, water-retaining foliage. *Coyote brush* is one of the most common and occurs throughout the Bay Area in dry locations—look for the small irregular leaves often found at the end of long bare stems, and their fuzzy white flowers in spring. *Chamise* sprouts a multitude of tiny, needle-like leaves along stiff woody stems and grows in thick stands. The smooth, blood-red wood of *Manzanita* is unmistakable. Dozens of subspecies exist, each intricately twisted and blooming with tiny, bell-shaped flowers in winter and early spring. Forty-three varieties of *Ceanothus* exist in California, many of which are found in the Bay Area. *Buckbrush* is a common variety, growing two small waxy leaves opposite each other that are lined with a prominent mid-vein. The shrub explodes with a coating of white flowers in the spring. Other common varieties include *deerbrush* and *blue*

SUDDEN OAK DEATH

A terrible scourge is sweeping through the oaks of the Bay Area, killing them by the tens of thousands. *Sudden Oak Death* (SOD) is a blight unlike any other to have struck the California woodlands, threatening to devastate vast tracts of our natural heritage. *You must do your part to prevent the spread of this epidemic.*

SOD is caused by *Phytophthora ramorum*, a destructive fungus that kills the food-distributing tissue beneath the bark of infected trees. Infection can be identified by the presence of cankerous sores on the main trunk, which bleed a dark-brown or amber-colored sap and mark the locations where the fun-

Boyd Camp oak,
Del Valle Regional Park

gus is doing its deadly work. As the disease weakens the tree, other organisms move in as well. Oak beetles burrow into the wood and leave a film of sawdust on the surface, joined by the black domes of another unrelated fungus. Withering away from the onslaught, the healthy-seeming foliage of an afflicted tree can abruptly turn from green to brown in a matter of weeks, signaling the tree's "sudden" death. Currently, the fungus is killing three species in the Bay Area—coast live oak, tanoak, and black oak—and can affect up to 80% of the trees in any given stand. However, it has also been found to be present on more than a dozen other plant species, including California bay, madrone, rhododendron, huckleberry, manzanita, and buckeye. While these hosts are not killed by the fungus, they likely represent important vectors for the spread of the disease. So far, none of the white oak species (blue, valley, and Oregon oaks) is known to be infected.

SOD was first observed in 1995 in a small Marin County grove of tanoak trees. Within a few years, hundreds of surrounding trees were dead and the mysterious disease began to attract widespread public attention and concern. As the dieback spread to other Bay Area counties, its cause remained a mystery despite increasing scientific scrutiny. Only in 2000 was the *Phytophthora* fungus identified as the

blossom, both of which are adorned in springtime with long sprays of fragrant white, pale blue, or pink flowers. *Rabbits* and other small rodents hide in the thick brush, avoiding the watchful eyes of *red-tailed hawks* and other raptors overhead.

Coastal Scrub flourishes along the coastal margin of the Bay Area, where the ravages of salt-laden air and strong winds make life impossible for redwoods causal agent, a hitherto unknown species in a genus harboring the same fungus responsible for the Irish Potato Blight of the mid-19th century. Today, SOD has been found in nearly every county of the Bay Area and continues to spread rapidly. The fate of California's oak trees in the years ahead is frighteningly unknown.

While the precise means by which the disease is spread remain a mystery, it appears increasingly likely that the fungus is spread through three primary mediums—water, soil, and infected wood. Of these, soil is of greatest concern for Bay Area hikers, campers, and mountain bikers. Soil from afflicted areas will often contain fungal spores capable of infecting new areas. Contaminated dirt stuck to hiking boots, animals, car tires, or bicycles is easily transferred to another area on a later adventure and can spread the blight to previously unaffected areas. In this book, the presence of SOD is mentioned in every campground and backpacking trip that visits infected areas.

In order to prevent the spread of SOD, *please* adhere to the following recommendations:

- Accumulations of soil or mud should be washed from shoes, mountain bikes, and animals' feet prior to leaving an infected site. If this is not possible, wash them in an area at home that will not result in mud being washed directly towards other trees or waterways.
- If possible, avoid driving or parking vehicles in areas where they may accumulate contaminated soil or mud. Vehicles that have mud in the tires from an infected area should be run through a car wash.
- Do not remove plant material of any kind from an infested area.
- Avoid transporting oak wood for use in campfires as the fungus can remain active in infected dead wood for a considerable length of time.

For more information and current updates on SOD, visit the California Oak Mortality Task Force web site at www.suddenoakdeath.org.

Primary Source: Garbelotto, Matteo, Pavel Svihra, and Davie M. Rizzo. *Sudden Oak Death Syndrome Fells 3 Oak Species.* California Agriculture, Jan.-Feb. 2001, pp. 9-19.

and other interior trees. Instead, a tangled and intricate world of shrubbery exists, a wide range of species interlocking in a tight web of life.

Many plants common to chaparral environments thrive here as well, including coyote brush and ceanothus. Joining the tangled web are the thorny vine tangles of *blackberry*; the abundant but inedible berries of *coffee berry*, which progress from green to red to black as they ripen; the vines of *honeysuckle*, whose terminal leaves sprout as one diamond-shape before splitting into two as it grows; the tough, spiny leaves of the diminutive *scrub oak*; and the hardiest of all ferns, the *bracken fern,* whose fronds curl under at the margins. *Poison oak* is extremely common in coastal scrub as well. The treeless expanse of coastal scrub extends as far as a mile inland before the first trees appear. These include coast live oak, cypress, and the gnarled architecture of *Monterey pine,* festooned with lop-sided, smooth-scaled cones. *Rabbits, deer,* and *bobcats* are common, as is a wide variety of birdlife that finds shelter in the impenetrable brush.

WHO RUNS THE PARKS OF THE BAY AREA?

There are more than 200 parks and preserves in the Bay Area managed by no fewer than a dozen different governing agencies. Of these, six agencies maintain facilities for overnight outdoor adventures and are consequently featured in this book. They run the gamut from federal to state to county government groups, each of which has unique procedures and regulations. Since communication between the governing agencies is minimal, figuring out who runs what from where by what rules can be a mind-bending process. Here, each of the six featured agencies are discussed in greater detail to help you select the perfect outdoor destination. General contact information is provided for each governing agency. For specific park contact information, please see the corresponding camping or backpacking trip description.

The National Park Service is a federal agency (a division of the Department of the Interior) and manages the Golden Gate National Recreation Area (GGNRA) and Point Reyes National Seashore through its Pacific West Regional Office. Dedicated to protecting the natural and historic beauty of its parklands, the NPS is generally well staffed and its facilities nicely maintained. Several excellent visitor centers are open daily for research and education. The GGNRA includes the Marin Headlands and is the largest urban national park in the nation, protecting more than 75,000 acres of open space. Point Reyes National Seashore includes 30,000-acre Phillip Burton Wilderness, where the land is managed to maintain its wilderness qualities. Backpacking reservations are handled through the respective park visitor centers—Bear Valley Visitor Center (Point Reyes) and the Marin Headlands Visitor Center. Dogs are not permitted on the NPS lands featured in this book. For general NPS information contact the National Park Service, Pacific West Region, at One Jackson Center, 1111 Jackson St., Oakland, CA 94607, (510) 917-1300, www.nps.gov.

California State Parks are run by the State of California from its headquarters in Sacramento. In the Bay Area, state parks are scattered broadly and account for more than half of Bay Area campgrounds and backpacking trips. While each park unit is largely a self-contained entity, they all strive to preserve parklands in as natural a condition as possible. None of them allow dogs on park trails, all operate under the same reservation system (see below), and costs are more or less uniform from park to park. Staffing and facilities vary widely by location, however, and the park system is in constant need of additional funding. In January 2003, fees were increased at all state parks—expect prices to fluctuate in the years to come. For more information contact California State Parks, Communications Office, Box 942896, Sacramento, CA 94296, 1-800-777-0369, fax (916) 657-3903, www.parks.ca.gov, email: info@parks.ca.gov.

Humanity fades in Henry Coe State Park

Reservations for state park campgrounds are handled by a completely separate entity, Reserve America. A for-profit company, Reserve America was acquired in 2001 by an even larger corporate juggernaut, TicketMaster (2001 revenue: $675 million). As of 2003, the company handles camping reservations for 15 state park systems and several federal and county agencies. Both phone and online reservations are possible. While Reserve America's California operations are based in Sacramento, it does not seem to communicate much with the individual parks. This separation can be frustrating to deal with—conflicting information between Reserve America and park sources is common. (In this book, information obtained directly from park staff was given priority.) Although completely redesigned in Spring 2002, the web site can still be cumbersome and frustrating to use; the author has found that phone reservations are considerably easier to make. One advantage of the web site, however, is the ability to see what bookings are available weeks and months ahead of time. Online reservations can be made at any time, while phone reservations can only be made daily 8 A.M.–5 P.M. PST. A reservation fee is charged. Contact and reservation information: www.reserveamerica.com; (800) 444-7275 (800-444-PARK); international phone number: (916) 638-5993; customer service: (800) 695-2269, TTY: (800) 274-7275.

The East Bay Regional Park District includes both Alameda and Contra Costa counties and protects more than 91,000 acres of open space spread over 59 designated parks. Established in 1934, it is one of the oldest regional park districts in the country and manages its lands for a range of activities, from wilderness hiking to golf courses to motor boating. It is the dog-friendliest park agency in the Bay Area and canines can run off-leash through the undeveloped areas of almost all EBRPD lands (The Ohlone Trail is an exception). In addition to three family campgrounds (Anthony Chabot, Del Valle, and Sunol) and two backpacking opportunities (the Ohlone Trail and Black Diamond Mines), the

EBRPD offers a large number of group campgrounds that may be used by anybody (see Appendix A: *Group Campgrounds of the Bay Area*). All campsites and trail camps may be reserved through the park's reservation office at (510) 636-1684. While always in need of new funding, park facilities are generally in good shape and staffing is decent. Every other month the park district publishes *Regional in Nature,* an informative newsletter highlighting upcoming events and interpretive activities across the district. It is available for free at EBRPD visitor centers and many East Bay outdoor stores, or can be ordered for home delivery. The EBRPD web site is comprehensive and provides details and maps for every park in the district. For more information contact East Bay Regional Park District, 2950 Peralta Oaks Court, Oakland, CA 94605-0381, (510) 562-PARK, www.ebparks.org.

Santa Clara County Parks encompass both sides of the Santa Clara Valley in the southern Bay Area. Stretching from the crest of the Santa Cruz Mountains on the west to the heart of the Diablo Range on the east, the park district protects 40,000 acres in 28 parks and offers good facilities for hiking, camping, boating, archery, golf, and other outdoor activities. Dog regulations vary by park—some allow dogs (leashed) on all trails while others restrict dogs to small areas at park entrances (see individual descriptions for more information). In summer 2002 the park district inaugurated a new reservation system for all five of its family campgrounds: Sanborn, Mt. Madonna, Uvas Canyon, Joseph D. Grant, and Coyote Lake county parks. Reservations can be made through the

Joseph D. Grant County Park

park district by calling (408) 355-2201. Online reservations should be available in the years to come. No backpacking trips are possible in the Santa Clara County Park District but numerous group campgrounds are available for use by non-profit youth groups (see Appendix A: *Group Campgrounds of the Bay Area*). The Santa Clara County Parks web site is comprehensive and provides excellent maps for each of its parks. For more information contact Santa Clara County Parks and Recreation Department, 298 Garden Hill Dr., Los Gatos, CA 95032, (408) 355-2200, fax (408) 355-2290, www.parkhere.org, email: parkinfo@mail.prk.co.santa-clara.ca.us.

San Mateo County Parks protect 14,000 acres in 17 parks, the smallest amount of land among the featured park districts. While the majority of its small park units are located on the northern San Francisco peninsula, a large complex of three parks in the redwood forest of the Santa Cruz Mountains—Memorial,

Pescadero Creek, and Sam McDonald—provide overnight outdoor opportunities and backpacking trailheads. All sites are first-come, first-serve at both Memorial campground and Pescadero Creek trail camps; dogs are not permitted at either. The San Mateo County Park district seems most in need of funding relative to other local park districts. Facilities are wanting, the park maps difficult to use or find, and staffing minimal. Tracking down specific information can be a challenge. While Memorial County Park is popular, Pescadero Creek County Park is one of the least traveled parks in the Bay Area. For more information contact San Mateo County Parks and Recreation, 455 County Center, 4th Floor, Redwood City, CA 94063, (650) 363-4020, fax (650) 599-1721, www.eparks.net, email: ParksandRecreation@co.sanmateo.ca.us.

Midpeninsula Regional Open Space District is an independent special district established in 1972 for the sole purpose of preserving open space land in its natural condition. Centered along the long spine of Skyline Ridge in the Santa Cruz Mountains, the district currently includes nearly 50,000 acres of land in more than 25 preserves. Dogs are generally not allowed. Entrance is free to all preserves. Only one overnight opportunity is available—Black Mountain Trail Camp in Monte Bello Open Space Preserve. For more information contact Midpeninsula Regional Open Space District, 330 Distel Circle, Los Altos, CA 94022-1404, (650) 691-1200, www.openspace.org, email: info@openspace.org.

A SEASON-BY-SEASON PLAYBOOK

Winter (December-February)

It is a magical time. Slaked with moisture after months of dry weather, open landscapes blush a luminescent green. The air of the Bay Area is purged by wind and cleansed by rain, creating sparkling and far-reaching views. In the redwood forest, countless mushrooms explode as orange-bellied newts clamber across the eternally damp forest floor. Streams and waterfalls flow strong across the land, gushing at peak volume. The naked limbs of deciduous oaks, sycamores, and big-leaf maples twist toward the sky in fantastic form. Winter waves break large and powerful upon the coastal shore. And very few people are out enjoying it.

This is the time of the year to savor views, waterfalls, and those regions overrun with people during the rest of the year. With incredible vistas of the entire Bay Area, Mt. Diablo and Angel Island are prime destinations between storms. In the crowded and popular North Bay parks—Mt. Tamalpais, Point Reyes, and

Point Reyes National Seashore

Samuel P. Taylor especially—visitation is as light as it ever gets. Waterfalls are at their peak in Uvas Canyon County Park and Big Basin Redwoods. Impressive winter swells and warm sunny stretches make the coast an inviting place. Watch the weather report closely for multi-day adventures—strong winter storms make for an intense camping experience suitable only for the properly-equipped.

Spring (March-May)

The rains of winter pour into the wildflowers of spring and open hillsides dance in a radiance of color. The riot of springtime progresses rapidly. By early to mid-March, wildflowers and new oak leaves have begun to appear at lower elevations. By the end of March, wildflowers start to peak at elevations below 500 feet. As April progresses, Spring marches up the hills to higher elevations—by mid-April in a typical year, it has reached the 2000-foot elevation and by the end of the month has reached the highest crests of the Bay Area. In May, wildflowers continue to bloom, but sun has already started to turn the lush green hillsides to a rustling brown.

Shooting stars

Spring is a fabulous time throughout the Bay Area and it is virtually impossible to go wrong when selecting a destination. The coast is alive with sunshine and wildflowers are abundant on open coastal bluffs. While fog does begin to arrive in step with the increasing temperatures of late spring, it is usually infrequent. The Marin Headlands and Point Reyes beckon. East of the Bay, one of the narrowest windows of all swings open. Regions that scorch intolerably in summer and crackle brown in fall are green, inviting, and flush with water. Watch the dazzling progression of spring as your elevation changes on Mt. Diablo or the Ohlone Trail. The backcountry of Henry W. Coe State Park has plentiful water sources, but hurry, they'll be gone by the end of May.

Summer (June-August)

A season of dramatic climactic contrast, it is also summer vacation for students and their families. From Memorial Day through Labor Day, visitation at Bay Area campgrounds increases markedly. Securing a campsite at many destinations requires reserving a site months in advance—especially for weekends and holidays—and crowds can dominate many an overnight experience.

It is the time for shady inland spots, sheltering redwood forests, and less-traveled destinations. Campers should avoid the popular, well-known parks such as Big Basin Redwoods and Mt. Tamalpais and opt instead for lesser-traveled parks such as the walk-in sites at Sanborn County Park; the first-come, first-serve sites at Austin Creek State Recreation Area; or the shady world of China Camp State Park. Backpackers are encouraged to steer clear of popular Point Reyes and avoid the heat of Henry W. Coe State Park and the Ohlone Trail. Focus instead on the shady, seldom-trod trail camps of the Santa Cruz Mountains. Castle Rock and Butano state parks, Pescadero Creek County Park, and the trail camps in Big Basin closer to the ocean (Twin Redwoods, Alder, and Camp Herbert) are good bets for availability during this busiest of outdoor times.

Fall (September-November)

Following the mania of Labor Day weekend, schools reopen their doors and absorb the children who have filled parks all summer long with their families. While weekends remain busy in September at many parks, use begins to drop off in October, and securing a weekend spot in the shoulder month of November is generally not a problem. Weekdays are almost completely empty. The great weather and sudden reduction in crowds make fall a prime time for exploring nearly everywhere in the Bay Area. Conditions are dry and brown across much of the region, but the pleasant weather means all parks are open for outdoor play.

The empty Mt. Diablo foothills,
Black Diamond Mines Regional Park

View of Mt. Tam
from Angel Island State Park

Camping Trips
& Campgrounds

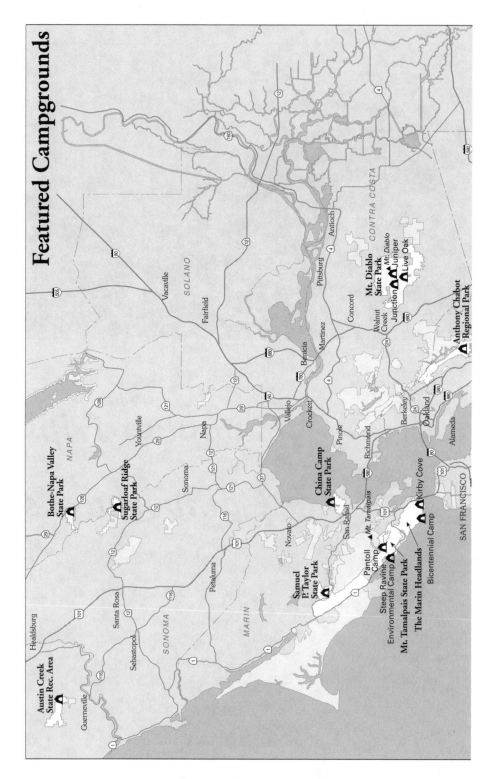

Featured Campgrounds

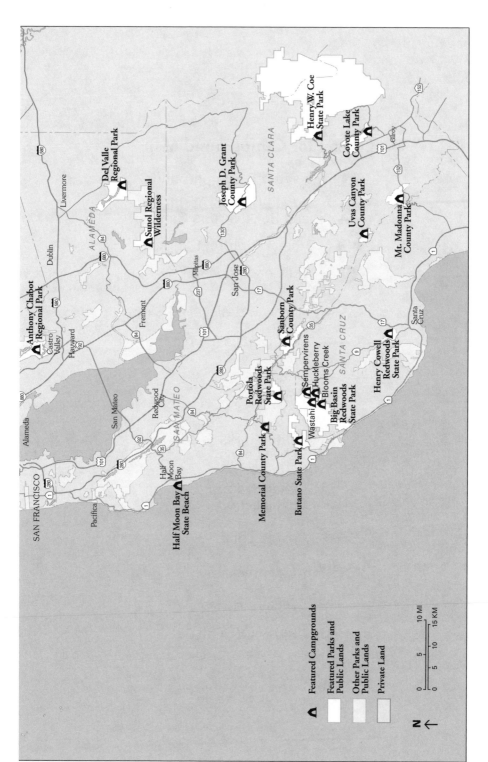

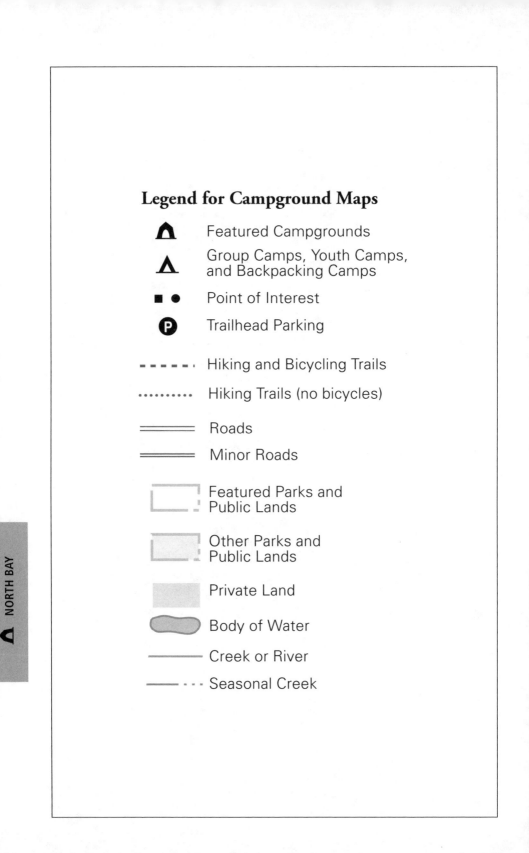

Legend for Campground Maps

⛺ Featured Campgrounds

⛺ Group Camps, Youth Camps, and Backpacking Camps

■ ● Point of Interest

🅟 Trailhead Parking

- - - - - Hiking and Bicycling Trails

.... Hiking Trails (no bicycles)

═══ Roads

═══ Minor Roads

Featured Parks and Public Lands

Other Parks and Public Lands

Private Land

Body of Water

─── Creek or River

──··· Seasonal Creek

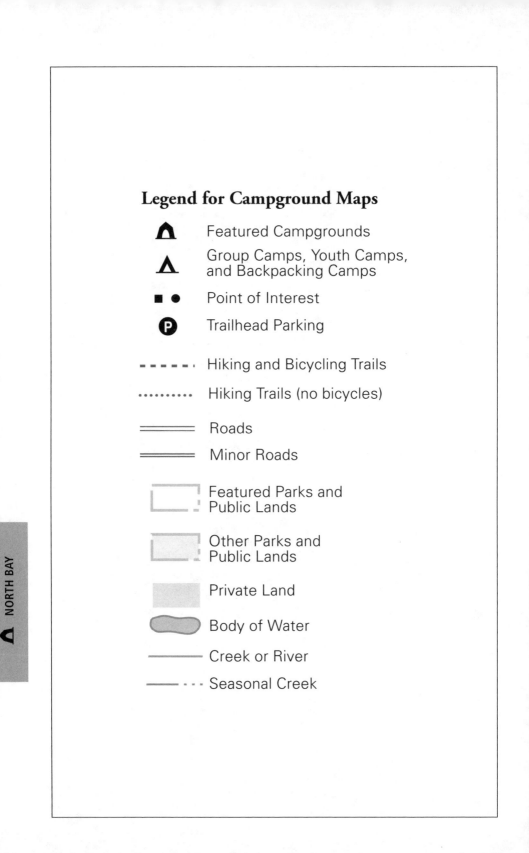

NORTH BAY

Mt. Tamalpais State Park

*Sweeping variety on the roof and
shores of Marin County*

Prominent, fascinating, and damn near irresistible, Mt. Tamalpais (2571′) rises high above Marin County. Mt. Tamalpais State Park rolls down its southern and western flanks, 6300 acres of wildland stretching from ocean cliffs to airy slopes. Additional protected land surrounds the state park, forming a great swath of open space that includes the upper slopes and summit of the mountain, as well as nearby Muir Woods. More than 200 miles of trails lace through this vast natural world, encompassing virtually every ecosystem found in the Bay Area.

Mt. Tamalpais State Park offers two distinct camping opportunities. Centrally located **Pantoll Walk-in Campground** is a forested destination in the heart of the park, and with six different trailheads nearby it makes an ideal base camp for exploring every aspect of the mountain. **Steep Ravine Environmental Campground** is located on the coast and is an isolated natural sanctuary featuring 10 rustic cabins and six walk-in campsites, optimal for peace and relaxation. Each campground is described in detail below.

PANTOLL WALK-IN CAMPGROUND

The Campground

Pantoll Walk-In is situated at an elevation of 1500 feet and spreads up the slopes adjacent to Pantoll Ranger Station at the intersection of Panoramic Highway and the road to the Mt. Tamalpais summit (Ridgecrest Blvd.). Sixteen sites shelter beneath a shady forest of Douglas-fir, coast live oak, canyon live oak, and tanoak with a sparse understory of huckleberry and sword ferns, blocking views from camp. All the sites are walk-in only, requiring campers to leave their vehicles in the Pantoll parking area and carry supplies the short distance to the sites (50-150 yards). Store all food in the provided food lockers—the raccoons and other camp raiders are determined creatures. Sudden Oak Death has been identified in the park—please take precautions against spreading this blight to other areas (see "The Living Bay Area" section in the *Where Should I Go?* chapter for more information).

Peace, quiet, and privacy are hard to find here. Many sites are located close together; Pantoll Ranger Station and parking area is one of the main hubs of the mountain and receives heavy visitor use; and the nearby traffic on Panoramic Highway is visible from a few sites and audible from them all. More than 2 million people visit the park each year, weekends are particularly manic year-round, and it is difficult to escape the sounds of humanity. Come during the week if possible.

That said, the campground has several things going for it. It is a first-come, first-serve campground and no reservations are accepted, making it possible to secure a site year-round with an early enough arrival (see below). Pantoll is also one of the best trailheads in the park and visitors can spend endless days exploring the wide variety of mountain trails. With its central location, dayhikes radiate in all directions—Muir Woods, the Pacific shore, and the mountain summit are all readily accessible. Lastly, public transportation is available directly to Pantoll on weekends and holidays, ideal for those without a vehicle.

En route camping is available for self-contained vehicles even when the campground is full. "Self-contained" means that the vehicle must have a permanently installed gray-water holding tank. En route campers park in the day-use lot and must sleep in their vehicles (no tents or fires); sleeping in "normal" cars is not allowed. Check-in for en route camping begins at 6 P.M., check-out is at 9 A.M., and there is a stay limit of only one night.

Crowds and Reservations

For such a popular park, it is surprisingly simple to obtain a site here—just arrive early. The campground usually fills on weekends year-round and daily from late April to late September. On weekends, especially during summer, the park recommends arriving by 8 A.M. to secure a site. On summer weekdays (Sunday-Thursday), a noon arrival is usually adequate to obtain a site. On weekdays from October to late April, space is almost always available. Check at Pantoll Ranger Station upon arrival. While it's always worth calling ahead for availability, the park will not hold a site for you.

Trails

Mt. Tamalpais is laced with a vast network of interconnecting trails, a half dozen of which converge on Pantoll. A map of the park and its myriad trails is essential (see below). Recommended hiking trails include: Matt Davis Trail, which traverses a wide range of ecological variety both east and west from

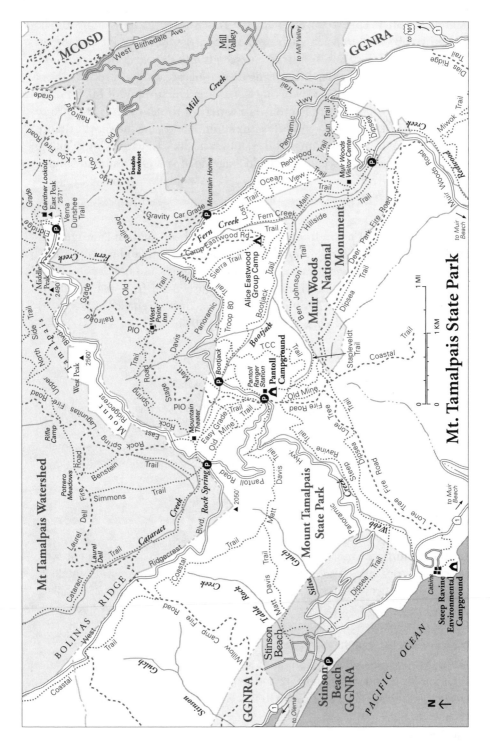

Mt. Tamalpais State Park

Pantoll and offers epic views; Steep Ravine Trail, which descends along lush and vibrant Webb Creek to reach Highway 1 and accesses Steep Ravine and the coast (see below); and Bootjack Trail, which descends into the old-growth redwoods of Muir Woods. Round-trip hikes using these trails are generally in the range of 5-6 miles, perfect for a half-day hiking adventure. The summit of Mt. Tamalpais can be reached on foot from Pantoll via a variety of routes but it is easier to drive Ridgecrest Blvd. to its end below the summit and hike the short distance from there. Those with mountain bikes, however, can easily ride almost all the way to the summit on nicely graded Old Stage Road and Old Railroad Grade, a 7-mile round-trip.

To Reach Pantoll

Take Highway 1 north from Highway 101 and bear right on Panoramic Highway, following it for 5 miles to Pantoll Ranger Station and parking area on your left. *Public Transportation* is available weekends and holidays on Golden Gate Transit Route 63, which runs up to eight buses a day from Marin City to Stinson Beach via Pantoll. For more information and current schedules, go online at www.transitinfo.org or call (415) 455-2000.

PANTOLL WALK-IN CAMPGROUND DETAILS

Governing Agency: Mt. Tamalpais State Park, 801 Panoramic Highway, Mill Valley, CA 94941, (415) 388-2070, www.parks.ca.gov.

Visitor Center: Pantoll Ranger Station (415) 388-2070. Open daily in summer and on most weekends approximately 9 A.M.–5 P.M., open intermittently during the off-season.

Sites: 16 walk-in sites. 1 handicapped-accessible site.

Costs: $13/site, includes 1 vehicle. $4 per additional vehicle. *Seniors 62+:* $2 discount. *Day-use parking fee for Pantoll lot:* $4/vehicle.

Group Campground: Alice Eastwood Group Campground, located just above Muir Woods near the eastern edge of the park. 15-minute drive from Pantoll. 2 sites. *Site A:* maximum 50 people and 15 vehicles. *Site B:* maximum 25 people and 10 vehicles. By reservation only, (800) 444-7275 or www.reserveamerica.com. Very popular, reserve far in advance.

Months Open/Closed: Open year-round.

Maps: Mt. Tamalpais State Park Map ($1) is available at the ranger station and is sufficient for hiking within the park and surrounding open space. Best map for the area is Olmsted's *A Rambler's Guide to the Trails of Mt. Tamalpais and the Marin Headlands.*

Facilities: Flush toilets in tiled bathrooms, pay phone, firewood available for purchase ($5/bundle).

Regulations: *Fires* permitted in fire rings, no wood collecting. *Dogs* prohibited on all state park trails, allowed leashed in the campground and picnic areas only and on trails in the Marin Municipal Water District, north of the state park; leashes must be no longer than 6 feet. *Bikes* allowed on fire roads and designated trails only. *Maximum number of people per site:* 8. *Maximum number of vehicles per site:* 2. *Check-out time:* noon. *Check-in time:* 2 P.M. *Maximum length of stay:* 7 consecutive days, 30 days total annually.

STEEP RAVINE ENVIRONMENTAL CAMPGROUND

The Campground

In contrast to bustling Pantoll, Steep Ravine is remote, isolated, and a world away from reality. Ten diminutive cabins and six walk-in campsites perch above breaking waves and rugged cliffs, providing far-reaching views up and down a battered and emergent coastline. With few amenities, abrasive weather, and minimal availability, this is a special place for only the determined few.

Steep Ravine is situated just above sea level on a small bluff at the end of Rocky Point Road, a gated, one-lane road dropping abruptly from Highway 1. The ten small cabins cluster close together on the north shore of the bluff and are equipped with wooden sleeping plat-

Steep Ravine, Mt. Tamalpais State Park

forms, a table, cooking area, and wood-burning stove. A barbecue grill is available outside. No electricity is provided and guests need to bring a cookstove, lantern, and sleeping bag and padding.

The six campsites are well spaced and private, each in a unique location offering a nice mix of views and shelter from the wind. Site 1 is exposed but offers good views north. Sites 2 and 3 tuck close to each other in a copse of Monterey pine, with 2 offering shelter but no views and 3 providing the opposite. Sites 4 and 5 nestle among fascinating sandstone outcrops and are the most removed. Both offer views south with some wind protection. Site 6 is farthest inland, near the parking area, and has both decent shelter and views amid the brush.

Sitting on the edge of California above the mighty Pacific, Steep Ravine gets some exciting waves and weather. Wind is a common companion, its cold blustery breath making a strong, wind-worthy tent essential for campers. Wet winter storms can pack a powerful—and powerfully exciting—punch. Summer fog is

NORTH BAY

common. Bring warm clothes and a windbreaker year-round. Due to limited space and efforts to preserve Steep Ravine as a natural sanctuary, certain regulations are strictly enforced. First, dogs are prohibited in order to preserve and protect the unusually wild nature of this location. Second, each site or cabin is allowed only one vehicle. Additional vehicles are not permitted past the gate (even to unload) and must park in the small lot near the gate on Highway 1. Due to the narrow, twisting access road, RVs and trailers are not permitted.

Crowds and Reservations

Steep Ravine is reputedly the most popular unit in the entire state park system. Reservations can be made year-round from 10 days to seven months in advance by calling (800) 444-7275 or going online at www.reserveamerica.com. On the first day of each month at 8 A.M. PST, the entire month seven months later opens up for reservations (for example, on March 1 all the days in September open for reservation). All cabins are usually booked within the first 30 minutes of becoming available! Tentsite reservations are not quite as difficult to obtain, but weekends fill almost immediately from March through October and all sites are usually completely booked three months in advance. The winter months (December-February) are the only time that campsites won't be fully reserved. No more than one site or cabin per night may be reserved by an individual.

If you aren't able to plan more than six months in advance, don't despair— there is still hope. Each day at 2 P.M. a lottery is held at Pantoll Ranger Station (see above) if any cabins and campsites are available due to cancellations, no-shows, or early departures. You must be present at the time of the drawing and no preference is given to those who submit their names earlier in the day. Some days several campsites and/or cabins become available, on other days nothing. Contact the ranger station in the morning to find out if a lottery will be held. Those lucky enough to get a spot in Steep Ravine may stay there as long as the given cabin or site is available. The unlucky have the option of staying at Pantoll Walk-In Campground and trying again the next day.

Trails

The rocky headlands and rugged shore around Steep Ravine make for thrilling exploration. Be careful as you scramble on rocks; never turn your back on the sea, and exercise good judgment while exploring the hazardous shoreline. Trails wind around the area; please stay on existing paths to minimize your impact. Interested in exploring beyond Steep Ravine? The only trail access to the greater network of state park trails is Steep Ravine Trail, starting immediately south of Rocky Point Road on Highway 1. A beautiful trail that steadily climbs 1100 feet along perennial Webb Creek, it reaches Pantoll Ranger Station in 2 miles. Extended dayhikes run from Steep Ravine to Muir Woods via Dipsea Trail or to the very summit of Mt. Tam via various heart-pounding routes.

To Reach Steep Ravine Environmental Campground

Take Highway 1 for one mile south of Stinson Beach or five miles north of Muir Beach to reach gated Rocky Point Road. After putting in the gate code provided with your reservation materials, descend 0.7 mile on the narrow road to the small parking area. Remember, only one car per site is allowed and extra vehicles must be left in the small dirt lot on the east side of Highway 1.

STEEP RAVINE ENVIRONMENTAL CAMPGROUND DETAILS

Governing Agency: Mt. Tamalpais State Park, 801 Panoramic Highway, Mill Valley, CA 94941, (415) 388-2070, www.parks.ca.gov.

Visitor Center: Pantoll Ranger Station (see above).

Sites: 10 cabins, 6 walk-in campsites. 1 handicapped-accessible cabin and campsite.

Costs: *Cabins:* $27/night. *Campsites:* $9/night, April-Oct.; $7/night, Nov.-March.

Group Sites: None.

Months Open/Closed: Open year-round.

Maps: Mt. Tamalpais State Park and Olmsted maps (see above).

Facilities: No phones or electricity. Outhouses are provided and firewood is available for purchase ($5/bundle).

Regulations: *Fires* permitted in fire rings, no wood collecting. *Dogs* are prohibited in Steep Ravine. *Bikes* allowed on paved access road only. *Fishing* allowed in the Pacific Ocean with valid California fishing license. *Maximum number of people per cabin or campsite:* 5. *Maximum number of vehicles per site:* 1 (strictly enforced). Vehicles without a permit are not permitted past the gate, even to unload. *Check-out time:* noon. *Check-in time:* 2 P.M. *Maximum length of stay:* 7 consecutive days, 30 days total annually.

▲ NORTH BAY

Giving Back

Mt. Tamalpais Interpretive Association is a volunteer organization whose purpose is to promote the conservation, education, and interpretation of Mt. Tamalpais State Park. Box 3318, San Rafael, CA 94912, (415) 258-2410, www.mttam.net.

The Marin Headlands

*A powerful geographic nexus on
the shores of the Golden Gate*

The forces of nature and humanity converge on the Golden Gate. On its southern end the workings of humanity cover San Francisco with a blanket of technological triumph, a city of concrete and skyscrapers home to a rich collection of society and its trappings. Spanning the Gate, the Golden Gate Bridge is human genius incarnate, a marvel of beauty and ingenuity. Through the Gate rushes restless natural energy, a flood of California water mingled with the salty pulse of the Pacific Ocean. And north of the Gate, nature is free to exist, a shining example of outdoor wonder secluded and protected within the coastal wilds of the Marin Headlands.

Unlike other destinations listed in this book, the Marin Headlands provide only a few sites for overnight camping adventures. However, their unique qualities and the epic views of the surrounding area make them extremely desirable places to visit. In total, there are seven sites in the Marin Headlands amenable to car camping, and all still require at least a 100-yard walk from the parking area. (There also are two backpacking trail camps with a total of eight sites—see the backpacking chapter *Marin Headlands* for details.) Sites are divided between two camping areas—Kirby Cove and Bicentennial Camp. Each is described in detail below.

KIRBY COVE CAMPGROUND

The Campground

Kirby Cove Campground is situated in a secluded valley immediately west of the Golden Gate Bridge by the shores of the Golden Gate. Accessed via a 0.9-mile one-lane dirt road off-limits to non-campers and inaccessible to RVs and trailers, the campground offers four spacious sites beneath the tall branches of a sheltering forest. Each site is equipped with picnic tables, tent platforms, and a fire ring, but *water is not provided*; campers need to bring an adequate supply for their stay. Site 1 is located closest to the coast (but farthest from the parking area), offers the most privacy, and has tent sites that look directly onto the Golden Gate Bridge. Sites 2 and 3 are adjacent to each other on the smooth forest floor, centrally located, and can be reserved together for large groups. Site 4 is the smallest,

Camping at Kirby Cove

located close to the parking area, and is tucked peacefully away in the back corner. The raccoons here are almost predatory—be sure to secure all food items in the provided lockers at night.

Kirby Cove is one of the foggiest places in the Bay Area. While this can make for chilly, damp, and windy conditions (come prepared), the bigger drawback is the deafening foghorns that guard the towers of the Golden Gate Bridge. When visibility is obscured for ships approaching the bridge, the foghorns bellow on regular 40-second cycles, an overpowering discordant presence that easily blots out all other sounds. When active, they can make for a restless night of minimal sleep. And you can't escape them by coming in the fog-free off-season—due to rain, Kirby Cove is closed for camping November through March. April and October are your best bets for avoiding the fog and its accompanying power symphony.

Within Kirby Cove Campground the forest is dominated by tall Monterey pine, joined on the periphery by eucalyptus and Monterey cypress. The understory is thick in places with coyote brush, California sage, coffee berry, willow, toyon, and poison oak. A thin trickling stream flows through camp on occasion,

its moist green bed filled with ferns, vetch, horsetail, and wild cucumber. A small beach can be found in Kirby Cove, guarded by the concrete bulwark of Battery Kirby. Built at the turn of the century as part of an extensive chain of coastal fortifications surrounding the Golden Gate, these days the abandoned battery makes for fun scrambling—a narrow brick-lined tunnel still connects through the fortifications to the beach.

Kirby Cove

Surprisingly tranquil waters appear to lap the sandy beach but beware—swimming at Kirby Cove is risky. Less than a hundred yards offshore, powerful tidal currents can move in excess of 7 knots, quickly sweeping the unwary to sea.

NORTH BAY

Enjoy the incredible beach views instead. The unique color of the sand is due to the extensive bands of red chert common in this region of the Headlands. Formed over millions of years on the bottom of the sea floor from the settling skeletons of microorganisms, chert is extremely resistant to erosion and forms the sheer topography found in these coastal cliffs. Excellent exposures can be seen on the south end of the beach and along Conzelman Road above Kirby Cove.

Crowds and Reservations

Given its proximity, small size, and unique location, Kirby Cove is nearly always full. Advance reservations are essential and can be made up to a maximum of 90 days and a minimum of seven days in advance by calling (800) 365-2267 between 7 A.M. and 7 P.M. daily. Weekends are the most popular and require calling the moment sites open up for reservations. Weekday reservations are easier to secure but still require calling several weeks (sometimes more than a month) in advance. After securing a reservation, all appropriate materials, including parking permits and the code for the gated access road, will be mailed to you. Registration at the Marin Headlands Visitor Center is not required. Any sites not reserved are available on a first-come, first-serve basis at the visitor center.

Other Fun Activities

See Exploring the Marin Headlands below.

To Reach Kirby Cove from the South

Take Highway 101 to the Alexander Avenue Exit, the first off-ramp north of the Golden Gate Bridge. Turn left at the stop sign and drive under the freeway overpass. After a short distance, bear right up steep Conzelman Road and follow it 0.3 mile to the gated gravel road on your left, located immediately past the viewing point pullout. From Conzelman Road, the thrilling access road rapidly drops 350 feet to the parking area.

To Reach Kirby Cove from the North

From Highway 101 take the last Sausalito exit immediately before the Golden Gate Bridge, turn left at the stop sign, bear right up steep Conzelman Road, and proceed as above.

Monterey Pine above Kirby Cove

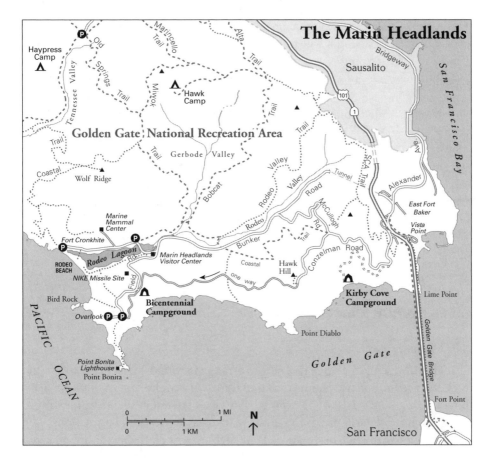

KIRBY COVE DETAILS

Governing Agency: Golden Gate National Recreation Area, Special Park Use Group, Marin Headlands Visitor Center, Building 948, Fort Barry Chapel, Sausalito, CA 94965, 1-800-365-2267, www.nps.gov/goga.

Visitor Center: Marin Headlands Visitor Center, located on Bunker Rd. in nearby Rodeo Valley, (415) 331-1540; open 9:30 A.M.–4:30 P.M. daily.

Sites: 4 walk-in sites.

Costs: $25/site.

Group Sites: Sites 2 and 3 are adjacent to each other and can be used together for larger groups. Maximum 20 people.

Months Open/Closed: Closed Nov.-March.

Maps: Free Golden Gate National Recreation Map is available at visitor center and adequate for hiking. Best map for the Headlands and surrounding area is Olmsted's *A Rambler's Guide to the Trails of Mt. Tamalpais and the Marin Headlands.*

NORTH BAY

Facilities: Pit toilets, no water. A wheeled cart is provided for each site and can be picked up at the parking area. For most of the season, a camp host resides in Kirby Cove and can help answer any questions.

Regulations: *Fires* permitted in fire rings. All firewood must be brought in, no wood collecting. No beach fires. *Dogs* prohibited. *Bikes* allowed on fire roads only, prohibited in posted areas around campsites. *Trailers and RVs* prohibited. *Fishing* permitted from Kirby Cove Beach. *Maximum number of people per site:* 10. Up to 15 people may visit the registered campers at the site but must leave by 10 P.M. Groups must have a responsible leader 21 years or older for every 10 people under 18. *Maximum number of vehicles per site:* 3. Additional vehicles must park in the commuter lot on the north side of the Golden Gate Bridge. Sleeping in vehicles is prohibited. *Check-in time:* 1 P.M. *Check-out time:* noon. *Maximum length of stay:* 3 nights total per season, only 1 weekend night (Friday-Saturday) per group per season.

BICENTENNIAL CAMPGROUND

The Campground

This tiny refuge of three tent sites is arranged around a small clearing, with each site accommodating a maximum of only two people. Privacy is minimal but camping here is free! While spectacular views are not available from within the campground itself, proximity to the many nearby views and attractions make this a worthwhile destination. Picnic tables, tent platforms, and food lockers are provided, but water is not available at the campground itself. Expect cool, windy conditions year-round, with the added bonus of regular fog from May through September.

A short walk is required to reach the campground. From the parking lot, a wide fire road descends 50 feet in about 100 yards to the sites. Good views south of San Francisco can be had as you descend—on San Francisco's northwest Pacific shore the Cliff House and adjacent Seal Rocks can be spotted, the antenna-lined ridge of San Bruno Mountain is farther south, and Montara Mountain defines the southern horizon more than 18 miles away beyond the long sandy line of Ocean Beach. By the roadside and around the campground, wind-lashed cypress trees extend above thick coastal brush populated primarily by coyote brush, sticky monkey flower, lupine, wild cucumber, poison oak, blackberry brambles, and California sage.

Lupine at
Marin Headlands

Crowds and Reservations

It only takes six people to completely fill Bicentennial, and it is fully reserved most summer days and weekends year-round. Reservations can be made up to 90 days in advance by contacting the Marin Headlands Visitor Center at (415) 331-1540 between 9:30 A.M. and 4:30 P.M. daily. On the day of their reservation, campers are required to check in at the visitor center during open hours before heading to the campground. All unclaimed reservations are cancelled at 4:30 P.M. unless advance notification is given to arrange an after-hours pick-up.

Other Fun Activities

See Exploring the Marin Headlands below.

To Reach the Campground

Campers will need to first register at the visitor center. From the south, take Highway 101 to the Alexander Avenue exit (the first off-ramp north of the Golden Gate Bridge) and follow signs toward the Marin Headlands, turning left to pass through the one-lane tunnel and then continuing straight on Bunker Road for approximately 2.0 miles to the visitor center. Approaching from the north, take the last Sausalito exit immediately before the Golden Gate Bridge, turn left at the stop sign, bear right up steep Conzelman Road and continue on Conzelman Road for 3.0 miles to the intersection by Battery Alexander. Turn right and continue 0.5 mile to the visitor center. The parking area for Bicentennial is located across from Battery Alexander.

Public Transportation is available to the Marin Headlands from San Francisco on Sundays and holidays aboard Muni Bus 76, which departs once an hour from downtown and makes stops throughout the Headlands. Go online at www.transitinfo.org/Muni or call (415) 673-MUNI for current schedules and information.

NORTH BAY

BICENTENNIAL CAMPGROUND DETAILS

Governing Agency: Golden Gate National Recreation Area, Marin Headlands Visitor Center, Building 948, Fort Barry Chapel, Sausalito, CA 94965, (415) 331-1540, www.nps.gov/goga.

Visitor Center: Marin Headlands Visitor Center, located on Bunker Rd. in nearby Rodeo Valley, (415) 331-1540; open 9:30 A.M.–4:30 P.M. daily.

Sites: 3 walk-in sites.

Costs: Free.

Group Sites: None.

Months Open/Closed: Open year-round.

Maps: See Kirby Cove Details above.

Facilities: Pit toilet, no water.

Regulations: *Fires* permitted in fire rings. All firewood must be brought in, no wood collecting. *Dogs* prohibited. *Bikes* allowed on fire roads and paved roads only, prohibited in posted areas around campsites. *Maximum number of people per site:* 2. *Maximum number of vehicles per site:* 2. *Check-out time:* noon. *Maximum length of stay:* 3 nights total per year.

EXPLORING THE MARIN HEADLANDS

There are enough trails and destinations in the Headlands to keep visitors occupied for weeks. Dozens of trails crisscross the Headlands and a near-infinite variation of dayhikes are possible. In the southern half of the Headlands, recommended are all trails that approach the dramatic coastline, as well as the 5-mile loop hike around wild and open Gerbode Valley. In the northern half, Wolf Ridge offers outstanding views of nearly the entire Headlands and towers almost 1000 feet above secluded Tennessee Valley to the north. (See the backpacking chapter *Marin Headlands* for more information on Gerbode and Tennessee valleys.) Most trails in the Headlands are old ranch roads open for biking—check with the visitor center for current information and trail closures.

Kirby Cove, Marin Headlands

For those less interested in hiking or biking, the long list of exciting nearby possibilities includes: A short stroll to the farthest reaches of the Bay Area at Point Bonita Lighthouse (open 12:30-3:30 P.M. Saturday-Monday; free guided walk at 12:30 P.M.); visiting rescued sea creatures at the Marine Mammal Center by Rodeo Lagoon (open 10 A.M.–4 P.M. daily, (415) 289-7330); a stop at Hawk Hill to view the myriad raptors and other migratory birds that travel south over the Golden Gate in fall; exploring the numerous batteries and bunkers along the coastal bluffs which once protected the Golden Gate from marine invasion; or experiencing a once-active NIKE Missile Site to learn about Cold War military defense strategy (open 12:30-3:30 P.M. Wednesday-Friday). The Headlands Visitor Center has detailed information about all these activities, and more.

Giving Back

The Golden Gate National Parks Conservancy is a non-profit membership organization dedicated to the preservation and public enjoyment of the Golden Gate National Parks. Golden Gate National Parks Association, Building 201, Fort Mason, San Francisco, CA 94123, (415) 561-3000, www.parksconservancy.org, email: tellmemore@parksconservancy.org.

Marin Headlands view

NORTH BAY

Samuel P. Taylor State Park

*Barnabe's bones and redwood forest
in the heart of Marin County wild*

Astride crystalline Lagunitas Creek, shadowed by redwood
trees, surrounded by protected open space, Samuel P. Taylor
State Park awaits. Few campgrounds can match its proximity to
so many beautiful outdoor destinations and visitors could easily
spend weeks exploring the vast possibilities of trails and adventures in this park and the surrounding region.

Today's parkland was once the haunt of Barnabe, a retired
white army mule owned by Samuel P. Taylor in the 1860s. Too
wily to be penned, he regularly escaped from his fenced confine
and would wander on the lofty slopes of the 1466-foot hill that
today bears his name. Following his death, he was reputedly
buried on the selfsame hill and could witness later changes from
his ethereal perch.

While alive, Barnabe could look over the drainage of Lagunitas Creek and espy the original 100 acres of prime creekside tim-
berland purchased by his owner in the early 1850s with the profits
realized from 6173 pennyweight of Sierra Nevada gold. He may
have seen the small community that surrounded Taylor's paper
mill, built in 1856 on the stream banks. The first such mill west
of Pennsylvania, it transformed burlap, linen rags, paper scrap,
old rope, and cotton bits into manila paper, newsprint, and wrapping paper for use in the exploding city of San Francisco. Had he
not died beforehand, Barnabe probably would have been startled
by the clamor of the narrow gauge railroad which began operation in 1874 along Lagunitas Creek, hauling produce, paper, and
passengers from the coast to San Rafael until the great 1906 quake
collapsed one of its principal tunnels. Barnabe likely would have
panicked in 1874 when Samuel P. Taylor's profitable black-pow-
der mill accidentally detonated and permanently shut the creekside operation down. Were he not decaying, Barnabe also might
have been a popular guest at Camp Taylor, a resort that developed

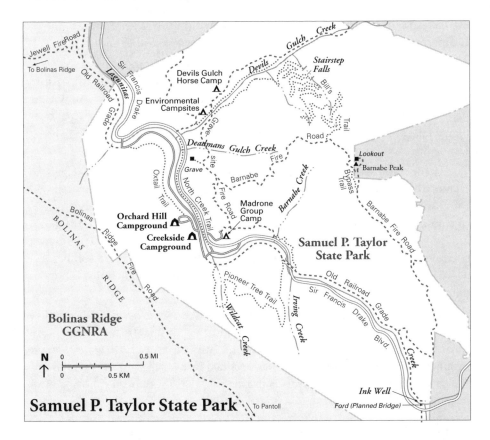

Samuel P. Taylor State Park

during the 1870s and '80s along the eastern boundary of today's park. Drawing up to 3000 people at a time by the late 1880s, Camp Taylor was one of the first places in the country to offer camping as a recreational activity (alongside less-rustic amenities like a massive hotel and dance floor). In 1946, the state of California purchased Camp Taylor and created the park that today encompasses nearly 3000 acres and forever protects Barnabe's bones.

SAMUEL P. TAYLOR STATE PARK CAMPGROUND

The Campground

Sites are situated at an average elevation of 200 feet and divided into two areas: Creekside (sites 1-24) and Orchard Hill (sites 25-58). As their names imply, Creekside lines mellifluous Lagunitas Creek and offers more closely spaced sites perched along the edge of somewhat steep cutbanks, while Orchard Hill offers better-spaced sites a short distance uphill and away from passing vehicles. Overall, site privacy is fair to good with the thick foliage providing extra cover between sites. Located completely within the redwood forest, the campground is generally cool and shady—bring warm clothes year-round.

Within the campground the branches of redwood, Douglas-fir, tanoak, California bay, and madrone intertwine in a shady mosaic, while an understory of huckleberry, California hazel, sword fern, elderberry, blackberry, and poison oak completes the forest. Sudden Oak Death has been identified in the park— please take precautions against spreading this blight to other areas (see "The Living Bay Area" in *Where Should I Go?* for more information).

The forest provides habitat for a raucous collection of birdlife—Steller's jays chatter all day, great horned owls call at night, and acorn woodpeckers hammer incessantly on tree trunks. Unusual in the avian world, acorn woodpeckers live in communal family groups of up to a dozen individuals and cooperatively store and protect massive quantities of acorns in tree trunks. A keen eye will discover several such caches within the campground. Slightly smaller than a robin, the acorn woodpecker can be identified by its red head, black body, and white patches on the wings, cheeks, and rump.

Along Lagunitas Creek, big-leaf maple is joined by the occasional coast live oak. Coho salmon and steelhead trout still journey up this stream to reproduce during the winter months when rains sufficiently swell the creek. Statewide, the number of spawning coho salmon has declined by a staggering 94% within only the past 60 years and the Central California populations of both coho and steelhead are now listed as threatened under the Endangered Species Act. Today, Lagunitas Creek supports an estimated 10% of the entire Central California wild coho population, or approximately 500 fish. Visitors in January have the best chance to spot these survivors as they battle their way upstream; the park's creekside trails offer several good vantage points. From December through mid-February, the Marin Municipal Water District also opens a parking area by Shafter Bridge on the eastern edge of the park for fish viewing. Call (415) 459-5267 for more information.

Crowds and Reservations

Samuel P. Taylor is one of the most popular campgrounds in the Bay Area, and to get a site during the summer months and on most weekends requires considerable advance planning. Weekends are fully reserved in advance from April through October and the campground is totally booked every day from Memorial Day through Labor Day. Reserve months ahead of time for popular summer weekends and holidays. Outside of these times, space is usually available. Reservations can be made year-round, up to seven months in advance, by calling (800) 444-7275 or going online at www.reserveamerica.com.

A few additional tips: The campground provides one hike/bike site to accommodate those traveling under their own power. Also, the campground offers en route camping for those merely passing through. En route campers

cannot enter until 9 P.M., must completely vacate by 9 A.M., and can stay only
one night. Lastly, there are two primitive group sites (capacity 10) located near
Devils Gulch Horse Camp, 1 mile west of the main park entrance. Both lack the
amenities of the main campground (pit toilets and water only) and are close to
the horse camp corrals, but they are removed from the central campground
bustle.

Trails

More than 20 miles of trails can be found within the park, half of which are
singletrack and reserved for hikers only. The remainder are wide fire roads and
open to bike use. For those intrigued by the area's human history, a short historical trail can be found past the campground, at the end of the paved road on the
south side of the creek, and is interpreted with the help of numbered posts and
a free brochure (available at the ranger station). Other recommended hikes: the
3-mile Pioneer Tree Trail loop, which passes through peaceful redwood forest
and by the Pioneer Tree, the largest redwood in the park; and the more strenuous 6-mile loop hike to the spectacular views atop Barnabe Peak via Devils
Gulch, Bill's Trail, Barnabe Fire Road, and Gravesite Fire Road. Casual cyclists
can follow the old railroad grade on an easy and level 3-mile paved bike trail
that runs the length of the park, while the more ambitious can choose from a
variety of loops through the park and surrounding open space.

Other Fun Activities

Swimming is possible in Lagunitas Creek at both ends of the park—ask
about the Ink Well near Shafter Bridge by the park's eastern boundary. Campfire
programs are usually offered during the summer months on Wednesday and
Saturday evenings. Lastly, the park makes an ideal base camp for excursions to
other nearby parks. Point Reyes National Seashore is particularly close—Bear
Valley Visitor Center is only 6 miles away (see the backpacking chapter *Point
Reyes National Seashore* for more information).

To Reach the Park

Take Sir Francis Drake Blvd. 5 miles east from Highway 1 in Olema or
15 miles west from Highway 101 in San Rafael. It is also possible to reach the
park by *public transportation*. Weekdays, Marin Stagecoach runs a round-trip
shuttle four times a day between the San Anselmo hub and Inverness. It stops
in front of the Samuel P. Taylor entrance en route. For more information and
current schedules, call Marin Stagecoach at (415) 454-0964, or go online at
www.marin-stagecoach.org.

THE DETAILS

Governing Agency: Samuel P. Taylor State Park, Box 251, Lagunitas, CA 94938, (415) 488-9897, www.parks.ca.gov.

Visitor Center: No visitor center. Entrance station provides information and sells maps for the park.

Sites: 61 drive-in sites. 1 hike/bike site for those without vehicle. 3 handicapped-accessible sites. 25 sites can accommodate RVs and trailers up to 27'. 10 additional sites for trailers and RVs to 20'.

Costs: $12/site, includes 1 vehicle. *Additional vehicle:* $4. *Hike/bike site:* $2/person. *Devils Gulch primitive sites:* $14. *Seniors 62+:* $2 discount. *Day-use fee:* $4/vehicle.

Group Sites: *Madrone #1:* maximum 50 people and 20 vehicles, $67. *Madrone #2:* maximum 25 people and 10 vehicles, $33. Sites are located together, away from the campground on the other side of Sir Francis Drake Blvd., and are very popular.

Months Open/Closed: *Orchard Hill area:* open year-round. *Creekside area:* closed December-February.

Maps: The State Park Map ($1) is available at the entrance station and is sufficient for hiking within the park. Tom Harrison's *Point Reyes National Seashore* map provides the best overview for the park and surrounding region.

Facilities: Free hot showers, flush toilets in tiled bathrooms, pay phone, dump station, firewood ($5/bundle).

Regulations: *Fires* permitted in fire rings, no wood collecting. *Dogs* prohibited on all park trails, allowed leashed in the campground and on fire roads and paved roads; leashes must be no longer than 6 feet. *Bikes* allowed in campground and on paved roads and fire roads. *Fishing* prohibited in Lagunitas Creek and its tributaries. *Maximum number of people per site:* 8. *Maximum number of sites per group:* 2. *Maximum number of vehicles per site:* 2. *Check-out time:* noon. *Maximum length of stay:* 30 days per calendar year, maximum 7 consecutive days during summer months, 14 consecutive in off-season, must leave for 48 hours before returning. Hike/bike site maximum 2 consecutive days.

NORTH BAY

Giving Back

Salmon Protection and Watershed Network (SPAWN) works to protect the endangered coho salmon and steelhead, as well as the creeks of the Lagunitas watershed. It provides public education programs, restoration projects, and site monitoring. Box 400, Forest Knolls, CA 94933, (415) 488-0370, www.spawnusa.org, email: spawn@igc.org.

NORTH BAY

China Camp State Park

*Bayside seclusion and vibrant
human history*

China Camp State Park tumbles from panoramic ridges to the historic bayshore, delightfully isolated from neighboring San Rafael by intervening topography. Located on the shores of San Pablo Bay, this quiet haven features a mild micro-climate that escapes the summer fog and makes it a pleasant camping destination year-round. Add to this its close proximity to San Francisco and Marin County sights and you have a campground ideal for just about everybody.

Home to a thriving population of grass shrimp, shallow San Pablo Bay (the broad northern arm of San Francisco Bay) attracted a large community of Chinese immigrants in the late 19th century. Utilizing skills learned in their coastal homeland of Kwangtung province, the Chinese harvested the shrimp for sale in San Francisco and export to China. They established more than 20 fishing camps around the Bay, including a bustling location in today's state park. In 1880, nearly 500 people called the small village at China Camp home. Fishing from traditional junks and sampans constructed from local redwoods, the successful Chinese soon raised the ire of non-Chinese fishermen. Beginning in 1901, a series of increasingly restrictive laws were passed which culminated in the total elimination of the Chinese industry by 1911. The few buildings that remain at China Camp Village (see below) are the last vestiges of this era of California history.

BACK RANCH MEADOWS WALK-IN CAMPGROUND

The Campground

Situated near sea level in a small, nicely shaded valley, all 30 sites are walk-in only, with the distance from parking lot to campsites ranging from 100-300 yards. There is also a cheap hike/bike site for those traveling under their own power. The pleasant sites

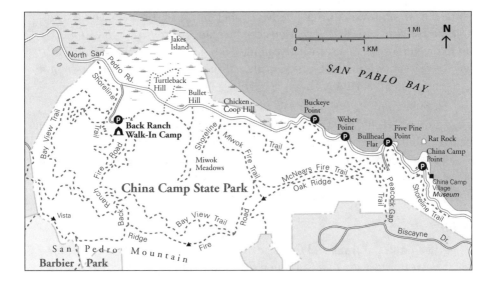

are reasonably spaced, offer fair to good privacy, and come equipped with a
food locker and barbecue grill. A quarter mile inland from the main park road,
the melody of local songbirds is more audible than the sounds of traffic. The
recently remodeled campground includes immaculate tiled bathrooms and hot
showers. Weather is mild year-round (more than 200 days per year are entirely
fog-free) and the summer heat found in parks farther east is pleasantly moder-
ated by nearby maritime influences. Note that the campground gate is locked
9 P.M.–8 A.M. daily and no entry or exit is possible during this time—plan
accordingly.

The campground and entire park is infested with Sudden Oak Death. More
than 100 dead or dying trees have been removed from the campground area in
recent years and it is critical that you take precautions against spreading this
blight to other areas (see "The Living Bay Area" in *Where Should I Go?* for more
information). While California bay trees predominate overhead, coast live oak
and smooth, bark-peeling madrones are also found in the area. A small stream
trickles through camp after winter rains and a few buckeye and valley oak can
be found along the streambed lower down. The large concrete ring in the lower
campground is a legacy from the days when the park was part of McNear
Ranch. The principal ranch area was located over the ridge west of the park,
but non-milking heifers were often herded into the region of today's campground to graze (the "Back Ranch") and watered in the concrete cistern whose
outline remains today.

Crowds and Reservations

The campground is popular in summer with both locals and tourists, but
demand is not as extreme as in other parks of the Bay Area. Weekends are fully

NORTH BAY

booked from mid-May through early October, but space on weekdays is available almost year-round. Reservations can be made from April 1 to October 31 up to seven months in advance by calling (800) 444-7275 or going online at www.reserveamerica.com. Outside of these times, sites are available first-come, first-serve and are virtually always available.

En route camping is available for self-contained vehicles even when the campground is full. "Self-contained" means that the vehicle must have a permanently installed gray-water holding tank. En route campers park in the day-use lot and must sleep in their vehicles (no tents or fires); sleeping in "normal" cars is not allowed. Check-in for en route camping begins at 6 P.M., check-out is at 9 A.M., and there is a stay limit of only one night.

Trails

Fifteen miles of trails and fire roads wind through the park. Unusual for the Bay Area, nearly every trail is open for mountain biking as well as hiking. Designed with bikers in mind, the singletrack trails are slightly wider (4') than normal, making the park a popular biking destination. For casual walkers the short loop on Turtle Back Hill is less than a mile long, designated for hikers only, and offers an interpretive trip through the park's ecosystems. A multitude of shorter and longer loops can be made with the Bay View and Shoreline trails, both of which pass through the campground and offer intermittent views of the San Pablo Bay and northern Bay Area. The best view, however, is found atop the hill at the intersection of Miwok and McNear fire trails, where an exotic stand of eucalyptus trees was recently removed. The panorama encompasses all of San Pablo Bay as well as nearly the entire Bay Area south of the park.

Other Fun Activities

The rustic fishing shanties of China Camp Village make for a fun exploration of history; a free museum details the story. Located 3 miles east of the campground turnoff, the Village is also accessible by trail from the campground via a 4-mile, one-way hike on Shoreline Trail. Swimming and fishing in the bay are possible from the village beach and several other shoreline locations—sturgeon and striped bass are popular targets.

To Reach the Park

Take Highway 101 for 3 miles north from the 580/101 junction to the Civic Center/North San Pedro Road exit (signed for China Camp State Park), located just north of central San Rafael. Follow N. San Pedro Road east for 3.0 miles to the campground entrance on the right. China Camp Village is 2.9 miles farther ahead on the left.

THE DETAILS

Governing Agency: China Camp State Park, Route 1, Box 244, San Rafael, CA 94901, (415) 456-0766, www.parks.ca.gov.

Visitor Center: *China Camp Village Museum:* open 10 A.M.–5 P.M. daily. *Park ranger station:* located just inland from Bullhead Flat a half mile west of China Camp Village, open intermittently.

Sites: 30 walk-in sites. 1 hike/bike site. 2 handicapped-accessible sites.

Costs: $12/site, includes 2 vehicles. *Additional vehicle:* $5. *Hike/bike site:* $1. *Seniors 62+:* $2 discount. There is no day-use fee for the park.

Group Sites: None.

Months Open/Closed: Open year-round.

Maps: China Camp State Park Map ($1) is sufficient for hiking within the park and available outside the ranger station and at the museum and campground entrance station when staffed. *Trails of Northeast Marin County* by Ben Pease (Pease Press) covers the park and other nearby open spaces.

Facilities: Hot showers ($.50/5 minutes), flush toilets in tiled bathrooms, pay phone, firewood available for purchase from the campground host by the parking area ($5/bundle). There also is a fun snack bar in China Camp Village, open weekends and holidays.

Regulations: *Fires* permitted in fire rings, no wood collecting. *Dogs* prohibited on all park trails, allowed leashed in the campground and picnic areas only; leashes must be no longer than 6 feet, dogs must sleep in tent or vehicle at night. *Bikes* allowed in campground and on all park trails except Turtle Back Hill Nature Trail. *Fishing* permitted in the bay from the park beaches. *Maximum number of sites per group:* 2. *Maximum number of people per site:* 8. *Check-out time:* noon. *Check-in time:* 2 P.M. *Maximum length of stay:* 7 consecutive days, April-October; 14 consecutive days, Nov.-March; 30 days total annually.

Giving Back

Friends of China Camp is a non-profit organization
dedicated to supporting the interpretive needs of the park.
16 Heritage Dr., San Rafael, CA 94901, (415) 454-8954.

Bothe–Napa Valley State Park

Natural, historic, pleasant Napa Valley

Tucked against the western edge of upper Napa Valley, secluded Bothe–Napa Valley State Park provides relief from the area's endless flow of vineyards, traffic, and tourist activity. The only public campground in the area, Bothe (BO-thee)–Napa makes an ideal base camp for exploring the diverse woodlands of the surrounding hills, marveling at America's largest wooden waterwheel, and savoring the wines of nearby vintners.

In the years preceding the California Gold Rush, fields of wheat and livestock—not grapes—filled Napa Valley, providing sustenance to San Francisco de Solano Mission in neighboring Sonoma Valley. Dr. Edward Turner Bale, an Englishman turned Mexican citizen, acquired a land grant of nearly 18,000 acres in the area around today's park and constructed one of the first mills in the region for processing wheat into flour. A colorful character known for his drinking habits, Dr. Bale was a Surgeon-in-Chief for the Mexican army in the early 1840s. He married the niece of General Mariano Vallejo, was publicly flogged in Sonoma for questioning the honesty of General Vallejo's younger brother Salvador Vallejo, subsequently shot Salvador in the back, was pardoned by the Mexican governor of California, ran off to the gold fields in 1848, got sick, and died the following year at age 38. His land was slowly divided up over time and in 1929 Reinhold Bothe acquired the land of today's state park, developing it as a private camping resort until it was turned over to the state park system in 1960. Bale's mill passed through a variety of owners, was upgraded with a huge 36-foot-diameter waterwheel in the early 1850s, and used to commercially process wheat until the turn of the century. Today, the nearby mill has been painstakingly restored—it houses a visitor center and museum (see below) and its giant waterwheel turns again.

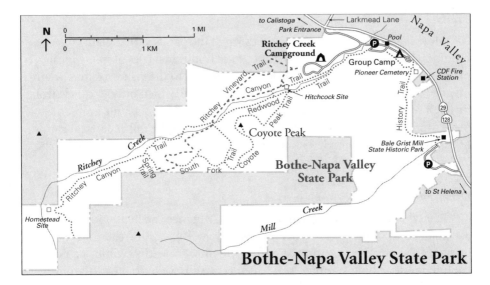

Bothe-Napa Valley State Park

RITCHEY CREEK CAMPGROUND

The Campground

Ritchey Creek, a perennial stream whose waters give life to a thin strip of redwood forest, forms a lush riparian corridor that contrasts markedly with the dry oak woodlands just beyond. Straddling this sharp ecologic divide, the campground offers spacious and relatively secluded sites whose vegetation varies dramatically by location. Closer to the creek, a thick canopy of Douglas-fir, madrone, California bay, buckeye, black oak, big-leaf maple, and coast live oak arc overhead, while second-growth redwoods line the streambed. Farther from the water grow dry chaparral and oak woodland where manzanita, coyote brush, blue oak, canyon live oak, buckbrush, toyon, gray pine, and scrub oak dominate. Nearly all sites offer shade from the baking summer sun, which can reach temperatures in excess of 100°F. Fall, winter, and spring are mild, and a profusion of wildflowers colors the landscape from March through May. Poison oak is common in the area—beware!

Crowds and Reservations

Popular Napa Valley is busy nearly every weekend of the year. Friday and Saturday nights from April through September, expect the campground to be fully reserved in advance. Weekdays year-round are seldom full, however. Reservations can be made from April 1 to October 31 up to seven months in advance by calling (800) 444-PARK or going online at www.reserveamerica.com.

Trails

More than 10 miles of trails wind through the park's varied plant communities. Before heading out, learn about the traditional uses of many local plants in the Native American Garden, located next to the visitor center. Recommended hikes include short and easy Redwood Trail, which offers a quiet stroll through redwoods along gurgling Ritchey Creek; and the 4.4-mile loop on Coyote Peak, South Fork, and Redwood trails, which runs the full ecological gamut of the area and provides views north from Coyote Peak (1170′) of upper Napa Valley and Mt. St. Helena (4343′).

Other Fun Activities

Plenty! For the camping oenologist, eight wineries can be found within a 4-mile radius of the park—perfect for a bicycle wine-tasting tour. The park offers regular weekend evening campfire programs, a nearby swimming pool cools in the scorching summer heat (open weekends Memorial Day to mid-June, daily mid-June to Labor Day, closed rest of year, $1/person, under 17 free), and horse riding tours are available from the adjacent Sonoma Cattle Company and Napa Valley Trail Rides, (707) 996-8566.

Bale Grist Mill State Historic Park adjoins Bothe-Napa and protects Bale's storied mill. The park is open 10 A.M.–5 P.M. daily (the excellent visitor center is open 10 A.M.–5 P.M. weekends only), and can be reached on foot from the Bothe-Napa picnic area via the 1.2-mile History Trail or by driving 1.5 miles south of the park entrance on Highway 29. Live milling demonstrations are offered several times a day on weekends. Contact Bothe-Napa Valley State Park for more information.

To Reach the Park

Take Highway 29 5 miles north of St. Helena or 4 miles south of Calistoga; the park entrance is posted on the west side of the highway. *Public transportation* to the park is available daily with Napa County's VINE bus service, which runs regularly from the Vallejo Ferry terminal to the park entrance. For current schedule and fare information, call (800) 696-6443 or go online at www.nctpa.net/vine.

NORTH BAY

THE DETAILS

Governing Agency: Bothe-Napa Valley State Park, 3801 St. Helena Highway North, Callistoga, CA 94515, (707) 942-4575, www.parks.ca.gov.

Visitor Center: Housed in a beautiful former ranch house by the park entrance—open sporadically as staffing allows.

Sites: 50 total sites: 42 drive-in, 8 walk-in. Sites can accommodate trailers to 24 feet and RVs to 31 feet. 1 hike/bike site. 1 handicapped-accessible site.

Costs: $12-15/site, depending on season, includes 1 vehicle. *Extra vehicle:* $4. *Hike/bike site:* $1/person. *Seniors 62+:* $2 discount. *Day-use fee:* $4.

Group Sites: 1 site, maximum 30 people and 10 vehicles. No trailers or motorhomes. Popular in summer. Reservations required. Call (800) 444-7275 or go online at www.reserveamerica.com.

Months Open/Closed: Open year-round.

Maps: The state park map ($1) is sufficient for hiking, available at the entrance station and visitor center.

Facilities: Flush toilets, hot showers ($.25/4 min.), swimming pool, pay phone, firewood available for purchase at the entrance station and camp host site ($5/bundle).

Regulations: *Fires* permitted in fire rings, no wood collecting. *Dogs* prohibited on all park trails, allowed leashed in the campground and picnic areas only. *Bikes* allowed in campground and on fire roads. *Fishing* prohibited in Ritchey Creek. *Maximum number of people per site:* 8. *Maximum number of vehicles per site:* 2. *Check-out time:* noon. *Maximum length of stay:* 15 consecutive days, 30 days total annually, 2 consecutive days for hike/bike site.

Giving Back

Napa-Valley Natural History Association is a non-profit organization dedicated to funding and supporting the interpretive needs of Bothe-Napa Valley, Bale Grist Mill, and Robert Louis Stevenson state parks. 3801 St. Helena Hwy. N., Calistoga, CA 94515, (707) 942-4745.

NORTH BAY

Sugarloaf Ridge State Park

Sonoma Valley escape in the
Mayacamas Mountains

The southern Mayacamas Mountains divide Napa and Sonoma valleys with a sheltered world of pristine California. A thin strip of asphalt winds upwards from Sonoma Valley into the heart of these hills, abandoning civilization as it dead-ends in isolated Sugarloaf Ridge State Park.

During the 19th century, sugar was sold not in granulated form, but rather in a large cone-shaped mass. The resemblance of the region's basaltic hills to this "sugarloaf" earned today's park its name. Largely inaccessible to ranching and containing soils too poor for farming, the region has been lightly used. The state purchased much of the park's land in the early 1920s, intending to dam Sonoma Creek to create a reservoir. Fortunately, the objections of nearby property owners precluded this and the land was used primarily for recreation, becoming a state park in 1964.

Reaching south from the Clear Lake region to divide the Napa and Sonoma valleys, the Mayacamas Mountains are but recently born. The north-trending San Andreas Fault has sheared adjacent lands into myriad faults over the last 10 million years, splitting the earth apart to form linear Napa and Sonoma valleys. Frequent volcanic activity accompanied this rifting, with basaltic lava flows occurring as recently as 2.7 million years ago. Prominent outcrops of this dark rock are visible on the slopes surrounding the park campground.

SUGARLOAF RIDGE STATE PARK CAMPGROUND

The Campground

Situated at an elevation of 1200 feet beside trickling Sonoma Creek, the shaded, semi-private sites surround two grassy fields. A few sites back up directly against the creek while the remainder

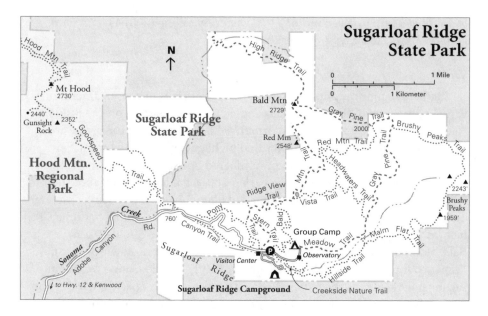

tuck beneath trees at the base of a steep forested slope. Summers are hot and dry, spring and fall are mild, and nights are cool year-round. Due to the higher elevation and near-ridgetop location, winters can be cold and unusually wet for a location so far inland—more than 40 inches of precipitation fall annually and the occasional snow flurry dusts the park during cold spells.

Three types of oaks surround the campground—black, coast live, and Oregon—joined by the drooping branches of Douglas-fir and namesake leaves of big-leaf maple on the north-facing hillside. *Sudden Oak Death* has been identified in the park—please take precautions against spreading this blight to other areas (see "The Living Bay Area" in *Where Do I Go?* for more information). Streamside, gnarled roots of California bay and white alder snake across the ground, joined overhead by the supple branches of willows and elderberry. Introduced cherry plum trees blossom white in the spring—one abuts the small bridge linking the campground and amphitheater. Flowers explode from March to May with California poppies, shooting stars, lupines, cream cups, and pentemons in abundance. Abundant birdlife infuses the park with peaceful melodies in mornings and evenings.

Crowds and Reservations

The park attracts fewer than 80,000 visitors a year (by contrast, Mt. Tamalpais State Park receives 2 million) and reserving a site on summer weekends requires considerably less advance planning than most Bay Area campgrounds. Space is often available only a few weeks ahead of time. The campground seldom fills on weekdays year-round. Reservations can be made from March 31

NORTH BAY

to October 31 up to seven months in advance by calling (800) 444-7275 or going online at www.reserveamerica.com.

Trails

To better enjoy the approximately 25 miles of trails that wind among the varied ecosystems of the park, hikers should consider starting on Creekside Nature Trail. An easy, 0.75-mile interpretive hike, it begins by the picnic area, ends at the upper campground loop, and highlights many of the common plants of the region with the help of numbered posts. The detailed natural history for this hike is included on the park map, available at the entrance station or visitor center ($1). Other recommended hikes include the 1.7-mile Canyon Trail/Pony Trail loop, which delves into the redwood forest lining Sonoma Creek below the campground, and the more strenuous 5.4-mile round-trip ascent of Bald Mountain (2729'), which on clear days yields views of downtown San Francisco more than 40 miles away. Finally, lightly-traveled Hood Mountain Regional Park adjoins the park on its western edge, but is open for use only on weekends and holidays and is entirely closed during fire season, providing an infrequent but tantalizing opportunity for deeper exploration on the slopes and summit of Mt. Hood (2730').

A shady Sugarloaf site

Other Fun Activities

An adjacent astronomical observatory adds a unique celestial flavor to the park. Located 100 yards from the stable parking lot at road's end, Ferguson Observatory houses two large telescopes and a classroom, and offers regular public programs. Call (707) 575-7813 for more information or go online at www.rfo.org. For the aspiring equestrian, a horse concession is located nearby in Kenwood and offers guided horseback rides through the park. Contact Sonoma Cattle Company & Napa Valley Trail Rides at (707) 996-8566.

To Reach the Park

Follow Highway 12 north from Sonoma for 11 miles to Adobe Canyon Road, located 4.5 miles north of Arnold Road. Turn east on Adobe Canyon Road and follow it uphill for 4 miles to the park entrance at road's end.

THE DETAILS

Governing Agency: Sugarloaf Ridge State Park, 2605 Adobe Canyon Road, Kenwood, CA 95452, (707) 833-5712, www.parks.ca.gov.

Visitor Center: By the park entrance and generally open 10 a.m.–2 p.m. (summer 10 A.M.–4 P.M.) on weekends only. Open sporadically at other times depending on volunteer staff.

Sites: 50 drive-in sites. Sites can accommodate trailers to 24 feet and RVs to 27 feet. 1 handicapped-accessible site.

Costs: $13/site. *Seniors 62+:* $2 discount. *Extra vehicle:* $2. *Day-use fee:* $4.

Group Sites: 1 site, located by the observatory. Maximum 50 people and 20 vehicles. $37/night. For reservations, call (800) 444-PARK or go online at www.reserveamerica.com.

Months Open/Closed: Open year-round, though occasionally closed in winter due to flooding.

Maps: The state park map ($1) is sufficient for hiking within the park, available at the entrance station and visitor center.

Facilities: Outhouses with flush toilets, pay phone, firewood available for purchase ($5/bundle).

Regulations: *Fires* permitted in fire rings, occasional fire closures due to weather, no wood collecting. *Dogs* prohibited on all park trails, allowed leashed in the campground and picnic areas only. *Bikes* allowed in campground and on most trails. *Fishing* permitted in Sonoma Creek (with a valid California fishing license) above the campground bridge from last Saturday in April until November 15, limit 5 (fish are scarce, however). *Maximum number of people per site:* 8. *Maximum number of vehicles per site:* 2. *Check-out time:* noon. *Maximum length of stay:* 15 consecutive days, 30 days total annually.

Giving Back

Valley of the Moon Natural History Association
is a nonprofit organization working toward the preservation and
enhancement of the state parks in Sonoma Valley. Valley of the Moon
Natural History Association, c/o Jack London State Historic Park,
2400 London Ranch Rd., Glen Ellen, CA 95442,
(707) 938 5216, www.parks.sonoma.net.

NORTH BAY

Austin Creek State Recreation Area

Isolation amid redwoods and wilderness on the Bay Area periphery

A hidden, wild world lurks in the rumpled Coast Range just north of the Russian River. Within easy striking distance of Santa Rosa and the North Bay, Austin Creek State Recreation Area is accessed via a thrilling, one-lane road that first passes beneath the gigantic old-growth redwoods of Armstrong Redwoods State Reserve before climbing more than 1000 feet at a 12% grade to dead-end atop a ridge with spectacular views.

The topography of the area is severe—a world of closely packed ridges rising more than 1000 feet above narrow canyons barely 200 feet above sea level. The San Andreas Fault slices along the coastal margin less than 10 miles away, slowly moving land west of the fault—such as nearby Bodega Head—north along the edge of California. While the majority of fault motion occurs directly along the San Andreas itself, some of the force is translated inland; nearby lands are thus sheared, compressed, squeezed upward, and riddled with smaller faults. The high rainfall of the area then dissected and eroded the folded landscape into the convoluted topography present today.

Within this tortured geography, Austin Creek SRA straddles an ecological divide between lush coastal redwood forest and drier oak woodland. Only 10 miles from the ocean, yet guarded from summer fog by several intervening ridges, the area receives significant precipitation (50"+) in the winter months yet bakes during the summer in temperatures that can approach 100°F. The results are perennial streams in narrow canyons lined with alders, bay, ferns, Douglas-fir, and redwoods; exposed hills of open grasslands dotted with twisting oaks and spring wildflowers; slopes with southern exposures cloaked with chaparral; and surprising pockets of redwood forest on shady north-facing slopes. Note that *Sudden Oak Death* has been identified in the park—please

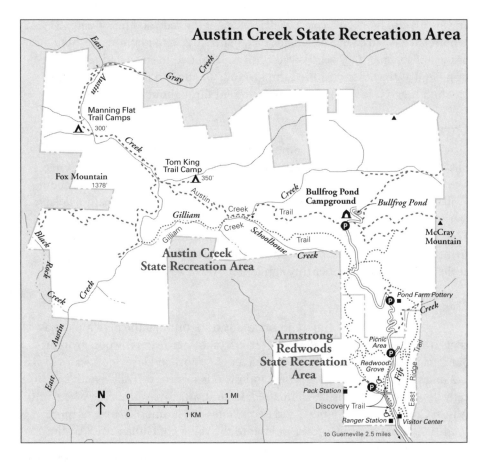

Austin Creek State Recreation Area

take precautions against spreading this blight to other areas (see "The Living Bay Area" in *Where Should I Go?* for more information).

BULLFROG POND CAMPGROUND

The Campground

Sites are situated at an elevation of 1200 feet amid an isolated pocket of redwood forest and are spacious with fair to excellent privacy. The campground is peaceful, a divide away from civilization. Due to the narrow, twisting, and hair-raising access road (there are several steep, 5 MPH hairpin turns), *trailers and vehicles longer than 20 feet are not permitted.* Conditions within the campground are shady and cool, perfect for the scorching days of summer and fall. However, be prepared for cool and very wet conditions in the winter and spring.

The bulk of the campground is sheltered beneath a forest dominated by redwoods, some of which are substantial (especially around sites 2 and 3). Tanoak, bay, and Douglas-fir are also present, with a sparse understory of vetch and sword and bracken ferns. The drier edge of the redwood forest (sites 21-24) is populated by coast live oak, black oak, manzanita, and madrone. Fishing for bass, sunfish, and other warm-water fish is permitted in small and reedy Bullfrog Pond at the bottom of the campground. Or you can just look for turtles and bullfrogs. Note that poison oak is present throughout the campground.

Crowds and Reservations

The campground is first-come, first-serve. The small campground usually fills every weekend and holiday from May through September, making it necessary to arrive early to secure a site. Call ahead to check with the rangers about availability (although they will not hold a site). While space is usually available weekdays year-round, arriving early in the day during summer is recommended. The campground is lightly used from October through April. Register at the Armstrong Redwoods entrance station April through September; self-register at the campground October through March.

Trails

Close to 20 miles of trails and fire roads trace through the park and adjacent Armstrong Redwoods Reserve (the largest old-growth redwood grove in Sonoma County). Exploring the grove is easy—short and level loop walks of 1-2 miles begin by the visitor center and include Discovery Trail, a path specifically designed for the visually impaired. In contrast, adventuring anywhere into Austin Creek SRA is strenuous and necessitates an elevation change of more than 1000 feet. Loops of 5 to 11 miles into the valleys of Gilliam and Austin creeks are described in detail in the backpacking chapter *Austin Creek State Recreation Area.* Mountain bikers have access to nearly 10 miles of fire roads, but riding is strenuous and the drop into the drainages is steep. Fire roads are generally level at the valley bottoms, however.

To Reach the Park

Take either Highway 116 or River Road west from Highway 101 to Guerneville and turn north on Armstrong Woods Road, located 0.1 mile west of the Russian River Bridge. The park entrance and visitor center is reached in 2.5 miles, the campground a thrilling 2.5 miles later.

Swimming newts

THE DETAILS

Governing Agency: Armstrong Redwoods State Reserve and Austin Creek State Recreation Area, 17000 Armstrong Woods Road, Guerneville, CA 95446, (707) 869-2015, www.parks.ca.gov.

Visitor Center: Located at the park entrance, (707) 869-2958. Open 11 A.M.– 3 P.M. daily, longer hours in the summer. The park entrance station is open in summer approximately 8 A.M.–sunset daily, weekends only in spring and fall, sporadically in winter.

Sites: 23 drive-in sites. 1 handicapped-accessible site.

Costs: $12/site, includes 2 vehicles. *Extra vehicle:* $2. *Seniors 62+:* $2 discount. *Day-use fee:* $2/vehicle.

Group Sites: None.

Months Open/Closed: Open year-round.

Maps: An informative and accurate State Park Map is available at the visitor center and entrance station ($1) and is sufficient for hiking within the park.

Facilities: Flush toilets, pay phone, firewood available for purchase at the entrance station ($5/bundle).

Regulations: *Trailers and vehicles over 20 feet* prohibited. *Fires* permitted in fire rings, but prohibited during wildfire season (varies by year, generally late June through October, call ahead to check current regulations), no wood collecting. *Dogs* prohibited on all park trails, allowed leashed in the campground and on paved roads only; leashes must be no longer than 6 feet. *Bikes* allowed in campground, on paved roads, and on fire roads only. *Fishing* prohibited in Austin Creek and its tributaries, permitted in Bullfrog Pond with valid CA fishing license. *Maximum number of people per drive-in site:* 8. *Maximum number of vehicles per site:* 2. *Check-out time:* noon. *Maximum length of stay:* 7 consecutive days, 30 days total annually.

NORTH BAY

Giving Back

Stewards of Slavianka is a non-profit organization that works in partnership with California State Parks to protect and interpret the natural and cultural resources of the Russian River District. Box 221, Duncan Mills, CA 95430, (707) 869-9177, ww.stewardsofslavianka.org.

Half Moon Bay State Beach

The only drive-up beachside camping in the Bay Area

Stroll from your campsite directly to a sandy beach extending miles in either direction. The energy of crashing waves, the extensive coastal views, the beauty of the open ocean—these are the reasons to come here. Those looking for an isolated destination away from civilization, however, should head elsewhere.

A tale of mankind's collision with the natural world, the story here features two human constructs at odds with Nature's way—the Ocean Shore Railway and Pillar Point Harbor. Only a hundred years ago, Half Moon Bay was difficult to access and nearly empty, isolated by rugged topography too challenging for roads. In fact, the only means for the few resident farmers to ship their produce to San Francisco was by boat! Enter the Ocean Shore Railroad, designed to connect San Francisco and Santa Cruz by rail along the coast. Beginning operation in 1908, the railroad soon stretched as far south as Half Moon Bay. Suddenly new real estate was available for development! Where once had been fields of potatoes now were the fantasies of capitalism. Numerous small towns were laid out along the line of the Ocean Shore Railroad—most with catchy marketing names like Princeton-by-the-Sea and Miramar—and lots were sold to the general public. Visitors streamed in from San Francisco to sample the newly created resort world. However by 1920, long before the tracks made it to Santa Cruz, nature overpowered the poorly designed railway; flooding winter streams wiped out weak bridges and landslides repeatedly damaged the roadbed on the sheer cliffs of Devils Slide, closing the railway for good. Yet its existence reverberates today in the surrounding towns and adjacent Coastside Trail (see below), which in many places follows the old railbed.

Half Moon Bay is sheltered from prevailing northwest winds in summer by the outstretched arm of Pillar Point. Winter storms rage from the south, however, and vent their full energy on the

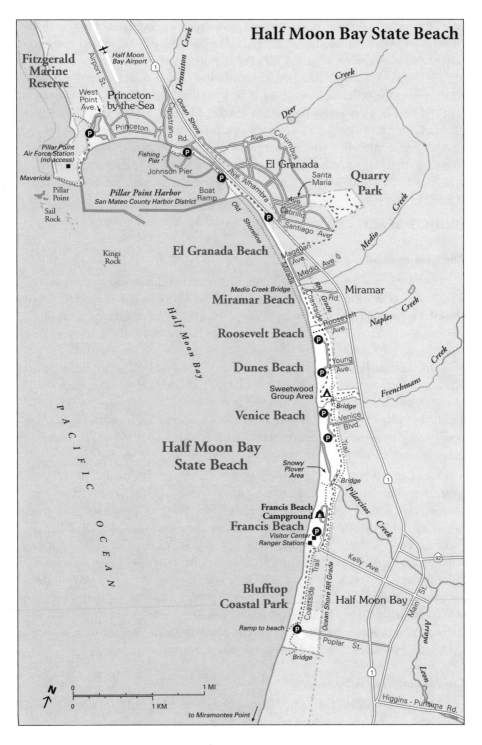

Half Moon Bay State Beach

bay. The first protective breakwater for the harbor was constructed in the 1950s, yet strong swells continued to slam boats. The breakwater also altered the direction of swells wrapping around Pillar Point, refocusing wave energy along Miramar and El Granada beaches. This instantly caused an accelerated rate of erosion—on the order of more than 10 feet per year! An additional breakwater arm was constructed across the harbor entrance in 1967. The waves still rocked the boats on nasty storm surges, however, calling for the construction of yet another breakwater, this one in the inner harbor (1982). Still the beach eroded, reducing what was once an extensive flat beach backed by rolling dune fields into a steep narrow beach hemmed by cliff faces. The erosion continues today.

FRANCIS BEACH CAMPGROUND

The Campground

Sites are located immediately inland from the beach around a large grassy field dotted with young Monterey cypresses. The campground is generally open and sites are often close together, making for little privacy. Of the 58 total sites, 39 are open to tents, RVs, and trailers; 4 are for tents only; and the rest are reserved for self-contained vehicles only. Wind is common year-round—its predominant northwest direction bends the cypresses inland—and little windbreak is available at the campsites. A solid tent and warm clothes are highly recommended. Spring and fall offer the best chance for warm sunny days, summer brings regular fog (at its thickest in July and August), and winter brings big swells and powerful storms interspersed with crisp beautiful days. The frigid ocean is treacherous year-round and swimming is not recommended.

Views encompass rolling hillsides of coastal scrub, with small Douglas-firs appearing inland away from the harsh salty air of the immediate coastline. Looking north, the sweeping curve of Half Moon Bay and its railroad-spawned towns terminates in elevated Pillar Point. Atop the point sits the small Pillar Point Air Force Station, a tracking station used to monitor polar-orbiting space satellites and missile launches from Vandenberg Air Force Base. Just west of Pillar Point is Mavericks, site of the West Coast's largest waves and playground for some of the world's best surfers. Occurring only a handful of times each winter, the required big swells explode in foam and are often visible from the campground more than 4 miles away. The beach near the campground is also a popular spot for surfing and spectating when the waves are firing.

Crowds and Reservations

All sites are available on a first-come, first-serve basis only; no reservations are accepted. The campground seldom fills up except on weekends from Memorial Day to Labor Day. When the campground is full, the park maintains a waiting list at the entrance kiosk (opens 8-8:30 A.M.) and begins filling sites as they are vacated (check-out is noon). For those traveling in self-contained vehicles (defined by the presence of an on-board bathroom), en route camping is permitted when the campground is full. En route campers can stay for only one night (check-in 6 P.M., check-out 9 A.M.), but stand an excellent chance of securing a site the following day. For those traveling under their own power, space is always available in the hike/bike area for only $1/night.

Trails

Half Moon Bay State Beach is small and trail options are limited to two scenic areas—the beach and Coastside Trail. It is possible to walk north along the sandy and surprisingly isolated beach for 3 uninterrupted miles to the edge of Pillar Point Harbor. While the beach is continuous, it is divided into several different sections. From south to north, they are Francis, Venice, Dunes, Roosevelt, and Miramar beaches. The startling erosion caused by the construction of the Pillar Point breakwater is increasingly evident in the beachside bluffs as you travel north. Within the campground, please be respectful of the fenced-off breeding area for the snowy plover. Reduced to an estimated population of only 1500, this threatened bird needs to be left alone.

The Coastside Trail is a pathway tracing just inland from the beach and stretches for 6 miles from Miramontes Point south of the campground to the end of Pillar Point. A popular bike ride, it is mostly paved and for much of its distance either follows or closely parallels the roadbed of the Ocean Shore Railroad.

To Reach the Park

Take Highway 1 a quick 0.3 mile south from Highway 92 in Half Moon Bay, turn right on Kelly Avenue, and follow it 0.5 mile to the park entrance. *Public transportation* is available to the junction of highways 92 and 1 in Half Moon Bay on SamTrans Bus 294 from the Hillsdale CalTrain station. Call (800) 660-4287 or go online at www.samtrans.com for current schedules and fare information.

THE DETAILS

Governing Agency: Half Moon Bay State Beach, 95 Kelly Ave., Half Moon Bay, CA 94019, (650) 726-8819, www.parks.ca.gov.

Visitor Center: Newly-built visitor center, open weekends 10 A.M.–4 P.M., sporadically on weekdays. The entrance kiosk is the best source of information, open approximately 8:30 A.M.–5 P.M. daily year-round, hours vary with season, (650) 726-8820.

SANTA CRUZ MTNS

Sites: 58 total sites. 53 sites accommodate RVs and trailers. 43 sites available for tents. 1 hike/bike site. 1 handicapped-accessible site.

Costs: $13/site, includes 1 vehicle. *Hike/bike site:* $1. *Extra vehicle:* $4. *Seniors 62+:* $2 discount. *Day-use fee:* $4/vehicle.

Group Sites: Sweetwood Group Campground, located 1.5 miles north of the main campground in a grove of eucalyptus. The only drive-up group camp by the beach between Santa Cruz and Bodega Bay. Tent camping only. Maximum 50 people and 12 vehicles, $37. By reservation only. Call (800) 444-PARK or go online at www.reserveamerica.com.

Months Open/Closed: Open year-round.

Maps: Ben Pease's *Trails of the Coastside and Northern Peninsula* (Pease Press) features the park and surrounding region. In addition, a free and very basic map is available at the entrance station. Also try USGS 7.5-min *Half Moon Bay.*

Facilities: Hot showers ($.25/2 minutes), flush toilets in tiled bathrooms, pay phone, dump station, firewood available for purchase at the entrance station ($5/bundle).

Regulations: *Fires* permitted in fire rings, no beach fires, no wood (or driftwood) collecting. *Dogs* allowed leashed in the campground and on the beach; leashes must be no longer than 6 feet. *Bikes* allowed in campground and on Coastside Trail. *Fishing* permitted from the beach, prohibited in Pilarcitos Creek. *Maximum number of people per site:* 8. *Maximum number of vehicles per site:* 2. *Check-out time:* noon. *Maximum length of stay:* 7 consecutive days in summer, 15 consecutive days in the off-season, 30 days total annually.

Giving Back

San Mateo Coast Natural History Association supports the interpretive programs at state park units in San Mateo and San Francisco counties. They recently provided funding for the completion of a visitor center at Half Moon Bay State Beach. Box 3245, Half Moon Bay, CA 94019, (650) 879-2030.

SANTA CRUZ MTNS

Butano State Park

A secluded campground in a
redwood canyon microcosm

The entire upper drainage of Little Butano Creek flows protected through peaceful Butano State Park. The watershed fills
a verdant canyon cut between steep ridges nearly a thousand feet
high and offers deep camping seclusion. Unlike most parks in the
Santa Cruz Mountains, 3560-acre Butano State Park does not
directly connect with the vast network of protected open space
surrounding it and is consequently an entirely self-contained
natural world. Tucked within, surrounded by redwood forest,
a small campground hides away from it all.

Like most regions of the Santa Cruz Mountains, the park was
extensively logged during the late 19th century, leaving a second-
growth redwood forest remarkable for its size and stature. Fortunately, a few stands of old-growth trees also still exist and shelter
sections of magnificent trail.

BEN RIES CAMPGROUND

The Campground

This haven is situated at an elevation of approximately 500
feet on a rare patch of semi-level ground far above Little Butano
Creek. Named for the park's first ranger, the campground is small
and split evenly between very private drive-in sites (1-21) and a
community of walk-in sites (22-39) located a very short distance
from the parking area. At the end of a narrow, twisting road,
under the hushed forest canopy, and nicely removed from drive-
through traffic (the walk-in sites especially), the campground is
usually a peaceful place. In the shady depths of a redwood forest
cloaked by regular summer fog and saturated by winter rains,
conditions are usually cool and damp—bring warm clothes
year-round.

Tall, second-growth redwoods tower overhead, joined by sizable Douglas-firs up to 5 feet in diameter (a striking specimen can be found in the middle of the road by site 1). The undergrowth is dominated by huckleberry bushes and sword ferns, with the large spiny leaves of tanoak fluttering throughout.

Crowds and Reservations

The campground is popular in the summer months and, given its small size, is often full from Memorial Day to Labor Day. Weekends and holidays during these times require reservations far in advance. Space is often available on weekdays, however, especially in the walk-in sites. Reservations can be made from mid-May until Labor Day up to seven months in advance, by calling (800) 444-7275 or going online at www.reserveamerica.com. Outside of these times, sites are first-come, first-serve and are usually available, although weekends remain busy in April, September, and October.

Trails

Butano offers more than 30 miles of diverse hikes along trembling creeks, airy slopes, and redwood paths. Given the steep nature of the canyon, most trails involve some elevation gain. Pleasant exceptions to this are the Six Bridges and Creek trails, the only paths that follow the verdant world directly alongside Little Butano Creek. Among the many other trails in the park, Doe Ridge Trail is highly recommended for its level journey beneath some of the park's grandest trees (the shortest access from the campground is on nearby Goat Hill Trail).

An extended 10-mile hike to the park's backcountry trail camp circles the entire canyon of Little Butano, passes through diverse ecological communities, and provides great views—see the backpacking chapter *Butano State Park* for more information. Bike trails are more limited, with 13 miles of strenuous fire road open for riding.

Spectacle of quivering blubber

SANTA CRUZ MTNS

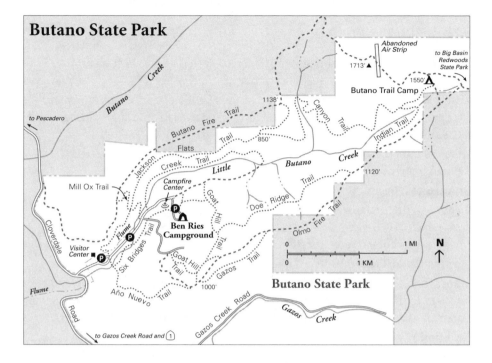

Other Fun Activities

Butano State Park is the closest campground to Año Nuevo State Park and its wintertime population of enormous growling, belching, mating elephant seals. Congregating each winter by the hundreds, these blubbery animals come to breed on the sandy shores of Point Año Nuevo from December through March and can only be observed by taking part in the numerous daily ranger-guided walks. These walks are extremely popular and advance reservations are often necessary. For recorded information, call (650) 879-0227; for reservations, contact Reserve America (see above). The park entrance is located on Highway 1, 12 miles south of Pescadero Road and 4 miles south of Gazos Creek Road (see directions below).

To Reach the Park

From the north, take Highway 1 south from Half Moon Bay for 16 miles to Pescadero Road and turn left. In 2.5 miles, turn right on Cloverdale Road and proceed for 4 miles to the park entrance on the left. The campground is located a mile past the entrance station at road's end. *Approaching from Santa Cruz,* take Highway 1 north from Davenport for 14 miles and turn right on Gazos Creek Road, located immediately north of the Beach House gas station. Follow Gazos Creek Road for 2.0 miles, turn left on Cloverdale Road, and follow the narrow, twisting road for 1.0 mile to the park entrance on the right.

SANTA CRUZ MTNS

THE DETAILS

Governing Agency: Butano State Park, 1500 Cloverdale Rd., Pescadero, CA 94060, (650) 879-2040, www.parks.ca.gov.

Visitor Center: A small nature center is located by the entrance station. Open daily during the summer, hours vary depending on available staffing. Closed in the off-season.

Sites: 39 total sites. 21 drive-in sites. 18 walk-in sites. 17 sites can accommodate RVs and trailers up to 24 feet.

Group Sites: None.

Costs: $12/site, includes 2 vehicles for drive-in sites, 1 vehicle for walk-in sites. *Extra vehicle:* $2. *Seniors 62+:* $2 discount. *Day-use fee:* $2/vehicle, collected only when the entrance station is staffed.

Months Open/Closed: Open year-round.

Maps: The free Butano State Park Map is available at the entrance station and is sufficient for hiking within the park. The Sempervirens Fund *Trail Map of the Santa Cruz Mountains 2* covers Butano and the entire complex of surrounding parks.

Facilities: Flush toilets, pay phone, firewood available for sale ($5/bundle).

Regulations: *Fires* permitted in fire rings, no wood collecting. *Dogs* prohibited on all park trails, allowed leashed in the campground, picnic areas, and on fire roads only; leashes must be no longer than 6 feet; dogs must be in a tent or vehicle at night. *Bikes* allowed on paved roads and some fire roads; prohibited on all single-track trails. *Fishing* prohibited in Little Butano Creek and its tributaries. *Ball games, horseshoes, Frisbee, badminton, and similar activities* prohibited. *Maximum number of people per site:* 8. *Maximum number of vehicles per drive-in site:* 2. *Maximum number of vehicles per walk-in site:* 1. *Check-out time:* noon. *Maximum length of stay:* 15 consecutive days, 30 days total annually.

Giving Back

Sempervirens Fund is a non-profit land conservancy dedicated to preserving, expanding, and linking parklands in the Santa Cruz Mountains. Drawer BE, Los Altos, CA 94023-4054, (650) 968-4509, www.sempervirens.org.

SANTA CRUZ MTNS

Memorial County Park

Camping beneath old-growth redwoods
deep in the Santa Cruz Mountains

A small parcel of redwood paradise, the campground at Memorial County Park is set beneath beautiful old-growth trees, a healthy second-growth forest, and a deeply incised creek canyon. Established to protect more than 200 acres of old-growth redwoods from encroaching lumber interests, Memorial County Park was the first of the San Mateo county parks, dedicated on July 4, 1924 to the memory of the San Mateo County residents who lost their lives in World War I.

MEMORIAL COUNTY PARK CAMPGROUND

The Campground

Situated at an elevation of 250 feet, the campground is completely enveloped by impressive redwood forest. Despite being one of the largest in the entire Bay Area, the well-designed campground offers many excellent sites with good privacy. Pescadero Creek splits the campground into two sections: Azalea and Sequoia Flat. Most sites are located in Sequoia Flat, the nicer of the two areas by dint of better site spacing and seclusion among the large, old-growth trees. However, Sequoia Flat also is surrounded on three sides by Pescadero Creek, which rises dramatically in the rainy season and regularly drowns the access road; the area is closed from the first rains in late October until the rains taper off in late April or May. Located among second-growth forest, Azalea is open year-round and is quiet and private in winter. Here in the heart of the redwood forest, conditions are usually shady, cool, and damp—bring warm clothes year-round.

Within the campground, the redwoods are joined by their regular companions of Douglas-fir, tanoak, canyon and coast live oak, madrone, and huckleberry bushes, while red alders and bigleaf maples can be found arcing over Pescadero Creek. Draining

81 square miles, Pescadero Creek is the second largest watershed in the Santa Cruz Mountains after the San Lorenzo River and still supports a winter run of steelhead. Unfortunately, massive flooding occurred during the torrential rains of 1982-83 and severely impacted the creek's fish populations. They are closely monitored today.

Crowds and Reservations

The campground is hugely popular in the summer months and, despite its massive size, is always full on weekends from Memorial Day to Labor Day. All sites are first-come, first-serve. In order to assure a site for a summer weekend it is recommended that you arrive by 10 A.M. on Friday morning. After this point, the campground begins to completely fill and the park maintains a waiting list for those few sites that open up early Friday and Saturday afternoons. Weekends remain busy and often full through September and early October. Space is almost always available on weekdays, even during the summer months.

Trails

Though small, Memorial Park still offers 7 miles of trails ideal for brief adventure strolls. Short, singletrack Creek and Wurr trails line the sheer slopes along Pescadero Creek below the campground and are fun to explore. The 3.5-mile loop on Pomponio Trail, as well as the shorter 1.6-mile loop to Mt. Ellen Summit (680'), offer views north. Pescadero Creek County Park borders the park to the east and offers opportunities for longer hikes and overnight trips (see the backpacking chapter *Pescadero Creek County Park* for more information). While all trails in Memorial Park are closed to bicycles, Old Haul Road stretches 5 miles through the length of Pescadero Creek County Park to reach Portola Redwoods State Park, an excellent and easy ride that begins from Wurr Road on the eastern park boundary.

To Reach the Park

Take curvaceous Highway 84 to Pescadero Road, located 1.1 miles east of the small town of La Honda, and turn west. Follow Pescadero Road 6 miles to the park entrance on the left, bearing sharp right at the intersection with Alpine Road 1.1 miles from Highway 84.

THE DETAILS

Governing Agency: San Mateo County Parks and Recreation Division, 455 County Center, 4th Floor, Redwood City, CA 94063, (650) 363-4020, www.eparks.net.

SANTA CRUZ MTNS

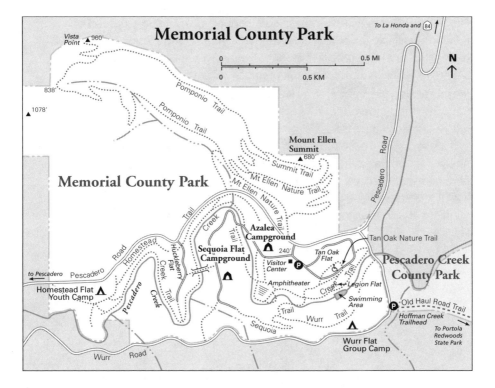

Park Contact Information: Memorial County Park, 9500 Pescadero Creek Rd., Loma Mar, CA 94021, (650) 879-0212.

Visitor Center: Henry H. Blomquist Visitor Center, located immediately past the entrance station, open 10 A.M.–4 P.M. daily, May-September.

Sites: 157 drive-in sites. Only 22 sites can accommodate RVs and trailers, maximum length 35 feet. 2 handicapped-accessible sites.

Costs: $15/site, includes 1 vehicle. *Extra vehicle:* $5. *Day-use fee:* $4/vehicle.

Group Sites: Wurr Group Campground, 2 sites, maximum 75 people and 20 vehicles per site, $100/night. Also Homestead Youth Group Camp for youth groups only. 6 sites, maximum 50 people, $1.50/child/night. All group campgrounds are fully booked every day during the summer and are available by reservation only. Call (650) 363-4021 up to a year in advance.

Months Open/Closed: *Azalea area:* open year-round (52 sites). *Sequoia Flat area:* closed mid-October through late April or May depending on rain conditions.

Maps: Basic park map available free at the entrance station and visitor center is sufficient for exploring the park. The *Pescadero Creek County Park Map* is also available ($1) and covers the large complex of Memorial, Pescadero, and Sam McDonald county parks.

SANTA CRUZ MTNS

Facilities: Hot showers available in summer only ($.25/2 min.), dump station, firewood available for purchase ($4/bundle). A camp store inside the park sells basic provisions—open daily mid-June to early September; weekends only mid-May to mid-June and the rest of September; closed rest of year.

Regulations: *Fires* permitted in fire rings, no wood collecting. *Dogs* prohibited in the park and campground. *Bikes* allowed in campground and on paved roads only, prohibited on all park trails, helmets required for youths under 14. *Fishing* prohibited in Pescadero Creek and its tributaries. *Alcohol* is limited to beer and wine only, no hard liquor. *Campsites* must be physically occupied each night. *Drinking fountains* and *water faucets* are not to be used for washing dishes. *Quiet hours:* 10 P.M.–8 A.M., no generators until 10 A.M. *Park gates:* closed and no entry allowed midnight–8 A.M. *Maximum number of people per site:* 8. *Maximum number of vehicles per site:* 2. *Check-out time:* 2 P.M., re-register by noon. *Day Visitors* must leave by 10 P.M. *Maximum length of stay:* 14 days within any 4 week period.

Giving Back

San Mateo County Parks Foundation
provides financial support for the recreational,
environmental, and educational programs and projects of
the San Mateo County Parks and Recreation Department.
215 Bay Road, Menlo Park, CA 94025, (650) 321-5812,
www.supportparks.org.

SANTA CRUZ MTNS

Portola Redwoods
State Park

*Redwood wilderness heartland in
the canyon of Pescadero Creek*

Slicing through the western Santa Cruz Mountains, Pescadero Creek flows through a canyon more than 2000 feet deep. Portola Redwoods State Park protects a wilderness core of this secluded drainage, offering opportunity to commune with a vibrant redwood forest.

In many ways the park preserves a historical record typical of the Santa Cruz Mountains. In the 1860s, following the California Gold Rush, a homesteader arrived named Christian Iverson. Hewing a simple cabin from the surrounding redwoods, Iverson lived a rugged life in a towering old-growth forest populated by grizzly bears. Arrive Page Mill, a logger eager to provide the burgeoning city of San Francisco with lumber. Reducing to shingles the redwoods along nearby Peters Creek and then Slate Creek in the late 1860s and '70s, Mill was the vehicle of capitalism and constructed roads to carry out his valuable merchandise. Next enter the private citizens to buy smaller parcels of land in logging's ecological wake. San Francisco banker John A. Hooper purchased land and built a summer retreat on Pescadero Creek, then in 1924 sold 1600 acres to the Islam Temple Shrine of San Francisco. After building a cavernous recreation hall on the property, the Shriners sold their holdings to the state in 1945. Converting the area for public use, the state transformed the recreation hall into a beautiful visitor center. Exit Portola Redwoods State Park, which today has grown to a splendid 2800 acres.

PORTOLA REDWOODS STATE PARK CAMPGROUND

The Campground

The sites are situated at an elevation of 450 feet along Peters Creek, a tributary of Pescadero Creek. Spread lengthwise on the limited level ground found along the creek, the campground offers pleasant camping within a beautiful redwood forest. The thick foliage maintains a high level of privacy between the sites. Conditions are shady, cool, and typically damp to sopping wet depending on season—bring warm clothes year-round. Note that the campground is closed December-February.

The common constituents of the redwood forest surround the campground: redwoods, Douglas-fir, tanoak, canyon and coast live oak, madrone, and huckleberry bushes. A few big-leaf maples arc over Peters and Pescadero creeks as well, blushing yellow in the late fall as they coat the ground with an intricate leaf mosaic. For those unfamiliar with the plants of the redwood forest, the easy 0.75-mile Sequoia Nature Loop begins at the Visitor Center, is interpreted on the back of the state park map, and winds its way across Pescadero Creek beneath some impressive old-growth redwoods—an easy way to learn more about the flora of the redwood forest.

Crowds and Reservations

While summer weekends and holidays require reservations well in advance, weekday space is surprisingly available. Reservations can be made from mid-May until Labor Day weekend up to seven months in advance by calling (800) 444-7275 or going online at www.reserveamerica.com. Outside of these times, sites are first-come, first-serve and are usually available, although weekends remain busy in April, September, and October.

Trails

Eighteen miles of excellent hiking trails radiate in all directions. Short but stimulating Iverson Trail explores the waters and steep slopes of Pescadero Creek on an undulating singletrack that passes by secretive Tip-Toe Falls. For an all-day adventure, Peters Creek Grove—a stand of magnificent old-growth redwoods—can be reached via a strenuous, 12-mile round-trip adventure on Slate Creek and Bear Creek trails (see the backpacking chapter *Portola Redwoods State Park* for more information). Portola Redwoods is joined to the west by Pescadero Creek County Park, which provides a 10-mile round-trip bike ride along Old Haul Road to Memorial County Park and back; follow the Park Service Road to its end to access this gem. Lastly, Portola Redwoods is smack in the middle of several backpacking routes and it is possible to complete long-distance hikes to both Big Basin Redwoods State Park and Highway 35 (see the backpacking chapter *The Traverse* for more information).

To Reach the Park

Take Highway 35 to the turnoff for Alpine Road, located 6 miles north of the junction with Highway 9 and 7 miles south of the junction with Highway 84. Head south on Alpine Road and in 2.5 miles bear left on Price Avenue

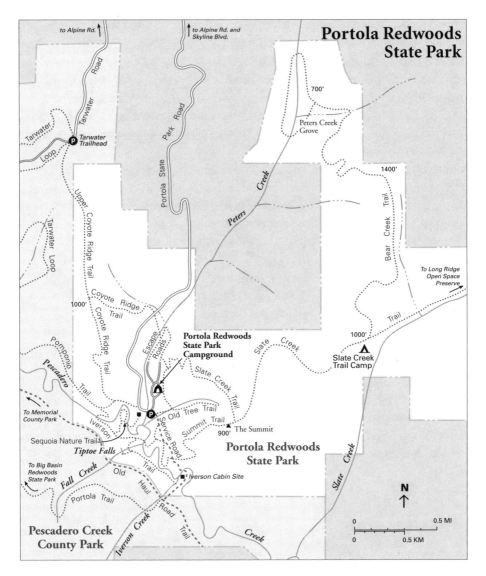

Portola Redwoods State Park

to Alpine Rd.

to Alpine Rd. and Skyline Blvd.

Tarwater Road

Tarwater Loop

Tarwater Trailhead

700'

Peters Creek Grove

1400'

Portola State Park Road

Peters Creek

Bear Creek Trail

To Long Ridge Open Space Preserve

Upper Coyote Ridge Trail

1000'

Coyote Ridge Trail

Coyote Ridge Trail

Pomponio Trail

Pescadero Trail

Escape Roads

Portola Redwoods State Park Campground

Slate Creek

Trail

1000'

Slate Creek Trail Camp

Slate Creek Trail

To Memorial County Park

Iverson Trail

Sequoia Nature Trail

Old Tree Trail

Service Road

Summit Trail

900'

The Summit

Tiptoe Falls

Portola Redwoods State Park

To Big Basin Redwoods State Park

Fall Creek

Trail

Old Haul Road

Iverson Cabin Site

Slate Creek

N

0   0.5 MI

0   0.5 KM

Portola Trail

Pescadero Creek County Park

Iverson Creek

Creek Trail

Creek

(Portola State Park Road). From here, the road drops steeply and abruptly for 3 miles to the campground, located just past the visitor center on the left.

THE DETAILS

Governing Agency: Portola Redwoods State Park, 9000 Portola State Park Rd., Box F, La Honda, CA 94020, (650) 948-9098, www.parks.ca.gov.

Visitor Center: Located just past the entrance station on the right. Open daily in summer and on weekends year-round. Open sporadically on off-season weekdays depending on staffing.

SANTA CRUZ MTNS

Sites: 53 drive-in sites. 7 walk-in sites. 1 hike/bike site. 11 sites can accommodate RVs and trailers up to 24 feet. 1 handicapped-accessible site.

Costs: $16/site, includes 1 vehicle. *Extra vehicle:* $5. *Hike/bike site:* $2/person. *Seniors 62+:* $2 discount. *Day-use fee:* $5/vehicle.

Group Sites: Four sites in redwood forest. *Circle, Point, and Hillside:* maximum 50 people and 12 vehicles, $135. *Ravine:* maximum 25 people and 6 vehicles, $67. Reservations required. Very popular in summer. Call (800) 444-PARK or go online at www.reserveamerica.com.

Months Open/Closed: Campground closed December–February/March. Park open year-round.

Maps: Excellent State Park Map is available at the visitor center and sufficient for hiking within the park ($1). The Sempervirens Fund *Trail Map of the Santa Cruz Mountains 1 & 2* covers the entire complex of parks that surrounds Portola Redwoods.

Facilities: Hot showers ($.25/2 min.), flush toilets in tiled bathrooms, pay phone, firewood ($6/bundle) and ice ($2/bag) are available for purchase at the visitor center.

Regulations: *Fires* permitted in fire rings, no wood collecting. *Dogs* prohibited on all park trails, allowed leashed in the campground and picnic areas only; leashes must be no longer than 6 feet. *Bikes* allowed in campground and on paved roads only. *Fishing* prohibited in Pescadero Creek and its tributaries. *Skates and Skateboards* prohibited. *Ball games, horseshoes, Frisbee, badminton, and similar activities* prohibited. *Hammocks* cannot be attached to a tree less than 12 inches in diameter. *Maximum number of people per site:* 8. *Maximum number of vehicles per site:* 2. *Check-out time:* noon. *Maximum length of stay:* 15 consecutive days, 30 days total annually. Maximum 1 night stay for hike/bike site.

Giving Back

Portola and Castle Rock Foundation publishes maps, brochures, and interpretive materials, and supports interpretive projects at Portola Redwoods and Castle Rock state parks through fundraising efforts. 9000 Portola State Park Rd., Box F, La Honda, CA 94020, (650) 948-9098.

SANTA CRUZ MTNS

Big Basin Redwoods State Park

A vast stand of forest primeval

Protecting the largest stand of old-growth redwoods south of Humboldt County, Big Basin Redwoods State Park features a forest world like no other in the Bay Area. The first state park in California—the first park anywhere to protect the magnificent coastal redwoods—Big Basin celebrated its one hundredth anniversary in 2002 and features four campgrounds, numerous tent cabins, and more than 80 miles of trails. You can transcend the temporal world of mankind beneath this ever-living forest and experience nature on its own, seemingly eternal, terms.

In the late 19th century, the Santa Cruz Mountains were being stripped of their glorious old-growth redwoods to feed the insatiable construction needs of a booming new state. In 1884 alone there were 28 sawmills operating along the San Lorenzo Valley and nearby coast, producing 34 million board feet of lumber annually. A railroad connecting Oakland and Felton opened up the region for mass lumber production, and by the turn of the century nearly the entire San Lorenzo watershed had been denuded. As the inexorable logging push continued into the less-accessible regions of the mountains, cries rang out to protect the last great stands of old-growth trees. Big Basin, a uniquely level area of towering redwoods at the headwaters of Waddell Creek, became the focus of preservation efforts. The newly formed Sempervirens Club, dedicated to protecting the remaining untouched redwood forest in the Santa Cruz Mountains, convinced the state to appropriate funds for the purchase of land in this area. After much political wrangling, 3800 acres—2500 of which were old-growth redwood forest—were purchased in 1902 to form the core of California's first state park. Over the ensuing decades the park slowly expanded piece-by-piece through the continuing efforts of the Sempervirens Club and today includes more than 18,000 acres stretching from the very headwaters of Waddell Creek to the Pacific Ocean, some 6000 of which are old-growth forest.

The Campgrounds

Big Basin offers nearly 150 campsites spread among four adjacent campgrounds: Sempervirens, Blooms Creek, Huckleberry, and Wastahi. Located in the heart of the original park acreage at an elevation of roughly 1000 feet, each campground (described in detail below) has hot showers, convenient access to park trails, and is located within redwood forest. Keep in mind, however, that when making reservations you will only be securing a general guaranteed spot; your specific campground and site will be determined upon registering in person with park staff. Huckleberry campground also offers 36 tent cabins for rent (see information at end of chapter). While the park is often bustling and campgrounds full, the quiet dignity of the surrounding redwood forest hushes sound, making even crowded weekends a more peaceful experience than might be expected.

The park receives as much rain as any place in the Bay Area—more than 40 inches annually—and remains wet from November to the following summer. Camping during the winter can be an exciting experience as mushrooms, newts, and banana slugs take over the forest floor and crowds are almost entirely absent; be prepared for heavy downpours and the perpetually cold dampness, however. Waterfalls rush loudest after spring and winter storms, and a few wildflowers appear in March and April. While summer does bring fog, the campgrounds are far enough inland to receive a good amount of sun and warm temperatures (70°+ F). Fall brings the most regular sunny weather and a pleasantly dry forest.

Blooms Creek Campground offers 54 sites spread parallel to its small namesake creek. Though the sites are positioned somewhat close together, the thick forest increases site privacy and the creek muffles the sounds of camp activity. Pleasant 0.2-mile Blooms Creek Trail follows the opposite creek bank, traveling beneath the large redwoods and Douglas-firs that dominate the forest here. Sword ferns and huckleberry bushes are common undergrowth and a few twisting madrones fill in the middle story.

Sempervirens Campground is the smallest of the drive-in campgrounds, providing 32 sites. Many of the small sites are close together or are exposed to Highway 236 and its accompanying traffic, making this a more hectic campground when the park is full. The forest is more open here, and several canyon live oaks intermix with the large redwoods.

Wastahi Walk-in Campground offers the most removed camping experience, with 27 walk-in sites spread across an almost completely undeveloped forest floor. The most distant sites are approximately 200 yards from the parking area but most are within an easy 100-yard walk. The impressive surrounding redwood forest heightens privacy. Campers are limited to only one vehicle per site. Sempervirens Falls is a short half-mile walk from the campground on Sequoia Trail.

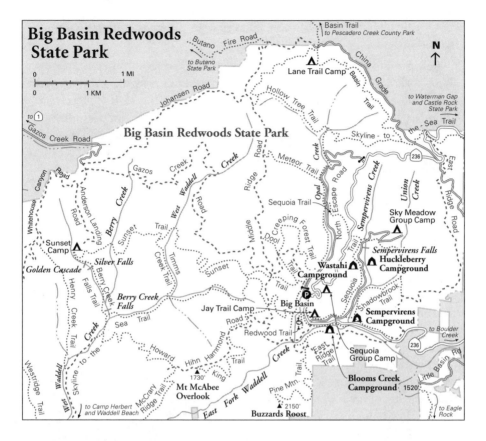

Big Basin Redwoods State Park

Huckleberry Campground is the largest of the campgrounds and is evenly split between 34 tent sites (26 drive-in, 8 walk-in) and 36 cabin sites (see below). Located on Sky Meadow Road more than a half mile from Highway 236, the campground avoids much of the bustle of the headquarters area. The redwood forest here is thicker, younger, and not as towering, but site privacy is good.

Crowds and Tent Camping Reservations

Big Basin attracts a million visitors each year, making it by far the most visited outdoor destination in the Santa Cruz Mountains. Unusual for the Bay Area, it also is a destination more akin to popular national parks—a self-contained world complete with camp store and amenities where families come to stay and recreate for longer periods of time. The campgrounds are full nearly every day of the week from early May through the beginning of October and it is usually necessary to make reservations several weeks in advance for weekdays, and months in advance for weekends. On weekdays, a limited number of sites are occasionally not reserved and available on a first-come, first-serve basis—arrive as early as possible. Holiday weekends are typically completely booked more than three months in advance. In April and October, weekends still

SANTA CRUZ MTNS

occasionally fill but outside of these times space is generally available without reservations.

Reservations can be made year-round, up to seven months in advance, by calling (800) 444-7275 or going online at www.reserveamerica.com. When making reservations, note that a site *type* (walk-in, car camping, or RV) is secured but not a specific campground or site number. Upon arrival, campers must register at the headquarters window adjacent to the visitor center and may request specific campgrounds and sites, depending on availability. The registration window is open in summer 8 A.M.–10 P.M. daily, with reduced hours the rest of the year. Those arriving after-hours need to check the dry-erase board posted by the registration window to find out which site they've been assigned.

Trails

With more than 80 miles of trails and fire roads in the park, there are enough hiking and biking opportunities to satisfy anybody. Several hikes are spectacular and recommended despite their popularity. Located across the highway from headquarters, the 0.6-mile loop on Redwood Trail passes beneath some of the largest trees in the park and is an easy, level stroll. The 11.0-mile loop to Berry Creek Falls via Skyline-to-the-Sea and Sunset trails is more strenuous, but circuits almost continuously through old-growth forest and passes the misty cascades of three beautiful waterfalls. For those who like waterfalls but not 11-mile hikes, all of the campgrounds directly access the loop on Sequoia and Shadowbrook trails to nearby Sempervirens Falls—a 4.0-mile round-trip from headquarters, made shorter by beginning at one of the campgrounds. For cyclists, several fire roads radiate from the headquarters area. While few loops are possible, one exception is the round-trip ride on Gazos Creek, Johansen, and Middle Ridge roads. Lastly, Big Basin has five backcountry trail camps and the latter half of the 26-mile Skyline-to-the-Sea Trail winds from headquarters to the ocean. (See the backpacking chapter *Skyline-to-the-Sea* for more information on camping and backpacking in the Big Basin backcountry.)

Biking inland from the sea,
Skyline-to-the-Sea Trail

Other Fun Activities

Interpretive campfire talks are given every Friday and Saturday night from May through September. There also are regularly scheduled guided hikes throughout the year—call (831) 338-8861 for information on upcoming hikes.

To Reach the Park

Take Highway 236 west from one of the two junctions on Highway 9. Located 6 miles south of Highway 35, the northern junction is the start of a one-lane twister that reaches the visitor center in 8 miles and is not recommended for RVs and trailers. The southern junction is located in the town of Boulder Creek, reaches the visitor center in 9 miles, and makes for easier driving.

Public transportation to the park is available on Santa Cruz Metro bus #35A from the Metro Center in downtown Santa Cruz on weekends from April through October. For current schedules and fare information, call (831) 425-8600 or go online at www.scmtd.com.

TENT CAMPING DETAILS

Governing Agency: Big Basin Redwoods State Park, 21600 Big Basin Way, Boulder Creek, CA 95006, (831) 338-8860 (recorded message) or (831) 338-8861, www.bigbasin.org, www.parks.ca.gov.

Visitor Center: Located near Highway 236 in the main park complex. Great displays, including a very informative multi-media video kiosk. Open 8 A.M.–8 P.M. daily in summer; reduced hours the rest of the year depending on staffing.

Sites: 146 total sites. 69 car camping sites, 31 RV sites, 38 walk-in sites. 8 handicapped-accessible sites. Maximum vehicle length 27 feet.

Costs: $16/site during peak season (roughly May-September), $13/site rest of year, includes 1 vehicle. *Extra vehicle:* $5. *Seniors 62+:* $2 discount. *Day-use fee:* $5/vehicle.

Group Sites: 4 sites in redwood forest. *Sky Meadow:* 2 sites, maximum 40 people and 15 vehicles, $108/site. *Sequoia:* 2 sites, maximum 50 people and 18 vehicles, $108/site. Reservations required. Call (800) 444-7275 or go online at www.reserveamerica.com. Very popular, reserve far in advance.

Months Open/Closed: Open year-round.

Maps: Excellent State Park Map ($2) is available at the visitor center and is sufficient for hiking within the park. It can also be ordered by contacting the Mountain Parks Foundation at (831) 335-3174. The Sempervirens Fund *Trail Map of the Santa Cruz Mountains 2* covers the entire park as well as surrounding parkland.

SANTA CRUZ MTNS

Facilities: Hot showers ($.25/2 min.), flush toilets, pay phone, laundry facilities; camp store sells firewood, ice, and basic supplies, (831) 338-4745.

Regulations: *Fires* permitted in fire rings, no wood collecting. *Dogs* prohibited on all park trails, allowed leashed in the campground; leashes must be no longer than 6 feet, dogs must be in tents or vehicles at night. *Bikes* allowed in campground, on paved roads, and on fire roads only, prohibited on trails. *Fishing* prohibited in the park. *Maximum number of people per drive-in or walk-in site:* 8. *Maximum number of vehicles per site:* 2; extra vehicles must park in overflow area. *Check-in time:* 2 P.M. *Check-out time:* noon. *Maximum length of stay:* 30 consecutive days, maximum 30 days combined in all Santa Cruz County state parks.

TENT CABINS

Tent cabins are available at 36 sites in Huckleberry Campground. Brown and green with wood frames and canvas roofs, each cabin measures approximately 12 by 14 feet, can comfortably sleep four people, and comes equipped with two double platform beds, a wood-burning stove, and a small table. Other than the cabins, the sites are similar to others in the park and include an outdoor picnic table, fire ring, and space to pitch an additional tent. The watertight cabins are warm and dry during the rainy season. Linens and lanterns are available for rental (see below), or you can bring your own.

Redwood enormous over Big Basin site

Tent Cabin Reservations

The cabins are operated by a private concessionaire, The Big Basin Redwoods Park Company, and thus operate on a reservation system entirely separate from the state park system. Reservations can be made two months to 24 hours in advance by calling (800) 874-TENT (8368) 10 A.M.–4 P.M., Monday-Friday. From May 1 through October 31 there is a two-night minimum stay on regular weekends and a 3-night minimum on holiday weekends. Register at either the camp store or after hours at the host site in Huckleberry Campground.

TENT CABIN DETAILS

Governing Agency: Big Basin Redwoods Park Company, (831) 338-4745.

Sites: 36 tent cabin sites, 3 handicapped-accessible sites.

Costs: *May-October:* $49/night, includes 1 vehicle. *November-April:* $35/night. *Extra vehicle:* $6/night. *Dogs:* $1/night. *Linen package (2 blankets, 2 sheets, 2 pillows):* $10. *Lantern rental:* $6/night.

Months Open/Closed: Open year-round.

Regulations: Same as tent camping above.

Giving Back

Sempervirens Fund, a non-profit land conservancy dedicated to preserving, expanding, and linking parklands in the Santa Cruz Mountains. Drawer BE, Los Altos, CA 94023-4054, (650) 968-4509, www.sempervirens.org.

Mountain Parks Foundation supports educational activities and facilities in the park. 525 N. Big Trees Park Rd., Felton, CA 95018, (831) 335-3174, www.mountainparks.org.

SANTA CRUZ MTNS

Sanborn County Park

Outdoor play and walk-in wild on the eastern escarpment of the Santa Cruz Mountains

Mixing a landscape of afternoon recreation with the steep slopes and diverse woods of the Santa Cruz Mountains, Sanborn County Park offers something for everybody. Tendrils of redwood forest trail down damp stream gullies and shelter a delightful campground, a huge grassy field perfect for play extends from forest's edge, and a small RV camping lot tucks in between.

The park's topography is dramatic—from the park entrance, the steep slopes rise more than 1500 feet in less than a mile to Skyline Ridge and the crest of the Santa Cruz Mountains. Responsible is the San Andreas Fault, which passes through the park and traces directly beneath the grassy field and park entrance. Marking the division between the North American and Pacific tectonic plates, the fault has been steadily slipping for 28 million years. The land west of the fault was submerged beneath the Pacific Ocean for much of its journey northward and sediments collected on its underwater surface, forming thick layers of sandstone and shale. Approximately 3-4 million years ago, the Pacific and North American plates slightly changed their direction of motion and suddenly were being compressed together as well as sliding past each other. The new element of compression forced the once-submerged layers of sandstone and shale above the sea, squeezing the rocks upwards and creating the Santa Cruz Mountains. This geologic power is particularly evident in places like Sanborn County Park where the land has been pushed dramatically upwards. (It's no accident that the highest peaks of the Santa Cruz Mountains are found along the San Andreas Fault.) The resulting steep slopes and high ridges are made even more dramatic by the easily eroded material ground up in the fault itself. Quickly washed away, it leaves behind deep troughs adjacent to sheer slopes—Lyndon Canyon in the eastern half of the park is a textbook example.

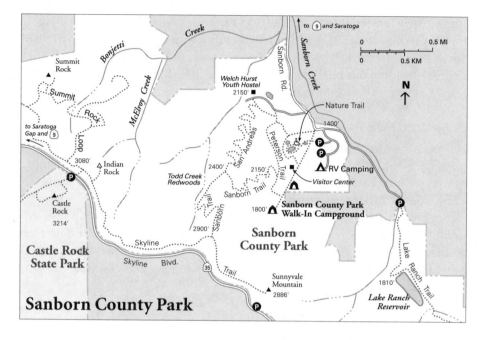

SANBORN COUNTY PARK WALK-IN CAMPGROUND

The Campground

Only walk-in campsites are offered here, spread over nearly 300 feet of vertical rise on the steep slopes bordering small Sanborn Creek. While a few distant sites are up to a half-mile walk from the parking lot, most are much closer. The lack of vehicular traffic is nice, and the good to excellent privacy available in many sites is another bonus. The nearby RV camp is essentially just a large parking lot with full hook-ups—no tent camping allowed.

Here on the east side of the Santa Cruz Mountains the weather is generally mild. While fog does form during summer months, it is far less frequent and burns off more regularly than at parks only a few miles away on the western slopes. The walk-in campground is closed during the rainy season, from mid-October until the last Saturday in March. The RV camp is open year-round. Note that the park gates close after sunset and no re-entry is allowed—plan accordingly.

The campground shelters beneath a nicely regenerating second-growth redwood forest, joined by Douglas-fir, California bay, and tanoak. Wood ferns and wood rose are common constituents of the understory. Perennial Sanborn Creek trickles along the edge of the campground and big-leaf maples, alders, and elderberry bushes shade the watercourse. Numerous mossy sandstone boulders, once at the bottom of the ocean (see above), add texture to the forest floor.

SANTA CRUZ MTNS

Immediately beyond the riparian alley of Sanborn Creek, the redwood forest transforms into slopes of madrone, coast and canyon live oak, and chaparral. *Sudden Oak Death* has been identified in the park—please take precautions against spreading this blight to other areas (see "The Living Bay Area" in *Where Should I Go?* for more information).

Crowds and Reservations

With the exception of summer holiday weekends, tent sites are almost always available. RV camping is more popular, however, and the limited number of sites are full nearly every weekend and many weekdays. In 2002, the Santa Clara County Park District inaugurated a new reservation system for its family campgrounds. Reservations can be made six months to 48 hours in advance by calling (408) 355-2201, 8:30 A.M.–3:30 P.M. Monday-Friday. A $6 reservation fee is charged and there is a minimum two-night stay required for weekend reservations. Online reservations may be possible in the coming years—check www.parkhere.org for current information.

Trails

Although the park is substantial at 3400 acres, the steep and often inaccessible slopes limit hiking trails to only about 12 miles, many of which are not easily accessed from the campground area. That being said, the few trails found nearby are rewarding. The short Nature Trail begins by the visitor center and makes an easy loop through a forest interpreted with the help of numbered posts and a free brochure (available at the visitor center and entrance station). A more strenuous 4-mile loop begins at the back of the walk-in campground and follows the Sanborn, San Andreas, and Peterson trails. Highlights are 1400 feet of total elevation gain and loss, twisting stands of peeling madrone, and brief glimpses east of the South Bay. It is possible to continue all the way to the top of the ridge on Sanborn Trail, a 2-mile hike which rapidly climbs a heart-pumping 1500 feet.

To Reach the Park

Take Highway 9 two miles west from the town of Saratoga or 4.5 miles east from Highway 35 to Sanborn Road. Located on the east side of the remarkable bridge over Todd Creek, the turn-off is small and easy to miss—keep an eye out. Follow Sanborn Road south 1.0 mile to the park entrance on the right. Parking for the walk-in campground is located in the upper parking lot by the RV campground.

SANTA CRUZ MTNS

THE DETAILS

Governing Agency: County of Santa Clara, Parks and Recreation Department, 298 Garden Hill Drive, Los Gatos, CA 95032-7699, (408) 358-7146, www.parkhere.org.

Park Contact Information: Sanborn County Park, 16055 Sanborn Road, Saratoga, CA 95070, (408) 867-9959.

Visitor Center: Housed in a unique building constructed from the sandstone found on the surrounding hillsides and located on the edge of the Upper Picnic Area. Open year-round, hours vary depending on volunteer staffing availability.

Sites: 33 walk-in sites, 13 RV sites.

Costs: Walk-in site $8, includes 1 vehicle. RV sites $25. *Extra vehicle:* $6. *Seniors 62+:* 50% discount Sunday-Thursday. *Day-use fee:* $4/vehicle.

Group Sites: 1 site, non-profit youth groups only. 0.4-mile walk to site. Maximum 35 people, $30/first night, $10/each additional night. Reservations required, call (408) 358-3751, 9 A.M.–4 P.M., Monday-Friday.

Months Open/Closed: Walk-in campground closed from the third Saturday in October through the third Saturday in March. Park and RV Campground open year-round.

Maps: Informative and free park map available at the entrance station and visitor center is sufficient for hiking.

Facilities: Hot showers ($.50/5 min., located by the RV lot), large restroom facilities, pay phone, 3 group picnic areas (can be reserved). There also is a wonderful youth hostel in the park (see Appendix C: *Hostels of the Bay Area*).

Regulations: *Fires* allowed in fire rings, no wood collecting. *Dogs* prohibited on all park trails, allowed leashed in the campground and picnic areas only; leashes must be no longer than 6 feet. *Bikes* prohibited in campground and on trails. *Fishing* prohibited. *Gates* close at sunset—no re-entry after gates are closed. *Maximum number of people per walk-in site:* 6. *Maximum number of people per RV site:* 8. *Maximum number of vehicles per site:* 2. *Check-out time:* 1 P.M. *Maximum length of stay:* 14 total days, Memorial Day through Labor Day; 14 days within a 30-day period during the remainder of the year. *Persons under 18* may not camp without an adult.

Giving Back

Silicon Valley Parks Foundation works with
the Santa Clara County Park District to improve the quality
of life for all citizens of Santa Clara County by generating
funding and support for projects and programs that
enhance the enjoyment, education, and inspiration of the
regional park and outdoor recreation experience.
Box 320038, Los Gatos, CA 95032-0100,
(408) 358-3741 x137, www.siliconvalleyparks.org.

Those interested in *volunteering* for Sanborn
County Park—or in any other unit of the Santa Clara
County Park system—should contact the district's
volunteer coordinator at (408) 846-5761
for more information.

Henry Cowell Redwoods State Park

An ecological mixer on the rim of the San Lorenzo River canyon

Draining a huge portion of the southern Santa Cruz Mountains, the San Lorenzo River cuts a narrow gorge 500 feet deep less than 10 miles from downtown Santa Cruz. Lush redwood forest fills this moist and secluded canyon, while a surprising world of gnarled ponderosa pine and chaparral grows on the mostly level plateau above the river canyon. Sheltered in this unusual ecological world, a campground lies adjacent to peaceful redwood forest and a nearby grove of massive old-growth trees.

An unusually sandy formation known as the Santa Cruz Sandhills rests upon the plateau immediately east of the river canyon. Once found on the bottom of a shallow sea, the loosely consolidated sand is porous, retains little water, is poor in nutrients, and tends to magnify temperatures near ground level. These unusual conditions, coupled with the high precipitation of the area, create a unique biological island for those species able to adapt to such harsh conditions. Many rare and endemic plants grow alongside plant species typically found far away from the Santa Cruz Mountains. The most striking example is the presence of ponderosa pine. Ubiquitous in the Sierra Nevada foothills, the large, plated trunks of these unusually gnarled pine trees thrive around the campground area. (Ponderosa pines are found in only one other Bay Area location: Henry Coe State Park.) A remarkable diversity of other species more common to drier environments is also present: coffee berry, coast live oak, canyon live oak, blackberry, poison oak, scrub oak, California bay, bracken ferns, knobcone pine, manzanita, golden chinquapin, monkey flower, yerba santa, chamise, coyote brush, and honeysuckle. Plus, outliers from the moister redwood environment are found in the nearby river canyon: Douglas-fir, madrone, tanoak, hazel, and huckleberry. Add a few species that grow nowhere else—silverleaf manzanita and the Ben Lomond wallflower—and it all equals a fascinatingly diverse ecosystem.

HENRY COWELL REDWOODS STATE PARK CAMPGROUND

The Campground

Sites are situated at an elevation of 650 feet in the middle of the Santa Cruz Sandhills formation, fewer than 2 miles by trail from one of the most impressive old-growth redwood groves in the Santa Cruz Mountains. For such a large, close-knit campground, the sites are pleasantly spacious and surprisingly unique. While at least one nearby site is usually visible from each location, privacy is fair to good and the thick twisting foliage enhances the feeling of isolation. The campsites are arranged in four loops, with sites on the outer edge more removed from other sites as well as from the sound of cars traveling on nearby Graham Hill Road. The region receives heavy precipitation, but the porous nature of the soil and often open forest canopy mean that the campground is usually considerably drier and warmer than the shady, damp conditions common to the redwood forest. This makes Henry Cowell a great place to visit during the cool months of winter, spring, and late fall. Nevertheless, bring warm clothes year-round. While fog is common in the summer, it often burns off by afternoon. Unlike most state parks, dogs are allowed on approximately 10 miles of park trails (see Trails below). Note that alcohol is prohibited within the park.

Most of the plant members of the Sandhills community outlined above can be found in the campground. Moss-coated oak and madrone branches twist and interlace among the platy trunks of ponderosa pines on the eastern half of the campground, while drier (and sunnier) chaparral is common along the western perimeter close to the canyon slopes and provides the few limited views available from the campground. The cones of ponderosa pine are easily identified by their prickly scales. Knobcone pine is known by its wispy, multi-trunked architecture and the namesake knobby scales on its curved cones, often seen growing directly out of the tree's branches.

Ponderosa pine by a Henry Cowell site

Crowds and Reservations

Despite the campground's large size, it is popular enough to be completely reserved on every weekend and holiday from May through October. Space is usually available on a first-come, first-serve basis on summer weekdays, but these often fill quickly in summer. Outside of these times, securing a site is not a problem. Reservations can be made from mid-March through October up to seven months in advance by calling (800) 444-7275 or going online at

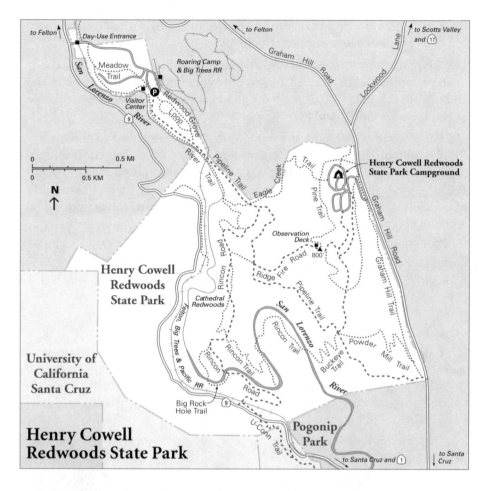

to Felton
Day-Use Entrance
to Felton
to Scotts Valley
and (17)
Graham Hill Road
Lockwood Lane
Meadow Trail
Roaring Camp & Big Trees RR
San Lorenzo River
Visitor Center
Redwood Grove Loop
River Trail
Pipeline Trail
Eagle Creek
Trail
Pine Trail
Henry Cowell Redwoods State Park Campground
0   0.5 MI
0   0.5 KM
N
Observation Deck
800
Henry Cowell Redwoods State Park
Rincon Road
Ridge Fire Road
Pipeline Trail
Graham Hill Road
Graham Hill Trail
Cathedral Redwoods
Felton, Big Trees & Pacific RR
Rincon
Rincon Trail
San Lorenzo River
Rincon Trail
Powder Mill Trail
Buckeye Trail
University of California Santa Cruz
Big Rock Hole Trail
Road
U-Conn Trail
Pogonip Park
Henry Cowell Redwoods State Park
to Santa Cruz and (1)
to Santa Cruz

www.reserveamerica.com. A reservation secures a spot, but not a specific site—they are all first-come, first-pick, making it worthwhile to arrive early during busy times to secure a prime location. While the campground has been closed December through mid-February in recent years, it may now be open year-round—contact the park for current information if you are plotting a winter visit.

Trails

The park offers more than 20 miles of excellent trails for hikers, bikers, and even dog-lovers. Four trails begin within the campground and the following hikes are recommended.

To explore the ecology of the Sandhills formation, take the 3-mile Pine Trail loop around the campground, which passes the Observation Deck atop the highest point in the park (800′). Offering views of Monterey and the Santa Lucia Range across Monterey Bay as well as glimpses of the upper San Lorenzo

River basin, this viewpoint can also be accessed in less than a half mile on the spur trail beginning between sites 47 and 49.

To commune with the redwoods and visit the old-growth grove near the main park entrance, take Eagle Creek Trail to either Pipeline Road or River Trail and take the 0.8-mile loop through the grove. This easy, 4-mile round-trip hike begins between sites 82 and 84.

For an exciting and more strenuous journey, drop into the San Lorenzo River canyon on the 5-mile loop via Powder Mill Fire Road, Buckeye Trail, Big Rock Hole Trail, and Ridge Fire Road. The hike has an elevation change of 1000 feet, fords the river twice (there are no bridges—expect shin- to knee-deep water depending on season), and visits a rivercourse strewn with granite boulders and flood debris.

Ten miles of trail are open to dogs (on leash): Graham Hill Trail (closest to campground), Pipeline Road, and Meadow Trail near the main entrance station. Bikers will enjoy the park's 10 miles of fire roads and Pipeline Road, which is paved and connects to the main entrance area.

Other Fun Activities

Campfire programs are offered in the campground Friday and Saturday nights from mid-June until Labor Day. Nearby Roaring Camp Railroad abuts the park's northern boundary; it recreates the region's logging heyday of the late 19th century and offers rail journeys to the top of nearby Bear Mountain

Contemplate the ever-living

SANTA CRUZ MTNS

aboard a narrow-gauge steam train dating from 1890 (daily service from mid-June through November, weekends and holidays only in the off-season). A standard-gauge railroad also makes the round-trip to the Santa Cruz Beach Boardwalk on weekends in summer. Call (831) 335-4484 or go online at www.roaringcamp.com for more information.

To Reach the Campground

From the South Bay, take Highway 17 toward Santa Cruz. After you go over the mountains and pass Scotts Valley, turn right on Mt. Hermon Road. Follow Mt. Hermon Road until it ends at Graham Hill Road and turn left. The campground entrance is 3.0 miles ahead on the right. *From Santa Cruz,* take Highway 9 for 6.5 miles north from its junction with Highway 1 to Graham Hill Road in Felton. Turn right and proceed 3.0 miles to the posted campground entrance on your right. Note that the prominently signed main park entrance on Highway 9 is for day-use only and does not provide access to the campground. It is possible to reach the park area using *public transportation* from Santa Cruz, although there is no direct service to the park. The Santa Cruz Metropolitan Transit serves the Henry Cowell area from the Metro Center in downtown Santa Cruz via Route 30, which comes closest to the campground entrance on Graham Hill Road; and Route 35, which stops in downtown Felton and is about a mile walk through Roaring Camp to the main park entrance. Call (831) 425-8600 or go online at www.scmtd.com for current route and schedule information.

THE DETAILS

Governing Agency: Henry Cowell Redwoods State Park, 101 North Big Trees Park Rd., Felton, CA 95018, (831) 335-4598, www.parks.ca.gov.

Visitor Center: Located in the main day-use entrance area at the Redwood Grove trailhead. A Nature Center highlights park history and redwood ecology, (831) 335-7077. Open 10 A.M.–4 P.M. daily in summer and on weekends year-round; 11 A.M.–3 P.M. Monday-Friday in the off-season. The entrance kiosk to the campground also is usually staffed.

Sites: 113 drive-in sites. 1 bike site. 5 handicapped-accessible sites. Most sites can accommodate RVs and trailers up to 31 feet.

Costs: $16/site March 15-October 31, $13/site otherwise, includes 1 vehicle. *Extra vehicle:* $5. *Seniors 62+:* $2 discount. *Bike site:* $1/night. *Day-use fee:* $/vehicle, valid for all state parks and beaches in Santa Cruz County.

Group Sites: None.

Months Open/Closed: Closed December 1-February 14. This may change in the future and is worth double-checking if interested in camping here in the winter months.

Maps: Excellent State Park Map ($2) is available at the entrance kiosks and is sufficient for hiking within the park.

Facilities: Hot showers ($.25/2 min.), flush toilets in tiled bathrooms, pay phone, firewood available for purchase at the campground entrance kiosk ($5/bundle). Mountain Parks Foundation runs a gift store in the main day-use area: open 10 A.M.–6 P.M. daily, April-September; 11 A.M.–5 P.M. daily in the off-season; (831) 335-3174.

Regulations: *Fires* permitted in fire rings, no wood collecting. *Dogs* allowed leashed in the campground and on Meadow Trail, Pipeline Road, and Graham Hill Trail. *Bikes* allowed in campground and on Pipeline Road and all fire trails; youths under 18 must wear a helmet. *Fishing* for steelhead permitted in the San Lorenzo River during the winter months on certain days, check current regulations as they change frequently. It is the angler's responsibility to know and obey all fishing laws. *Maximum number of people per site:* 8. *Maximum number of vehicles per site:* 2. *Check-in time:* 2 P.M. *Check-out time:* noon. *Maximum length of stay:* 7 consecutive days, maximum 30 days total annually within all state parks in Santa Cruz County.

Giving Back

Mountain Parks Foundation publishes books, park maps, and educational brochures, and sponsors events and exhibits, to help visitors more fully experience and understand the characteristics of these beautiful protected forests. 525 North Big Trees Park Rd., Felton, CA 95018, (831) 335-3174, www.mountainparks.org.

Uvas Canyon County Park

*A box-canyon ecological sampler
replete with tumbling waterfalls*

Hidden at road's end on the steep eastern flanks of the Santa
Cruz Mountains, Uvas Canyon County Park sits near the headwaters of Uvas Creek in a deep, narrow canyon laced with perennial
streams and pattering waterfalls. The canyon slopes exist on rain
shadow's edge and provide habitat for a wide variety of trees and
plants, perfect for a full ecological taste of the region.

In winter, storms blowing eastward are forced to rise more
than three thousand feet over the Santa Cruz Mountains. As the
rising air cools, it disgorges heavy rains on the western slopes, but
relatively little on the steep eastern slopes above Uvas Canyon. In
summer, the range's high ridgeline prevents thick coastal fog from
spilling into the park, depriving the area of shade and moisture
in a period when temperatures routinely soar into the 90s. The
result is a patchwork of ecosystems determined by extreme differences in moisture. Fingers of lush redwood forest line perennial
creeks, mixed-evergreen forest and oak woodland intermingle
on shady slopes, and desiccated chaparral bakes in the hot sun.

UVAS COUNTY PARK CAMPGROUND

The Campground

A lack of level ground in the park compresses the campground into a small clearing above Uvas Creek at an elevation
of 1000 feet. The closely-spaced sites offer limited privacy and
a full campground makes for a crowded experience. In summer,
sweltering heat and crowds are common, and the pleasant waterfalls of the park all but disappear. In the mild temperatures of fall,
winter, and spring, however, an emptier campground makes for a
peaceful experience, and the waterfalls rush loudly as they drain
heavy storms.

Within the campground a wide variety of flora makes for an interesting stroll. Representatives of the lush environment to the west (tanoak, madrone, big-leaf maple, Douglas-fir, California bay, and a few small redwoods) intermix with denizens more common to drier environments found inland (coast live oak, black oak, manzanita, and knobcone pine). The unique ecologic transition zone offers the chance to learn about the most common plants and trees of the Santa Cruz Mountains in one place. The Waterfall Loop (see below) is ideal for this.

Crowds and Reservations

The small campground tends to fill quickly on summer and holiday weekends, but is surprising empty during off-season weekends and weekdays year-round. In 2002, the Santa Clara County Park District inaugurated a new reservation system for its family campgrounds. Reservations can be made six months to 48 hours in advance by calling (408) 355-2201 8:30 A.M.–3:30 P.M. Monday-Friday. A $6 reservation fee is charged and there is a minimum two-night stay required for weekend reservations. Online reservations may be possible in the coming years—check www.parkhere.org for current information.

Trails

Seven miles of trail wind through the slopes, all easily accessible from the campground. Below the campground, the brief half-mile jaunt along Uvas and Swanson creeks rewards with redwoods, twisting California sycamores, and a waterfall. Above the campground, the 1-mile Waterfall Loop Nature Trail passes several cascades while educating hikers on the flora of the park with the help of numbered posts and a free interpretive brochure. For those seeking effort, several trails climb steeply through dense chaparral and offer intermittent views down Uvas Creek Canyon. The 1700-foot climb through chaparral and knobcone pines to Nibbs Knob (2694') is the steepest, most strenuous hike in the park.

Shady Uvas site

To Reach the Park

Take Highway 101 or Highway 85 south from San Jose and exit on Bernal Road, located a few miles north of the Highway 85/101 junction. Follow Bernal Road west and turn left on Santa Teresa Blvd. Head south for 3 miles and turn right onto Bailey Road. Travel on Bailey Road for 2.3 miles and then bear left onto McKean Road, which becomes Uvas Road 2 miles south and reaches Croy

SANTA CRUZ MTNS

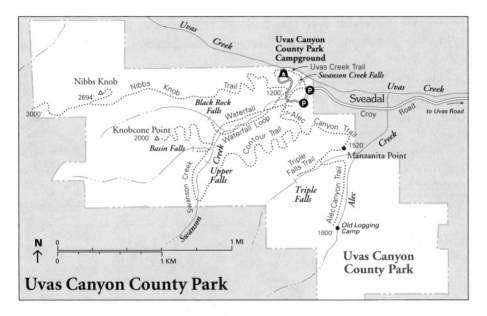

Uvas Canyon County Park

Road in 6 miles. Head west on Croy Road for 4.5 miles to the park entrance, passing through a private resort of the Swedish American Patriotic League called Sveadal. Please respect their privacy as you drive this final, narrow, surreal section of road.

To reach the park from points south, take Highway 152 to Watsonville Road and head north. In 3.5 miles, turn left onto Uvas Road, follow it for 5.7 miles to Croy Road, and then proceed as above.

THE DETAILS

Governing Agency: County of Santa Clara, Parks and Recreation Department, 298 Garden Hill Drive, Los Gatos, CA 95032-7699, (408) 358-7146, www.parkhere.org.

Park Contact Information: Uvas Canyon County Park, 8515 Croy Rd., Morgan Hill, CA 95037, (408) 779-9232.

Visitor Center: Termites have closed the park visitor center indefinitely.

Sites: 25 sites. 1 handicapped-accessible site.

Costs: $15/site, includes 1 vehicle. *Extra vehicle:* $6. *Seniors (60+) and disabled:* 50% discount, Monday-Thursday. *Dogs:* $1/day. *Day-use fee:* $4. The electronic ranger collection box takes cash and credit cards.

Group Site: Upper Bench Youth Group Area, non-profit youth groups only. Maximum 40 people, $30/first night, $10/each additional night. Reservations required, call (408) 355-2201, 9 A.M.–4 P.M. Monday-Friday.

SANTA CRUZ MTNS

Months Open/Closed: Open year-round.

Maps: Free and informative park map available at the entrance station is sufficient for hiking.

Facilities: Flush toilets, pay phone, no RV facilities.

Regulations: *Fires* prohibited during fire season (roughly June–November), otherwise permitted in fire rings, no wood collecting. *Dogs* allowed leashed on all park trails and in campground. Maximum 2 dogs per site. *Bikes* prohibited on all trails. *Fishing* and *swimming* prohibited in Uvas Creek. *Maximum number of people per site:* 8. *Maximum number of vehicles per site:* 2. *Check-out time:* 1 P.M. *Maximum length of stay:* 14 days total between Memorial Day and Labor Day, 14 days within any 30-day period during the rest of the year.

Giving Back

Silicon Valley Parks Foundation works with the Santa Clara County Park District to improve the quality of life for all citizens of Santa Clara County by sponsoring and supporting projects and programs that enhance the enjoyment, education, and inspiration of the regional park and outdoor recreation experience. Box 320038, Los Gatos, CA 95032-0100, (408) 358-3741 x137, www.siliconvalleyparks.org.

Those interested in *volunteering* for Uvas Canyon County Park—or any other unit of the Santa Clara County Park system—should contact the district's volunteer coordinator at (408) 846-5761 for more information.

SANTA CRUZ MTNS

Mt. Madonna County Park

*Easy access, full facilities,
and human history*

Perched atop a ridge within easy striking distance of Monterey Bay and Santa Clara Valley, Mt. Madonna County Park is a fully-developed recreation area where young redwood forest veneers dense campgrounds and house ruins whisper memories a hundred years old.

The park's 3219 acres surround the former residential estate of Henry Miller, a wealthy man who once owned more than a million acres of California ranchland roamed by more than a million head of cattle. Miller purchased the land around today's park beginning in 1859 and eventually owned 13,000 acres of the surrounding slopes. In the late 19th century, Miller converted the highest region of his land—the summit of 1897-foot Mt. Madonna—into a summer family retreat that included a 3600-square-foot ballroom and seven-bedroom house. Miller died in 1916 and Santa Clara County began purchasing parcels of his Mt. Madonna estate in 1927. The Civilian Conservation Corps of the 1930s followed, developing the park with many of the roads, trails, and campsites available to visitors today.

MT. MADONNA COUNTY PARK CAMPGROUND

The Campground

Sites are divided into four separate units—Valley View #1-3 and Tan Oak Camp—situated between 1500 and 1800 feet of elevation. All four units offer closely packed sites with limited privacy among a dense forest dominated by tanoak and young redwood trees. A few madrone and coast live oak provide some limited ecologic diversity overhead. Of the four units, Tan Oak Camp feels the most removed while Valley View #1 is the only unit that provides RV facilities. Valley View #2 and #3 are alike and close to the "Giant Twins," an intertwined pair of old-growth redwoods and one of the park's highlights. Given the park's ridgetop location, soupy summer fog and sopping winter rains are common—come prepared for cool, wet conditions.

Crowds and Reservations

Mt. Madonna's location on well-traveled Highway 152 makes it better known than other parks. The few sites with electric hook-ups are popular and are booked far in advance. Also, the close proximity of sites to the highway means that the sounds of nature are drowned out on busy weekends. In 2002, the Santa Clara County Park District inaugurated a new reservation system for its family campgrounds. Reservations can be made six months to 48 hours in advance by calling (408) 355-2201 8:30 A.M.–3:30 P.M. Monday-Friday. A $6 reservation fee is charged and there is a minimum two-night stay required for weekend reservations. Online reservations may be possible in coming years— check www.parkhere.org for current information.

Trails

Spanning more than 1200 feet of elevation, the park offers 20 miles of trails to explore and hikers can find oak woodlands, open chaparral, and views of Monterey Bay, the Santa Clara Valley, and beyond. Try the upper Merry Go Round trail for views east and Bayview Trail for a glimpse west. Bikes are not permitted on park trails.

Other Fun Activities

Stroll on the winding paths among the rock-wall ruins of Miller's hundred-year-old summer retreat, located in the shade near the visitor center. Adding to the developed atmosphere of the park are an archery range and a pen of exotic white fallow deer, descended from a pair contributed by William Randolph Hearst in the 1930s. Both are located near the visitor center, which offers historical information and some stuffed wildlife. Finally, Sprig Lake is located 3 miles east of the park entrance on Highway 152 and provides kids ages 5-12 the chance to catch stocked fish from April through June.

Redwoods shade a Mt. Madonna site

To Reach the Park

Take Highway 152 west from Highway 101 for 10 miles to reach the park entrance on the right. The park also can be accessed from Highway 1 by Hecker Pass; take Highway 152 east as it winds through and then above Watsonville.

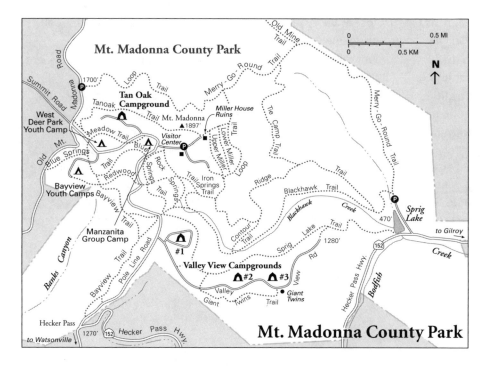

THE DETAILS

Governing Agency: County of Santa Clara, Parks and Recreation Department, 298 Garden Hill Dr., Los Gatos, CA 95032-7699, (408) 358-7146, www.parkhere.org.

Park Contact Information: Mt. Madonna County Park, 7850 Pole Line Rd., Watsonville, CA 95076, (408) 842-2341.

Visitor Center: In the center of the park, open sporadically.

Sites: 117 total drive-in sites. 17 sites with electric hook-ups. 1 handicapped-accessible site.

Costs: $15/site, includes 1 vehicle. Sites with electric hook-ups $25. *Extra vehicle:* $6. *Dogs:* $1/day. *Seniors (60+) and disabled:* 50% discount Monday-Thursday. The electronic ranger collection box takes cash and credit cards.

Group Sites: 2 sites. *Manzanita:* maximum 30 vehicles, $150, includes 10 vehicles, each additional vehicle $15/night. *Huckleberry:* maximum 20 vehicles, $225, includes 12 vehicles, each additional vehicle $15. Reservations required—call (408) 358-3751, 9 A.M.–4 P.M. Monday-Friday. There also are three sites for use by non-profit youth groups only. Maximum 50 people per site, $30/first night, $10/each additional night.

Months Open/Closed: *Valley View #1* is open year-round. *Valley View #2-3 and Tan Oak Camp* are sometimes closed during winter.

Maps: Free and informative park map available at the entrance station is sufficient for hiking.

Facilities: Hot showers ($.50/5 min.) with bonus heat lamps, pay phone, electric hook-ups, dump station. Firewood is available for purchase ($5/bundle).

Regulations: *Fires* permitted in fire pits year-round, no wood collecting. *Dogs* allowed leashed in the campgrounds and on all trails. Maximum two dogs per site. *Bikes* allowed in campground and on paved roads, but prohibited on all trails. *Swimming* prohibited. *Fishing* is permitted in Sprig Lake April-June for children ages 5-12 only. *Maximum number of people per site:* 8. *Maximum number of vehicles per site:* 2. *Check-out time:* 1 P.M. *Maximum length of stay:* 14 days within any 30-day period.

Giving Back

Silicon Valley Parks Foundation works with the Santa Clara County Park District to improve the quality of life for all citizens of Santa Clara County by sponsoring and supporting projects and programs that enhance the enjoyment, education, and inspiration of the regional park and outdoor recreation experience. Box 320038, Los Gatos, CA 95032-0100, (408) 358-3741 x137, www.siliconvalleyparks.org.

Those interested in *volunteering* for Mt. Madonna County Park—or any other unit of the Santa Clara County Park system—should contact the district's volunteer coordinator at (408) 846-5761 for more information.

SANTA CRUZ MTNS

Mt. Diablo State Park

*The flanks, recesses, views, and
thrills of a dominating mountain*

A monolithic mountain with eye-popping views, Mt. Diablo
(3849') towers over the surrounding East Bay landscape and
harbors three distinct campgrounds upon its vibrant slopes.

For millions of years, the Mt. Diablo region—as well as most
of western California—lay beneath the ocean, collecting thick
layers of sand, mud, and other sediment on its surface. Roughly
3.5 million years ago, the geometry of the San Andreas Fault system changed slightly, adding an element of compression between
the Pacific and North American tectonic plates. As a result, these
extensive beds of sediment were pushed upward to form the
mountainous topography of the Bay Area and Coast Range.
Approximately 2 million years ago, the region around Mt. Diablo
was compressed and the young mountain and its layers of sediment pushed skyward. During this process an old piece of the sea
floor—an *ophiolite*—was squeezed through the crust and into the
core of Mt. Diablo. Today the elements have weathered the overlying sediment to expose the ophiolite around the summit, an
erosion-resistant rock estimated to be 165 million years old.
Younger sediments also ring the mountain core and striking
outcrops of sandstone are common on Diablo's lower slopes.

Surrounded by encroaching civilization and isolated from
other nearby mountains, Mt. Diablo is an oasis of unique plant
and animal life. Due to variations in elevation, precipitation,
and exposure to the sun, a variety of ecosystems are present on
the mountain slopes. Oak woodlands and chaparral are most
common, yet a few lush riparian alleys trace through deeper
stream canyons. Common trees include gray pine, California
bay, buckeye, and a wide diversity of oaks—coast live, blue,
valley, interior live, and canyon live oak. Wildflowers explode
from March through May, slowly advancing up the mountain
slopes with the progression of spring.

MT. DIABLO STATE PARK CAMPGROUNDS

The Campgrounds

Each of the park's three campgrounds—Juniper, Live Oak, and Junction—resides in a separate ecosystem. All three offer sites with good to excellent privacy and are described in greater detail below. Note that *the park is closed and gated from sunset until 8 A.M* and campers are locked in the park during these hours—arriving before nightfall is essential.

While the mountain and its campgrounds are year-round destinations, each season is radically different. Summer is the least recommended time. Intense heat bakes the mountain a tawny brown, confining visitors to shady areas; and brown haze can obscure the incredible views. Also, summer is a time of great wildfire danger and the park closes entirely during times of extreme risk—call (925) 837-0904 a day in advance of your visit to ensure that the park will be open. As fall approaches, temperatures moderate pleasantly and the first winds and storms of approaching winter begin to cleanse the surrounding air, yielding far-reaching views. Winter is spectacular on Mt. Diablo as regular storms flush the air to crystalline

Junction Campground

purity. The slopes explode with green grasses and ephemeral creeks and waterfalls burst forth. Crowds are all but non-existent. Spring brings dazzling displays of wildflowers that slowly creep up the mountain slopes. Oak trees and buckeyes send forth their gentle new leaves and the mountain is cloaked in a velvet of green. Warmer weather, increased daylight, and good air quality attract many visitors in this most desirable season.

Juniper Campground is the largest campground of the three and, situated at an elevation of 3000 feet, is the Bay Area's highest drive-in campground. Views are everywhere, sweeping a remarkable 180-degree vista down Diablo's western flanks—downtown San Francisco, Mt. Tamalpais, the Sacramento/San Joaquin river delta, and Mission Peak are all visible beyond the cities of Walnut Creek and Danville.

Sites are interspersed within a low-lying chaparral plant community and many are exposed to wind and weather, although several offer good protection in the winter months. Here on the western flanks of the mountain the dry slopes bake in the late afternoon sun. Chamise, buckbrush, and scrub oak are common members of this hardy community, along with several live oaks and junipers. A magnificent live oak grows at the back of the campground.

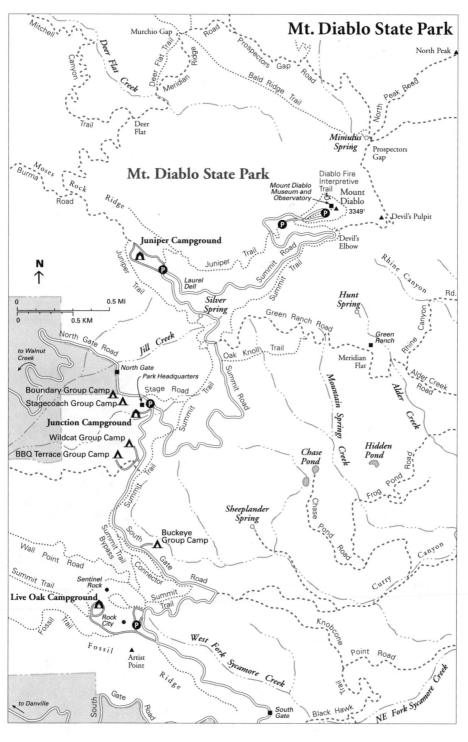

Mt. Diablo State Park

Mitchell

Murchio Gap

Road

Prospectors Gap Road

North Peak

Deer Flat Creek

Deer Flat Trail

Meridian Ridge

Bald Ridge Trail

North Peak Road

Trail

Deer Flat

Mimulus Spring

Prospectors Gap

Moses Burma Road

Rock Ridge

Mt. Diablo State Park

Diablo Fire Interpretive Trail

Mount Diablo Museum and Observatory

Mount Diablo 3349'

Devil's Pulpit

Juniper Campground

Juniper Trail

Juniper Trail

Summit Trail

Summit Road

Devil's Elbow

Rhine Canyon

N

Laurel Dell

Silver Spring

Summit Trail

Hunt Spring

Rd.

0   0.5 MI

0   0.5 KM

North Gate Road

Jill Creek

Green Ranch Road

Green Ranch

Rhine Canyon

to Walnut Creek

Oak Knoll Trail

Meridian Flat

Alder Creek Road

North Gate

Park Headquarters

Boundary Group Camp

Stage Road

Summit Trail

Summit Road

Mountain Springs Creek

Alder Creek

Stagecoach Group Camp

Junction Campground

Wildcat Group Camp

BBQ Terrace Group Camp

Chase Pond

Hidden Pond

Summit Trail

Frog Pond Road

Sheeplander Spring

Chase Pond Road

Wall Point Road

Summit Trail Bypass

South Gate Connector Road

Buckeye Group Camp

Summit Trail

Canyon

Curry

Sentinel Rock

Summit Trail

Live Oak Campground

Rock City

Summit Trail

Knobcone Point Road

Fossil Trail

Artist Point

West Fork Sycamore Creek

Fossil Ridge

Trail

to Danville

South Gate Road

South Gate

Black Hawk

NE Fork Sycamore Creek

Live Oak Campground is located at an elevation of 1400 feet within a thick and shady mix of canyon and coast live oak, gray pine, manzanita, and chamise. Despite the dense foliage, the sites are pleasantly open. The campground is peacefully small with only 22 sites, well-sheltered from the elements, and near the interesting geologic exposures of Rock City. Bulbous and pitted, these large sandstone outcrops protrude above the foliage around and to the east of the campground. The rocks, part of the sedimentary layers that ring Mt. Diablo (see above), are fun to scramble on with many a view on top. A popular and exciting excursion is the 200-foot, cable-aided climb to the top of Sentinel Rock. The trail begins behind Site 20.

Junction Campground is located at an elevation of 2200 feet just south of the North Gate Road/South Gate Road junction. The smallest of the park's campgrounds, Junction offers six large sites beneath a shady canopy of blue oak and gray pine. Unlike Juniper and Live Oak, Junction is first-come, first-serve only—no reservations are accepted—making it possible to secure a site with a sufficiently early arrival on even the busiest days. Beware the thick poison oak in the small creek gully on the edge of camp, joined by more inviting stands of California bay and buckeye. Views are sparse in the sites themselves but plentiful nearby, overlooking the South Bay and the distant Santa Cruz Mountains on clear days.

Crowds and Reservations

All sites in Juniper and Live Oak campgrounds are subject to reservation, while Junction is first-come, first-serve only. All three campgrounds are most popular during spring and often fill up on weekends in April and May. At all other times—even on summer weekends—space is usually available with little advance notice. Reservations can be made year-round up to seven months in advance by calling (800) 444-7275 or going online at www.reserveamerica.com. Note that all campers must register at the South Gate Entrance Station upon arrival (see below).

Summit Visitor Center, Mt. Diablo State Park

Trails

Mt. Diablo is a hiking and biking paradise. Free brochures outlining the numerous easy, moderate, and strenuous trips are available at the Summit Visitor Center, entrance stations, and park headquarters. Countless adventures await, but of all the trails on the mountain, the one not to be missed is the short and easy 0.7-mile Fire Interpretive Trail on top of the mountain. Circling the summit, it offers one of the most incredible and far-reaching views to be found anywhere on Earth—more than 40,000 square miles of California roll out beneath you.

To Reach the Park and Campgrounds

Note that it is most convenient to approach from the south on South Gate Road as all campers must register at the South Gate Entrance Station. Registration is not permitted at the North Gate Entrance Station.

To reach the park on South Gate Road, take Interstate 680 to the Diablo Road/Danville exit in Danville. Follow Diablo Road east for 3.0 miles to Mt. Diablo Scenic Blvd., then turn left. Follow Mt. Diablo Scenic Blvd.—which becomes South Gate Road inside the park—for 3.5 miles to South Gate Entrance Station. Live Oak Campground is 1 mile past the entrance station on the left and Junction Campground is 3 miles past the entrance station immediately below the junction with North Gate Road. To reach Juniper Campground, continue up the mountain on Summit Road for another 2 miles past Junction Campground.

To reach the park on North Gate Road, take the Ygnacio Valley Road exit immediately north of the Interstate 680/Highway 24 junction and head east on Ygnacio Valley Road for 3.5 miles to Oak Grove Road. Turn right on Oak Grove Road and then turn left onto North Gate Road after 1 mile. North Gate Road twists up the mountain for 7.5 miles to the junction with South Gate Road. Bear right on South Gate Road and descend just over 3 miles to register for camping.

THE DETAILS

Governing Agency: Mt. Diablo State Park, 96 Mitchell Canyon Rd., Clayton, CA 94517, (925) 837-2525, www.parks.ca.gov, www.mdia.org.

Visitor Center: Summit Visitor Center, (925) 837-6119, located on the actual summit of the mountain. Open March-October 11 A.M.–5 P.M. Wednesday-Sunday; November-February 10 A.M.–4 P.M. Wednesday-Sunday.

Sites: Juniper, 36 sites. Live Oak, 22 sites. Junction, 6 sites. Sites can accommodate RVs and trailers up to 20 feet.

Costs: $15/site, May-October; $12/site, November-April; includes 1 vehicle. *Extra vehicle:* $4. *Seniors 62+:* $2 discount. *Day-use fee:* $4/vehicle.

Group Sites: Five group sites, each located away from the family campgrounds in pleasant seclusion. *Stagecoach and Boundary:* maximum 20 people and 7 vehicles, $27. *Buckeye and Wildcat:* maximum 30 people and 10 vehicles, $40. *BBQ Terrace:* maximum 50 people and 17 vehicles, $67. Reservations required. Call (800) 444-PARK or go online at www.reserveamerica.com.

Months Open/Closed: All campgrounds open year-round. Subject to closure in summer during periods of extreme fire hazard and in winter during periods of snow.

Maps: Best is the *Trail Map of Mount Diablo State Park and Adjacent Parklands* ($5.50), published by the Mt. Diablo Interpretive Association and available at the Summit Visitor Center, outdoor shops, and online at www.mdia.org. The official Mt. Diablo State Park Map is available at the entrance stations and visitor center for $1. It indicates all trails and facilities but not topography.

Facilities: Free hot showers available at Live Oak and Juniper, pay phone.

Regulations: *Alcoholic beverages* prohibited. *Fires* permitted in fire rings, no wood collecting. Campfire restrictions in effect during fire season; call (925) 837-2525 for current information. *Dogs* not recommended—prohibited on all park trails, allowed leashed in the campground and picnic areas; dogs must be in tent or vehicle at night. *Bikes* allowed on paved roads, fire roads, and certain designated trails only. Check at ranger station or visitor center for current regulations. *Skateboards, roller skates, inline skates* and other gravity-propelled devices are prohibited. *Electric generators* prohibited 8 P.M.–10 A.M. *Maximum number of people per site:* 8. *Maximum number of tents per site:* 2. *Maximum number of vehicles per site:* 2. *Check-out time:* noon. *Check-in time:* 2 P.M. *Maximum length of stay:* 14 consecutive days, 30 days total annually.

The flanks and recesses of Mt. Diablo

Giving Back

Mount Diablo Interpretive Association (MDIA) is a non-profit volunteer organization that assists the California Department of Parks and Recreation in maintaining and interpreting Mt. Diablo State Park for its 700,000 visitors each year. It maintains one of the most informative web sites about the park at www.mdia.org. Box 346, Walnut Creek, CA 94957-0346, (925) 927-7222.

Save Mt. Diablo works to secure through acquisition, protection, and preservation, the open space necessary to support the full range of biological diversity and to ensure the integrity of Mount Diablo's natural beauty. 1196 Boulevard Way, Suite 10, Walnut Creek, CA 94595, (925) 947-3535, www.savemountdiablo.org, email: sendinfo@savemountdiablo.org.

Anthony Chabot Regional Park

*Seclusion and proximity
in the East Bay Hills*

A mere ridge away from East Bay cities, Anthony Chabot (Shuh-BO) campground shelters beneath a canopy of whispering eucalyptus and offers an easy excursion into a surprisingly secluded natural world. City lights are nicely hidden by intervening topography and convenience to metropolitan areas is the advantage here, making it a popular choice for both out-of-town visitors and East Bay residents.

In 1875, Anthony Chabot bottled up the waters of San Leandro Creek behind an earth-fill dam and created the lake that would bear his name. Off-limits to public use for the ensuing 91 years, the reservoir was first opened for limited recreation in 1966. Today it is one of the best fishing grounds in the East Bay, regularly stocked by the park district and home to some very large trout (5+ lbs.). See *Other Fun Activities* below for more information on fishing and boating opportunities. Unfortunately, swimming is not permitted—the reservoir serves as an emergency water supply for the East Bay.

ANTHONY CHABOT CAMPGROUND

The Campground

Located at an elevation of 600 feet on a long ridge shaded by eucalyptus trees, the numerous sites are closely situated and offer limited privacy. Amenities like free hot showers and a few full hook-up sites for RVs are bonuses. The weather is pleasant here year-round; winter rains are the only real inconvenience. The park gate closes at 10 P.M., making it necessary for campers to arrive beforehand or risk being locked out.

While the watchful can find a few small specimens of coast live oak, coffee berry, redwoods, and big-leaf maple around the

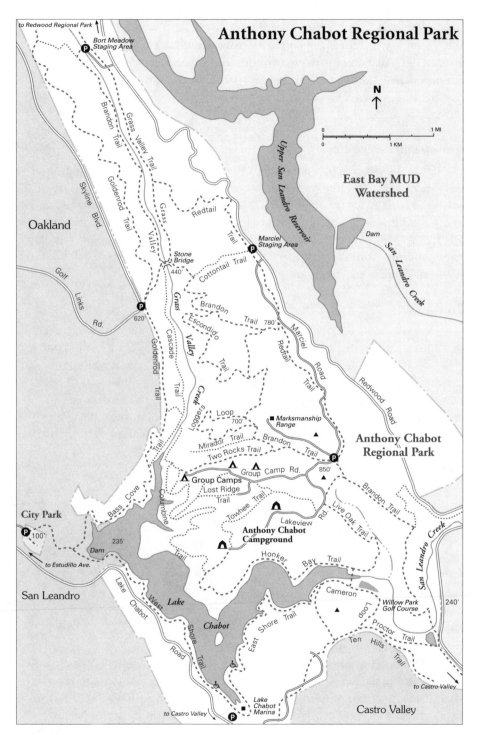

EAST OF THE BAY

Anthony Chabot Regional Park

to Redwood Regional Park

Bort Meadow
Staging Area

N

0   1 MI
0   1 KM

Upper San Leandro Reservoir

East Bay MUD
Watershed

Dam

San Leandro Creek

Oakland

Skyline Blvd.

Brandon Trail

Grass Valley Trail

Goldenrod Trail

Redtail

Grass Valley

Golf Links Rd.

Stone Bridge
440'

620'

Marciel
Staging Area

Cottontail Trail

Brandon

Escondido

Trail

Trail 780'

Marciel   Road

Redtail

Trail

Redwood   Road

Cascade

Trail

Goldenrod   Trail

Grass   Valley   Creek

Loop

Loop
700'

Marksmanship
Range

Anthony Chabot
Regional Park

Mirador   Trail

Brandon   Trail

Two Rocks Trail

Group   Camp Rd.

850'

Brandon   Trail

Group Camps

Lost Ridge
Trail

Towhee Trail

Lakeview Rd.

Live Oak Trail

Bass   Cove

Columbine

City Park

100'

235'

Dam

to Estudillo Ave.

Anthony Chabot
Campground

Honker   Bay   Trail

San Leandro Creek

San Leandro

Trail

Lake   Chabot

West   Shore   Trail

Lake
Chabot

Cameron

Willow Park
Golf Course

240'

Proctor   Trail

East   Shore   Trail

Ten   Hills   Trail

Loop

Road

Lake Chabot
Marina

to Castro Valley

Castro Valley

to Castro Valley

campground, eucalyptus forest dominates. In the early 1900s, the controlling water company for the lake planted extensive stands of non-native eucalyptus around the lake. Soon discovered commercially worthless and consequently left untouched, the alien forest now provides a world of tremulous trees and rustling leaves, the air awake with the resonant calls of great horned owls and red-tailed hawks.

Crowds and Reservations

Given the closely-spaced nature of the sites, a fully occupied campground feels very crowded. While weekends are generally full in summer and busy in spring and fall, space is available on most weekdays. Reservations can be made year-round up to 12 weeks in advance by calling the East Bay Regional Park District at (510) 562-2267 and are especially recommended for holiday weekends and from April through September for the limited number of full hook-up RV sites. There is a $6 reservation fee.

Trails

Lake Chabot is the obvious destination 300 feet below and several trails descend quickly to its shore from the campground. Huck's Trail, located past the walk-in campsites, provides the steepest and most direct access, while a pleasant 2.5-mile loop hike along the lakeshore and through the campground can be done by combining the Live Oak and Honker Bay trails. The motivated can circumnavigate the entire lake using the Honker Bay, Columbine, Bass Cove, West Shore, and East Shore trails, a 9-mile undertaking. While a vast network of trails can also be found north and west of Lake Chabot, the distance from the campground encourages driving to an alternate trailhead to explore this area—try Marciel Gate or Bort Meadow Staging Area along Redwood Road.

Canoe across Lake Chabot

Other Fun Activities

While swimming—or even any contact with the water—is not allowed in Lake Chabot, fishing and boating are permitted and popular. The park district regularly stocks the lake with thousands of rainbow trout, many of which grow to be large and delicious, and fishing is possible from the lakeshore in several spots below the campground. In order to fish, you need both a valid California fishing license *and* an East Bay Regional Park District fishing access permit ($4 per day), available at the campground entrance kiosk. For the latest on the angling excitement, call the fishing hotline at (510) 562-PARK. The park district also publishes a bi-weekly fishing bulletin called *Angler's Edge,* available at the marina or by subscription ($8/year, contact park district headquarters).

While rather inaccessible from the campground, the park marina is the central hub of lake activity. Located on the south corner of the lake, the marina provides a small store and offers boat rentals—rowboats, canoes, electric boats, pedal boats, and one- and two-person kayaks—by the hour, half-day, or day. (Prices range from $13-16/hour, $33-$36/half day, and $32-49/full day. Call (510) 892-2177 for more information.) Canoes, kayaks, and sculls under 20 feet can be carried in and launched ($2 fee). To reach the marina from the campground, take Redwood Road south to Seven Hills Road and turn right. After 1 mile on Seven Hills Road, bear right onto Lake Chabot Road and watch for the marina entrance on the right.

To Reach the Park

Take the Redwood Road exit off Highway 13 and follow Redwood Road up the hill to its intersection with Skyline Blvd. Continue straight (east) on Redwood Road for 6.2 miles to the Marciel Gate park entrance on the right. The campground is located 2 miles inside the park. Approaching from eastbound Interstate 580 in Oakland, take the 35th Avenue exit and turn left. 35th Avenue becomes Redwood Road and climbs up to Highway 13. Continue as above.

Approaching from eastbound Interstate 580 closer to Castro Valley, take the Redwood Road exit, turn left (north) on Redwood Road and proceed 4.5 miles to Marciel Gate on the left. From westbound I-580 in Castro Valley, take the east Castro Valley Blvd. exit to Castro Valley Blvd., turn right on Redwood Road, and proceed as above.

THE DETAILS

Governing Agency: East Bay Regional Park District, 2950 Peralta Oaks Court, Oakland, CA 94605-0381, (510) 562-PARK, www.ebparks.org.

Park Contact Information: Anthony Chabot Regional Park, 9999 Redwood Rd., Oakland, CA 94546, (510) 636-1684; Lake Chabot Marina, 17930 Lake Chabot Dr., Castro Valley, CA 94546, (510) 247-2526.

Visitor Center: No visitor center. Entrance kiosk usually open for information.

Sites: 75 total sites. 53 drive-up family sites. 10 walk-in sites. 12 full hook-up sites. 3 handicapped-accessible sites.

Costs: $15/site, includes one vehicle. *Sites with hook-ups:* $20. *Second vehicle:* $6. *Trailered vehicle:* $3. Dog fee: $1. *Dump station fee:* $5.

Group Sites: 7 sites. 5 primitive sites with pit toilets located just north of campground on Group Camp Road, 1 developed site within campground, 1 site

(Bort Meadow) at north end of park by Redwood Road. Site capacity 35-150 people except Bort Meadow (up to 500). Fees vary depending on county of residence and size of group. Reservations required at least 14 days in advance. Call (510) 562-2267, 9 A.M.–4 P.M. weekdays.

Months Open/Closed: Open year-round.

Facilities: Free hot showers, flush toilets, pay phone, dump station, firewood available for purchase ($5/bundle).

Regulations: *Fires* permitted in fire rings, no wood collecting. *Dogs* allowed in campground but must be confined within a vehicle or tent, or securely leashed with a maximum leash length of 6 feet. Limit 2 dogs per site. Dogs allowed off-leash in undeveloped areas of the park. *Bikes* allowed in campground and on most park trails. *Fishing* is allowed (see above). *Hard liquor* prohibited, beer and wine permitted. *Maximum number of people per site:* 10. *Maximum campsites per family:* 2. *Maximum number of vehicles per site:* 2. *Check-out time:* noon. *Maximum length of stay:* 15 consecutive days, 30 days maximum per year. After 15 consecutive days, campers must leave for 48 hours before returning. *Maximum Trailer Length:* 39 feet.

Giving Back

The Regional Parks Foundation supports and funds the acquisition, development, and stewardship of parklands in the East Bay Regional Park District through private contributions. Box 21074, Crestmont Station, Oakland, CA 94620, (510) 544-2200, www.regparksfdn.org.

Those interested in *volunteering* in Anthony Chabot Regional Park—or in any other unit of the East Bay Regional Park District— should contact the district's volunteer coordinator for more information, (510) 544-2515, email: volunteers@ebparks.org.

Del Valle Regional Park

Swimming, fishing, hiking, chilling

Softly flowing through a broad valley, ephemeral Arroyo del Valle shimmers through an inviting campground before reaching the waters of Lake Del Valle. Surrounding the lake are nearly 4000 acres of parkland and outdoor recreation in a land of intense seasonal change: lush rain and baking heat, vibrant greens and tawny browns, pressing crowds and empty trails. Secluded in the hills, removed from suburban sight, the park invites year-round.

Formed by a dam in 1968, Lake Del Valle is a substantial body of water and the largest featured in this book with more than 15 miles of shoreline. A prime attraction, it offers visitors the chance to swim, fish, and boat in its refreshing waters. The fishing is considered some of the best in the Bay Area, the swimming a respite from summer heat, and the boating a pleasant escape from the terrestrial world. See *Other Fun Activities* below for more information. Surrounding the lake are miles of trails for both hiking and biking, skirting the lakeshore and winding through the oak woodlands that cloak the landscape. There is something at Del Valle for everyone.

DEL VALLE CAMPGROUND

The Campground

Situated at an elevation of 700 feet at the southern end of Lake Del Valle, the campground is divided into three separate areas with most sites arranged around the perimeters of large grassy lawns ideal for play. Sites are often close together, but the campground's size and numerous shady trees add an air of privacy. A few choice sites border the creek and 21 sites have water and sewage hook-ups (but no electricity). Within the campground, stately gray pines branch upward and shed enormous pine cones on the ground. The mottled gray boles of sycamores line Arroyo del Valle, dangling spiny seed balls in the fall. And throughout, coast live, blue, and valley oaks offer shade beneath sheltering branches.

Crowds reach their peak in summer and the park is a giant playground for every type of activity. Spring is the best time to experience the park as wildflowers dot the landscape and new leaves bud above a luminescent green landscape. Crowds are surprisingly light. Fall in the far East Bay means continued warm temperatures, extremely dry conditions, and reduced crowds, making Del Valle one of the hottest Indian Summer destinations going. In winter, dedicated anglers hunt their prey as the cooler lake temperatures translate to excellent fishing. Naked oak branches twist above an explosion of green grass, and overnight use is minimal.

Crowds and Reservations

The campground books up quickly on summer weekends and holidays. Space is often available on summer weekdays, however, and at all times during fall, winter, and spring. Reservations can be made up to 12 weeks in advance by calling (510) 562-2267. There is a $6 reservation fee.

Trails

The majority of park trails wind through oak woodlands in the rolling landscape found on the eastern lakeshore. Numerous loops are possible—recommended is the 5-mile circuit on East Shore and Ridgeline trails which begins north of the boat launch. Del Valle Regional Park also marks the terminus of the 17-mile Ohlone Trail, a two- to four-day backpacking trip that begins in Sunol Regional Wilderness and travels the most remote lands of the East Bay Regional Park District (EBRPD). The last few miles approaching Del Valle are some of the steepest of the entire trail, but the opportunity to camp overnight in a backcountry graced with monstrous oaks is a just reward. (See the backpacking chapter *The Ohlone Trail* for more details.) With the exception of the Ohlone Trail, most paths are open to bikers.

Other Fun Activities

Fishing, fishing, fishing. Rainbow trout, largemouth bass, smallmouth bass, catfish, stripers, and bluegills all can be caught. Trout are regularly stocked from October through May by California Fish and Game and supplemented with trophy plants made possible by the District's fishing permit program. These

lunkers are no joke—the lake's record trout weighed in at 20 pounds, and 5+ pound trout are regularly pulled from the waters. Other lake records (in

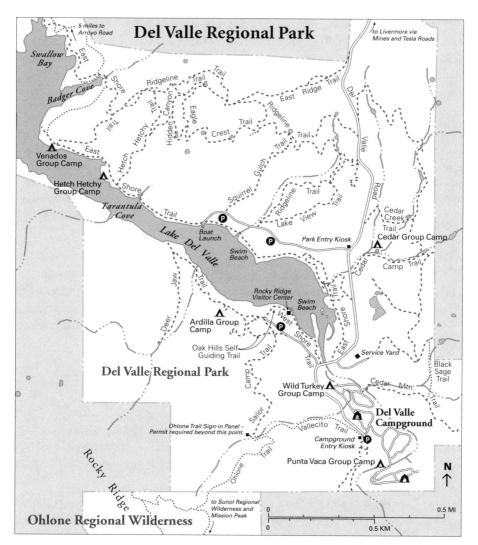

Del Valle Regional Park

pounds): catfish, 30; striped bass, 40; largemouth bass, 14.5; smallmouth bass, 5.75; bluegill, 2.75. Bait fishing is popular from both shore and boat, and the easily accessible south end of the lake generally offers good fishing. Get the latest at the EBRPD fishing hotline, (510) 562-PARK. All anglers 16 years or older must have both a current California sport fishing license *and* an EBRPD fishing access permit ($4 per day), available at the entrance station, marina, and visitor center.

Boats, boats, boats. For those with their own watercraft, a public launch is located on the east side of the lake. There is a launch fee of $3 and a speed limit of 10 MPH. Boats must be off the water a half-hour before sunset, and jet skis are not allowed. A variety of watercraft can be rented at hourly, half-day, and full-day rates—rowboats, motorboats, patio boats, two-person kayaks, and four-person pedal boats are all available ($33-140 per day depending on watercraft, contact Urban Park Concessionaire, (925) 449-5201). Windsurfing equipment also can be rented—call (925) 455-4008 for more information. On summer weekends and holidays, a tour boat makes twice daily hour-long journeys on the lake and provides the most affordable way to venture onto the water ($5/person).

Swimming is permitted but limited to two designated areas at the south end of the lake (south of the boat launch). Lifeguards are regularly on duty in the summer months. Swimming is allowed north of the boat launch but is less accessible and performed at your own risk. While sitting and soaking in Arroyo del Valle is possible, the stream usually dries up in May.

To Reach the Park

Take the North Livermore Avenue exit from Interstate 580. Head south and proceed through town (North Livermore Avenue becomes South Livermore Avenue). About 1.5 miles outside town, turn right at Mines Road, go about 3.5 miles and continue straight on Del Valle Road as Mines Road turns left. The park entrance is about 4 miles ahead.

THE DETAILS

Governing Agency: East Bay Regional Park District, 2950 Peralta Oaks Court, Box 5381, Oakland, CA 94605-0318, (510) 562-PARK, www.ebparks.org.

Park Contact Information: Del Valle Regional Park, 7000 Del Valle Rd., Livermore, CA 94550, (925) 373-0332.

Visitor Center: Rocky Ridge Visitor Center, located on the lake's southwest shore, open daily in summer, weekends in the off-season, and sporadically at other times. The park entry kiosk also is usually staffed and can answer most questions.

Sites: 150 drive-in sites, 21 sites have sewer/water hook-ups (no electricity). Most sites can handle large RVs and trailers. 2 handicapped-accessible sites.

Costs: $15/site, includes 1 vehicle. *Sewer/water hook-up sites:* $18. *Extra vehicle:* $6. *Trailer:* $3. *Dog:* $1. *Day-use fee:* $4/vehicle, October-March; $5/vehicle, April-September.

Group Sites: 6 sites. 2 sites (Wild Turkey and Punta Vaca) located within the campground. 4 sites (Ardilla, Venados, Hetch Hetchy, and Cedar) are removed from the main campground area and are hike-in or boat-in only (0.5-1 mile walk). Capacity varies from 35-150. Fees vary depending on county of residence and size of group. Reservations required at least 14 days in advance—call (510) 562-2267, 9 A.M.–4 P.M. weekdays.

Months Open/Closed: Open year-round.

Maps: Free and accurate park map is sufficient for hiking, available at entrance station and visitor center.

Facilities: Free hot showers and flush toilets in nice, open-air bathrooms; pay phone; boat launch and rentals (see above); two snack bars (open summer only). Camp store by the campground entrance sells ice, wood, and tasty snacks (open daily in summer, weekends only April-May and September-October, closed November-March).

Regulations: *Fires* permitted in fire rings, no wood collecting. *Dogs* allowed on nearly all park trails, must be leashed in the campground, leashes must be no longer than 6 feet. *Bikes* allowed in campground and on most trails. *Fishing* permitted year-round in Lake del Valle (see above) and permitted in Arroyo del Valle from the last Saturday in April until November 15. *No alcoholic beverages* except beer and wine. *Rope swings, hammocks, and other activities that require hanging ropes from trees* prohibited. *Water activity* prohibited at night. *Maximum number of people per site:* 10. *Maximum number of vehicles per site:* 2. *Check-out time:* noon. *Maximum length of stay:* 15 consecutive days, 30 days total annually.

Giving Back

The Regional Parks Foundation supports and funds the acquisition, development, and stewardship of parklands in the East Bay Regional Park District through private contributions. Box 21074, Crestmont Station, Oakland, CA 94620, (510) 544-2200, www.regparksfdn.org.

Those interested in *volunteering* for Del Valle Regional Park—or in any other unit of the East Bay Regional Park District—should contact the district's volunteer coordinator for more information, (510) 544-2515, email: volunteers@ebparks.org.

Sunol Regional Wilderness

A tiny campground on the banks of Alameda Creek

Behind the massif of Mission Peak, hidden from the bustling human landscape of the Bay Area, Sunol exists peacefully on nature's terms, on nature's time. The perennial tumble of Alameda Creek beneath the stalwart arms of sycamores, the cycle of seasons in radiant greens and gentle browns, the patient wheeling of raptors across the sky, the steadfast grip of oaks upon hillsides rounded by time. . . . Sweet Sunol.

SUNOL CAMPGROUND

The Campground

Situated at an elevation of 400 feet, the campground consists of nothing more than four sites stacked together in a small clearing by Alameda Creek. Located adjacent to the visitor center parking lot and with no privacy between sites, this is not the place to come during busy times. Weekends and holidays attract crowds to the park and curious visitors regularly wander near the campsites during the day. Relaxation is difficult and theft a concern; staying here at these times is not recommended. However, those who arrive late and break camp early can largely avoid these hassles and still enjoy the park's hiking opportunities. Weekdays (especially October-March) are lightly-traveled, and those who stay overnight may feel they have the place to themselves. While Sunol is an all-seasons destination, summer heat can be oppressive. *The park gates are locked at dusk*—campers must arrive beforehand or will be unable to enter the park.

The campsites lie beneath the shady branches of California bay and coast live oak; water-loving sycamores and alders draw sustenance along the nearby margin of Alameda Creek. The largest drainage in the East Bay, the Alameda Creek watershed drains more than 600 square miles before emptying into San

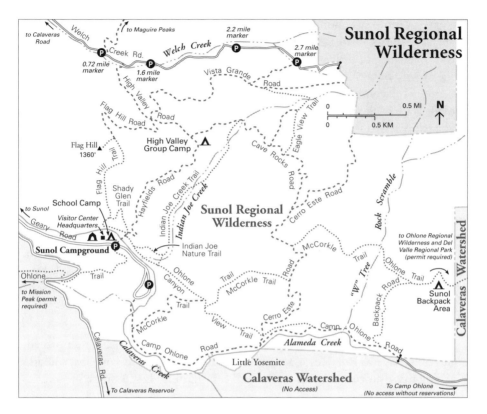

Francisco Bay just north of the Dumbarton Bridge. Spring wildflowers are abundant in Sunol, typically peaking in the park's lower elevations during the last week of March and first week of April.

Crowds and Reservations

The campground is popular in the summer months and, given its microscopic size, full most days. Weekends remain busy year-round, but weekday space is usually available September-May. Reservations can be made up to 12 weeks in advance by calling (510) 636-1684; there is a $6 reservation fee. Groups wishing to have the entire campground to themselves can reserve all four sites at once.

Trails

The exceptional hiking opportunities are the main reason to come here. The hilly landscape means significant elevation change—most hikes are moderate to strenuous. The exception is wide Camp Ohlone Road, a broad and level fire road/trail that parallels Alameda Creek for just over a mile before reaching the cataracts of Little Yosemite. The easy, 2.5-mile out-and-back hike to this narrow, boulder-strewn section of Alameda Creek is the most popular hike in the park. A more strenuous option is the 5.0-mile loop along Indian Joe Nature Trail, Cave Rocks Road, Cerro Este Road, and Camp Ohlone Road. With a total elevation change of nearly 1500 feet, this hike explores a small creek, passes a pile of wild basalt boulders, offers far-reaching views, and includes Little Yosemite at the end. Sunol also marks the beginning of the Ohlone Trail and provides one of the nicest trail camps in the Bay Area, perfect for a two-day backpacking trip (see the backpacking chapter *The Ohlone Trail* for more information).

Other Fun Activities

Housed in an original ranch building, the visitor center provides numerous free and informative handouts, including basic guides for identifying the multitude of birds, flowers, and trees that line Alameda Creek. Specimens of all the park's wildflowers are carefully preserved here. In addition, the park offers regular naturalist-led programs and hikes in the park. Check the latest schedule by phone at (925) 862-2601 or online at www.ebparks.org/events/byloc/sunol.htm.

To Reach the Park

Take Interstate 680 east of Fremont to the Calaveras Road exit and proceed south on Calaveras Road for 4.3 miles to Geary Road. Turn left on Geary Road, reaching the visitor center parking lot and campground in 1.9 miles.

THE DETAILS

Governing Agency: East Bay Regional Park District, 2950 Peralta Oaks Court, Box 5381, Oakland, CA 94605-0318, (510) 562-PARK, www.ebparks.org.

Park Contact Information: Sunol Regional Wilderness, 1895 Geary Rd., Sunol, CA 94516, (925) 862-2244.

Visitor Center: Open 10 A.M.–5 P.M. weekends year-round, closed weekdays, (925) 862-2601.

Sites: 4 sites, all handicapped-accessible.

Costs: $11/site, includes 1 vehicle; fee for extra vehicles. *Dog fee:* $1. *Day-use fee:* $4/vehicle, $3/trailer.

Group Sites: 5 hike-in group sites available April-October. *High Valley Camp:* a steep 1-mile hike from the visitor center, no vehicles permitted, maximum 50 people. *School Camp:* located in main entrance area, maximum 60 people and 5 vehicles. *Camp Ohlone:* 3 sites located a 7-mile drive from the park entrance and set up for the disabled, 2 sites require a 0.2-mile walk from the parking area. Maximum 50 people and 7 vehicles per site. Fees vary depending on county of residence and size of group ($30-70). Reservations required at least 14 days in advance—call (510) 562-2267, 9 A.M.–4 P.M. weekdays for more information.

Months Open/Closed: Open year-round, subject to closure during fire season (June-October).

Maps: Free and accurate park map available at entrance station and visitor center is sufficient for hiking.

Facilities: Pay phone.

Regulations: *Fires* permitted in fire rings, no wood collecting, restrictions may be in effect during fire season (June-October). *Dogs* allowed on all park trails and may be off-leash outside of developed areas, must be leashed in the campground area, leashes must be no longer than 6 feet. *Bikes* allowed in campground and on most trails. *Swimming* permitted in Alameda Creek, prohibited in Little Yosemite area. *Fishing* prohibited in Alameda Creek and its tributaries. *Alcoholic beverages* prohibited. *Maximum number of people per site:* 10. *Maximum number of vehicles per site:* 2. *Check-out time:* noon. *Maximum length of stay:* 10 consecutive days, 30 days total annually.

Giving Back

The Regional Parks Foundation supports and funds the acquisition, development, and stewardship of parklands in the East Bay Regional Park District through private contributions. Box 21074, Crestmont Station, Oakland, CA 94620, (510) 544-2200, www.regparksfdn.org.

Alameda Creek Alliance is a community watershed group dedicated to preserving and restoring the natural ecosystems of the Alameda Creek drainage basin. Box 192, Sunol, CA 94516, (510) 845-4675, www.alamedacreek.com.

Those interested in *volunteering* for Sunol Regional Wilderness— or any other unit of the East Bay Regional Park District— should contact the district's volunteer coordinator for more information, (510) 544-2515, email: volunteers@ebparks.org.

Joseph D. Grant County Park

Pastoral oak woodlands on the flanks of Mt. Hamilton

Hidden in the swales east of San Jose are grassy fields of oaken delight, a quiet world nestled in the foothills of the Bay Area's highest mountains. Largest of the Santa Clara County Parks at nearly 10,000 acres, Joseph D. Grant County Park lies in an isolated valley on a seldom-traveled road and protects a swath of oak woodlands remarkable for its seclusion.

The park exists as a legacy to Joseph Grant, a successful businessman and early environmentalist who acquired most of today's parkland in the late 19th century. As an early environmentalist, he served as president of the Save-the-Redwoods League for 21 years and passionately believed in the preservation of open space for future generations. As an influential business man, he was a life trustee of Stanford University, had the sway to move Mt. Hamilton Road a half mile from his house, and entertained guests as important as Herbert Hoover and Leland Stanford at his ranch. Following his death in 1942, the land passed to his wife and then to his daughter Josephine, who donated the land of today's park to the Save-the-Redwoods League and the Meninger Foundation following her death in 1972. Purchased by Santa Clara County in 1975, the park opened to the public in 1978.

JOSEPH D. GRANT COUNTY PARK CAMPGROUND

The Campground

Situated at an elevation of 1600 feet along a small ridgelet, the campground overlooks an undeveloped pastoral landscape. Most of the semi-private sites offer shade beneath twisting oak branches, the free hot showers are a refreshing bonus, and the small size of the campground means that crowds do not completely dominate the experience even when all sites are full. Sites tend to be small, however, and squeezing in more than one tent

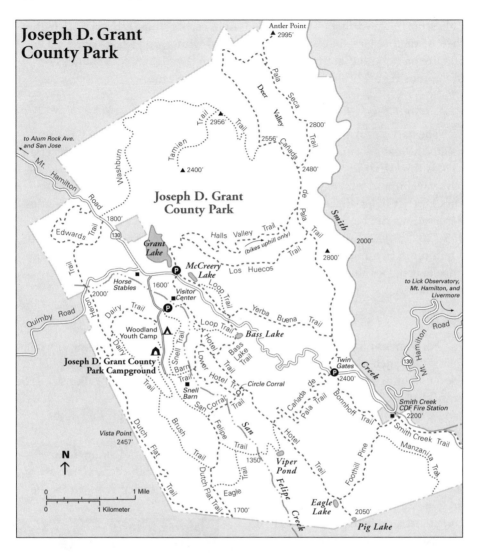

Joseph D. Grant County Park

can be challenging. Winter and spring the land is cloaked with the soft greens of grass, wildflowers, and new oak leaves. Summer and fall are dry, with the baking temperatures of June through August tapering into the more mild days of September and October. Note that the park gates close a half hour after sunset and that no entry is permitted once the gates are closed—plan accordingly.

Within the campground the dominant trees are large black oaks, identified by their large and pointy (4-8″), spine-tipped leaves; and valley oaks, known by their smaller (3-6″), rounded, and deeply lobed leaves. As the leaves of black oak first appear in March, they emerge soft and fiery red, an unusual sight. Intermixed with the oaks are a few Coulter pines, producers of the largest cones of any conifer and identified by their needle clusters of three; some enormous

California buckeye, first of the trees to bud in early spring (February), dangling their distinctive large buckeye seeds in fall and winter; and a few California bay and live oaks, both evergreen species that retain their leaves year-round. The ubiquitous coyote brush is scattered around in between.

Crowds and Reservations

The park's proximity to San Jose, the most populous city in the Bay Area, means the campground is usually full on weekends and holidays from the end of May through mid-September. Outside of these times, weekend space is usually available and weekdays are lightly used. In 2002, the Santa Clara County Park District inaugurated a new reservation system for its family campgrounds. Reservations can be made six months to 48 hours in advance by calling (408) 355-2201 8:30 A.M.–3:30 P.M. Monday-Friday. There is a $6 reservation fee and a minimum two-night stay required for weekend reservations. Online reservations may be possible in coming years—check www.parkhere.org for current information.

Trails

Forty miles of trails weave through the park's varied terrain, many of which follow old ranch roads and are well graded and easy to follow. The park offers a good mix of ridges and valleys, and hikers can choose either easy valley strolls or more challenging ridgetop excursions with far-reaching views. Oak woodlands can be found throughout, and occasionally you will see cows grazing in the park. Bikes are permitted on most trails (helmets are required).

Numerous short loop trips emerge from the campground along the Snell, San Felipe, Barn, and Hotel trails, passing over trickling San Felipe Creek as they loop around the lower elevations. For views and more exercise, go for the 6.5-mile loop formed by the Dairy, Dutch Flat, and Brush trails, which offers expansive views of the park and distant South Bay as it follows a segment of the Bay Area Ridge Trail. Finally, those who like to avoid cows while exploring remote destinations will enjoy Deer Valley in the far northeastern corner of the park.

Please Close the Door when you Leave so the Animals Don't Come In.

Other Fun Activities

Anglers can catch bass and catfish from sizable Grant Lake and smaller Bass and McCreery lakes, all located along Mt. Hamilton Road. Although outside the park, the white dome of Lick Observatory is clearly visible perched atop the summit of nearby Mt. Hamilton (4213'). The narrow, twisting drive to the top is not soon forgotten. Open daily to the public, the observatory offers free guided tours of its unique, 36-inch telescope dome every half hour (tours begin at 1 P.M. weekdays, 10:30 A.M. weekends, last tour at 4:30 P.M.). For more information, contact the observatory at (408) 274-5061 or go online at www.ucolick.org/public/visitors.html.

To Reach the Park

Take Alum Rock Road (Highway 130) east from Highway 101 or Interstate 680 to Mt. Hamilton Road, located 2 miles from I-680, and turn right. From there it's a narrow and twisting 7.5-mile escape from civilization to the park entrance, located on the right side of the road.

Beating the crowds in February

THE DETAILS

Governing Agency: County of Santa Clara, Parks and Recreation Department, 298 Garden Hill Drive, Los Gatos, CA 95032-7699, (408) 358-7146, www.parkhere.org.

Park Contact Information: Joseph D. Grant County Park, 18405 Mt. Hamilton Rd., San Jose, CA 95140, (408) 274-6121.

Visitor Center: Located by the former ranch house, open sporadically.

Sites: 22 drive-in sites. An overflow area of 16 sites is opened if the main campground is full. Most sites can accommodate small trailers and RVs. 1 handicapped-accessible site.

Costs: $15/site, includes one vehicle. *Extra vehicle:* $6. *Day-use fee:* $4. *Dog:* $1.

Group Sites: 3 sites (Woodlands, Arrowhead, Buckhorn), non-profit youth groups only. Limited shade. *Woodlands:* maximum 200 people. *Arrowhead:* maximum 40 people. *Buckhorn:* maximum 30 people. $30/first night, $10/each additional night. Reservations required, call (408) 355-2201, 9 A.M.–4 P.M. Monday-Friday.

Months Open/Closed: Open year-round.

Facilities: Flush toilets, free hot showers, pay phone, dump station.

Regulations: *Gates* locked half-hour after sunset, no re-entry once gates are closed. *Fires* permitted in fire rings outside of wildfire season. Fires prohibited during most of summer and fall due to wildfire risk, exact times determined by the state. No wood collecting. No firewood for sale in the park. The park encourages the use of charcoal and artificial logs to minimize the risk of introducing Sudden Oak Death to the park (see "The Living Bay Area" in *Where Should I Go?* for more information). *Dogs* allowed leashed in campground and on Edwards Trail only;

leash must be 6 feet or less. *Bikes* allowed on many park trails as posted, helmets required. *Fishing* permitted year-round in Grant, McCreery, and Bass lakes; valid California fishing license required. *Swimming* prohibited in all lakes, streams, and reservoirs. *Maximum number of people per site:* 8. *Maximum number of vehicles per site:* 2. *Check-out time:* 1 P.M. *Maximum length of stay:* 14 days total from Memorial Day through Labor Day. Rest of year: 14 days in a 30-day period, with a gap of 30 days required between stays.

Giving Back

The Silicon Valley Parks Foundation works with the Santa Clara County Park District to improve the quality of life for all citizens of Santa Clara County by sponsoring and supporting projects and programs that enhance the enjoyment, education, and inspiration of the regional park and outdoor recreation experience. Box 320038, Los Gatos, CA 95032-0100, (408) 358-3741 x137, www.siliconvalleyparks.org.

Those interested in *volunteering* for Joseph D. Grant County Park—or any other unit of the Santa Clara County Park District—should contact the district's volunteer coordinator for more information, (408) 846-5761, or go online at www.parkhere.org/volunteer.htm.

Henry W. Coe State Park

*Breathtaking ridges and valleys
in Northern California's
largest state park*

In the heart of the Diablo Range lies a park vast and beautiful, creased with ridges, sliced by canyons, infused with an incredible variety of life. With 87,000 acres, 700 plants species, 137 bird species, and a lifetime of trails and adventure, Henry W. Coe State Park beckons.

HEADQUARTERS CAMPGROUND

The Campground

For a park so huge, it's ironic that the sheer topography of the entrance region allows for only a small campground of 20 sites. Situated at 2650 feet near the top of steep Pine Ridge, the sites are close together and offer minimal to no privacy. The campground is not a destination in itself, and should be considered primarily a gateway to the exceptional hiking opportunities that radiate in all directions. Winter and spring are by far the best times to visit the park as rain turns the landscape a vibrant green and gives life to a profusion of wildflowers from March through May. Summer and fall are hot, hot, hot! and the campground offers minimal shade, although each site is equipped with a simple wooden shelter above the picnic table for some sun protection.

Crowds and Reservations

The campground is popular from March through May and weekends are usually fully reserved in advance. Throughout the rest of the year, however, space is available at most times—even on summer weekends. Reservations can be made year-round up to seven months in advance by calling (800) 444-7275 or going online at www.reserveamerica.com. Note that RVs and trailers are not recommended due to the narrow and twisting nature of the park's access road.

Coe backcountry

Trails

With rare exception, trails in Henry Coe are *very* steep; elevation changes on most hikes will exceed 2000 feet. The delightful exception is the mostly level 3.5-mile loop formed by the Corral, Forest, and Spring trails, a pleasant ramble which also offers the opportunity to learn about the area's flora. Forest Trail educates with the help of numbered posts and an interpretive brochure, available at the visitor center and Manzanita Point Road/Forest Trail junction. For the fit and motivated, other day hike recommendations include the 7.5-mile loop formed by the Corral, Fish, Middle Ridge, Frog Lake, and Flat Frog trails (2000' elevation gain/loss); and any of the loops that access the swimming spot at China Hole. The park offers some of the wildest, deepest, and most extensive backpacking options in the entire Bay Area—see the backpacking chapter *Henry W. Coe State Park* for details.

To Reach the Park

Take Highway 101 to Morgan Hill and exit at East Dunne Avenue. Head east and follow East Dunne Avenue for 11 miles to the visitor center parking lot at road's end. After leaving the residential area of Morgan Hill, the ascent road is narrow, twisting, and exciting.

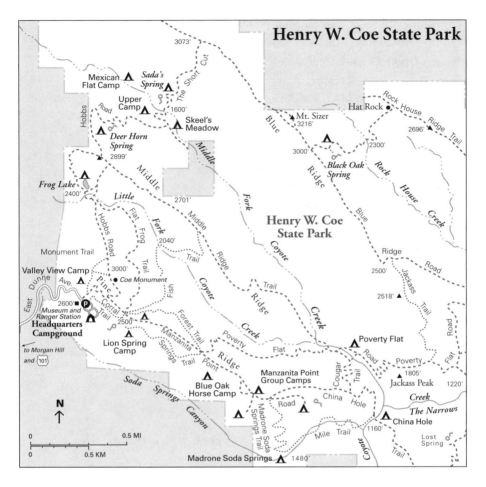

THE DETAILS

Governing Agency: Henry W. Coe State Park, Box 846, Morgan Hill, CA 95038, (408) 779-2728, www.coepark.org.

Visitor Center: Located at the park entrance in a beautifully restored original ranch building. Great bookstore sells state park maps and all the USGS quads for the area. Open spring and summer 7 A.M.–8 P.M. Friday-Sunday, sporadically other days and during fall and winter.

Sites: 20 drive-in sites. 1 handicapped-accessible site. 9 sites can accommodate RVs and trailers up to 20 feet for those who braved the access road.

Costs: $7/site, includes 1 vehicle. *Extra vehicle:* $4. *Seniors 62+:* $2 discount. *Day-use fee:* $4/vehicle.

Group Sites: Manzanita Point, 10 large hike-in sites located a relatively easy 2-3 miles from the visitor center. A single support vehicle is allowed to make one trip in to haul water, food, and supplies. Pit toilets, no water. Minimum 10 and maximum 50 people, $15. Reservations required—contact the park directly.

Months Open/Closed: Open year-round.

Maps: The only map covering the entire park and its trails is the *Henry W. Coe Park Trail & Camping Map,* available at the visitor center or by sending a check for $6.50 to: The Pine Ridge Association, Map Request, Box 846, Morgan Hill, CA 95038. USGS 7.5-min *Mt. Sizer* covers the western region of the park around the entrance.

Facilities: Pit toilets, pay phone, firewood available at visitor center ($5/bundle).

Regulations: *Fires* permitted in fire rings, no wood collecting, occasional restrictions during wildfire season (June-October). *Dogs* prohibited on all park trails, allowed leashed in the campground only; leashes must be no longer than 6 feet. *Bikes* allowed in campground and on fire roads, prohibited on singletrack trails. *Fishing* permitted in several lakes and creeks in the park, with good bass fishing in most lakes; access is difficult. *Maximum number of people per site:* 8. *Maximum number of vehicles per site:* 2, additional vehicles must park in overflow area. *Check-out time:* noon. *Maximum length of stay:* 30 consecutive days.

Giving Back

The Pine Ridge Association assists park staff in designing interpretive materials and presenting educational programs to the public. A uniformed-volunteer training program is offered and membership ($15) has many benefits. Box 846, Morgan Hill, CA 95038, (408) 779-2728.

Coyote Lake County Park

*Reservoir wild in the foothills
of the Diablo Range*

Filling an oaken valley with the dammed waters of Coyote Creek, 635-acre Coyote Lake is a secluded world on the edge of the greater Bay Area. The park is small, the campground closely packed, and swimming or wading in the lake is not permitted. However those in search of fishing, boating, water skiing, or questing into the southern wilds of Henry W. Coe State Park will find this a pleasant destination.

In the early 1900s the burgeoning population of the South Bay was sapping underground water reserves and lowering the water table of the Santa Clara Valley. To combat this, the Santa Clara Valley Water Conservation District was formed in 1929 to collect and regulate the runoff of the County's creeks and recharge the diminishing aquifers. Six dams were built in the county, two of them on Coyote Creek. Coyote Lake dam was completed in 1936, and a dam creating Anderson Lake 5 miles downstream was finished a few years later. Following the creation of Coyote Lake, the surrounding lakeshore passed through a variety of leases and was slowly developed for recreation. By the 1960s more than 90 small, leased cabins dotted the shore, accompanied by numerous docks and private concessionaires. In 1969, Santa Clara County Parks acquired the land and over time demolished the cabins and turned the lake into a county park. By 1979, all the cabins were gone and the park resembled much of what it is today.

The deep and narrow trough in which Coyote Lake sits owes its existence to the Calaveras Fault, a large off-shoot of the San Andreas Fault that parallels the Santa Clara Valley in the western foothills of the Diablo Range. Since the mid-1800s, more than two dozen earthquakes of magnitude 5.0 or greater have occurred along the Calaveras Fault. Its relentless grinding pulverizes the rock along its trace, creating a trough of loose material that was easily eroded away by Coyote Creek to form the valley present today. Within the park, the Calaveras Fault runs directly beneath the lake…and directly under the dam's foundation. Seriously.

COYOTE LAKE COUNTY PARK CAMPGROUND

The Campground

While the park is remarkably isolated with little sign of human intrusion, the campground does not share the same sense of privacy. Situated at an elevation of 800 feet at the lake's southwest shore, the entire campground is visible from most sites and a fully occupied weekend feels very crowded. Sites lining the outer perimeter of the campground offer a bit more privacy, with those closest to the lake offering unobstructed views of the water and opposite shore. Roughly half the sites offer some shade, while the other half bake in the summer sun; expect hot, dry conditions from June through the first rains of winter. Spring is a delight as the surrounding oak trees bud amid fields of green grass.

Within the campground, the curled and spiny round leaves of coast live oak are common, joined by the lobed leaves of several stately valley oak. California bay, coyote brush, and small elderberry trees are joined by buckeye and wild cucumber vines in the moist stream gully on the eastern border of the campground. The smooth gray boles of twisting sycamores also can be found nearby and poison oak is unfortunately common as well. Birdlife is abundant—food-grubbing yellow-billed magpies, gobbling wild turkeys, and coveys of bobbing quail join the birdsong of many other species in the campground. Bald eagles and osprey occasionally are spotted. Do not leave food unattended even for a minute—the magpies are well trained.

Crowds and Reservations

The park is a popular weekend getaway for local anglers and boaters, filling up every weekend and holiday from Easter until the end of September. Reservations are recommended. Outside of these times, space is generally available; weekdays in spring, winter, and fall find only one or two campsites occupied. The lake is popular year-round for day-use fishing and boating—noisy enthusiasts often arrive early in the morning. In 2002, the Santa Clara County Park District inaugurated a new reservation system for its family campgrounds. Reservations can be made six months to 48 hours in advance by calling (408) 355-2201, 8:30 A.M.–3:30 P.M. Monday-Friday. A $6 reservation fee is charged and there is a minimum two-night stay required for weekend reservations. Online reservations may be possible in the coming years—check online at www.parkhere.org for current information.

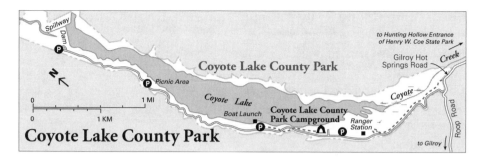

Coyote Lake County Park

Trails

With only 2 miles of trails that closely parallel the road, hiking is not much of an attraction in the park. However, Henry W. Coe State Park—and its hundreds of miles of trails—is only 4 miles away. See the backpacking chapter *Henry W. Coe State Park* for more information. Cyclists can enjoy 3-mile-long paved Coyote Reservoir Road to the dam or pleasant rides along Gilroy Hot Springs Road outside the park.

Other Fun Activities

Fishing, boating, water skiing. Open year-round for fishing, Coyote Lake is regularly stocked with rainbow trout by the California Department of Fish & Game (the biggest plants occur May-June; see www.dfg.ca.gov/fishplant for current stocking information) and also harbors non-stocked bass, crappie, catfish, and bluegill. Shore fishing is good everywhere except the east shore and a boat launch is provided a mile north of the campground. Both non-power and power boating are permitted—sailboats, ski boats, and jet skis all play here. See *Boating Regulations* below for the details.

To Reach the Park

Take the Leavesley Road exit from Highway 101 in Gilroy and follow Leavesley Road 1.8 miles east to New Avenue. Turn left and follow New Avenue 0.6 mile to Roop Road and turn right. Roop Road becomes Gilroy Hot Springs Road and reaches the park entrance on the left 3.0 miles past New Avenue.

THE DETAILS

Governing Agency: County of Santa Clara Parks and Recreation Department, 298 Garden Hill Drive, Los Gatos, CA 95032-7699, (408) 358-7146, www.parkhere.org.

Park Contact Information: Coyote Lake County Park, 10840 Coyote Lake Rd., Gilroy, CA 95020, (408) 842-7800.

Visitor Center: Located by the entrance station. Open 8 A.M.–5 P.M. daily in summer, sporadically in the off-season.

Sites: 75 drive-in sites, most accommodate RVs and trailers. 1 handicapped-accessible site.

Costs: $15/site, includes 1 vehicle. *Additional vehicle:* $6. *Seniors 62+:* $7.50/site Sunday-Thursday. *Dogs:* $1 each. *Gas-powered boats:* $5/day. *Electric and self-powered boats:* $3/day. *Day-use fee:* $4/vehicle.

Group Sites: None.

Months Open/Closed: Open year-round.

Maps: Free and useful park map available at entrance station.

Facilities: Flush toilets, pay phone, firewood available for purchase ($5/bundle). No RV facilities.

Camping Regulations: *Swimming* prohibited in Coyote Lake and Creek. *Fires* permitted year-round in fire rings, no wood collecting. *Dogs* allowed leashed in the park south of San Ysidro Picnic Area only (second picnic area above boat launch), leashes must be no longer than 6 feet, maximum two dogs per site. *Bikes* allowed in campground and on paved roads only, helmets required for youths under 18. *Fishing* permitted year-round in Coyote Lake with valid CA fishing license. *Maximum number of people per site:* 8. *Maximum number of vehicles per site:* 2, additional vehicles must park in overflow lot. *Check-out time:* 1 P.M. *Maximum length of stay:* 14 days within any 45-day period. *Youths under 18* are not permitted to camp without an adult.

Boating Regulations: *Boats* permitted on the lake from 8 A.M. until 30 minutes before sunset. *Non-MTBE Fuel* required; boaters must show a receipt to confirm this. *Current registration* required for all motor-driven vessels and for sailboats over 8 feet. *Life Jackets* required for all water skiers, users of personal watercraft and children under 12 in boats 26 feet or less. *Passengers* must be inside the passenger compartment when vessel is underway. *Maximum speed* 35 MPH, observe "no wake zones." *Direction of travel* is counter-clockwise. No 360-degree or trick turns except for picking up a downed water skier. *Youths under 16* may not operate a vessel which is over 15 HP, unless between the ages of 12 and 15 and accompanied by an adult 18 or older. A *Red Ski Flag* must be displayed when equipment and/or a skier is down in the water. An *observer* at least 12 years of age must be in the vessel watching water skiers at all times.

Giving Back

The Silicon Valley Parks Foundation works with the Santa Clara County Park District to improve the quality of life for all citizens of Santa Clara County by sponsoring and supporting projects and programs that enhance the enjoyment, education, and inspiration of the regional park and outdoor recreation experience. Box 320038, Los Gatos, CA 95032-0100, (408) 358-3741 x137, www.siliconvalleyparks.org.

Those interested in *volunteering* for Coyote Lake County Park—or any other unit of the Santa Clara County Park District—should contact the district's volunteer coordinator for more information, (408) 846-5761, or go online at www.parkhere.org/volunteer.htm.

The Alameda Creek drainage,
Ohlone Wilderness

Backpacking Trips

Above Tennessee Valley Beach,
Marin Headlands

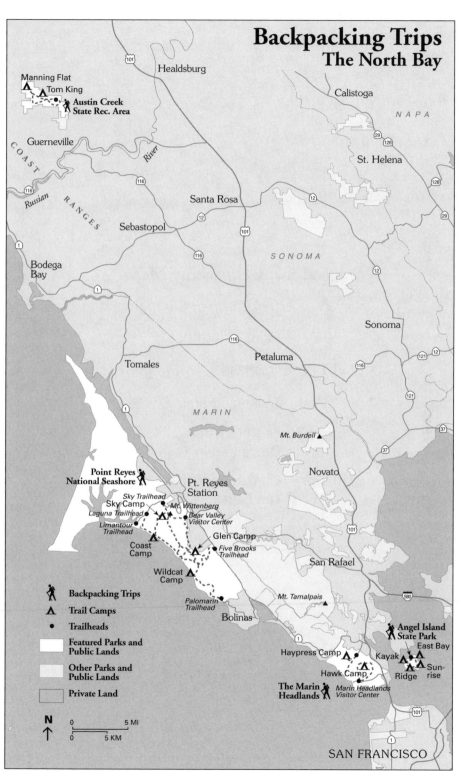

Backpacking Trips
The North Bay

Manning Flat
Tom King
Austin Creek
State Rec. Area

Healdsburg

Calistoga

NAPA

Guerneville

St. Helena

COAST

Russian River

Santa Rosa

RANGES

Sebastopol

Bodega
Bay

SONOMA

Sonoma

Tomales

Petaluma

MARIN

Mt. Burdell

Novato

Point Reyes
National Seashore

Pt. Reyes
Station

Sky Trailhead
Sky Camp
Laguna Trailhead
Limantour
Trailhead
Coast
Camp

Mt. Wittenberg
Bear Valley
Visitor Center

Glen Camp

Five Brooks
Trailhead

San Rafael

Wildcat
Camp

Mt. Tamalpais

Palomarin
Trailhead
Bolinas

Angel Island
State Park
East Bay

Haypress Camp

Kayak

Sun-
rise

Hawk Camp

Ridge

The Marin
Headlands

Marin Headlands
Visitor Center

SAN FRANCISCO

Legend
🚶 Backpacking Trips
⛺ Trail Camps
● Trailheads
　 Featured Parks and
　 Public Lands
　 Other Parks and
　 Public Lands
　 Private Land

N
0   5 MI
0   5 KM

NORTH BAY

Legend for Backpacking Maps

▲ Trail Camp or Campground

■ ● Point of Interest

T Trailhead

P Trailhead Parking

——— Featured Trail,
Described in Text

┈┈┈► Connecting Trail,
Not Described in Text

Angel Island State Park

*Epic views, rich history, and
camping in the middle
of San Francisco Bay*

The Park: Angel Island State Park
Distance: 2.6-3.0 miles round-trip
Total Elevation Gain/Loss: 300/300 to Ridge Sites,
500/500 to East Bay and Sunrise
Trip Length: 2 days
Difficulty: ★
Best Times: Year-round
Recommended Maps: *Angel Island State Park
Map,* USGS 7.5-min *San Francisco North*

In the middle of the Bay, less than 5 miles from downtown San
Francisco, Angel Island rises like a jewel. Accessible only by boat,
the island offers a backpacking experience unlike any other, where
vistas sweep 360 degrees around the Bay, gentle paths mingle with
history, and unique rock outcrops tell unusual tales.

Angel Island has witnessed its share of human activity during
the past 300 years. Prior to Spanish colonization it was a fishing
and hunting outpost for the native Ohlone tribe. The first Euro-
pean to explore the island was Lt. Juan Manuel de Ayala in 1775.
It became a Spanish cattle ranch during the 1840s and later
housed a Union fort during the Civil War. It was an infantry
camp through the late 1800s (Camp Reynolds) and in the early
1900s contained numerous gun batteries (Wallace, Ledyard, and
Drew) built to protect the Golden Gate. Through the 1940s Angel
Island was a quarantine station (Ayala Cove) and processing center (Fort McDowell) for overseas troops and ships. It also held a
prison site for German POWs during WWI and WWII and was
an immigration station for more than 150,000 arriving Chinese,
detained here two weeks to six months while their applications
for citizenship were verified. Finally in 1954 the beginnings of a

state park formed at Ayala Cove and grew to encompass nearly the entire island in 1962 after the Army shut down an active NIKE Missile base.

Hike Overview

Short and easy trails take different routes to reach four separate campsites scattered around the island. The island is small—only 1.5 miles across at its widest—and each campsite serves as an excellent base camp for exploring the many natural and historic sites. All the sites are accessible via bicycle and many of the island's trails are smooth, level, and perfect for relaxed cycling. Paved Perimeter Road rings the island in a level 5.0-mile loop and passes most historic sites. Note that dogs are prohibited on the island and that poison oak is common throughout.

Ferries travel to the island year-round but far less frequently in winter when views are at their most spectacular. On a winter weekday trip you may be the only visitor on the entire island! While weekend use in the mild weather of spring and fall picks up markedly, the weekdays remain quiet. The island is extremely popular every day in summer, however, and its location just inside the Golden Gate means fog regularly streams over the island, obscuring views and chilling the air. Bring a windbreaker and warm clothes year-round.

The Trail Camps

A total of nine campsites and one group site are open year-round, situated in four separate locations around the island. Each campsite (described in greater detail below) accommodates up to eight people and is equipped with a nearby potable water faucet, picnic table, food locker, outhouse, and barbecue grill. There also is one additional site designated for disabled campers only. Sites are $7/night except for Kayak Camp, which is $15. While campfires are not allowed, charcoal may be used in the grills. Note that roughly half the island—those areas around historic buildings in particular—is off-limits at night.

Reservations for specific sites can be made up to seven months in advance by calling Reserve America at (800) 444-7275 or going online at www.reserveamerica.com. Expect weekends in spring, summer, and fall to be booked several months in advance. While space is generally available weekdays year-round on a first-come, first-serve basis (always call ahead to check with the visitor center), the popular Ridge sites are often not available.

Ridge Sites are located on the windier, western side of the island and offer the most striking views of San Francisco, the Golden Gate Bridge, and much of the Bay Area. Site 4 has the best views but no shelter and is totally exposed to wind. Site 5 hides beneath Monterey pine and cypress next to Battery Wallace and provides good wind protection and nearby views. Site 6 is in a grassy clearing just below the ridgeline next to Battery Wallace; it has the most space and good wind protection, but offers no views from the site itself.

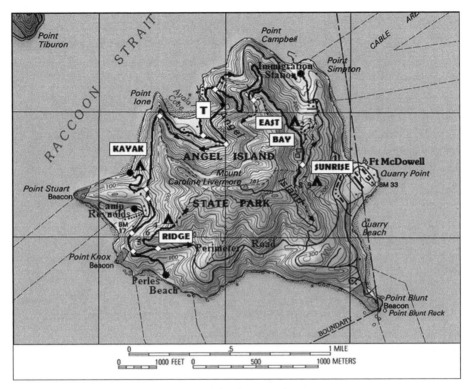

Angel Island State Park

Kayak Camp is a group site located 80 feet above a small beach on the west side of the island, slightly closer to Ayala Cove than Ridge sites. The site is an open clearing surrounded by coast live oak, toyon, and coyote brush that gets soggy in winter. Unlike other sites, the capacity here is 20 people. The rocky beach is a bit of a scramble from the camping area and is a popular destination for paddlers. A separate handicapped-accessible site is located just above Kayak Camp.

East Bay and **Sunrise Sites** are closely situated on the east side of the island and provide views of the early morning sun peeking over the East Bay hills (Oakland, Berkeley, and the eastern Bay Bridge are all visible). Both camping areas also are in close proximity to Mt. Livermore, Fort McDowell, and the Immigration Station, where interpretive programs are regularly offered in summer. The East Bay sites (1-3) provide good privacy but limited views, and shelter beneath the boughs of Monterey pines and coast live oak. Site 1 is the largest, site 2 the most secluded, and site 3 the most open. The Sunrise sites (6-9) are packed together in a wind-swept, level clearing with open views east. While the use of all three sites together is ideal for large groups, there is no privacy between the sites for individual users.

To Reach the Trailhead

A short ferry trip is required. Depending on season, ferries depart from three locations: Tiburon, Pier 41 in San Francisco, and Oakland/Alameda. Call ahead or check the web sites below for current fares and schedules.

From Tiburon, the closest and most frequently served dock, Angel Island-Tiburon ferries depart hourly on weekends March-November; less frequently on weekdays March-November and weekends December-February; and by special request only weekdays December-February. The terminal is located on Main Street in downtown Tiburon ($6 round-trip, (415) 435-2131, www.angelisland-ferry.com).

Pier 41 and Alameda/Oakland are served by Blue & Gold Fleet ferries (415) 705-5555, www.blueandgoldfleet.com). *From Pier 41* (located adjacent to popular Pier 39 on San Francisco's Embarcadero), ferries depart daily year-round ($11 round-trip) with increased service on weekends and during the summer. Pier 41 is the only weekday option December-February.

From Oakland/Alameda, ferries run weekends only from Mid-May through September. Terminals are located in Oakland at the foot of Clay Street in Jack London Square, and in Alameda at Gateway Center, 2991 Main Street ($13 round-trip).

Trail Description to Ridge and Kayak Sites

From the ferry landing at Ayala Cove and its accompanying gift shop, snack bar, and bike rental station (0.0/0), proceed toward the large grassy picnic area and informative visitor center to register with park staff. Housed in an original structure dating from the cove's use as a quarantine station during the early to mid-1900s, the visitor center is shadowed by large Monterey pines and offers a good survey of island history. At the three-way junction behind the visitor center, bear right toward Camp Reynolds. Passing a few residences (for the roughly 30 state park staff and family who live on the island), the paved road soon becomes dirt and narrow as it climbs steeply via large steps to reach wide and level Perimeter Road (0.3/160). Bear right. Epic views north to Mt. Tamalpais (2571') and the Tiburon peninsula slowly widen to encompass San Francisco and the Golden Gate. Coast live oak, lupine, sage, coyote bush, and monkey flower dominate the dry nearby hillsides, while pockets of bay and sword fern grow in the lush shade of north-facing slopes.

Sandstone outcrops are common on this initial stretch of trail. Typical of the *Franciscan Formation* (see "Bay Area Geology" in *Where Should I Go?*), the sandstone here has been slightly deformed by the pressure of tectonic forces and is visibly layered. However, as the trail proceeds past the first buildings of Camp Reynolds and the junction to Kayak site (0.7/170), it passes into a realm of unusual rock formed deep within the Earth. As a tectonic plate is forced beneath an adjacent continent—or *subducted*—it dives for 10-30 miles into the inner layer of the Earth (the mantle) where temperatures are hot enough to melt all rocks. However, since the diving plate is cool and warms slowly, not all of it may melt. Instead, portions may be altered into new rock-forms by extreme pressure, and re-emerge much later at the site of the now dormant subduction zone— tell-tale indicators of its previous existence. At Camp Reynolds look for blueschist, a vibrantly dark-blue stone, that was created in such a way. Also striking are the altered serpentine outcrops (above Ridge sites) and pillow basalt exposures (Perles Beach and below Kayak Camp).

Perimeter Road passes above Fort Reynolds (an obvious access road leads down to the historic structures), then curves east to reach the junction for Perles Beach on the right just before the junction for Ridge sites on the left (1.3/180). The campsites are spread out along the ridge above (1.4/200-270) and Perles Beach is a great place to enjoy views south toward San Francisco and the Golden Gate. To access Mt. Livermore (781') from camp, head directly up the ridge behind the water tank, past the fascinating serpentine outcrops, across the first road, and all the way to Sunset Trail. The best views on the island can be found on the summit.

Trail Description to East Bay and Sunrise Sites

After registering with park staff (see description above), proceed to Perimeter Road on the paved road leading uphill from behind the visitor center (0.0/0). Turn left on Perimeter Road to reach the four-way junction with Northridge

Looking west from Ridge Site 4

Trail (0.4/150), located near a picnic table beneath eucalyptus trees. This junction also may be accessed via Northridge Trail from the ferry dock, a more direct singletrack option that begins at the north end of Ayala Cove and climbs steeply beneath coast live oak and Monterey pine. From Perimeter Road, bear right (uphill) on the singletrack Northridge Trail as it begins a slow climb through the denser vegetation common on the shadier north slopes of the island. Here bay, sword fern, hazel, and wood rose join the more common coast live oak, sage, and sticky monkey flower. Intermittent views north are possible across narrow Raccoon Strait, named for the 1814 repair of the British man-of-war *HMS Raccoon* in Ayala Cove and not the critters that visit Angel Island campsites nightly.

As the winding trail reaches a drier, more exposed ridge, the vegetation changes accordingly to manzanita, coyote brush, ceanothus, scrub oak, and chamise. The trail then reaches another paved road (1.0/450). Bear left on the pavement (continuing straight on Northridge Trail leads to the island's summit). The fire road contours around to the east side of the island and soon reaches the posted junction for East Bay Sites by a large metal-roofed dome structure (1.3/400). To reach Sunrise Sites, continue past the fenced-off water supply area and follow the road down to join yet another road (1.5/360). Go right toward Mt. Livermore to immediately reach Sunrise Sites on the left.

PARK CONTACT INFORMATION

Angel Island State Park, Box 318, Tiburon, CA 94920, (415) 435-1915, www.angelisland.org. Visitor center usually open 8 A.M.–sunset daily, (415) 435-5390.

Giving Back

The Angel Island Association supports the preservation and interpretation of history, structures, and natural resources of Angel Island State Park.
Box 866, Tiburon, CA 94920, (415) 435-3522,
www.angelisland.org.

The Marin Headlands

Wildflowers, wildlife, wildland:
so close, so far away

The Park: Marin Headlands, Golden Gate National Recreation Area
Distance: 1.5-7.3 miles round-trip
Trip Length: 2 Easy Days
Best Times: Year-round
Recommended Maps: Olmsted's *A Rambler's Guide to the Trails of Mt. Tamalpais and the Marin Headlands,* USGS 7.5-min *Point Bonita*

It is as it was. Rolling hills cleft by valleys, split by ridges, battered by the sea. A land of sweeping vistas, vibrant life, and dramatic geology in a protected natural world isolated from the bustle of the Bay Area. The Marin Headlands await.

Two trail camps are available in the Marin Headlands, each offering a special overnight experience. Hawk Camp, one of the most remote destinations in the Headlands, is accessed on a loop around untrammeled Gerbode Valley. Haypress Camp is easily reached and ideal for exploring one of the Bay Area's outdoor gems—Tennessee Valley. Both camps and the recommended adventures for each are described in greater detail below.

GERBODE VALLEY LOOP TO HAWK CAMP

Distance: 7.0 miles round-trip
Total Elevation Gain/Loss: 1500/1500
Difficulty: ★★

With a trailhead in close proximity to the Headlands Visitor Center, a wide and well-graded trail on a full loop around a self-contained natural world, and a lightly used backcountry trail camp, this hike is a great introductory experience to the world of Bay Area backpacking opportunity. Add a dash of wildflower glory in the Spring and merriment at all times.

Hawk Camp

The camp shelters beneath a small stand of Monterey pine at an elevation of 800 feet and offers three small sites in the uppermost reaches of Gerbode Valley. Each site can accommodate a maximum of 4 people. An outhouse and picnic tables are available but *no water is provided,* there are no reliable sources on the hike, and no water is available at the trailhead—all necessary water must be packed in. While this limits the duration one can stay in the backcountry, it also seems to reduce crowds (a pleasant compromise). Located at the end of a half-mile spur trail, Hawk Camp is pleasantly secluded and escapes the foot and bike traffic common throughout the Headlands.

The trail camp is free. Reservations can be made up to 90 days in advance by calling the Marin Headlands Visitor Center at (415) 331-1540 any day of the week 9:30 A.M.–4:30 P.M. While summer weekends regularly fill, space is surprisingly available at most other times. Arriving backpackers are required to register at the Headlands Visitor Center by 4:30 P.M. or the entire reservation will be cancelled. Those arriving later should notify the visitor center in advance to arrange an after-hours pick-up. Campers are limited to no more than three nights at Hawk Camp per year.

Hike Overview

The hike follows wide fire roads around Gerbode Valley on a full loop with excellent views throughout. Given its immediate proximity to San Francisco, crowds are common on weekends and dozens of mountain bikers will likely pass you on the trail. While the occasional warm sunny day does occur, expect cool, breezy conditions with lots of fog during the summer months. Dogs are not permitted. While the hike can be easily completed in either direction, it is described below in clockwise direction. It is possible to bikepack to the site via Bobcat Trail, but the full loop can't be completed as a 1.5-mile section of Miwok Trail is closed to bikers.

To Reach the Trailhead

Backpackers will need to first register at the Visitor Center. Approaching from the south, take Hwy. 101 to the Alexander Avenue Exit (the first off-ramp north of the Golden Gate Bridge) and follow signs toward the Marin Headlands, turning turn left to pass through the one-lane tunnel and then continuing straight on Bunker Rd. for approximately 2 miles to the visitor center. Approaching from the north, take the last Sausalito exit immediately before the Golden Gate Bridge, turn left at the stop sign, bear right up steep Conzelman Rd. and continue straight on spectacular Conzelman Rd. for 3 miles to the intersection by Battery Alexander. Turn right and continue 0.5 mile to the visitor center. After registering, bear left out of the parking lot and then

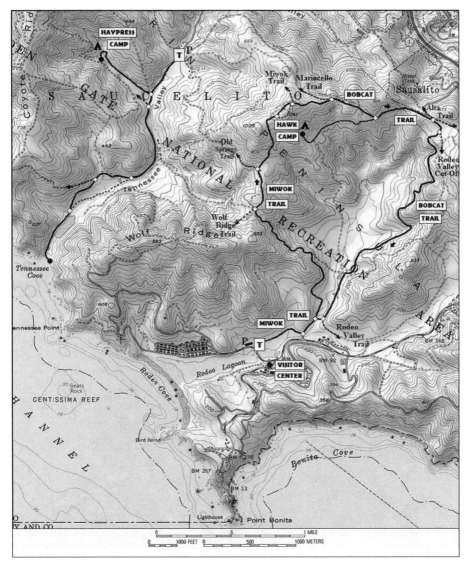

The Marin Headlands

immediately left again towards Fort Cronkhite to reach the trailhead on the right in a quarter mile.

Trail Description

From the trailhead (0.0/20), begin on broad Miwok Trail as it passes through open grassland punctuated with coyote brush, blackberry brambles, and a brilliant seasonal display of lupine, poppies, paintbrush, checkerbloom, irises, and other common wildflowers. Throughout the hike, watch for quail and jackrabbits in the brush; black-tailed deer and the elusive bobcat in open clearings; and red-tailed hawks and other raptors overhead. The trail briefly enters a small riparian alley and reaches a small feeder trail on the right from nearby Bunker Rd. (0.4/20). Filled with willows, stinging nettle, wild cucumber vines, horsetail, elderberry, dogwood, bracken fern, vetch, and other moisture-loving plants, this dense world contrasts markedly with the surrounding dry slopes.

Continue straight on Miwok Trail to quickly reach the junction with Bobcat Trail—your return trail—on the right (0.5/30). Remain on Miwok Trail as it next turns towards the valley slopes and begins steadily climbing. Passing some folded and layered chert outcrops as it ascends, Miwok Trail passes a junction with Wolf Ridge Trail on the left (1.6/600) and views north into adjacent Tennessee Valley appear. As the trail briefly undulates along the ridgeline, downtown San Francisco begins to peek over the hills to the south and the long spine of Mt. Tamalpais slowly starts its rise above the hills to the north. Miwok Trail narrows to single-track shortly before reaching the junction with Old Springs Trail (1.9/640)—continue straight on Miwok. Note that no bikes are allowed along the next mile of trail.

Now climbing steeply toward the FAA facilities atop Hill 1041, the trail rises above it all and offers stratospheric views across the Bay Area. To the south, Gerbode Valley, the Golden Gate Bridge towers, downtown San Francisco, antenna-lined San Bruno Mountain, and distant Montara Mountain (1831′). To the east, Mt. Diablo (3849′), the Bay Bridge, Oakland, Berkeley, and the entire East Bay hills. To the north, Mt. Tamalpais (2571′) dominates above Mill Valley, the Tiburon peninsula, and Angel Island. To the west, the vast Pacific Ocean, pimpled with the Farallon Islands on clear days. The trail splits and rejoins around the fenced-off FAA facilities, which remind you that INTERRUPTION OF SERVICE MAY RESULT IN THE LOSS OF HUMAN LIFE.

Continue straight past the FAA hilltop on Bobcat Trail as Miwok Trail splits left to descend into Tennessee Valley (2.5/1000). Dropping from the hilltop, Bobcat Trail next reaches the junction with Marincello Trail (2.8/900)—bear right, noting the small coast live oaks below the junction. After a brief downhill, Bobcat Trail reaches the junction for Hawk Camp (3.1/780). Bear right to head toward the small copse of trees that marks the camp location (3.7/800). While Monterey pine are most common around camp, the odd introduced incense cedar, eucalyptus, and palm tree mix it up. Excellent views down San Francisco's Pacific shore to Pedro Point in southern Pacifica (a distance of nearly 20 miles) are visible from camp.

After a night of outdoor perfection, return to the earlier junction with Bobcat Trail (4.3/780) and marvel at the completely protected world of Gerbode Valley so enjoyed last night. Now imagine that instead of this beautiful undeveloped valley before you, there are 30,000 people living in a self-contained community called Marincello. Hundreds of homes line Wolf Ridge, 19 high-rise buildings rise 16 stories tall above the valley, and schools, churches, shopping centers, and light industry complete the development. During the 1960s, it almost happened. A master development plan was drawn up for the privately held valley, an access road (Marincello Trail) was built, and construction loomed nigh. Thankfully, financial and bureaucratic delays slowed the project and a key court decision in the late 1960s ultimately stopped the project altogether. The land was then purchased by the Nature Conservancy for $6.5 million and bequeathed to the National Park Service, forever protected for public enjoyment. Hooray! (Dunham, 1989)

To return, follow Bobcat Trail as it dips beneath power lines and passes junctions on the left for Alta Trail (4.8/730) and Rodeo Valley Cut-off Trail (4.9/720). As Bobcat Trail begins its slow descending traverse back toward the trailhead, note the different vegetation which grows in the moist, protected, north-facing gullies by the trail—bay, hazel, coast live oak, elderberry, and the odd Douglas-fir can all be spotted. Bobcat Trail passes the junction with Rodeo Valley Trail (6.7/50) shortly before reaching the earlier junction with Miwok Trail (6.8/30) and the final return stretch to the trailhead (7.3/20).

TENNESSEE VALLEY AND HAYPRESS CAMP

Distance: 1.5 miles round-trip
Total Elevation Gain/Loss: 250/250
Trip Length: 2 days
Difficulty: ★

Less than a mile from the trailhead, at the end of a lightly-traveled spur trail, in a world secluded from everything, Haypress Camp is as close and easy as it gets. Add on 3 miles of day-hiking to explore Tennessee Valley and its isolated beach at the base of 400-foot-high cliffs, and you have an adventure remembered forever.

Haypress Camp

The camp is located at trail's end in the back of a small valley at an elevation of 250'. A stand of eucalyptus provide shade and shelter from the wind for 5 grassy sites enclosed by a rustic zig-zagging wooden fence. Located adjacent to each other in a pleasant clearing, each site offers a picnic table, food locker, and two designated tent sites for a maximum of 4 people per site. Privacy is minimal, however. An outhouse is available but note that *no water is provided* and there are no reliable sources on the hike or at the trailhead—all necessary water must be packed in.

The trail camp is free and open year-round. Reservations can be made up to 90 days in advance by calling the Marin Headlands Visitor Center 9:30 A.M.–4:30 P.M. at (415) 331-1540. While summer weekends regularly fill, space is surprisingly available at most other times. Arriving backpackers are required to register at the Headlands Visitor Center (a minor detour from the trailhead) by 4:30 P.M. or the entire reservation will be cancelled. Those arriving later should notify the visitor center in advance to arrange an after-hours pick-up. November-March, groups can reserve all 5 sites at once. April-October, no more than 3 sites may be reserved per group. There is a maximum stay at Haypress Camp of 3 nights per year.

Hike Overview

The hike is short and easy, can be traveled on bike, and makes for an excellent year-round destination. It also offers especially good (and dramatic) geologic exposures. While the trail down Tennessee Valley is extremely popular, Haypress Camp is a half mile removed from the main thoroughfare and is consequently much quieter. Cool, foggy conditions are common in summer, but Haypress Camp seems to escape much of the area's regular winds due to its sheltered location. Winter brings beautiful sunny stretches and a dramatic ocean but be prepared for damp, wet conditions at all times. Dogs are not permitted.

To Reach the Trailhead

Backpackers will first need to register at the Headlands Visitor Center (see directions above). After doing so, return to Hwy. 101, head three miles north, take the Hwy. 1 North/Stinson Beach exit, turn left on Hwy. 1, and then quickly left again on posted Tennessee Valley Rd. The often-crowded trailhead lot is two miles farther at road's end.

Trail Description

From the trailhead (0.0/200), cross the gate by the information sign and begin down the broad path to instantly leave the developed Bay Area behind. During the early 20th century, Tennessee Valley was the domain of Portuguese dairy ranches and the Headlands were a remote and rugged outpost divided from San Francisco by the unbridged Golden Gate (electricity did not arrive here until the 1930s). The few remaining structures in Tennessee Valley are relics of this period.

Briefly paralleling a moist, willow-choked riparian alley, the trail quickly reaches the posted junction for Haypress Camp (0.3/140). Bear right toward camp, and continue to the back of the valley to find the sites at trail's end (0.7/250). Striking bulbous rock outcrops and a lone Douglas-fir protrude from the coastal scrub of surrounding slopes, use trails wend everywhere for exploration, and an ephemeral camp-side trickle provides habitat for large sword and chain ferns, coffee berry, and poison oak. For being less than a mile from the trailhead, the sense of isolation is amazing.

To continue on the highly-recommended journey to the beach, return to the main trail and turn right. Passing an enviable private residence on the left, keep heading downvalley past junctions for Coastal Trail to reach the small pocket beach at trail's end—a single-track, hikers-only alternate trail splits and rejoins the main trail along the way. As you proceed, marvel at the 1000-foot high ridges to the north and south that together hem in this remarkable coastal valley.

Tennessee Valley is named for the 1853 shipwreck of the *S.S. Tennessee*, which foundered here on its way to San Francisco from Panama. Fortunately, all of its nearly 600 passengers and 14 chests of gold made it to safety. The boat sank, however, and its huge cast-iron engine can still be occasionally seen at the south end of the beach during low tides. A peep-hole pierces the towering cliffs of layered red chert and clearly-discernible pillow basalts north of the cove (see "Bay Area Geology" in *Where Should I Go?* for more information), while a fascinating realm of multi-hued boulders can be accessed to the south at lower tides. Use trails clamber up the steep slopes to the north, where stomach-queasing vertical drops and an abandoned bunker await discovery. Return the way you came.

NORTH BAY

GOVERNING AGENCY/PARK(S) CONTACT INFORMATION

Golden Gate National Recreation Area, Marin Headlands Visitor Center, Building 948, Fort Barry Chapel, Sausalito, CA 94965, (415) 331-1540, www.nps.gov/goga/mahe.

Giving Back

Golden Gate National Parks Conservancy is a nonprofit membership organization dedicated to the preservation and public enjoyment of the Golden Gate National Parks. Golden Gate National Parks Conservancy, Building 201, Fort Mason, San Francisco, CA 94123, (415) 561-3000, www.parksconservancy.org, email: tellmemore@parksconservancy.org.

Point Reyes National Seashore

An isolated world of forest and sea, Point Reyes National Seashore protects 30,000 acres of wild California within the boundaries of Phillip Burton Wilderness. Over 100 miles of trail interlace through this magical land, a web of countless adventures spread among four distinct backcountry campgrounds. Come here to camp on a wild shoreline, commune with haunting old-growth forest, and experience a vast tract of coastal wilderness unlike any other in California.

How to Use this Chapter

Information in this chapter is presented by campground rather than by trip, due to the abundance of trails, the numerous variations of backpacking routes, and the need to reserve specific campsites far in advance. Read the following background information about the Point Reyes backcountry first, then use the detailed campground descriptions to make the essential reservations. Once your campsite is secured, select a route based on available time, energy, and desired scenery.

At least two different access routes to each campground are described, ideal for those planning a simple overnight trip. If you are interested in planning a multi-day, multi-camp trip, you'll find descriptions of recommended routes that connect each of the campgrounds at the end of the chapter. Note that all mileage and elevation gain/loss data in the hike descriptions are one-way rather than round-trip.

Detailed topographic maps are included in the following pages; solid trails are covered in the various hike descriptions, dashed trails are not. A good overview map of the entire Seashore is extremely helpful—Tom Harrison's *Point Reyes National Seashore* is particularly recommended.

BACKPACKING IN POINT REYES NATIONAL SEASHORE: AN OVERVIEW

In the rugged southern half of the Point Reyes Peninsula, Phillip Burton Wilderness protects a vast swath of coastal and mountainous wild land. Myriad trails are laced through the wilderness, but backcountry camping is confined to four designated hike-in campgrounds—Coast, Sky, Glen, and Wildcat camps. Each is described in detail below. Roughly rectangular in shape, the wilderness is bounded by Limantour Rd. to the north, by the town of Bolinas to the south, and stretches west to east from the coast over 1200′ Inverness Ridge to Olema Valley.

Six principal trailheads ring the wilderness area. Clockwise beginning in the northwest they are: Limantour Beach, Laguna, Sky, Bear Valley, Five Brooks, and Palomarin. You'll find directions to the appropriate trailheads in the hike descriptions. While camping reservations are not required, they are usually necessary since sites often fill up months ahead of time. (See "Crowds, Facilities, and the Best Times to Go" below for more information.)

Reservations

Campsites can be reserved up to three months in advance by calling (415) 663-8054, 9 A.M.–2 P.M. Monday through Friday. Reservations can also be made in person at the Bear Valley Visitor Center anytime during open hours. You can also make a reservation by fax; download the appropriate form at www.nps.gov/pore/activ_camp_fax.htm and send it to (415) 464-5149. Most campsites have a capacity of only 6 people, but several larger group sites are also available (see individual camp descriptions below). Campsites cost $12/night for 1-6 people, $25/night for 7-14 people, and $35/night for 15-25 people. Payment by VISA or Mastercard is due at the time telephone reservations are made and reservations are non-refundable. *Permits must be obtained from the Bear Valley Visitor Center prior to leaving on your trip.* After-hours pick-up is allowed—permits are placed in a wooden box by the information board in front of the visitor center. If sites are available, walk-in registration is possible for same-day departures. See "Rules and Regulations" below for more information about the Seashore's wilderness policies.

Bear Valley Visitor Center

The primary source of information about the Seashore, Bear Valley Visitor Center is a required visit for obtaining your backcountry permit. Headquarters for Point Reyes National Seashore, the center offers extensive displays about the human and natural history of the Seashore. It is open 9 A.M.–5 P.M. weekdays, and 8 A.M.–5 P.M. weekends and holidays. A designated backcountry desk provides wilderness information and campsite reservations. For more information,

NORTH BAY

call the visitor center at (415) 464-5100, go online at www.nps.gov/pore, or write to Point Reyes National Seashore, Point Reyes, CA 94956.

To Reach Bear Valley Visitor Center

Head first to the small town of Olema on Highway 1; Olema is accessible by scenic but twisting Highway 1 itself or the more direct route along Sir Francis Drake Blvd. from Highway 101 in San Rafael. From the intersection of Highway 1 and Sir Francis Drake Blvd. in downtown Olema, proceed north on Highway 1 and turn left almost immediately on Bear Valley Road. In 0.5 mile, turn left again to reach the Bear Valley Visitor Center and trailhead parking.

Public Transportation is available weekends and holidays aboard Golden Gate Transit Bus 65. The bus makes two round-trips from the San Rafael Transit Center to Inverness, one in the morning and one in the

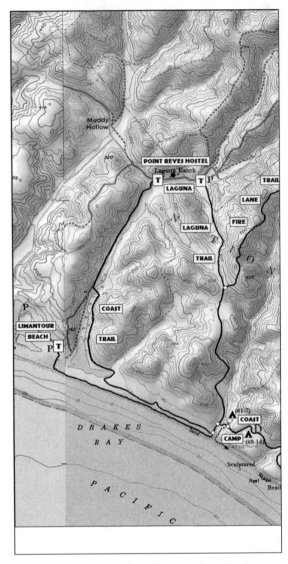

Point Reyes National Seashore: Northern Section

evening, with a stop at Bear Valley Visitor Center along the way. For more information and a current schedule, contact Golden Gate Transit at (415) 455-2000 or go online at www.transitinfo.org/GGT.

Crowds, Facilities, and the Best Times to Go

An estimated 2.5 million visitors pass through the Seashore each year. Weekends receive heavy use, the human torrents funnelling onto popular trails in discouraging numbers and usually filling the campgrounds to capacity.

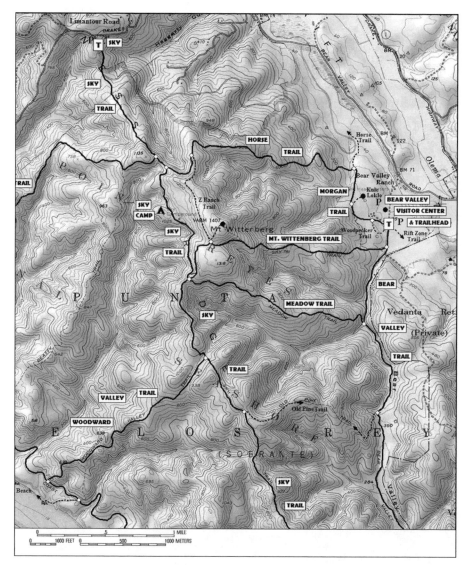

Point Reyes National Seashore: Northern Section

Advance planning is crucial. From April through October, it is difficult to secure a campsite for a weekend night with less than two months advance planning. During summer months, securing a campsite on *any* day of the week can be challenging; they are usually fully booked several weeks ahead of time. Note that the limited number of large group sites are usually the first to fill. Outside of these times, the campgrounds seldom fill and sites are generally available.

Each campground provides pre-fabricated pit toilets, picnic tables, food lockers, and water faucets. With the exception of Wildcat Camp, the provided water is potable (though not so palatable; powdered drink mixes are highly

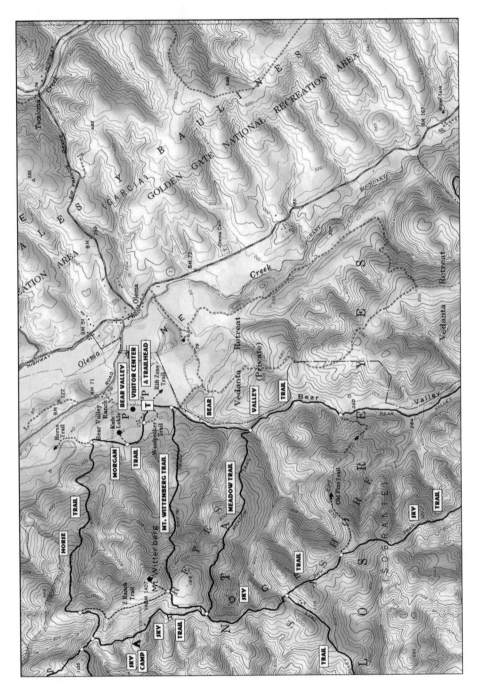

recommended). Each campsite offers nice level ground for at least one tent (usually two or more) but many sites are exposed to the elements and morning dew is usually heavy. A strong weather-proof tent is an oftentimes crucial item. Marauding skunks, raccoons, and foxes nightly scavenge the campground and

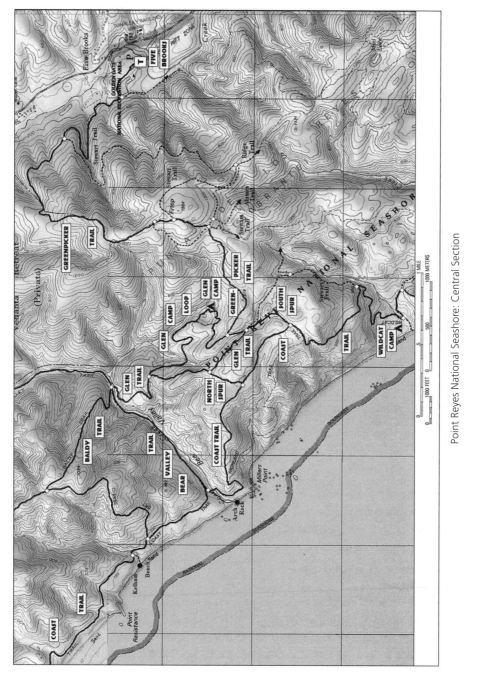

Point Reyes National Seashore: Central Section

have been known to invade tents with food (and sleeping people) inside—it is critical that all food and scented items be placed inside the provided food lockers.

The Seashore is a year-round destination. Summer means fog, crowds, and

NORTH BAY

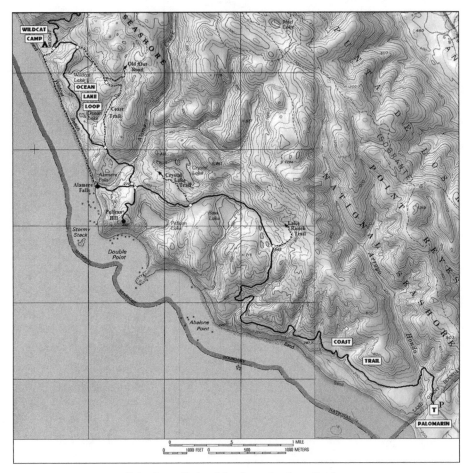

Point Reyes National Seashore: Southern Section

unseasonably cold conditions, but long hours of daylight. Spring explodes with wildflowers, lush green hillsides, and highly variable weather. Fall provides frequent sunshine, warm days, and a golden, dry landscape. Winter offers crystalline air and powerful surf, but is interspersed with torrential storms.

Rules and Regulations

Camping is by permit only and violators are subject to a $150 fine. Overnight use is limited to a maximum of four nights per visit and 30 days per year. *Dogs* are prohibited at the campgrounds and throughout the wilderness. *Wood fires* are prohibited at the campsites, although charcoal may be used in the provided grills. Camp stoves are permitted. *Driftwood fires* are allowed on sandy beaches below the high tide line; however, a permit obtained from Bear Valley Visitor Center is required. *Bicycles* are prohibited on most trails in the wilderness, but permitted on the dirt access roads that service each backcountry camp.

A Note on Bikepacking

Each backcountry camp can be accessed on bicycle via the service roads that Seashore staff use for maintenance purposes. With the exception of Glen and Wildcat camps, however, it is not possible to connect between the camps through the wilderness. The bike-able access routes to Sky and Coast camp are described below, but the heart-pumping access route over Inverness Ridge from Olema Valley to Glen and Wildcat camps (Stewart Trail) is not covered in detail.

THE NATURAL HISTORY OF POINT REYES: A BRIEF SURVEY

Weather

Point Reyes National Seashore experiences the full range of conditions like nowhere else in the Bay Area. From April through October, thick blankets of fog bury the low-lying coastal regions and strong onshore winds are common. The encroaching fog encounters a formidable obstacle at Inverness Ridge, however, and is often unable to overcome the thousand-foot rise in elevation, leaving eastern regions to bask in more frequent sunshine. It may be sunny, calm, and 80°F at Bear Valley, but foggy, breezy, and in the low 50s just a few miles west. In the winter, incoming storms are forced over Inverness Ridge. The higher elevation results in lower temperatures and increased moisture from the storm clouds; thus ridgelines are the wettest places in the region, with the upper slopes of Inverness Ridge averaging twice the annual precipitation as received on the coast and in Olema Valley.

Overall, average daily temperatures fluctuate little throughout the year. You may be surprised by warm, sunny days during any month of the year, but always prepare for the most common conditions—wind, wet, and temperatures in the 50s.

Flora

Weather is a major factor in shaping the dramatic ecology of Phillip Burton Wilderness. Fed by heavy winter precipitation and nourished by moisture strained from summer fog, the high ridges harbor dense mixed-evergreen forest. Throughout the year, a rich tapestry of ferns, elderberry, and huckleberry bushes fill a surprisingly open understory beneath majestic Douglas-fir, while California bay, hazel, and coast live oak thicken the forest on the lower slopes. Along the coast, regular winds and salty seaside air preclude forest growth, giving rise instead to thick, low-lying coastal scrub where the ubiquitous coyote brush, coffee berry, and blackberry vines are among the predominant species. Wildflowers appear as early as late February; Douglas iris, California poppy, bush lupine, checkerbloom, and tidy tips are particularly abundant. Unfortunately, the toxic leaves of *poison oak* and wicked needles of *stinging nettle* are adapted to life in both environments and common nemeses throughout the backcountry.

Wildlife

A variety of native and introduced species live here, including 37 land mammals and a dozen native marine mammals; an impressive 45% of all bird species in North America have also been sighted here. Native black-tailed deer are populous, regularly seen, and easily identified by their namesake appendage. Two introduced deer species also live here—axis deer, native to India and identified by its reddish-brown coat interspersed with white spots; and fallow deer, native to Europe and easily distinguished by its large moose-like antlers and white color. Small mammals roam and scurry everywhere and campers are guaranteed a visit from scavenging skunks, raccoons, and gray foxes.

Along the coast, harbor seals that have hauled themselves out on several beaches are a common sight—the inaccessible cove at Double Point usually has a sizeable community. California gray whales migrate south past Point Reyes on their way to Baja each winter and north to the Gulf of Alaska in spring. The southern migration peaks in mid-January, the northern in mid-March. Watch for their spouts from coastal viewpoints throughout the wilderness. *Note: it is illegal to disturb marine mammals onshore. If they are altering their behavior due to your presence, you are too close.*

The Vision Fire

In October 1995 a major human-caused wildfire burned more than 12,000 acres of the Seashore, including a large segment of northern Phillip Burton wilderness. Sparked from the smoldering embers of an illegal campfire atop Mt. Vision, the fire spread rapidly over the dry hillsides. In the wilderness area, the fire reached as far south as Sky Trail and left regions north heavily charred. Fortunately, the land is rapidly recovering from the fire's effects. Young trees, especially bishop pines, are everywhere. Expect to see burnt tree skeletons everywhere in the fire zone which makes the area seem desolate, especially in the dry months of summer and fall.

Geology

Point Reyes National Seashore is a migrant piece of land. Its deepest bedrock is granite, formed in the region of southern California approximately 85 million years ago. When the San Andreas Fault became active 28 million years ago, pieces of the North American continent located west of the emergent fault began to slowly migrate north at the rate of 2-3 centimeters per year. These land chunks traveled hundreds of miles over the ensuing millennia. One was granitic Point Reyes, which became covered by thick, waterborne sediments while submerged beneath the sea for almost 10 million years on its journey north. Roughly four million years ago, a slight change in the geometry of the San Andreas Fault system increased compression on either side of the fault, pushing Point Reyes (and most of the Coast Ranges) well above sea level. Erosion then began stripping away the overlying sediment, exposing the erosion-resistant granite found on northern Inverness Ridge, Tomales Point, and Point Reyes itself. In Phillip Burton Wilderness, most of the granite is still deeply buried beneath the deep layers of sediment known as the *Monterey Shale.* A few isolated outcrops of granite can be found on Horse Trail north of Sky Camp, but most geologic exposures (including the many spectacular coastal cliffs) are layers of Monterey Shale. In some coastal sections of the northern wilderness, however, the *Drakes Bay Formation* overlays Monterey Shale. Deposited in a shallow sea environment roughly 8 million years ago, it is loosely-consolidated and shows no obvious layering. This formation is dramatically exposed at Sculptured Beach by Coast Camp.

Human History

Once the site of more than 100 Coast Miwok Indian villages, Point Reyes peninsula was conquered by the Spanish by the early 19th Century. The indigenous population was devastated by the introduction of western diseases and their numbers further reduced as many Miwok left the area for nearby Mission San Rafael (est. 1817). Left to fend for themselves following the secularization of the missions in the 1830s, most remaining Miwok died.

Following the 1821 overthrow of its Spanish governors, Mexico began giving out massive land grants. Several large parcels on Point Reyes peninsula were distributed, but became the subject of controversy due to loosely-defined property boundaries. Once America acquired California in the late 1840s, a long series of complicated legal battles eventually put the entire peninsula in the hands of just three (American) men—Oscar and James Shafter, and Charles Webb Howard. The three quickly began leasing their land to dairy farmers. Soon these ranches were producing high-quality butter for shipment to San Francisco. In the 1860s, these numerous ranches were called by the letters of the alphabet; starting with A Ranch by the lighthouse, the ranches progressed clockwise around the peninsula to Z Ranch on Mt. Wittenberg.

Wilderness

Over one-third of Point Reyes National Seashore is wilderness. Congress designated these areas beginning in 1976 to retain the

Sign at Bear Valley

After World War II, local conservationists began lobbying for the creation of a national park. On September 13, 1962, President Kennedy signed the bill creating the National Seashore and authorizing acquisition of 53,000 acres.

Over the ensuing decade, the land was slowly acquired although existing ranches continued operation under long-term leases. The wilderness area of the Seashore was designated in 1976, and named for Congressman Phillip Burton in 1985, a long-time Representative from San Francisco who had worked hard to expand the acreage in the national park system. Existing ranch structures in the wilderness were torn down, their legacy inscribed in the network of roads and trails that criss-cross the wilderness area.

Coast Camp

Coast Camp

The easiest campground to access, Coast Camp is a mecca for large family groups and for those looking for the shortest route to an overnight backcountry experience. Located behind a small rise at the south end of Limantour beach, the camp marks the beginning of the spectacular bluffs and headlands that characterize the wilderness coastline. Sculptured Beach, a fascinating stretch of cliffs, crevices, and wave-washed promontories, is a short stroll south of camp and beckons visitors to explore its low-tidal zone. You can access Coast Camp by a short ocean-side stroll along Limantour Beach or by an easy 3-mile walk or bike ride down a wide fire road.

Coast Camp provides 14 sites split between two separate areas. Two sites are for large groups (capacity 25), while the other sites are smaller (capacity 6). Tucked within the coastal scrub, sites 1-7 offer privacy and some shelter from the incessant winds. They are the only sites with ocean views (1-4). The higher numbered sites are located farther from the water and restrooms, with site 7 offering the greatest seclusion and distance from fellow campers. Sites 8-14 spread around a large clearing, offer minimal privacy or shelter from the winds, and are located much closer to the water and restroom. Sites 10 and 14 are located farther back in the valley and offer some shelter, while sites 8-9 and 11-13 are entirely exposed, close to the main trail, and in high-traffic areas. Sites 8 and 13 are the group sites.

Wind and fog are regular companions at Coast Camp. Several sites take the full brunt of the northwest breezes; a strong tent is recommended. Camping crowds are common on the weekends and nearby Sculptured Beach is a popular destination for day-hikers. With little privacy, many sites at Coast Camp provide a less secluded backcountry experience.

The landscape around camp is in the process of regenerating following the 1995 Vision Fire. Blackened tree snags around camp stand as mute evidence of the fire's scorching effect. Thick coyote brush surrounds the campground and a few surviving alders line a trickling creek at campground's edge. Just south of camp, the unique geologic interface of Sculptured Beach provides a fascinating world to explore. Here, the easily-eroded Drakes Bay Formation rests on top of the more resistant Monterey Shale and is weathered into fantastic forms. At low tide, it is possible to walk (and scramble) nearly a mile along Sculptured Beach to reach a spur trail leading up to Coast Trail and an easy walk back to camp.

Approaches to Coast Camp

ALONG LIMANTOUR BEACH TO COAST CAMP

A short backpacking trip on the beach

One-Way Distance: 1.5 miles
Total Elevation Gain/Loss: 50/10
Hiking Time: 1 hour
⟶ **Difficulty:** ★

Hike Overview

This is the fastest approach to any of Point Reyes' backcountry camps, dimpling the sands of Limantour Beach as it meanders along the coastal margin. Note that during periods of high tide and big surf this route may be impassable.

To Reach the Trailhead

Take Bear Valley Rd. 1.5 miles north of Bear Valley Visitor Center, turn left on Limantour Rd., and follow it west for 7 miles. Immediately prior to reaching the main Limantour Beach parking lot at road's end, go left near the pay phone and follow the road 0.4 mile to the southernmost parking lot in the area. Parking space is limited. If the lot is full, park in the main lot and begin along the beach there.

The sweep of Drakes Bay

Trail Description

From the southernmost parking lot (0.0/30), head toward the beach along the obvious trail, passing coyote brush, coffee berry, blackberry, lupine, yarrow, ceanothus, cow parsnip, and a few creekside alders and bishop pines. The trail crests the grassy dunes, then emerges onto the beach. As you look west on clear days, Chimney Rock at the eastern end of the Point Reyes Headlands is visible across Drakes Bay. South down the beach, you'll see a large eucalyptus tree that marks both the location of Coast Camp as well as the start of the coastal wilderness headlands.

While Coast Camp is accessible by walking south entirely on the beach, the loose sand underfoot can make for strenuous going. Easier walking can be found along Coast Trail, easily reached approximately halfway to Coast Camp just past the marsh where a lone bishop pine rises from the sandy dunes. Look for harbor seals playing in the adjacent surf along the way and herons, ducks, and shorebirds in the marshy wetlands. Coast Camp awaits at the southern end of Limantour Beach (1.5/50).

LIMANTOUR ROAD TO COAST CAMP VIA COAST TRAIL

Easy walking, biking, and strolling along a wide fire road

One-Way Distance: 2.9 miles
Total Elevation Gain/Loss: 0/130
Hiking Time: 1-2 hours
⟶   **Difficulty:** ★

Hike Overview

Bikers with camping gear, hikers with wheeled equipment, and families with small children loaded into off-road power strollers use this route to bring in all the needed gear for their backcountry adventure. The trail is a wide fire road that skirts a lush riparian alley and marshy wetland before it passes just inland from the beach through open coastal plains that are still regenerating following the 1995 Vision Fire.

To Reach the Trailhead

Take Bear Valley Rd. 1.5 miles north of Bear Valley Visitor Center to Limantour Rd., turn left, and follow it west for 5.5 miles to the turn-off for Point Reyes Hostel. Turn left towards the hostel; the gated trailhead is 0.2 mile from Limantour Rd., immediately before the hostel on the right. There is limited roadside parking. If none is available continue for a further 0.3 mile, park in the Laguna trailhead parking lot on the right, and walk back along the road.

Trail Description

From the hostel trailhead gate (0.0/120), the wide trail descends between an unburned riparian alley of dense willow and alder, and scorched hillsides dotted with young bushy bishop pines. Bishop pines depend on the heat of wildfires to open their tightly-sealed cones, which then release seeds onto a nutrient-rich ashy soil surface, and then sprout as a new generation of trees. Coyote bush, lupine, blackberry, poison oak, and California sage fill the surrounding brush.

The trail crosses a thin creek (1.0/30) and takes you through a shady understory of lady ferns, horsetail, elderberry, and introduced foxglove stalks that bloom with pink bell-shaped flowers in spring and summer. Then, it edges along a hillside before curving in a broad **S**-turn around a large wetland popular with shorebirds. As it nearly reaches the beach by a lone bishop pine (1.8/10), the trail turns south, continues just inland from Limantour Beach, passes through low-lying coastal scrub dominated by coyote brush, then dips briefly across another trickling creek just prior to arriving at Coast Camp (2.9/50).

After a perfect night out, you can simply retrace your steps along Coast Trail (the easier route) or take a more direct route along Fire Lane and Laguna trails. The latter option, while nearly a mile shorter, adds several hundred feet of elevation change over a much rougher trail and passes through an area intensely burned by the Vision Fire. See this hike description below in "Connecting Routes Between Camps."

Sky Camp

A thousand feet high with views to match, Sky Camp features pleasantly secluded sites along the margin of the 1995 Vision Fire. Only three miles from the Pacific shore, the camp resounds with the echo of breaking waves and the closer-in vocalizations of scampering California quail. Access is a nice-and-easy hike from Limantour Road or a strenuous climb over Inverness Ridge from Bear Valley.

The fog cometh

The campground has 12 sites, including one large group site. Most sites, by virtue of their dense coastal scrub or Douglas-fir trees, are nicely private. Camping space is limited at most sites, however, and it can be difficult to squeeze in more than two tents. While expansive views are available from many points in the area, most vistas from the sites themselves are limited by surrounding brush. Site 2, the group site (capacity 25), offers less privacy but good views and nearby water and bathrooms. The sites with higher numbers are located farther from the water and toilet facilities.

Perched on the western slopes of Inverness Ridge, Sky Camp seems to flirt with the fog. Fog frequently blankets the low-lying coastal strand below the campground from April through October, obscuring the distant views north of Drakes Estero and Point Reyes itself. It often rushes over the ridge toward Olema Valley and buries Sky Camp in misty clouds. During the winter Sky

NORTH BAY

Camp receives more rain than the other campgrounds due to its higher elevation. Several good short trails radiate from Sky Camp, including the 2.6-mile loop to the summit of Mt. Wittenberg (described below) and the lush and mature mixed-evergreen forest just south of camp on Sky Trail (see *Connecting Routes between Camps* below).

Approaches to Sky Camp

LIMANTOUR ROAD TO SKY CAMP VIA SKY TRAIL

Sky Camp the easy way; bishop pines born by fire

One-Way Distance: 1.3 miles
Total Elevation Gain/Loss: 400/100
Hiking Time: 1 hour
Difficulty: ★

Hike Overview

Sky Trail formed a critical defense line during the 1995 Vision Fire, providing a staging area and access for fire-fighting trucks and equipment. While flames charred the trees west of Sky Trail, the forest east of the trail was largely saved. Hikers today can survey the unique contrast of old and new bishop pine forests, as well as benefit from the direct shot into Sky Camp with minimal elevation gain. Bicycles are permitted on this section.

To Reach the Trailhead

Take Bear Valley Rd. 1.5 miles north of Bear Valley Visitor Center to Limantour Rd., turn left, and follow it west for 3 miles to the Sky Trailhead parking lot, located on the left.

Trail Description

At the gated trailhead (0.0/670), note the bishop pines to the left. Distinguished by their clusters of two needles, bishop pines are a rare species, found only along a narrow coastal strip within a few miles of the ocean. They favor the well-drained soils weathered from the granite rock of the northern Point Reyes peninsula. The trail crosses the geologic divide between this granitic soil and the soil weathered from the Monterey Shale that underlies most of the wilderness, and is one of the best places in Phillip Burton wilderness to see these unique trees.

The broad trail quickly ascends beneath drooping Douglas-fir branches while coyote brush, blackberry, elderberry, thimbleberry, hazel, bracken fern, sword fern, and stinging nettle constitute impenetrable trailside thickets. The coast live oak also can be spotted occasionally next to the trail, their trunks bearded by green mosses. As the trail continues to climb, note the burn marks on the trunks of some trees. Soon blackened snags protrude from bare slopes to the right, and the fire zone is revealed.

Bishop pines are serotinous—they need the heat from wildfires to open their tightly-sealed cones and release the seeds of future generations. Fire also clears out the brushy understory that might otherwise impede the growth of young trees, and provides a generative ashy, nutrient-rich soil. Without regular wildfires, bishop pines would not survive as a species—most mature trees seldom live longer than 100-150 years before succumbing to old age and disease. The proliferation of countless young bishop pines to the west of the trail represents a natural ecologic succession.

A lush mixed-evergreen trail

As you continue past the burn zone, your trail enters an increasingly moist mixed-evergreen forest before it levels to a junction with Fire Lane Trail on the right (0.7/1060) and then Horse Trail on the left (0.8/1040). Immediately past Horse Trail on the left is an outcrop of layered Monterey Shale (topped by huckleberry bushes), illustrative of the rock type that underlies most of the wilderness area. Remain on Sky Trail as it descends slightly, briefly parallels the burn line again, and then reaches Sky Camp (1.3/1020).

BEAR VALLEY TO SKY CAMP: HORSE, WITTENBERG, AND MEADOW TRAILS

A heart-pumping climb over
Inverness Ridge through thick forest

One-Way Distance: 2.8-3.4 miles, depending on route
Total Elevation Gain/Loss: Via Wittenberg Trail, 1220/280; Meadow Trail, 1190/250; Horse Trail, 1100/160
Hiking Time: 2-3 hours
Difficulty: ★★★

Hike Overviews

An approach to Sky Camp from Bear Valley means climbing up, up, up and over Inverness Ridge via one of three different trails. All are about the same distance and pass through similar forest worlds, yet each trail provides a slightly different experience. *Meadow Trail,* the most direct option, follows Bear Valley Trail for its first 0.8 mile. It passes a lush riparian valley before ascending past its namesake meadow halfway up. *Mt. Wittenberg Trail* passes closest to the summit of Mt. Wittenberg (1407′), the highest point in Point Reyes National Seashore. Both Meadow and Wittenberg trails are knee-jarring on the descent. *Horse Trail,* the most rugged and removed, is consequently the least traveled. It visits interesting granite outcroppings near the ridgetop, and is a good choice for a return descent or busy weekend day.

To Reach the Trailhead

Park in one of the large parking lots near the Bear Valley Visitor Center (see directions above). For Mt. Wittenberg and Meadow Trails, proceed to the obvious gate marking the start of Bear Valley Trail. Horse Trail begins along the wooden fence behind the Horse Farm and to the right of the Bear Valley trailhead.

Trail Description, Mt. Wittenberg Trail

From the trailhead (0.0/80), begin on Bear Valley Trail as it immediately passes junctions for Rift Zone and Woodpecker trails on the right and left, respectively. You pass a large copse of Douglas-fir, California bay, coast live oak, and buckeye trees to the right, then quickly reach the junction with Mt. Wittenberg Trail where there are coast live oaks and a massive bay tree (0.2/80).

Bear right on Mt. Wittenberg Trail, which will have you climbing immediately as it enters the shade of bay trees and the forest, slowly transitioning into a mixed-evergreen forest of Douglas-fir, bay, hazel bushes, and sword ferns with the occasional buckeye and tanoak tree mixed in. The trail continues to rise and openings in the foliage let you glimpse Bolinas Ridge across Olema Valley. You eventually reach a clearing ringed by coast live oaks and dotted with coyote brush; this signals that you are halfway up the hill. After winding in and out of the clearing, the trail narrows then climbs three steep switchbacks before leveling momentarily to circle around a small drainage and crest Inverness Ridge. Now on the western slopes of Inverness Ridge, your northwest views finally open up out toward toward Limantour Beach, Drakes Estero, and Point Reyes itself. The junction for Z Ranch Trail and the spur to Wittenberg's summit (2.0/1260) is just ahead, at almost the exact spot of the 1995 Vision Fire boundary; note the regular size and age of the many young Douglas-firs regenerating in the burn area, as well as the burned trunks of nearby arboreal survivors.

It's a short 0.4 mile round-trip from here with a bonus 150 feet of elevation gain/loss to the top of Mt. Wittenberg (1409′), the highest point in Point Reyes National Seashore. While the summit is ringed by young Douglas-firs and no 360° view is available, a few tantalizing glimpses peek south to Olema Valley and beyond to the long spine of Mt. Tamalpais.

To reach Sky Camp, remain on Wittenberg Trail which curves down past a shrubby undergrowth of yerba santa and bracken fern before reaching the junction with Sky Trail (2.4/1120). Unburned, moist, and magnificent, the adjacent mixed-evergreeen forest sprouts huckleberry bushes, moss-coated bay trees, perennially green grass, elderberry, and large sword ferns. At this junction, turn right on broad Sky Trail and head gently north and down to reach Sky Camp (3.0/1000).

Trail Description, Meadow Trail

To reach Meadow Trail, continue on Bear Valley Trail past the junction for Mt. Wittenberg Trail (see above) and into the lush riparian world of Bear Valley. Sheltered beneath the rustling leaves of California bay, alders, and tanoak, a lush riparian world thrives. Above this sea of foliage rise mighty Douglas-firs, sentinels of this mature forest world, each majestically unique in form and character. Trickling water, bracken ferns, thimbleberry, blackberry tangles, sword ferns, elderberry, five-finger ferns, and gooseberry grow abundantly beneath their crooked branches. Note also the large stands of climbing poison oak and extensive stinging nettle that line the route in many places—staying on the trail is recommended.

At the junction with Meadow Trail (0.8/150), bear right, breathe deep, and start climbing! After first passing through a mature mixed-evergreen forest, the trail marches up a steeply graded slope to reach its namesake meadow (1.4/700). Ringed by Doug-firs, the meadow offers a nice rest stop with appetizing views of the Bear Valley drainage and the distant ridge of Mt. Tamalpais (seen cresting above the southwest skyline). After ascending 150 feet through the meadow, the trail widens through a corridor hemmed by thick huckleberry bushes and tanoak trees before circumscribing the level divide that separates the Vision Fire burn zone and a densely packed old-growth forest. Turn right on Sky Trail at the next junction (2.3/1050) and follow the wide fire road that will take you north and gently down to Sky Camp (2.8/1000).

Trail Description, Horse Trail

The Horse Trail adventure begins on Morgan Trail, located to the right (north) of the Bear Valley trailhead (0.0/80). Morgan Trail parallels the fenced margin of Morgan Horse Farm, passing the junction for Woodpecker Trail (0.1/170) en route. Established to breed and train horses for national parks around the country, Morgan Horse Farm once had a herd of nearly 80 animals. Today, since individual parks maintain their own stables, Morgan Horse Farm keeps only a few horses for trail patrol and maintenance in the Seashore. As you next enter the mixed-evergreen forest of Douglas-fir, tanoak, and bay, you'll be leaving these human structures behind. Continue straight on Morgan Trail at the junction for Kule Loklo (0.4/170), marked by a massive tanoak. A short side-trip to Kule Loklo will take you to a reconstructed Miwok village and a hint of the Seashore's deep human history. Remain on Morgan Trail as it descends gently to the junction with Horse Trail at a wooden bridge (0.6/90). Cross the bridge and prepare to ascend!

As you begin to climb, the sinuous curves of coast live oaks make them readily identifiable among the drooping arcs of bay trees and stout Doug-firs. Wreaths of poison oak climb the trees, while stinging nettle, fuzzy-leaved hazel bushes, blackberry tangles, soft thimbleberry leaves, and wood and sword ferns fill in the thick trailside understory. Tanoak is commonplace as the singletrack trail ascends and becomes steep and rutted. Poison oak and nettle also increase in hazardous abundance as the forest world lushifies at higher elevations. At 900′, the trail briefly levels out and granite rocks can be found in the trail. Part of the bedrock core of Point Reyes National Seashore (see "Geology" above), these exposures are the only granite outcrops visited in the wilderness area.

Making its final ascent through a moss-draped wetter environment, Horse Trail crests Inverness Ridge and contours south through a drier, more open area. It meets the junction with Z Ranch Trail (2.5/1110), at which point you continue straight on Horse Trail past some layered outcrops of Monterey Shale. This loose stone caps the bedrock granite throughout most of the wilderness area. At the junction with the wide fire road of Sky Trail (2.9/1050), go left. You pass another outcrop of Monterey Shale before Sky Trail descends and parallels the 1995 Vision Fire burn boundary before strolling into Sky Camp (3.4/1020).

Glen Camp

Glen Camp

Hidden within the forest, Glen Camp is the most sheltered of the four backcountry camps and escapes the incessant winds that whistle over much of the Seashore. With proximity to a wide variety of trails, Glen Camp makes an ideal base camp for dayhike exploration and is a good place to camp during times of inclement weather. Views from camp are non-existent, however, and the surrounding forest and tightly-spaced sites can make the camp feel crowded on busy weekends, yet space is often available here when the other campgrounds are full.

Located at an elevation of 540′, Glen Camp has twelve small sites arranged around an open clearing and is the only campground where large groups and equestrians are prohibited. Sites range from good to lousy and vary greatly in their privacy and shade. Located closest to the bathroom and water faucets, sites 1-2 are pleasantly shaded and offer decent privacy but nearby toilet aromas can assault the nose. Semi-private sites 3-4 are located adjacent to a monstrous coast live oak. One of the more private sites, site 3 is shady and tucked on the back edge of camp, while site 4 is situated beneath the behemoth tree itself which provides morning shade but less privacy. Sites 5-8 are hidden on the brushy slopes above the clearing; all offer decent privacy and some shade. Sites 9-12 surround the clearing with little to no shelter from the sun or fellow campers—site 10 is located smack in the middle of camp and is totally exposed.

The massive coast live oak highlights the wide diversity of flora within the campground. Its ponderous branches are so large that one lies broken on the ground like a gnarled elephant's leg. Douglas-firs and California bay complete the tree canopy, and a diverse understory of coyote brush, blackberry, poison oak, stinging nettle, cow parsnip, and huckleberry complete the vegetative world. A large patch of huckleberry bushes surrounds site 1 and explodes with delicious fruit in September. From your base at Glen Camp you can enjoy the 5.4-mile loop to Arch Rock and the coast via Glen Camp Loop, Glen, Bear Valley, Coast, and North Spur trails; and the 5-mile loop to Wildcat Camp and Beach via Glen Camp Loop, South Spur, Coast, and Stewart trails.

Approaches to Glen Camp

BEAR VALLEY TO GLEN CAMP
VIA BEAR VALLEY AND GLEN TRAILS

Fabulous forest and sheltered easy access

One-Way Distance: 4.6 miles
Total Elevation Gain/Loss: 490/100
Hiking Time: 2-4 hours
Difficulty: ★★

Hike Overview

The approach to Glen Camp from Bear Valley Visitor Center is a shady and straightforward route into the wilderness heartland. It journeys inland through perennially green Bear Valley and avoids the oft-windy open coastline.

To Reach the Trailhead

Park in one of the large parking lots near Bear Valley Visitor Center (see directions above) and proceed to the obvious gate that marks Bear Valley Trail.

Trail Description

From the trailhead (0.0/80), begin on wide Bear Valley Trail as it immediately passes junctions for Rift Zone and Woodpecker trails on the right and left respectively. You pass a large copse of Douglas-fir, California bay, coast live oak, and buckeye trees to the right, then quickly reach the junction with Mt. Wittenberg Trail shaded by coast live oaks and a massive bay tree (0.2/80). The open hillsides of Bolinas Ridge are briefly visible behind you as you continue straight into the shadier world of Bear Valley.

Sheltered beneath the rustling leaves of California bay, alders, and tanoak, a lush riparian world thrives. Above this sea of foliage rise mighty Douglas-firs, sentinels of this mature forest world, each majestically unique in form and character. Trickling water, bracken ferns, thimbleberry, blackberry tangles, sword ferns, elderberry, five-finger ferns, and gooseberry grow abundantly beneath their crooked branches. Note also the large stands of climbing poison oak and extensive stinging nettle that line the route in many places—staying on the trail is recommended.

Divide Meadow, Bear Valley

As you pass Meadow Trail on the right (0.8/150), continue through this lush environment to reach Old Pine Trail on the right (1.6/320) at the open clearing of Divide Meadow. The only low-elevation gap through Inverness Ridge, the meadow (and its outhouse) is a pleasant place for a rest stop. Here on the divide between the Olema Valley and coastal watersheds, temperatures often abruptly decrease as coastside winds and fog penetrate inland and reach the meadow. Ringed by coast live oaks, Divide Meadow was once the site of a hunting lodge owned by the Pacific Union Hunting Club of San Francisco. With its large kennel of hunting dogs, the lodge was a backcountry base for hunters pursuing bears and mountain lions from the 1890s to the Great Depression. Once located in the northwest corner of the meadow, the lodge has long since been removed; nothing remains but two huge introduced Monterey pines and patches of exotic pink flowers.

The trail gradually descends beside alder-choked Coast Creek and massive arching bay laurels. Coyote brush and bush lupine, members of the coastal scrub community, begin to appear as the trail reaches a four-way junction with

Glen and Baldy trails (3.1/170). A bike rack marks the farthest point cyclists may venture on Bear Valley Trail and is conveniently provided for those who wish to continue on foot. Hikers traveling south from Sky Camp also join the route here.

To continue to Glen Camp, bear left on wide Glen Trail. The trail climbs briefly, paralleling Coast Creek, then leaves the lush riparian world behind. As it curves left into an open clearing, the change in moisture and vegetation is apparent—coast live oak, coyote brush, thistle, poison oak, and coffee berry thrive here. Past the clearing, the trail continues its climb through a (drier) mixed-evergreen forest, levels out to provide brief glimpse of the ocean to the west, and finally reaches the junction with Glen Camp Loop Trail (3.7/460). Go left.

Glen Camp Loop Trail narrows to singletrack and passes by small Doug-fir, bay, sword ferns, and soft-leaved hazel bushes. You cross a small tributary of Coast Creek laced with five-finger and sword ferns. The trail then rises and skirts a clearing where willows, wood ferns, thimbleberry, and ocean spray bushes appear, until it rounds a clearing to traverse the slopes above a deep gully. It makes a final small descent past eucalyptus and huckleberry bushes to Glen Camp (4.6/540).

FIVE BROOKS TRAILHEAD TO GLEN CAMP VIA GREENPICKER TRAIL

Up, up, and over Inverness Ridge; crowd and equestrian dodging

One-Way Distance: 4.8 miles one way
Total Elevation Gain/Loss: 1100/800
Hiking Time: 2-3 hours
⟶ **Difficulty:** ★★

Hike Overview

Named for the five closely-spaced tributaries that pour into nearby Olema Creek, Five Brooks trailhead sits in the lee of pronounced Inverness Ridge and offers an over-the-top route to Glen Camp. The trailhead and camp are less than two miles apart as the crow flies, but the winding route travels more than double that distance to surmount Inverness Ridge. The advantages of Greenpicker Trail are that you can dodge the Bear Valley crowds and avoid the large equestrian troops on Stewart Trail.

To Reach the Trailhead

After you pick up your backcountry permit at Bear Valley Visitor Center (see above), return to Highway 1 and head south for 4 miles to the posted trailhead on the west side of the highway. A short 0.1-mile gravel road deposits you at the parking area where there are restrooms and potable water.

Trail Description

With popular Stewart Horse Camp only a quarter mile away and several popular riding trails in the vicinity, equestrians commonly gather at the trailhead (0.0/260). Bordered by coyote brush and coffee berry, the gated trailhead marks the start of the journey on Stewart Trail. Alder, willow, blackberry, coast live oaks, and young Doug-firs appear as you hike down the broad fire road and quickly pass the Rift Zone Trail junction on the right. The small lake on the left was created and used in the mid–20th century as a holding pond for logged Douglas-firs. You next come to a **T**-junction with Olema Valley Trail (0.1/260) where you bear right and enter a shady mixed-evergreen forest. Douglas-fir, big and small, arching bay trees, fluttering tanoak, clumps of sword fern, draping five-finger ferns, the soft leaves of hazel bushes, bushy huckleberry, creekside alder, chain ferns, and elderberry are the predominant plant species throughout the hike. They are joined intermittently by the spiny wood rose, honeysuckle vines, stinging nettle, and twisting madrone and canyon live oak trees as the trail rises in elevation.

After you cross a moist creek gully, the trail passes a turn-off for Stewart Horse Camp on the right (0.2/270) and begins to climb through thick forest. Briefly paralleling an alder-filled stream gully, the trail then curves up the opposite slope to reach the junction with Greenpicker Trail (0.9/450). Bear right on singletrack Greenpicker Trail as it traverses upwards along the slopes and passes a few vistas that look east of the rolling hills across Olema Valley. Greenpicker Trail begins a steady ascent as it winds along the boundary between Phillip Burton Wilderness and the private holdings of the Vedanta Society, who maintain a retreat here.

According to the web site of the Vedanta Society of Northern California (www.sfvedanta.org): "The basic teaching of Vedanta is that the essence of all beings and all things—from the blade of grass to the Personal God—is Spirit, infinite and eternal, unchanging and indivisible. Vedanta emphasizes that man in his true nature is this divine Spirit, identical with the inmost being and reality of the universe. There is, in short, but one reality, one being, and, in the words of the Upanishads, 'Thou art That.'"

The trail makes several switchbacks on its rise to the ridgetop before it dips slightly, passing a gate for the adjacent private property, and then reaching the junction for Fir Top (2.6/1310). Bear left here on the short 0.1-mile spur trail to the open clearing on the summit of Fir Top (1324). (Alternatively, continue straight on Greenpicker Trail to traverse around Fir Top and rejoin the route in 0.7 mile.) Although the meadowy summit lacks views, it makes a nice spot for a picnic. From here, you will turn right (west) on wide Stewart Trail to steeply descend Fir Top and reach the junction for Greenpicker and Ridge trails (3.1/1110). Bear right to rejoin Greenpicker Trail.

Stinging nettle and huckleberry are common along this section of trail, joined by the occasional coast live oak. As the trail descends, you gain northwest views allowing you to see Drakes Beach, Drakes Estero, and the bluffs beyond. Here on the seaward side of Inverness Ridge, the route soon enters an open clearing where coastal scrub plants appear. From here the rutted trail drops steeply before leveling out and dishing up views north past forested Bear Valley to beyond the bare hills on the other side of Tomales Bay. Another quick descent brings you to the junction with Glen Camp Loop Trail (4.1/820). Turn right and follow the wide fire road as it contours around to reach Glen Camp (4.6/540).

If you are returning to Five Brooks Trailhead, Stewart Trail is an alternate route that descends gently along a broad fire road—easy on the knees and a change of scene. To follow this route from Glen Camp, retrace your steps to the earlier four-way junction with Greenpicker, Ridge, and Stewart trails, follow Ridge Trail 0.5 mile to Stewart Trail, turn left onto Stewart Trail, and follow it all the way home.

Wildcat Camp

Perched on a bluff above two miles of untainted beach, adjacent to a singular point of coastal access, and ensconced in the heart of Nature's domain, Wildcat Camp is a delight. And yet its attributes are also the very things that make Wildcat Camp the least accessible of the backcountry camps: fog is frequent, coastal winds are constant, and strong winter storms rip into the unprotected camp. A strong tent is recommended year-round.

Wildcat Camp offers seven sites, including four group sites. The sites are well-spaced and often hidden behind tall grass or brush, which provide a strong sense of privacy and solitude. Sites 1-4 are the group sites (capacity 15-25, depending on site). All four are large, open, and essentially identical; the only difference between them is their proximity to the water and bathroom—sites 1 and 2 are closer. Located close to cliff's edge, sites 5-7 are smaller (capacity 6), but offer majestic coastal views; they are somewhat protected by patches of coyote brush—site 5 is the most sheltered. Note that group sites may be split among two smaller parties, making for potentially close quarters.

Wildcat Beach is arguably the most remote stretch of accessible coastline in the entire Bay Area. Bounded to the south and north by the sheer escarpments of Double Point and Millers Point, respectively, it is flanked by cliffs of twisted geology and can only be easily accessed in one spot—Wildcat Camp. It's easy to while away a day or more exploring this wonderful strand.

NORTH BAY

Approaches to Wildcat Camp

PALOMARIN TO WILDCAT CAMP VIA COAST TRAIL

Ocean vistas, lakes, and a beachside waterfall

One-Way Distance: 5.5 miles
Total Elevation Gain/Loss: 900/1100
Hiking Time: 3-4 hours
Difficulty: ★★

Hike Overview

As it winds along the coastal edge, this hike passes the only significant lakes in the wilderness, several epic viewpoints, and a short side-trip to Alamere Falls tumbling 40 feet directly onto the sands of Wildcat Beach. One of the most scenic hikes in the wilderness, it departs from distant Palomarin trailhead at the southern end of the Seashore.

To Reach the Trailhead

First proceed to the Bear Valley Visitor Center to pick up your wilderness permit (see above). From the visitor center, return to Highway 1 and head south 9 miles to the Olema-Bolinas Rd. junction (located immediately prior to the

Wildcat Camp, in the clearing on the right

northern edge of Bolinas Lagoon) and turn right. The turn-off is not posted so keep your eye out. In 1.2 miles, the road reaches a **T**-junction—go left, continuing on Olema-Bolinas Rd. for 0.5 mile before turning right again on Mesa Rd. Follow Mesa Rd. 4.6 miles to the large parking lot at road's end, passing a Coast Guard radar station and the Point Reyes Bird Observatory along the way. The last 1.3 miles are unpaved.

Trail Description

From the trailhead (0.0/280), the wide path immediately enters a thick eucalyptus grove where wild cucumber vines twine and a few enormous trees hulk in ethereal whispers—one huge Hydralike specimen is by far the largest eucalyptus visited in this book. Good views south open up next as the trail winds along open blufftops, and the Farallon Islands are visible southwest on a clear day. The trail turns inland, crossing two small creek gullies choked with willows, horsetail, watercress, monkey flowers, and bracken ferns before resuming ocean views. At the third significant creek gully, the trail continues inland, climbing over a small divide to the Lake Ranch Trail junction (2.2/570). Continuing ahead on Coast Trail, you meander through a dense forest of young Douglas-fir as the trail passes several swampy ponds full of lily pads before larger Bass Lake comes into view. Gradually descending along its northern shore, the trail leads to a short spur path on the left and an open space excellent for a break and a swim—this area provides the easiest access to the lakeshore. Beyond Bass Lake, the trail soon passes a junction for unexciting Crystal Lake (3.0/500) before traversing above beautiful Pelican Lake. Point Reyes and the long curving arc of beach and coastal bluffs appear north.

Descending, you reach a spur junction on your left (3.6/290) immediately after views north are hidden by coastal bluffs. This small trail climbs 0.3 mile to the top of Pelican Hill (480′) and the north end of Double Point, a spectacular and recommended side-trip. Besides far-reaching views south and north from the summit, the inaccessible cove beach below is often filled with hundreds of hauled-out seals.

The rock of this area is Monterey Shale, a sequence of sedimentary layers up to 8,000 feet thick that were deposited on the granite bedrock of Point Reyes National Seashore over the past 20 million years. In the region around Double Point, this shale has become involved in a huge landslide nearly four miles long and at least a mile wide. As this huge block of land slips slowly toward the sea, depressions are formed that fill with freshwater lakes such as Pelican and Bass lakes.

Immediately past the junction for Pelican Hill, another unposted spur trail splits left (3.7/270). This overgrown and brushy path leads 0.3 mile down to Alamere Falls, unseen until the very end, where some scrambling is required to reach the stream and its series of cascades. Some more challenging scrambling will take you down to the beach via a rocky chute. The bluffs are impressive, and the tilted, exposed layers of Monterey shale are spectacular south of the falls.

From the falls, it is possible to hike 1.3 miles north along the sands of Wildcat Beach to reach Wildcat Camp, a unique beach backpacking experience on a more direct and level route to camp. Note, however, that sections of the beach can be impassable during high tides and heavy surf, and that there is *no exit* from the beach between Alamere Falls and Wildcat Camp. The narrow beach section immediately north of the falls is a good indication of the feasibility of the route—if waves are reaching the cliff base, do not proceed. To continue inland, return to Coast Trail and head north to descend into the drainage of Alamere Creek where alder, elderberry, and thimbleberry thrive in the moister environment. Contouring past the creek, Coast Trail next reaches the junction with Ocean Lake Loop (4.2/240). While both trails lead equidistantly to camp, bear left on more scenic Ocean Lake Loop Trail (perhaps returning on Coast Trail for variety).

Singletrack Ocean Lake Loop Trail drops gently to bank around marshy Ocean Lake before climbing abruptly to reach a welcoming bench that offers great views of Wildcat Beach. After descending past brush-lined and inaccessible Wildcat Lake, Coast Trail rejoins from the right (5.3/220). Continue left on Coast Trail. The open field of Wildcat Camp appears before a final drop through a thick corridor of willow and vetch deposits you at camp (5.5/70).

BEAR VALLEY TO WILDCAT CAMP
VIA BEAR VALLEY AND COAST TRAILS

A verdant valley and euphoric coastal views

One-Way Distance: 6.8 miles
Total Elevation Gain/Loss: 1100/1140
Hiking Time: 4-6 hours
⟶   **Difficulty:** ★★★

Hike Overview

A journey with many wilderness highlights, this route travels beneath the lush canopy of Bear Valley, reaches the promontory of wave-cut Arch Rock, and then climbs above it all to provide eye-popping coastal views before it descends to camp. While not the most direct route to Wildcat Camp from the visitor center (see below), this longer variation is far more scenic.

To Reach the Trailhead

Park in one of the large lots near the Bear Valley Visitor Center (see directions above) and proceed to the obvious gate that marks the start of Bear Valley Trail.

Trail Description

First, review the description to Glen Camp (see above) and proceed to the junction with Glen and Baldy trails (3.1/150). Note that a more direct route to Wildcat Camp is to hike 1.3 miles on Glen Trail and then North Spur Trail to join Coast Trail. Although this variation saves a mile of hiking and a few hundred feet of elevation gain, it misses some spectacular scenery. It's a good option for the return to the Visitor Center parking area after a night at Wildcat.

To follow the more scenic route to camp, continue down Bear Valley Trail past Glen and Baldy trails. The route narrows slightly and descends more directly. Coast Creek becomes increasingly audible, stinging nettle is everywhere, and the softly green palmate leaves of buckeye glow as you approach the coast. After a brief rise, the trail emerges onto more open coastal plains where wind- and salt-stunted Douglas-firs appear among numerous coffee berry bushes. At the junction with Coast Trail (4.0/100), you may meet hikers who chose to travel south from Coast Camp along Coast Trail.

Bear left on Coast Trail towards Arch Rock, then quickly bear right and follow the short spur trail to cliff's edge atop Arch Rock itself. A wonderful picnic stop on calm days, the open blufftop provides views that stretch north along adjacent Kelham Beach to Point Resistance and beyond. On the south side of Arch Rock, a well-worn, narrow, and precarious use trail switchbacks tightly down into the mini-gorge of Coast Creek to reach sea level and fabulous views of the Arch itself. At low tide, you can access Kelham Beach through the Arch. South, a small pocket beach stretches a short distance to Millers Point and makes for fun exploring as well.

To continue to Wildcat Camp, return to Coast Trail and head south. While the round-trip to Arch Rock from the Visitor Center is one of the most popular hikes in the Seashore, few hikers continue on the next section of trail as it dramatically gains elevation. The route crosses Coast Creek among alders and elderberry, then curves briefly around the slopes before it climbs to the open ridgeline above. Increasingly expansive views open up as the trail reaches 300' elevation and encounters a use path on the right. A short 20-yard detour leads to a small knoll and gravestone marker for Clem Miller. As a local congressman, Miller was a great advocate for the creation of the National Seashore and worked tirelessly to achieve the reality. Miller Point below is named in his honor.

Return to Coast Trail and continue your ascent along the ridgeline. As you climb, the route makes a few small detours around sections that are being restored and the views become ever more thrilling. Reaching two large chert boulders, the trail finally levels out at 750' at one of the farthest-reaching viewpoints in the entire wilderness. Wildcat Beach and its southern terminus at Double Point are visible south beyond a deep and inaccessible drainage immediately below the ridge. Looking north, the long curving arc of Limantour Beach and Drakes Beach terminates in the prominent mass of Point Reyes itself (9 miles away). Just out of sight, Coast Camp and the northern wilderness boundary are located where the bluffs end at the south end of Limantour Beach. Just beyond nearby Arch Rock, Kelham Beach stretches north to Point Resistance. The bald slopes past the point were denuded by the 1995 Vision Fire. On clear days, the sharp points of the Farallon Islands are visible to the southwest. When the weather provides exceptional visibility, you'll be able to see the three lumpy rocks of the seldom-seen North Farallones to the west-southwest.

The singletrack route levels out and reaches the junction with North Spur Trail (5.4/740), where hikers taking the more direct path to Wildcat Camp via Glen Trail rejoin the route. Remain on Coast Trail as it abandons the beautiful vistas and enters a dense coastal scrub world of coyote brush, coffee berry, and blackberry and honeysuckle vines. The trail parallels the headwaters of the deep creek drainage that you saw earlier, then gently ascends to the junction with South Spur Trail (6.0/840). Bear right on Coast Trail as it turns south. Once again you can enjoy ocean views before you hike east above the deep valley holding Wildcat Camp at its mouth. Wildcat Lake and Pelican Hill are visible down the coast to the south. Shrubs and dense fields of poison oak line the trail as it curves down and past a knobby octopus of a Douglas-fir to the junction with broad Stewart Trail (6.9/420). Turn right and follow the wide fire road of Coast Trail winding through a thick creek forest of bay and Doug-firs. Leaving canyon bottom, you switchback steeply down past huge coffee berry bushes and willows and arrive at the open blufftop of Wildcat Camp (7.6/40).

Connecting Routes between Camps

Are you looking for a longer backpacking adventure than the overnight journeys highlighted above? The following connecting routes between backcountry camps allow you to customize unique multi-night backpacking experiences. Descriptions are point-to-point and one-way; therefore, depending on your route, it may be necessary to follow some descriptions in reverse.

For a multi-night trip that returns to the starting trailhead and avoids the need to shuttle cars, consider the Coast-Sky Camp loop or the round-trip journey to Glen and Wildcat camps from Palomarin. Most other trips involve beginning and ending at different trailheads, and consequently require shuttling vehicles. Driving to Point Reyes, picking up your permit in Bear Valley, and then shuttling cars can consume much of your day—consider staying at easily-accessible Coast or Sky camps on the first night of a multi-night, multi-trailhead trip. Located a short distance from their respective trailheads, each destination makes for an easy and short hike on the first day so that you can save the longer and more spectacular sections for ensuing days.

SKY CAMP AND COAST CAMP CONNECTING LOOP

A loop hike and single trailhead trip
with forest old and forest new

One-Way Distances: Coast Camp to Sky Camp 3.9 miles; Sky Camp to Coast Camp 4.2 miles

Total Elevation Gain/Loss: Coast Camp to Sky Camp 1300/330; Sky Camp to Coast Camp 230/1200

Hiking Time: 2-3 hours

→ **Difficulty:** ★★

Hike Overview

Sky and Coast camps connect via an eight-mile loop along Fire Lane, Sky, and Woodward Valley trails, to create an easy two-night backpacking journey that seldom retraces its steps. By beginning and ending the trip at the same trailhead (either Sky, Laguna, or Limantour Beach), you avoid the hassle of a car shuttle. While most of the loop traverses through regions that were intensely burned by the 1995 Vision Fire, some sections pass through delightful mixed-evergreen forest and provide a striking ecological contrast. The route description starts at Coast Camp, follows Fire Lane Trail to Sky Camp, and returns to Coast Camp along Sky and Woodward Valley trails.

Trail Description, Coast Camp to Sky Camp via Fire Lane Trail

From Coast Camp (0.0/50), cross the gurgling creek located north of camp to reach the junction with Fire Lane Trail (0.1/80). Turn right and climb steadily on wide and rutted Fire Lane Trail through a fire-cleared landscape thick with coyote brush, ceanothus, blackberry, and thistle. Young and bushy bishop pines that have been reborn from the fire appear as you approach the junction with Laguna Trail (1.1/360). (Laguna Trail descends 0.8 mile down another fire-ravaged drainage to the Laguna Trailhead and nearby Point Reyes hostel.) You continue, however, on Fire Lane Trail and bear right towards Sky Camp.

Fire Lane Trail climbs steeply to surmount the ridgeline, then gives you a broad view north past snaking Limantour Rd. The hike now remains on the ridgeline and passes numerous young bishop pines, Douglas-fir, and the occasional coast live oak. The rutted condition of the trail is partially due to the rapid run-off and erosion that occurred during the winter rains following the 1995 Vision Fire. As the rain fell on hillsides that had been cleared of protective vegetation, it washed away significant amounts of earth and caused the hillside to badly erode.

The trail narrows to singletrack and undulates along the ridgeline, passing through dense corridors of regenerating scrub oak, bay, coffee berry, deer brush, ocean spray, and sword and bracken ferns. Note the presence of surviving Douglas-fir in areas not completely burned over. During the summer, significant moisture drips around these trees as they strain water from the fog. This contrasts with the otherwise dessicated landscape and provides a good example of how some trees obtain water during rain-free months.

Vegetation noticeably increases shortly before the trail banks right to begin the steep and final ascent to Inverness Ridge 500 feet above. As you wind along the boundary of the Vision Fire, you pass through lush patches of mature mixed-evergreen forest. Intermittently, you can see views to the west and the ocean, until the path fully re-enters mature forest and reaches the junction with Sky Trail (3.4/1060). Turn right on Sky Trail and follow the wide fire road that quickly passes Horse Trail on the left (3.5/1040) and then gently descends into Sky Camp (3.9/1020).

Trail Description, Sky Camp to Coast Camp
via Sky and Woodward Valley Trails

From Sky Camp (0.0/1020), head south on broad Sky Trail to reach the junction with Mt. Wittenberg and Meadow trails (0.6/1120). Bear right on Sky Trail. You immediately pass the Vision Fire zone to enter a wonderful stretch of mature mixed-evergreen forest. Here dominant Douglas-firs strain moisture from the fog that flows over Inverness Ridge. The fog keeps the environment moist and green through the rain-free summer months. Water condenses on the trees' foliage, falls to the ground, and provides liquid sustenance for a vibrant understory (as much as a third of the area's total year-round moisture comes from fog drip). Moss-bearded branches and tree-bound ferns droop above abundant elderberry, huckleberry, blackberry tangles, and sword ferns. Poison oak and stinging nettle appear sporadically. In September huckleberry bushes explode with small delicious blue-black berries.

After delighting in this magical forest, you reach the junction with Woodward Valley Trail (1.3/890) where you should bear right. Burnt and dead trees appear as the trail descends through untouched virgin forest and fire-blackened snagscapes that were created by 1995 Vision flame. The gradient steepens abruptly as the trail passes into a burned zone marked by spottier undergrowth and fire-blackened trunks. After switchbacking downwards, the path levels and follows the contour above the fully-scorched drainage of Santa Maria Creek

Wildcat Beach

(north). Here you have far-reaching southern views; Point Resistance, the off-shore seas stacks by Arch Rock, and more distant Wildcat beach are all visible.

After entering the open world of coastal scrub, the trail descends its final switchback past numerous outcrops of Monterey Shale and reaches Coast Trail (3.3/180). Bear left (north) on Coast Trail as it winds around Santa Maria Creek and then descends into Coast Camp (4.1/50).

COAST CAMP TO GLEN AND WILDCAT CAMPS VIA COAST TRAIL

Going coastal

One-Way Distances: Coast Camp to Glen Camp, 6.7 miles; Coast Camp to Wildcat Camp, 7.9 miles
Total Elevation Gain/Loss: Coast Camp to Glen Camp, 680/180; Coast Camp to Wildcat Camp, 1000/1000
Hiking Time: 4-6 hours
Difficulty: ★★

Hike Overview

This section connects the northern and southern halves of the wilderness via the shoreline, allowing for 3-day, 2-night journeys that span the length of the wilderness. The trip from Limantour Beach or Laguna trailheads to

Palomarin, with overnight stays at Coast and Wildcat camps, traverses the entire length of wilderness coastline but requires a long car shuttle. A shorter shuttle allows you to hike from Limantour Beach or Laguna trailheads to Five Brooks or Bear Valley and provides a diverse experience of coastal and inland-forest environments. However, it requires several miles of back-tracking if you plan to stay at Wildcat Camp instead of Glen Camp. The hike takes place mostly along open coastal blufftops that offer minimal shelter on windy or wet days.

Trail Description

From Coast Camp (0.0/50), continue south on broad Coast Trail as it climbs above the small Coast Camp valley and begins its long blufftop journey south. For the next four miles, the coastline is hemmed by cliffs and steep drainages but your trail travels along the more level bluffs above the coast. After you curve around Santa Maria Creek—the first of numerous traversing **U**-curves around creek gullies—the trail reaches the junction with Woodward Valley Trail (0.6/180).

Continue straight on Coast Trail. You soon encounter a wide junction (0.8/150) that provides access to the southern end of Sculptured Beach. The side-trip to the beach descends a narrow path and stairway and deposits you in a small cove—leave your packs at the junction if you plan to continue south on Coast Trail. At the cove you can see outcrops of Monterey Shale; these are easily identified near sea level, but are dramatically overtopped by the high crenulated faces of the loosely-consolidated Drakes Bay Formation. During low tides, it is

Giant eucalyptus above Kelham Beach

possible to return to Coast Camp along Sculptured Beach. If you are going to do this, exercise extreme caution. If the tide appears to be on its way in, do not attempt a beach-walk back to Coast Camp—there is no exit from the beach to escape from encroaching waves. Also, some scrambling is in store after you pass a triple peninsula of razor sharp rocks where deep cavities echo detonating waves.

Sculptured Beach

Continue south as Coast Trail loops inland around a small creek and passes through an area affected by the Vision Fire: blackened snags and skeletal trees jut from the coastal scrub. Hardy coyote brush and bush lupine are predominant in the regenerating landscape, joined intermittently by sage and twining morning glory. The trail winds south around several small drainages before it gradually descends to an enormous eucalyptus situated by another small creek. A remnant of U Ranch, this arboreal gargantua marks the junction for the use trail to Kelham Beach (3.4/100). This solitary beach reveals excellent cliff faces and views south to distant Double Point and the closer sea stacks offshore from Arch Rock. Remaining on Coast Trail, you continue south and pass the junction with Sky Trail (3.6/130). Shortly before you reach Bear Valley Trail (4.1/110), there is a use path that splits to the right toward Arch Rock.

At this point, those who wish to continue to Wildcat Camp should refer to the hike description from Bear Valley Visitor Center to Wildcat Camp and follow it all the way to a good night's sleep. If, instead, you are heading to Glen Camp, you have two options. The more scenic, strenuous, and recommended route follows the Wildcat Camp description mentioned above for the next 1.4 miles, bears left at the junction with North Spur Trail, right on Glen Trail, and then left again to follow the wide fire road of Glen Camp Loop into camp. Alternatively, you can head inland on Bear Valley Trail for 0.9 mile

Arch Rock

to the junction with Glen Trail where you bear right. From here, refer to the hike description from Bear Valley Visitor Center to Glen Camp. This option is 0.4 mile shorter and avoids a few hundred extra feet of elevation gain.

SKY CAMP TO GLEN AND WILDCAT CAMPS VIA SKY TRAIL

Downhill through fantastic forest

One-Way Distances: Sky Camp to Glen Camp, 5.8 miles; Sky Camp to Wildcat Camp, 8.7 miles

Total Elevation Gain/Loss: Sky Camp to Glen Camp, 600/1080; Sky Camp to Wildcat Camp, 900/1880

Hiking Time: 3-6 hours

⟶   **Difficulty:** ★★

Hike Overview

This section connects the northern and southern halves of the wilderness via Inverness Ridge. It allows a 3-day, 2-night journey across the wilderness from either Sky or Bear Valley trailheads to Palomarin or Five Brooks. The most highly recommended backpacking trip in Phillip Burton Wilderness is the trip from Sky Trailhead to Palomarin, with overnights at Sky and Wildcat camps. You'll enjoy all the wilderness highlights with lots of downhill sections of trail; the only drawback is the long car shuttle that is required. The journey from Sky trailhead to either Five Brooks or Bear Valley trailheads necessitates a shorter car shuttle, but remains almost entirely within the inland forest if you plan to stay at Glen Camp (a trip to the coast adds at least an extra two miles).

Trail Description

From Sky Camp (0.0/1020), head south on broad Sky Trail to reach the junction with Mt. Wittenberg and Meadow trails (0.6/1120). Bear right on Sky Trail. You immediately pass beyond the Vision Fire zone and enter a wonderful stretch of mature mixed-evergreen forest. Douglas-firs tower overhead and strain moisture from fog flowing over Inverness Ridge, keeping the environment moist and green through the rain-free summer months. Water condenses on the trees' foliage, falls to the ground, and provides liquid sustenance for a vibrant understory (as much as a third of total year-round moisture here comes from fog drip). Moss-bearded branches and tree-bound ferns droop above abundant elderberry, huckleberry, blackberry tangles, and sword ferns. Poison oak and stinging nettle appear sporadically. In September huckleberry bushes explode with small and delicious blue-black berries.

You reach the next junction, which is Woodward Valley Trail (1.3/890). Continue straight on Sky Trail, climbing briefly to the junction with Old Pine Trail (1.6/1020). Stay on Sky Trail as it gently descends through the final stretch of green forest before cresting a small rise; here, the landscape transitions to coastal scrub as you approach the junction with Baldy Trail (3.0/870).

Bear left if you want to go to Glen Camp, then descend into Bear Valley on

NORTH BAY

Baldy Trail. A steady ridgeline descent, this trail offers occasional views into the deep drainage of Bear Valley before it switchbacks through a lush forest near the bottom to reach the four-way junction with Bear Valley and Glen trails (4.2/150). At this point, please refer to the hike description from Bear Valley Visitor Center to Glen Camp and follow it to a night's rest at Glen Camp (5.7/540).

If instead you wish to proceed to Wildcat Camp (or to Glen Camp via the longer, more scenic coastal route), remain on Sky Trail as it descends toward the increasingly visible ocean. After first passing along the margin of the Vision Fire where burnt snags still protrude, the trail reaches a small saddle where coyote brush covers the thick low-lying coastal scrub landscape. Continue your steady descent past coast live oaks, bay trees, stinging nettle, and a final sampling of mixed-evergreen forest. At last the trail makes its steepest drop on two switch-backs to the junction with Coast Trail (4.5/130). Turn left here and follow wide and sandy Coast Trail south toward Arch Rock. Shortly before you reach Bear Valley Trail (5.0/110), a shorter use path splits right toward scenic Arch Rock.

If you are continuing to Wildcat Camp, refer to the hike description from Bear Valley to Wildcat Camp. It will lead you all the way to a good night's sleep. For hikers heading to Glen Camp, you have two options: The more scenic and strenuous, but recommended, route follows the Bear Valley to Wildcat Camp description along Coast Trail for 1.4 miles to North Spur Trail. Bear left on North Spur Trail, right on Glen Trail, and then left again on Glen Camp Loop to follow the wide fire road into camp. Alternatively, you can head inland on Bear Valley Trail for 0.9 mile to Glen Trail and bear right. From here, refer to the hike description from Bear Valley Visitor Center to Glen Camp. This second option is 0.4 mile shorter and avoids a few hundred feet of elevation gain.

WILDCAT CAMP AND GLEN CAMP CONNECTION

Lightly-trod trails from the coast to the inland forest

One-Way Distance: 2.8 miles
Total Elevation Gain/Loss: 820/320
Hiking Time: 1-2 hours
Difficulty: ★★

Hike Overview

Between Wildcat and Glen camps, there is a tangled web of trails that lead from the open coast to an inland mixed-evergreen forest. While numerous routes are possible between the two camps, the description below takes you on the most scenic: Wildcat to Glen Camp along Coast, South Spur, and Glen Camp Loop trails.

Trail Description

From Wildcat Camp (0.0/40), follow the wide dirt road of Coast Trail inland past a well and water tank. On your way you will see an introduced Monterey pine that thrives by the side of the trail. Well-adapted to the windy, salty environment, these evergreens were planted along the California coast years ago, and several young trees dot the hills around camp. The broad trail heads inland, switchbacks upward, passes huge coffee berry bushes and willows, and then curves into the creek canyon where a shady forest of Douglas-fir and bay trees finds shelter and moisture. Turn left on Coast Trail where it meets with Stewart and Coast trails (0.7/420). You will immediately come upon a knobby octopus of a Douglas-fir.

The trail offers great views as it contours up the hill: the blue sea, Wildcat Lake, Pelican Hill, Wildcat Beach, Double Point, the Farallon Islands, and Point Reyes itself are all visible on a clear day. The route rises past fields of poison oak and Monterey pine, then levels out and turns inland. The coastal views are left behind as you approach the junction with South Spur Trail (1.6/840).

Continue straight on South Spur Trail as it narrows and enters the shade of a maturing mixed-evergreen forest. Greenery appears everywhere in the form of sword ferns, elderberry bushes, and rustling bay trees, all of which thrive beneath healthy Douglas-firs. You pass a marshy area of giant horsetails and thick stinging nettle, then reach the junction with Glen and Glen Camp Loop trails (2.0/720). Follow the wide road of Glen Camp Loop Trail. It passes the junction with Greenpicker Trail (2.1/700) and slowly descends through a young forest. After a short hike, Glen Camp is visible below shortly before the trail banks right and drops steeply into camp (2.8/540).

SOUTHERN INVERNESS RIDGE: NOTES ON RIDGE TRAIL

A vast tract of forest and inland trails covers the spine of Inverness Ridge south of Glen Camp. Stretching from Fir Top south to the Point Reyes Bird Observatory by Palomarin, Ridge Trail travels this long ridgeline and provides a remote and adventurous return trip to Palomarin from either Wildcat or Glen camps. While the pleasure of exploration and solitude are reasons to hike this route, it has drawbacks, including the scenery, distance, descent, and the mile-long road walk to Palomarin. The ridge is nearly covered by young mixed-evergreen forest that is still regenerating from recent logging. There are few views. This 9-mile journey from Wildcat or Glen Camp has more than a thousand feet of elevation change; the trail plummets in loose and knee-busting fashion at its end and the final mile takes you for a walk along dusty Mesa Rd. back to Palomarin. For these reasons, the route is not highly recommended or even featured on the included maps. It awaits the intrepid explorer.

NORTH BAY

Austin Creek State Recreation Area

The remote valleys of the northern Coast Ranges

The Park: Austin Creek State Recreation Area

Distance: 6.4-10.5 miles round-trip, depending on route

Total Elevation Gain/Loss: 1900/1900-2200/2200, depending on route

Trip Length: 2 Days

Difficulty: ★★★

Best Times March-November

Recommended Maps: *Austin Creek State Recreation Area Map,* USGS 7.5-min *Cazadero*

On the edge of the greater Bay Area resides a diverse natural world of oak woodlands, redwood groves, perennial streams, far-reaching vistas, and fantastic spring wildflowers, all tucked deep within secluded canyons. An overnight journey into the reaches of Austin Creek State Recreation Area takes you far from the bustling human world. (For more information about this region, see the campground chapter *Austin Creek State Recreation Area.*)

Hike Overview

The trail descends steeply from ridgeline to lush valley bottom, past four mellifluous streams, two different trail camps, and a wide diversity of ecosystems. The full 10.5-mile loop journey along East Austin Creek and Gilliam Creek trails to Manning Flat Trail Camp is described below, however shorter trips are possible. The quickest overnight excursion is the 6.4-mile out-and-back journey to Tom King Trail Camp on East Austin Creek Trail. Several other semi-loops are also possible that utilize only portions of Gilliam Creek Trail. East Austin Creek Trail is a broad service road; Gilliam Creek Trail is singletrack and open to hikers and equestrians only. While it is possible to bike into the trail camps, the drop into the canyons is steep and difficult.

The Trail Camps

As of 2003, two trail camps are available for overnight use: Manning Flat and Tom King. A third, Gilliam Creek Trail Camp, is currently closed but may reopen in the future (contact the park for its current status). Tom King is closest to the trailhead, located at the end of a 0.3-mile spur trail. There is only one site at Tom King, located beneath buckeye and bay trees and beside gurgling Thompson Creek, where a few redwoods grow in the streambed.

In the far western corner of the park, Manning Flat features two well-spaced sites beneath the shady boughs of Douglas-fir and bay trees near broad East Austin Creek. You must ford the bridgeless stream to reach Manning Flat, sometimes a challenge during the rainy season. Picnic tables, fire rings, and outhouses are provided at both trail camps, but water must be obtained from the adjacent creeks and purified. Campfires are not allowed during fire season (typically late July through October).

The trail camps are available on a first-come, first-serve basis, and all arriving backpackers must obtain a backcountry permit on the day of their trip. Permits can only be obtained from the park entry kiosk or from an on-duty park ranger. The volunteer-staffed Armstrong Redwoods visitor center (see below) may be able to help locate a ranger. There is a fee of $7 per site, and a maximum capacity of 16 people per site. Overall the trail camps are lightly used, but they occasionally fill on weekends in the fall and late spring. Call ahead to check Saturday night availability during these times, or consider arriving Friday evening and camping at Bullfrog Pond Campground to get an early start (and permit) Saturday morning. During winter, finding a ranger to issue a permit can be a challenge; call the day before to coordinate with park staff.

To Reach the Trailhead

Take either Highway 116 or River Road west from Highway 101 to Guerneville and turn north on Armstrong Woods Road, located 0.1 mile west of the Russian River Bridge. In 2.5 miles you reach the Armstrong Redwoods park entrance and visitor center. A thrilling 2.5 miles later you reach the East Austin Creek trailhead at Vista Point. This final 2.5 miles of road is narrow and twisting, with several steep (12% grade) 5 mph hairpin turns. *Vehicles longer than 20 feet are not permitted.* Park staff will advise you on where to park your vehicle overnight.

Trail Description

From the trailhead (0.0/1400), savor the sweeping view across the rolling terrain. Your journey down wide East Austin Creek Trail passes through a variety of ecosystems: coyote brush, manzanita, and several species of oak—coast, Oregon, and black—grow on the drier, sun-exposed west-facing slopes; bay trees, willow, buckeye, and poison oak are nourished by the moist shelter of

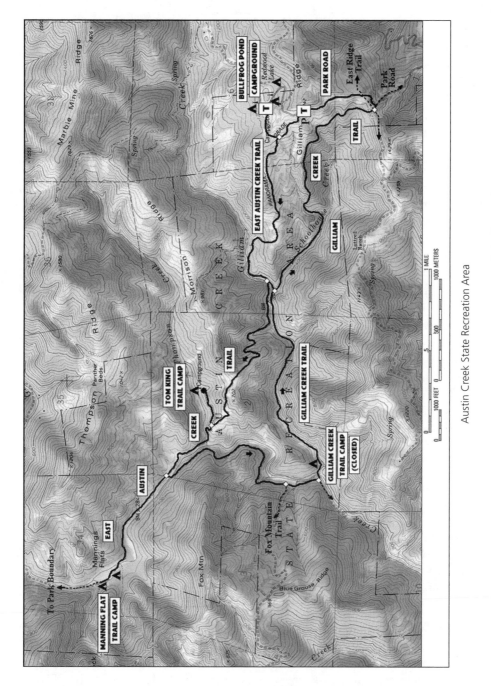

Austin Creek State Recreation Area

nearby gullies; and water-loving Douglas-fir and redwoods flourish on shady north and east-facing slopes.

Descending on East Austin Creek Trail, you soon pass a singletrack spur trail on the right, which comes from lower Bullfrog Pond Campground

(0.2/1150). Continue the steep drop on a hillside regularly rooted by wild pigs and seasonally flushed with wildflowers. Baby blue eyes, shooting stars, and brodeia are particularly abundant. Numerous rock outcrops of greenstone also are present, a geologic landscape rooted in the Franciscan Formation (see Bay Area Geology in the section *Where Should I Go?*). Near canyon bottom, the trail curves right and descends into a thickening mixed-evergreen forest. You briefly travel above crystalline Gilliam Creek, then reach it near a bridge and junction for the short spur trail that leads to nearby Gilliam Creek Trail (1.5/340).

Take it slow

Those fortunate to be here in March may witness orange-bellied newts congregating by the dozens to mate in these waters. Cross the bridge over Gilliam Creek and continue on wide East Austin Creek Trail as it climbs briefly up a small, unnamed drainage brimming with giant chain ferns (typically found only in dense redwood forests), big-leaf maple, and peeling madrone. You then climb above it all to open oak hillsides with exceptional views. The small linear valley of Thompson Creek is visible to the north (where Tom King Trail Camp resides) and the deep drainage of East Austin Creek twists southwest toward the Russian River. After cresting near coast live oaks (2.5/750), descend to the junction with Tom King Trail (2.9/450). If you're camping at Tom King, or just looking for an idyllic picnic spot, turn here and proceed a gentle 0.3 mile to camp at trail's end.

To continue to Manning Flat Trail Camp, remain on East Austin Creek Trail as it switchbacks twice and crosses Thompson Creek. Large, old-growth redwoods appear across the stream as the wide trail now parallels East Austin Creek to reach the unsigned junction (3.5/190) with Gilliam Creek Trail. Continue to camp on East Austin Creek Trail 0.7 mile beyond the junction. The sites are located immediately past the unbridged creek crossing. Along the way you pass through an area devoted to studying the environmental impact of introduced wild pigs.

Back at the trail junction (3.5/190), ford East Austin Creek on Gilliam Creek Trail to enter shadier east-facing slopes covered by an understory of sword, wood, and maidenhair ferns. Climbing briefly, the trail winds well above the rushing stream and its narrow canyon before descending again to reach Fox Mountain Trail on the right (4.6/290). Continue straight. Just past this section a portion of the trail has slid out; scramble down and then cross a small gully to find the continuing route. Note that the park has closed this section of trail in the past. If closed on your arrival, you can return the way you came and exit via East Austin Creek Trail.

The trail soon reaches the posted junction for Gilliam Creek Trail Camp (4.8/290). Bear left and descend the singletrack trail to reach the confluence of East Austin and Gilliam creeks. Ford East Austin Creek one last time to immediately reach the camp (4.9/240), located in a large grassy field near the creek. Picnic tables and a dilapidated outhouse are provided, making this a good resting spot.

Beyond camp, the trail winds through a narrow canyon beneath shady bay trees, oaks, buckeye, big-leaf maple, and Douglas-fir. You briefly climb a short distance above the creek, then descend to cross and re-cross the creek nine times over the next mile. The stream crossings are not always obvious (only a few are signed), but the trail is apparent; if you find yourself on a disappearing track, retrace your steps. At Schoolhouse Creek you encounter the unposted junction for the short connector to East Austin Creek Trail (6.5/360). The connector is the most direct route back to the trailhead, but if you want more variety and views continue straight on Gilliam Creek Trail.

Undulating Gilliam Creek Trail crosses the creek three more times before beginning a steep climb along a small feeder creek to an open, oak-studded ridge. Manzanita, toyon, and chamise line the trail as it steadily ascends the ridgeline before leveling and banking right to traverse the upper Schoolhouse Creek drainage (passing through several nice redwood groves en route). The trail alternately contours gently and ascends steeply to reach the junction with

The remote valleys of the northern Coast Ranges

East Ridge Trail and the park road (8.5/1300). Savor the beautiful vistas one last time as you bear left (north) and hike along the park road to return to the trailhead (9.1/1400).

PARK CONTACT INFORMATION

Armstrong Redwoods State Reserve and Austin Creek State Recreation Area, 1700 Armstrong Woods Rd., Guerneville, CA 95446, (707) 869-2015, www.parks.ca.gov. Visitor Center: (707) 869-2958, open 11 A.M.–3 P.M. daily, longer hours in the summer. Park entrance station open approximately 8 A.M.– sunset daily in summer, weekends only in spring and fall, sporadically in winter.

Giving Back

Stewards of Slavianka is a non-profit group that works in partnership with California State Parks to protect and interpret the natural and cultural resources of the Russian River District. Box 221, Duncan Mills, CA 95430, (707) 869-9177, www.stewardsofslavianka.org.

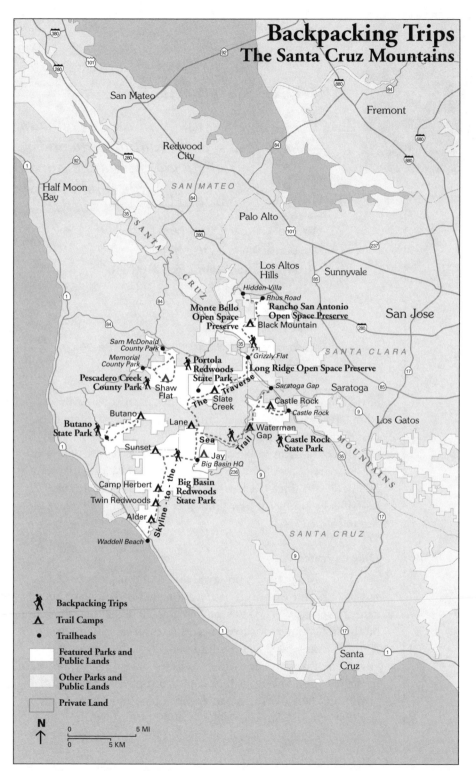

Backpacking Trips
The Santa Cruz Mountains

380

92

101

280

San Mateo

880

84

Fremont

Redwood
City

84

680

880

1

92

280

SAN MATEO

84

Half Moon
Bay

SANTA

280

Palo Alto

101

35

Los Altos
Hills

237

85

Sunnyvale

Hidden Villa

• *Rhus Road*

CRUZ

1

84

**Monte Bello
Open Space
Preserve**

**Rancho San Antonio
Open Space Preserve**

San Jose

Black Mountain

84

35

SANTA CLARA

280

*Sam McDonald
County Park*

Grizzly Flat

**Portola
Redwoods
State Park**

Long Ridge Open Space Preserve

17

*Memorial
County Park*

85

**Pescadero Creek
County Park**

Shaw
Flat

Saratoga Gap

Saratoga

The Traverse

Castle Rock

9

Slate
Creek

Castle Rock

Los Gatos

Butano

Lane

Waterman
Gap

MOUNTAINS

**Butano
State Park**

Sea

**Castle Rock
State Park**

1

Sunset

Trail

Jay

35

9

Big Basin HQ

236

9

Camp Herbert

**Big Basin
Redwoods
State Park**

17

Twin Redwoods

Skyline ~ to ~ the

SANTA CRUZ

Alder

Waddell Beach •

9

Legend

Backpacking Trips

Trail Camps

Trailheads

Featured Parks and
Public Lands

Other Parks and
Public Lands

Private Land

N
↑

0   5 MI

0   5 KM

1

17

Santa
Cruz

1

Butano State Park

*A remote trail camp, abundant
views, and beautiful redwoods; a
full circuit around the canyon
of Little Butano Creek*

The Park: Butano State Park
Distance: 9.8 miles round-trip
Total Elevation Gain/Loss: 2100/2100
Trip Length: 2 days
Difficulty: ★★★
Best Times: Year-round
Recommended Maps: *Butano State Park Map,*
USGS 7.5-min *Franklin Point*

Little Butano Creek slices westward in a narrow defile almost
completely protected within Butano (BOO-tah-no) State Park.
Less than 4 miles long yet brimming with ecological diversity, the
canyon contains an isolated and diverse world representative of
the entire region. A lightly used trail camp and a loop hike almost
exclusively on singletrack make this trip hard to resist. The park
also offers a family campground. (See the camping chapter
Butano State Park.)

Hike Overview

This journey travels on seven different trails to loop clockwise around the canyon. The elevation gain is significant but
generally gradual. The hike can be completed in either direction,
but hiking counter clockwise necessitates an extremely steep
climb of nearly 1000 feet (with full packs) at the start of the
adventure. Bikes and dogs are prohibited. As with all adventures
in the redwood forest, the hike can be completed year-round.
Spring and fall offer the most ideal combination of good weather
and light crowds. Summer is foggy and more crowded. Winter
and early spring are typically rainy, but the rewards are an explo-

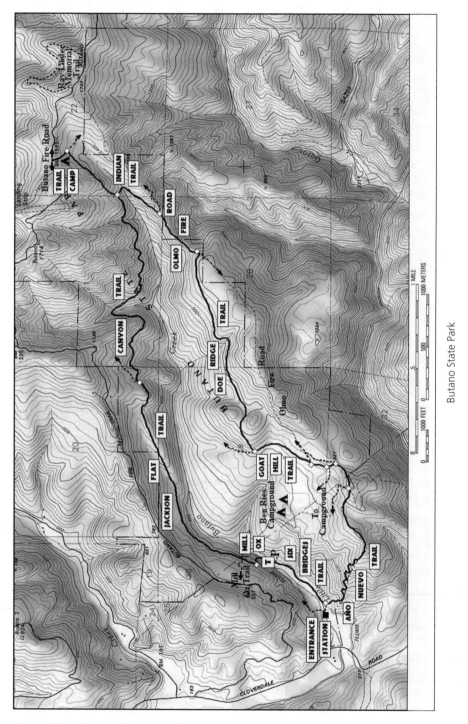

Butano State Park

SANTA CRUZ MTNS

sion of fascinating fungi, clambering newts, and the opportunity to discover the bloom of the purple calypso orchid.

The Trail Camp

Eight primitive sites are located at the ridgeline headwaters of Little Butano Creek in a thick canopy of young redwood forest. They consist of little more than small clearings with very basic chairs and tables made of planks and logs. An outhouse is located nearby but picnic tables and food lockers are not provided (there are reputedly few problems with raccoons and other nocturnal raiders). Campfires are not permitted and *water is not available within camp*—the closest source is a half mile away in perennial Little Butano Creek. Open year-round, the trail camp receives light use and, even when busy, offers good to excellent privacy. All sites are first-come, first-serve, and the seldom-visited trail camp reportedly never fills. There is a maximum of six people per site. Register at the park entrance station upon arrival.

To Reach the Trailhead

From the north, take Highway 1 south of Half Moon Bay for 16 miles to Pescadero Road and turn left. In 2.5 miles, turn right on Cloverdale Road and proceed 4 miles to the park entrance on the left. Approaching from Santa Cruz, take Highway 1 north of Davenport for 14 miles and turn right on Gazos Creek Road, located immediately north of the Beach House gas station. Follow Gazos Creek Road for 2 miles, turn left on Cloverdale Road, and follow the narrow twisting road for 1 mile to the park entrance on the right. The trailhead at Mill Ox Trail is a half mile past the entrance station by a large turn-out.

Trail Description

From the trailhead (0.0/230), begin on Mill Ox Trail as it crosses Little Butano Creek and quickly climbs northeast to reach the junction with Jackson Flat Trail (0.2/430). The route initially weaves through the typical mixer of redwoods, Douglas-fir, tanoak, and huckleberry bushes, with big-leaf maple, twisting madrone, the soft leaves of hazel, and sword and wood fern also appearing intermittently. Turn right on Jackson Flat Trail to begin a gradual rising traverse that runs along the moisture divide between a damp redwood forest (a few large old-growth trees can be spotted) and a drier mixed-evergreen forest.

Bear right onto Canyon Trail (1.7/800) at the junction as Jackson Flat Trail curves left, and continue through thick redwood forest. Soon the woods change to a shorter forest of canyon live oak and madrone, and then abruptly transform into an entirely different ecosystem as the trail crosses the threshold of the Santa Margarita Formation. Here xeric sandstone, poor in water and organic material, attracts species better adapted to these harsh conditions. Knobcone pine proliferates here, a spindly conifer with namesake cones that grow everywhere (including on branches and trunks). These pines survive through serotiny—their cones open only from the heat of wildfires. In an environment where fire frequency is every 20-40 years, this is a successful strategy that populates the newly charred, nutrient-rich soil with a massive sudden influx of seeds. Joining Knobcone pine are other members of the chaparral community: manzanita, golden chinquapin (look under the leaves), toyon berry, scrub oak (the mini-oak shrub), and chamise—one of the most common members of the driest chaparral communities.

As the trail winds through this open community, outstanding views reveal the depth of this diminutive canyon, just one of many to explore in the vast Santa Cruz Mountains. Next the trail banks left into a small tributary canyon and narrows, descending on steep slopes to cross a seasonally rushing creek (note the big-leaf maples and change of ecosystem as moisture again increases). Then it climbs back out via several switchbacks to rejoin the Santa Margarita Formation and

Doe Ridge Trail

accompanying views and flora. Contouring around several small drainages, the trail returns to thick forest and reaches the posted junction for the trail camp (3.7/1200). To reach the trail camp, bear left and head steeply uphill along the narrow overgrown trail to reach a junction with an unnamed fire road (4.2/1460) and turn left (uphill). The eight sites are well spread out to the left of the fire road between here and nearby Butano Fire Road. Ray Linder Memorial Trail is nearby, dedicated to a former park ranger.

After a night unlike any other, return to the junction with Canyon Trail (4.7/1200) and continue briefly up-canyon before the trail crosses young Little Butano Creek and begins the journey back out, soon reaching Olmo Fire Road (5.2/1240). Turn right. For the next 0.4 mile, the route follows Olmo Fire Road through private property owned by Ainsley Family Tree Farm. Please respect property rights and stay on the road as it descends to reach the posted junction with Doe Ridge Trail on the right (5.5/1050). Along the way, enjoy looking south into intriguing Gazos Creek drainage, the only views of the hike beyond Little Butano Creek.

The route turns right onto singletrack Doe Ridge Trail and passes through one of its most idyllic stretches—level, nicely contoured, and beneath old-growth redwoods (there are 315 acres of old-growth redwood forest protected within the park). At the junction with Goat Hill Trail (7.0/840), turn left and continue through a thick Douglas-fir forest recovering from recent logging. Goat Hill Trail passes a spur trail on the left (7.5/900) leading to adjacent Olmo Fire Road, and then another spur a short distance later (7.6/920). From here, Goat Hill Trail continues downhill to the right toward the campground and offers a more direct and less strenuous route back to trailhead—just follow the

SANTA CRUZ MTNS

road from the campground. However, it also necessitates dealing with vehicles and pavement.

To avoid the campground/road area and maximize singletrack hiking, return to Olmo Fire Road and bear right to reach the junction on the left for Año Nuevo Trail (8.0/1060). This is your last chance to choose the easier route to the trailhead—Olmo Fire Road also connects with the campground and road. Otherwise bear left on Año Nuevo Trail and contour briefly along a forested ridge of Douglas-fir. The trail banks right and down-canyon, then drops directly on switchbacks. The foliage becomes thick with elderberry and blackberry as airy views of the canyon's end and the entrance station appear. At the bottom (9.3/220), bear right at the bridge on Six Bridges Trail and proceed along the banks of Little Butano Creek to return to the trailhead. Enjoy the euphonious flow of this peaceful stream as you wind back and forth along level ground to end your journey (9.8/230).

PARK CONTACT INFORMATION

Butano State Park, 1500 Cloverdale Rd., Pescadero, CA 94060, (650) 879-2040, www.parks.ca.gov.

Giving Back

Sempervirens Fund is a non-profit land conservancy dedicated to preserving, expanding, and linking parklands in the Santa Cruz Mountains. Drawer BE, Los Altos, CA 94023-4054, (650) 968-4509, www.sempervirens.org.

SANTA CRUZ MTNS

Pescadero Creek County Park

Two journeys into the secluded canyon of Pescadero Creek

The Parks: Pescadero Creek, Memorial, and Sam McDonald county parks
Distance: From Memorial County Park, 4.6–10.5 miles round-trip, depending on route
Trip Length: 2 days
Best Times: Year-round
Recommended Maps: *Pescadero Creek County Park Map,* USGS 7.5-min *La Honda, Mindego Hill*

Deep and secluded, pocketed with untouched redwood groves and lined with gurgling streams, Pescadero Creek County Park shelters more than 6000 acres in the heart of the Santa Cruz Mountains. Amid it all hides Shaw Flat Trail Camp, a remote backcountry destination accessed via two different routes, each described in detail below.

The Trail Camp

Shaw Flat perches on a level shelf 100 feet above hidden Pescadero Creek and consists of eight sites spread beneath the branches of a healthy second-growth redwood forest. Potable water is not provided, but nearby Pescadero Creek can be accessed a quarter mile away. A few picnic tables are scattered among the sites and an outhouse is available. The camp is open year-round and conditions are usually the same at all times—cool and damp. While the rainy season brings more cold and wet, it also brings an explosion of fungi and migrating newts. The camp receives light use and is almost never full. Sites are first-come, first-serve; register at the Memorial County Park entrance station when staffed. Campfires and dogs are not permitted.

MEMORIAL COUNTY PARK TO SHAW FLAT TRAIL CAMP

Distance: 4.6 miles round-trip

Total Elevation Gain/Loss: 750/750

⟷   **Difficulty:** ★★

Hike Overview

Wide fire roads and narrow singletrack trails travel upstream from Memorial County Park near canyon bottom, passing through pleasant redwood forest. The hike's many positives include short and easy access to the backcountry, a trailhead adjacent to an excellent family campground (see the camping chapter *Memorial County Park*), and beautiful water and forest life.

To Reach the Memorial County Park Trailhead

Take Highway 84 to Pescadero Road, located one mile east of the small town of La Honda. Follow Pescadero Road south for 5 miles to the Memorial County Park entrance, bearing right at the sharp junction with Alpine Road a mile from Highway 84. After registering, proceed to Wurr Road—the intersection is 0.2 mile north of the Memorial Park entrance (turn right when leaving the park). Hoffman Creek Trailhead, your starting point, is located a short 0.2 mile down Wurr Road on the left.

Trail Description

From the trailhead (0.0/300), proceed across the narrow gully of Hoffman Creek, noting some of the flora common to the park's moist riparian alleys—alder, big leaf maple, sword fern, and thimbleberry. The trail continues on broad Old Haul Road, quickly entering a lush forest of Douglas-fir, redwood, tanoak, and moss-coated California bay, joined intermittently by the twisting limbs of live oaks. Hazel, huckleberry, and thick sword ferns fill in the understory. During the past 100 years much of Pescadero Creek County Park was logged, evidenced by the surrounding large stumps and springboard notches. Yet patches of the region's most superlative stands were protected from the saw by inaccessibility or purchase by San Mateo County. Their beauty and antiquity surprise at unexpected moments throughout the park.

After passing an unposted trail and then a fire road on the right, level Old Haul Road reaches the junction with Pomponio Trail (0.8/290). Bear left toward Worley Flat and follow Pomponio Trail down to Pescadero Creek. While a footbridge is provided during the dry season, Pescadero Creek must be rock-hopped or forded during the rainy season. Along the creek, large elderberry bushes join the riparian companions of alder and big leaf maple. A heron may be feeding in the streambed.

Climbing the opposite slopes, the trail soon leaves the redwood forest and

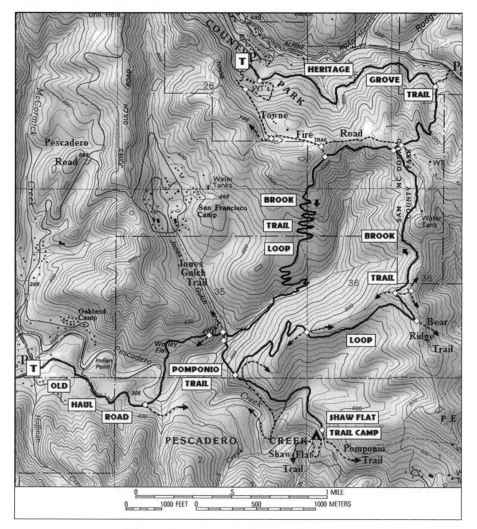

Pescadero Creek County Park

passes into a drier environment characterized by live oaks, before reaching the open fields of Worley Flat. During the 1960s this marked the location of a proposed dam which would have created a large reservoir and water supply for the Pescadero area by flooding nearly all of Pescadero Creek Canyon below 400' elevation. High costs and public opposition thankfully prevented this and the canyon instead became the protected land you tread on today.

Remain on Pomponio Trail as it bears right across the upper slopes of open Worley Flat and then branches left as a singletrack trail on the opposite side (1.2/380). Coyote brush and sticky monkey flower are indicative of a drier environment as you briefly climb through a dense oak forest and soon encounter an unposted and confusing four-way junction (1.3/440). Continue on narrow

Pomponio Trail across the wide trail/road, easily recognized by the wooden gate that prevents equestrians from using the narrow and muddy trail.

Dropping into the shady redwood-filled gully of Jones Creek, the trail makes two switchbacks and reaches the junction with Jones Gulch Trail on the left (1.4/360). Continue straight on Pomponio Trail as it descends to immediately encounter the first junction with Brook Trail Loop (1.4/280). Turn right and proceed downstream on Pomponio/Brook Trail to cross Towne Creek on a wooden bridge. Below, Jones Creek tumbles 10 feet into Towne Creek, a sparkling waterfall in a magic box canyon. Framed by redwood forest and bursting with chain, sword, and five-finger ferns, this isolated grotto is one of the region's deepest delights.

Continue on Pomponio Trail as it climbs beneath some impressive redwoods and crosses a well-marked fire road. The trail then reaches the second junction with Brook Trail Loop (1.7/400). From here, follow the numerous signs for Pomponio Trail as it closely parallels and then briefly follows an adjacent fire road before reaching a posted short spur trail to Shaw Flat Trail Camp (2.3/400). Shaw Flat Trail descends a short quarter mile past camp to Pescadero Creek and provides the easiest access to water. After a perfect night, return the way you came.

SAM MCDONALD COUNTY PARK
TO SHAW FLAT TRAIL CAMP LOOP

Distance: 10.5 miles round-trip
Total Elevation Gain/Loss: 1500/1500
Difficulty: ★★

Hike Overview

This more strenuous option offers a fuller backpacking experience and provides big-picture views of the area, descending from open ridgetop to lush redwood-filled canyon. Traversing first along a ridgeline above the Pescadero Creek drainage, this route then loops in and out of the canyon on impressive singletrack Brook Trail Loop. While Brook Trail Loop can be completed in either direction, it is described in the recommended counter-clockwise direction. Note also that the descent into the canyon via Sam McDonald County Park can be combined with an exit to Hoffman Creek trailhead (described above), making for an almost completely downhill point-to-point experience. A car shuttle would be required for this variation.

To Reach the Sam McDonald County Park Trailhead

Take Highway 84 to Pescadero Road, located one mile east of the small town of La Honda. Follow Pescadero Road south for 1.5 miles to the Sam

McDonald County park entrance, bearing right at the sharp junction with Alpine Road a mile from Highway 84. The park entrance comes up quickly on the right and there is a $4 parking fee per vehicle. Note that registration at Memorial County Park entrance station (when staffed) is required for overnight use of the trail camp—the entrance station is located 3.5 miles past the trailhead on Pescadero Road.

Trail Description

For the sake of staying on singletrack trails rather than fire roads, this description follows the more circuitous route through Heritage Grove rather than the direct route along Towne Fire Road. While this adds 1.6 miles to the total trip distance, the rewards of an old-growth redwood grove and bonus views into Pescadero Creek canyon merit the effort. For those in a hurry and wanting to avoid this extra distance, begin on Towne Fire Road and follow it just under a mile to the first junction for Brook Trail Loop, located on the right at the beginning of the open fields atop Towne Ridge.

At the trailhead, tall redwoods tower over the large parking lot (0.0/650) and several of the common redwood forest constituents can be identified in front of the intermittently staffed ranger station. Two big-leaf maple trees curve overhead, the fuzzy soft leaves of hazel bushes can be fondled, and clover-like redwood sorrel coats the ground with a miniature forest two inches high. While broad Towne Fire Road is prominently signed at the head of the parking area, our described hike begins on singletrack Heritage Grove Trail, found closer to the parking lot entrance by an area trail map.

California bay and canyon live oak grow overhead as the trail immediately drops to Pescadero Road. Cross it and continue through the gate. The large, spiny leaves of tanoak appear immediately, waving beneath several majestic ancient redwoods. Enormous sword ferns and a carpet of redwood sorrel enrich the world with green as the trail reaches the junction with Big Tree Trail (0.1/620). Bear left. Contouring slowly uphill through thick forest, the trail next reaches Heritage Grove and a posted junction (1.4/670)—bear right toward the Hikers' Hut. You may want to drop the packs for a moment before continuing, however, and turn left to stroll the short distance to the main flat of Heritage Grove, a 37-acre old-growth stand protected through the efforts of a local citizen's group.

Back on the main route, the trail steadily climbs, offering a few fleeting glimpses north across Alpine Creek drainage, and then encounters a gate immediately before reaching the ridgetop and intersection with Towne Fire Road (1.9/1150). The Hikers' Hut awaits here (call (650) 390-8411, ext. 8 for more information). Next cross Towne Fire Road to find the junction with Brook Trail Loop and turn right (the return route is on the left), passing along the edge of open meadows regularly rooted by non-native wild pigs. The trail parallels

SANTA CRUZ MTNS

telephone poles and the fire road as it winds along a mixed-evergreen environment populated by coyote brush, blackberry brambles, bracken fern, madrone,
ceanothus, Douglas-fir, and moss-festooned coast live oak. Excellent views south
into Pescadero Creek canyon open up along this section—the region of Portola
Redwoods State Park is visible a few miles upstream and lofty Butano Ridge
rises more than 1500 feet above Pescadero Creek on the opposite slopes.

After re-entering a shady forest of Douglas-fir, the trail reaches another
junction (2.3/1060) connecting back to Towne Fire Road. Bear left and begin
the steep descent on Brook Trail. A long series of switchbacks slowly drops into
an ever-wetter world and the mixed-evergreen forest of Douglas-fir abruptly
becomes dominated by redwood trees (3.5/700), their draping shields of foliage
coloring the forest a vibrant green. As the trail steadily descends into the Towne
Creek drainage, watch for some old-growth redwoods—several approach 8 feet
in diameter. Crossing the creek gully on a small bridge, the trail briefly parallels
the watercourse and then hits a road junction (4.5/300). Turn right here and
then take the immediate left on the spur trail posted for Brook Trail Loop to
cross above the deep gully of Jones Gulch and reach the intersection with Pomponio Trail (4.6/280). Head left (downstream) to cross above a magical waterfall
grotto on another Towne Creek Bridge.

Continue on Pomponio Trail as it climbs beneath some impressive redwoods and crosses a well-marked fire road until the trail reaches the second
junction with Brook Trail Loop (4.8/400)—your return trail. To reach the trail
camp from here, follow the numerous signs for Pomponio Trail as it closely

Sunset over the Santa Cruz Mountains

SANTA CRUZ MTNS

parallels and then briefly follows an adjacent fire road before reaching a posted short spur trail to the camp area (5.4/400). Shaw Flat Trail descends a short quarter mile past camp to Pescadero Creek and provides the easiest access to creek water.

After a revitalizing night, return to the closer Brook Trail Loop Junction (6.0/400) and bear right (uphill) to begin the climb back out. As you slowly ascend, so goes the transition from lush redwood forest—and some nice ancient groves—to a mixed-evergreen forest of massive Douglas-firs and moss-encrusted, Hydra-like bay trees. The trail crosses Towne Fire Road once as it ascends (6.8/780) to reach the junction with Bear Ridge Trail (7.5/1020). Turn left to remain on Brook Trail Loop as it crosses Towne Fire Road again and contours north just below the ridgeline. The slopes are steep around an enchanting redwood grove and a viewblazer picnic site offers vistas south as the trail winds among a much drier chaparral community of coffee berry, coyote brush, bracken fern, and sticky monkey flower to rejoin the earlier junction with Heritage Grove Trail (8.6/1150). From here, return either via Towne Fire Road to reach the parking lot in 1.2 miles (9.8/650), bearing right at the Horse Camp along the way; or along earlier Heritage Grove Trail to end your journey (10.5/650).

PARKS CONTACT INFORMATION

All three parks are managed by San Mateo County Parks and Recreation Division, 455 County Center, 4th Floor, Redwood City, CA 94063, (650) 363-4020, www.eparks.net.

Memorial County Park can be reached directly: 9500 Pescadero Creek Rd., Loma Mar, CA 94021, (650) 879-0212.

SANTA CRUZ MTNS

Giving Back

San Mateo County Parks Foundation provides financial support for the recreational, environmental, and educational programs and projects of the San Mateo County Parks and Recreation Department. 215 Bay Road, Menlo Park, CA 94025, (650) 321-5812, www.supportparks.org.

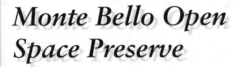

Monte Bello Open Space Preserve

Tranquil headwaters and rising ridges astride the San Andreas Fault

The Park: Monte Bello Open Space Preserve
Distance: 5 miles round-trip
Total Elevation Gain/Loss: 1200/1200
Trip Length: 2 days
Difficulty: ★★
Best Times: Year-round
Recommended Maps: *Monte Bello Open Space Preserve Map*, USGS 7.5-min *Mindego Hill*

Monte Bello lulls in more ways than one. A singletrack interpretive nature trail winds along the very headwaters of Stevens Creek. A steady climb reaches above the deep crease formed by the grinding San Andreas Fault. A trail camp awaits atop distinct Black Mountain (2800'). Savory, ever-changing views peer into a hidden valley and beyond. Monte Bello, que bello.

This preserve is a special place. Taller than neighboring Skyline Ridge to the west, Monte Bello Ridge is an anomalous rise on the eastern slopes of the Santa Cruz Mountains. At its base, sandwiched between the two steep ridges, the San Andreas Fault slices across the landscape and pulverizes the rock found along its trace. Stevens Creek, flowing eastward to enter the San Francisco Bay near Mountain View, easily cut through this loose material to carve a narrow, secluded canyon more than a thousand feet deep. The cool depths provide moisture and shelter for a mixed-evergreen forest more typical of regions farther west in the Santa Cruz Mountains, while the west-facing slopes of Monte Bello Ridge quickly transition to dry oak woodland, open grassland, and chaparral communities more commmon farther inland. Wildlife is abundant and varied as well—deer, newts, tarantulas, raptors, owls, lizards, frogs, coyotes, and bobcats all make the preserve their home.

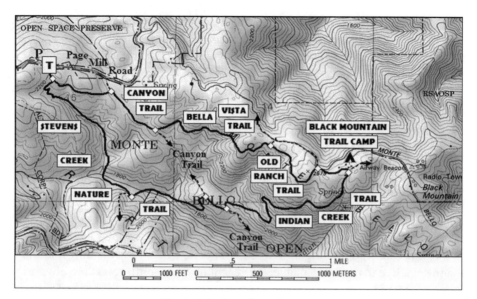

Monte Bello Open Space Preserve

Hike Overview

The loop to Black Mountain Trail Camp atop Monte Bello Ridge is a short and easy adventure along narrow trails and broad fire roads. Tucked in a narrow crease immediately east of the long axis of Skyline Ridge and Highway 35, this hike visits the only trail camp on the eastern slopes of the Santa Cruz Mountains. Considering its location only 8 miles from downtown Cupertino and Silicon Valley, the park is remarkably quiet and secluded. The hike is described counter-clockwise, beginning along educational Stevens Creek Nature Trail, which makes for a longer, more informative hike in and an easier hike out. While the hike can be completed year-round and the trail camp is shaded, trails above Stevens Creek corridor are exposed and hot in summer. Spring wildflowers are excellent. Dogs are prohibited in the preserve.

The Trail Camp

This is the only overnight camp in the Bay Area managed by the Midpeninsula Regional Open Space District. Advance reservations are required and can be made by calling MROSD at (650) 691-1200. There is a fee of $2 per person. Campfires are not permitted.

Situated a quarter mile from the summit of Black Mountain at an elevation of 2700 feet, the camp consists of four small sites (maximum four people per site) and one group site (24 maximum). While the sites are stacked close together, usage is light and it is unlikely that the camp will be full. For such a pristine-feeling park, the trail camp and surrounding area are surprisingly developed—radio towers dot the summit, a pay phone is available from camp, the bathroom is illuminated at night, and phone and power cables stretch overhead. Good views to the west are available nearby, but views of the often hazy South Bay are mostly obscured by vegetation. Non-potable water (bring a filter or boil it) and food lockers are provided, but there are no picnic tables.

To Reach the Trailhead

Take the Page Mill Road exit from Interstate 280 above Palo Alto, and follow Page Mill Road west for 7 miles to reach the main entrance and parking area on the left. Alternatively, take Highway 35 for 7 miles south of the Highway 84/35 junction, then bear left (east) on Page Mill Road and proceed 1.5 miles to the main entrance on the right.

Trail Description

At the trailhead parking lot (0.0/2230), the hike begins by the information sign where free maps are available. Far-reaching views south reveal the obvious trough formed by the San Andreas Fault. On the distant skyline are Mt. Umunhum (3486'), topped by a rectangular building; and slightly more distant Loma Prieta (3806'), epicenter for the namesake 1989 earthquake. The trail descends immediately and quickly reaches the junction with Stevens Creek Nature Trail (0.1/2200). Bear right.

Interpretive signs elucidate natural features as Stevens Creek Nature Trail descends via several short switchbacks. Bay, madrone, canyon live oak, and ferns fill the lush alley of dribbling Stevens Creek as the trail follows its drainage. Coast live oak and Douglas-fir soon join the forest as the trail skirts near the creek and then crosses it on a pretty wooden bridge. Tanoak appears as well before the trail briefly climbs to rise 30 feet above the increasingly steep gully.

Reaching the junction with Skid Road Trail (1.2/1800), bear left to remain on Stevens Creek Trail. Now wider, it briefly continues close to the creek before contouring upslope past some large firs and then passes through a gate

Black Mountain Trail Camp

to reach the junction with wide Canyon Trail (1.8/1920). The route turns right to briefly follow Canyon Trail through some open clearings before reaching the junction with Indian Creek Trail (2.0/1970). Head left toward Backpack Camp on Indian Creek Trail as Canyon Trail continues its journey downstream.

Buckeye, coyote brush, large twisting valley oaks, toyon, coffee berry, and yerba santa all appear on the drier, more exposed slopes as the trail steadily climbs, and large amounts of chamise grow closer to the top. Increasingly good views open up until the trail encounters the posted junction for the trail camp (3.0/2700). The antenna-clad summit of Black Mountain is a short 0.4 mile ahead but bear left instead to reach the campsites. The trail camp is located on the same site as the original buildings of Black Mountain Ranch, torn down following the acquisition of this property by MROSD in 1978. An interpretive placard providing further details can be found nearby, along with an active seismic monitoring station and views of distant Mt. Tamalpais.

Above Monte Bello Open Space Preserve

Following a perfect night under the stars, follow the road from camp northwest along the ridge, then go left at the junction with Old Ranch Trail (3.2/2660). Go left again at the junction with Bella Vista Trail (3.6/2540). Some of the farthest reaching views yet can be enjoyed along this section: Mt. Tamalpais in the North Bay, Mt. Diablo in the East Bay, and Dumbarton Bridge in the South Bay. Passing above several thin, oak-choked gullies, Bella Vista Trail passes numerous buckeye as it slowly descends to Canyon Trail (4.4/2130). Turn right on Canyon Trail and pass a small, marshy *sag pond* on the right filled with cattails. Sag ponds are common along the San Andreas Fault and are formed as fault motion pulls apart the ground to form small depressions. Bear left shortly before Canyon Trail reaches Page Mill Road (4.6/2100), and follow signs for the singletrack Nature Trail Return Loop. Many use trails crisscross this area before the trail rejoins the initial junction below the parking lot (5.0/2230).

SANTA CRUZ MTNS

PARK CONTACT INFORMATION

Midpeninsula Regional Open Space District, 330 Distel Circle, Los Altos, CA 94022-1404, (650) 691-1200, www.openspace.org, email: info@openspace.org.

Giving Back

For information about volunteer opportunities in Monte Bello Open Space Preserve and other MROSD lands, contact the district at (650) 691-1200, email: volunteer@openspace.org.

Castle Rock State Park

*Wild rocks and airy views into the
central core of the Santa Cruz
Mountains, plus guaranteed
trail camp availability*

The Park: Castle Rock State Park
Distance: 5.2 miles round-trip
Total Elevation Gain/Loss: 1200/1200
Trip Length: 2 days
Difficulty: ★★
Best Times: Year-round
Recommended Maps: *Castle Rock State Park Map*,
USGS 7.5-min *Castle Rock Ridge*

A short backpacking trip to a lightly-traveled trail camp, this
adventure rewards with fantastic sandstone boulders and towering views over the San Lorenzo River and Pescadero Creek
watersheds.

Castle Rock State Park perches on the tallest ridgeline in the
Santa Cruz Mountains and harbors a geologic wonderland. Heavy
winter precipitation (45-50" annually) falls upon the area's
unusually hard sandstone outcrops, creating conditions ideal for
some bizarre chemical weathering known as *tafoni*. As all this rain
falls upon the rocks, water seeps inside and dissolves the thin
matrix of calcium carbonate that binds the individual sand grains
together. When dry conditions return, the moisture trapped
inside the rocks is drawn back to the surface. Its evaporation
leaves behind the calcium carbonate as a hard and intricate surface residue. Without the calcium carbonate "glue" to hold them
together, the interior sand grains waste away to leave small cavities behind. Over time these cavities can become intricate cata-
combs, their puckered walls a fascinating honeycomb of pitted
rock. Examples of this unusual weathering can be seen close to
the park entrance.

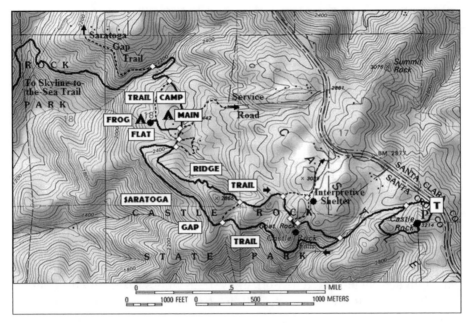

Castle Rock State Park

Hike Overview

The trail traverses the upper tier of the Santa Cruz Mountains, running high along the western slopes to reach a pleasantly secluded trail camp. Summer fog can obscure the hike's incredible views and winter storms can be heavy, but there is no bad time to visit. Snow occasionally falls during winter. While crowds on the trail are relatively light, the rock formations close to the park entrance usually attract large numbers of climbers and scramblers on the weekends.

The Trail Camp

One of the largest in the Bay Area, the trail camp offers 20 sites spread between two areas—Main Camp and Frog Flat Camp—and is tucked away at an elevation of 2400 feet in thick Knobcone pines and chaparral. A maximum of six people are allowed per site. The dense undergrowth allows for good to excellent site privacy, but obscures the exceptional views enjoyed on the approach. It is the only trail camp in the Bay Area that permits campfires—firewood is even available for purchase right at the trail camp ($5/bundle). Campfires are prohibited during wildfire season, however (typically June-November; call ahead for current information). Piped drinking water and a pay phone are available at the trail camp, as is a large sleeping shelter for use during inclement weather. *Reservations* may be made by calling (831) 338-8861 but are not necessary—the trail camp is reputed to never fill up and space is always available on a first-come, first-serve basis (a delightful rarity in the busy outdoor world of the Bay Area!).

Sites cost $5 per night and include trailhead parking for one vehicle (extra vehicle $2); register at the park entrance station upon arrival.

To Reach the Trailhead

Take Highway 35 south of the Highway 9 junction for 2.5 miles. The posted entrance and parking area are located on the west side of the road.

Trail Description

A small forest of signs marks the trailhead at the edge of the parking lot (0.0/3070). While the direct route to the trail camp proceeds straight on Saratoga Gap Trail, the fascinating sandstone formations are accessed via a short half-mile loop that rejoins the main trail a short distance ahead. Hours can easily be whiled away here—those arriving late in the day should consider exploring this area on the return trip. To begin among the boulders, bear left at the trailhead toward Castle Rock to quickly reach the first wild stone pile on the left. From here an interlaced network of use trails climbs past a variety of outcrops before reaching Castle Rock itself, an apartment-sized monolith deeply gouged by erosion. After exploring the *tafoni* world, proceed the short distance to Saratoga Gap Trail and bear left.

To head directly to the campground from the trailhead (0.0/3070), proceed straight on Saratoga Gap Trail as it passes through a mixed-evergreen forest dominated by the drooping evergreen branches of Douglas-fir, the large spiny leaves of tanoak, and the twisting trunks of madrone. A trailside understory of blackberry and poison oak discourages a departure from the soft path as it begins its descent into the Kings Creek drainage, one of the uppermost headwaters of the San Lorenzo River. Dropping into a dry gully, the trail quickly passes a junction on the left for Castle Rock (0.1/3000) where those exploring the sandstone formations can rejoin the main trail. The trail continues downward and a spring soon appears, feeding Kings Creek as the broad leaves of big-leaf maple appear overhead and thick clumps of sword ferns sprout along the moist creek bed. Crossing the creek, the trail reaches the junction with Ridge Trail (0.5/2730) and the beginning of the loop. While the hike can easily be completed in either direction, this description continues on Saratoga Gap Trail and returns via Ridge Trail.

A few young redwoods join large Douglas-firs as Saratoga Gap Trail continues briefly along the creek to reach the overlook for the thin cascade of Castle Rock Falls (0.7/2700). From here Kings Creek plummets downwards and drops over a thousand vertical feet in less than a mile. Heading away from the creek, the trail then quickly passes onto drier slopes where coffee berry, toyon, and fragrant California bay appear—plants better adapted to a world of less moisture.

The hike traverses steep slopes, passing through a world of chaparral protruded by sandstone boulders, and enters a stand of rustling black oaks shortly before reaching a connector trail on the right leading to nearby Ridge Trail (1.5/2560). Continue straight on Saratoga Gap Trail as spectacular views soon open into the heart of the Santa Cruz Mountains. Looking south beyond the vast drainage of the San Lorenzo River, the Monterey peninsula can be identified across Monterey Bay on clear days (a distance of more than 40 miles). To the west, the low ridge separating the San Lorenzo River and Pescadero Creek watersheds is apparent; the Skyline-to-the-Sea Trail follows this divide en route to Big Basin Redwoods State Park. Tall Bonny Doon Ridge hems the San Lorenzo River to the southwest, while Butano Ridge rises above Pescadero Creek to the west. The deep canyon of Pescadero Creek curves out-of-sight to the northwest, harboring many an overnight outdoor adventure in its recesses— Portola Redwoods State Park, Memorial County Park, and Pescadero Creek County Park all await exploration.

Now gradually descending, you pass through chaparral thick with coyote brush and poison oak. Narrow and rocky in places, the trail winds along sheer slopes before turning sharply right to pass through a suddenly thick forest of tanoak and madrone before reaching the junction with Ridge Trail (2.5/2400). To reach the trail camp, bear left, and then left again on the wide fire road to reach the main area (2.7/2400). Knobcone pines abruptly appear beside young Douglas-firs in this section, their twisted architecture and namesake cones making them easy to identify. The 15 sites of the Main Camp area are located nearby off Saratoga Gap Trail, while the five sites of more-removed Frog Flat Camp are

Mossy oaks and boulder thrills

located a quarter mile downhill on Service Road Trail, just below the intersection with Frog Flat Trail.

Following a night of outdoor perfection, return to the earlier junction with Ridge Trail (2.9/2400) and follow Ridge Trail as it climbs briefly through thick forest before breaking out at another incredible viewpoint of the Santa Cruz Mountains. Continue on Ridge Trail as it returns to the forest, climbs along the north side of the ridge, and then reaches the opposite end of the connector trail to Saratoga Gap Trail (3.7/2700). Remain on Ridge Trail as it climbs over a black oak-studded knoll to reach a fork (4.0/2900). Turn left for a short side-loop that rejoins Ridge Trail in 0.3 mile after passing an informative interpretive shelter. Ridge Trail continues to the right, passing the return trail from the interpretive shelter (4.2/2960), and then reaches the junction to exciting Goat Rock (4.3/2920). Another climbing destination, the rounded pinnacle of Goat Rock and its surrounding viewpoints can be accessed via numerous use trails and thrilling rock scrambles. After enjoying the most intense verticality of the trip, continue on Ridge Trail as it slowly descends along a narrow, rocky route to rejoin Saratoga Gap Trail (4.7/2730) and the final climb back to the parking lot (5.2/3070).

SANTA CRUZ MTNS

PARK CONTACT INFORMATION

Castle Rock State Park, 15000 Skyline Blvd., Los Gatos, CA 95030, (408) 867-2952, www.parks.ca.gov.

Giving Back

Portola and Castle Rock Foundation publishes maps, brochures, and interpretive materials, and supports interpretive projects at Portola Redwoods and Castle Rock state parks through fundraising efforts. 9000 Portola State Park Rd., Box F, La Honda, CA 94020, (650) 948-9098.

Sempervirens Fund is dedicated to preserving, expanding, and linking parklands in the Santa Cruz Mountains. Drawer BE, Los Altos, CA 94023-4054, (650) 968-4509, www.sempervirens.org.

Skyline-to-the-Sea

*Ridgeline to coastline through
the full spectrum of the
Santa Cruz Mountains*

The Parks: Castle Rock State Park, Big Basin
Redwoods State Park

Distance: 26-36 miles one way, depending on route

Total Elevation Gain/Loss: 2500/5100-3800/6400,
depending on route

Trip Length: 3-4 days

Difficulty: ★★★

Best Times: Year-round

Recommended Maps: *Castle Rock State Park Map,
Big Basin Redwoods State Park Map, Trail Map of the
Santa Cruz Mountains 1&2;* USGS 7.5-min *Mindego
Hill, Cupertino, Castle Rock Ridge, Big Basin, Franklin
Point, Point Año Nuevo*

From the ridgeline spine of the Santa Cruz Mountains, the
Skyline-to-the-Sea Trail descends through lush forest, passes
sweeping vistas, lines crystalline streams, explores magnificent
old-growth, visits beautiful waterfalls, and then reaches the
Pacific Ocean at Waddell Beach. It may be the best-known backpacking trip in the Bay Area, but the scenery and adventure are
irresistibly epic.

The 26-mile-long Skyline-to-the-Sea Trail begins at Saratoga
Gap at the Highway 35/9 junction, and closely parallels Highway
9 on its descent to the first available trail camp at Waterman Gap.
While this is the shortest and most direct route to the sea, there
are several drawbacks to starting the hike along the Skyline-to-
the-Sea Trail itself. Highway 9 and its accompanying traffic noise
are always nearby, and no overnight parking is permitted at the
trailhead, making it necessary to arrange a drop-off at the beginning of the hike. An alternate route begins at Castle Rock State
Park, avoids the highway for its first 6.7 miles, provides incredible

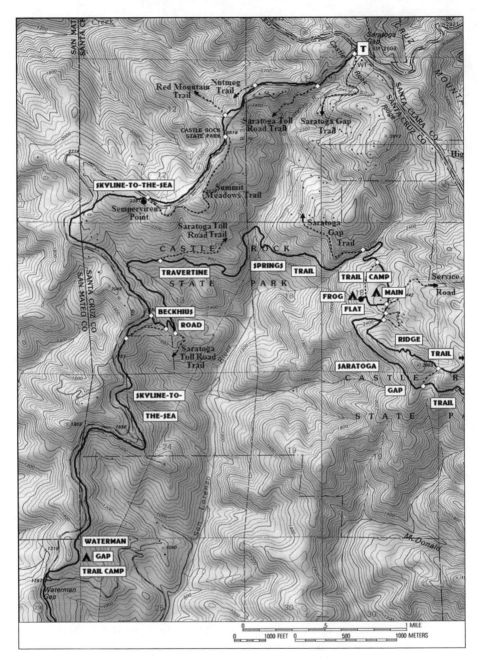

Skyline-to-the-Sea: Upper Section

views, includes an additional trail camp, and offers overnight parking at the trailhead. This variation adds 3 miles to the trip. Both routes are described in greater detail below. Note also that staying at Lane or Sunset trail camps increases the overall distance of the hike—see below for more information.

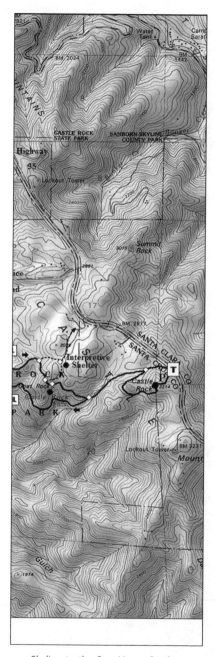

Skyline-to-the-Sea: Upper Section

Excellent single night trips are possible along sections of the Skyline-to-the-Sea Trail and adjoining trails. The overnight loop hike to Castle Rock Trail Camp and the journey inland from Waddell Beach are described in adjacent chapters, and several options begin from the visitor center in the heart of Big Basin Redwoods State Park. Recommended is the 11-mile loop to Sunset Trail Camp along the Skyline-to-the-Sea and Sunset trails, which tours a choice section of old-growth redwood forest and waterfalls. Also possible from the visitor center is the 10-mile hike to Lane Trail Camp along the Skyline-to-the-Sea, Basin, and Hollow Tree trails, highlighted by old-growth forest, big picture views, sandstone outcrops, and the absence of crowds.

THE TRAIL CAMPS

Seven trail camps are currently available for year-round overnight use along or close to the Skyline-to-the-Sea Trail. Each is described in detail below. With the exception of Castle Rock Trail Camp, all trail camps require advance reservations. *Reservations* can be made up to 60 days in advance by calling (831) 338-8861, 10 A.M.–5 P.M. Monday-Saturday. Sites cost $5 per night and there is a $5 non-refundable reservation fee that must be mailed to secure the site (21600 Big Basin Way, Boulder Creek, CA 95006). Overnight fees are paid upon arrival at the trailhead. A maximum of six people are allowed per site, campfires and pets are prohibited, outhouses are provided, and water is available at some locations (see below). Trail camps are designated for en route camping only and backpackers may only stay one night at each location. The sites themselves are first-come, first-pick upon arrival.

SANTA CRUZ MTNS

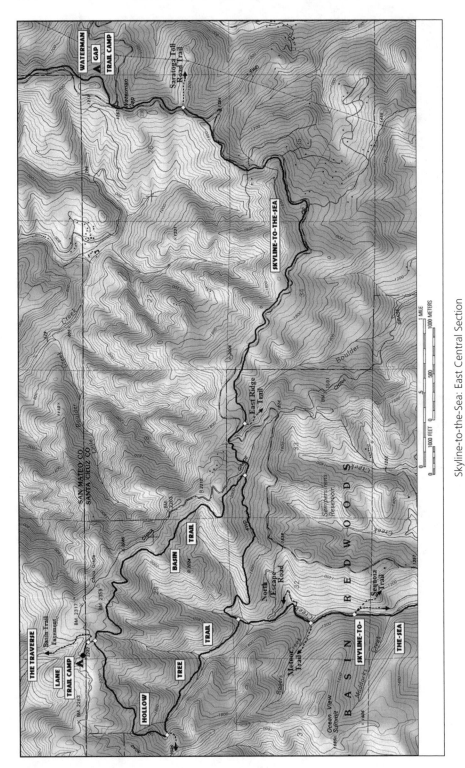

Skyline-to-the-Sea: East Central Section

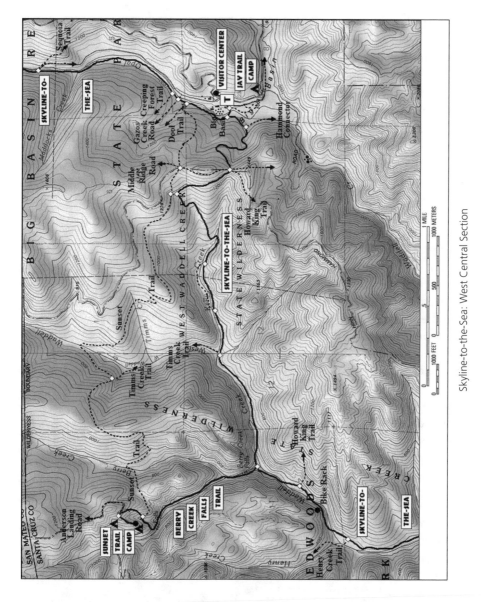

Skyline-to-the-Sea: West Central Section

SANTA CRUZ MTNS

With the exception of popular Sunset Trail Camp, the trail camps are sel-dom full and reservations are usually easy. For summer Saturdays and holiday weekends, however, always reserve as far in advance as possible.

Looking to complete the hike in two long days? The recommended overnight stops are Lane Trail Camp (quiet and isolated) or Jay Trail Camp (busy and noisy). For those taking three or more days, a variety of trail camp combinations can be utilized depending on preference.

Castle Rock Trail Camp is 2.7 miles from the Castle Rock trailhead and 6.9 miles from Waterman Gap Trail Camp. The largest trail camp along the route, it offers 20 sites tucked in the thick brush of a Knob-cone pine forest and is the best option for those starting the journey late in the day. Privacy is good to excellent, water is available, and a picnic table is provided at each site. This is the only trail camp in the entire Bay Area that allows campfires (outside of fire season only, typically December-May) and firewood is actually available for purchase on a self-serve basis at the camp itself ($5/bundle). Sites are first-come, first-serve, and the camp reputedly never fills—register at the Castle Rock main entrance.

Waterman Gap Trail Camp is 6.4 miles from Saratoga Gap, 6.9 miles from Castle Rock Trail Camp, and located a short distance from the Highway 236/9 junction. Six sites shelter beneath a young forest of live oak, Douglas-fir, madrone, and small redwoods. Privacy is fair to good and water is usually available, but no other facilities are provided.

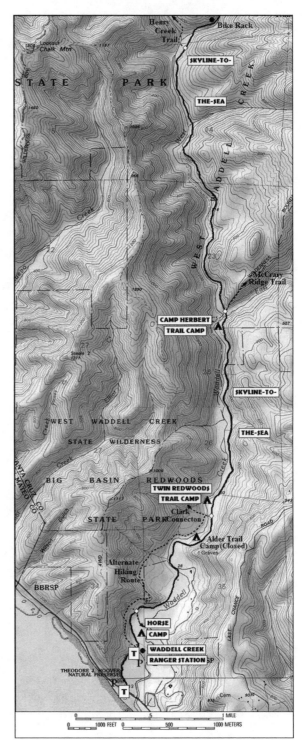

Skyline-to-the-Sea: Lower Section

SANTA CRUZ MTNS

While the nearby highways are not visible from camp, the regular traffic is intrusively audible and detracts from the wilderness experience.

Lane Trail Camp is 8.5 miles from Waterman Gap Trail Camp and 6.0 miles from Big Basin HQ on the northeastern border of Big Basin Redwoods State Park. Located 3.0 miles off the Skyline-to-the-Sea Trail, it is accessed via Basin and Hollow Tree trails. An overnight stay here adds an extra 4.2 miles and 700 feet of elevation gain to the overall journey. Six lightly used sites are available in a dense forest of tanoak with small live oaks, madrone, Douglas-fir, and redwoods interspersed. *Water is not available* anywhere near camp and the last reliable source is at Waterman Gap Trail Camp (a few ephemeral trickles can be found along Basin Trail during rainy season). Unfortunately, wild pigs regularly bulldoze the ground here and many sites have been completely dug up in the recent past.

Jay Trail Camp is 6.0 miles from Lane Trail Camp, 9.8 miles from Waterman Gap Trail Camp, and located in the main visitor complex surrounding Big Basin HQ. Situated adjacent to Highway 236 in redwood forest, the six sites are designated exclusively for backpackers heading to or from a trail camp. Advantages of staying here are the amenities—water is available, hot showers can be purchased in adjacent Blooms Creek Campground (\$.25/2 minutes), and basic provisions are available for purchase at the small camp store near HQ. Drawbacks are the crowds, noise, and lack of privacy that accompany its location in the busy heart of one of the Bay Area's most popular parks. Not the best wilderness experience.

Sunset Trail Camp is 5.3 miles from Big Basin HQ, 7.8 miles from Waddell Beach, and situated in a pleasant, second-growth redwood forest. Offering 10 sites spread between two areas, it is located 1.2 miles off the Skyline-to-the-Sea Trail (adding 2.4 miles to the overall journey) and accessed via fairy tale-perfect Berry Creek Falls Trail. Privacy is fair to good. Sunset is the most popular trail camp due to its location near the waterfalls, its access via beautiful old-growth redwood forest, and its ideal location for overnight loop trips from Big Basin HQ. It is often full. While water is not provided in camp, perennial Berry Creek is a third of a mile away.

Camp Herbert is 7.2 miles from Big Basin HQ, 4.5 miles from Sunset Trail Camp, and 3.0 miles from Waddell Beach. Located in a delightful, second-growth grove of redwoods and towering bay trees adjacent to mellifluous Waddell Creek, the six lightly-used sites offer good to excellent privacy. The substantial waterway (located below the confluence of East and West Waddell creeks) and surrounding scenery are evocative of the Sierra Nevada foothills. Water is not provided but Waddell Creek is accessible.

Twin Redwoods Trail Camp is 1.3 miles from Camp Herbert, 8.5 miles from Big

Basin HQ, and 1.7 miles from Waddell Beach in a shady copse of giant bay trees adjacent to Waddell Creek. On the edge of the redwood forest, the camp offers views up-canyon into ever thickening woods and provides open and spacious sites with good privacy. Water is not provided but Waddell Creek is readily accessible.

Alder Trail Camp is 1.5 miles from Waddell Beach, 0.2 mile below Twin Redwoods Camp, and 8.7 miles from Big Basin HQ. As of this writing, *Alder Trail Camp is closed indefinitely*—the torrential rains of the 1998-99 *El Niño* season flooded Waddell Creek, inundated the camp, and forced its closure. The camp is situated in an open area of young alders adjacent to Waddell Creek and may reopen in the future. Check with park staff for a current update.

DRIVING DIRECTIONS

To Reach the Trailhead at Saratoga Gap: Simply follow Highway 35 or Highway 9 to their intersection atop Skyline Ridge. Water is not available but a large parking area and picnic area makes for convenient last-minute packing. Note again that no overnight parking is permitted here.

To Reach the Trailhead at Castle Rock: Take Highway 35 south of the Highway 9 junction for 2.5 miles; the posted entrance is located on the west side of the road. Water is not available.

To Reach the Trailhead at Big Basin Headquarters: Take Highway 236 west from one of two junctions on Highway 9. Approaching from Highway 35 to the north, the upper turnoff is 5.8 miles below the Highway 35/9 junction. From this turnoff, Highway 236 is a one-lane twister that reaches the visitor center in 8.0 miles—RVs and trailers are not recommended. Approaching from the south, the lower turnoff is in Boulder Creek. This easier driving section of Highway 236 reaches the visitor center and headquarters complex in 9.0 miles. The trailhead is located across the road from the visitor center. Water is readily available. *Public transportation* is available to the park from downtown Santa Cruz on weekends from April through October. For more information and a current schedule, call Santa Cruz Metro at (831) 425-8600 or go online at www.scmtd.com.

To Reach the Trailhead at Waddell Beach: Take Highway 1 to Waddell Beach, located 4.0 miles north of Davenport. Turn inland at the closed (but unlocked) gate found north of Waddell Creek (not the Rancho del Oso Nature and History Center entrance). After closing the gate behind you, follow the road for a half mile to the Waddell Creek Ranger Station and parking lot. *Public transportation* is available daily to Waddell Beach from the Metro Center in downtown Santa Cruz on Santa Cruz Metro Route 40. For a current schedule call (831) 425-8600 or go online at www.scmtd.com.

TRAIL DESCRIPTIONS

The journey is divided into eight separate sections below. Five of them follow the Skyline-to-the-Sea Trail on its route from Saratoga Gap to Waddell Beach and list the hike's cumulative mileage at trail junctions and other land-marks. The remaining three sections describe the alternate route from Castle Rock State Park, the side-trip to Lane Trail Camp, and the return journey from Berry Creek Falls to Big Basin HQ via Sunset Trail Camp. Listed mileages in these sections are for the featured side-trips only. Note that the author found considerable discrepancies between the trail mileages listed in park literature, on trail signs, and as measured by topographic map. Given these inconsisten-cies, the distances included below have been made as accurate as possible.

Saratoga Gap to Waterman Gap Trail Camp

At the Highway 35/9 junction (0.0/2600), the large rest area offers a brief glimpse east of the developed Bay Area. To leave it all behind, cross the highway and follow signs toward the trailhead. Found on the south side of Highway 9, 50 yards from the junction, the posted start of your adventure includes an informative sign about historic Saratoga Gap Road.

Initial vegetation is mixed-evergreen forest: the drooping needles and rough bark of Douglas-fir; the fragrant scent of bay leaves; the smooth, peeling skin of twisting madrones; the large, spiny leaves of tanoak; the curling, cupped leaves of coast live oaks; the deciduous foliage of big leaf maple. Bear right to remain on the Skyline-to-the-Sea Trail at the junction with Saratoga Gap Trail (0.1/2500) and keep a close eye for the next junction with Saratoga Toll Road Trail (0.4/2480). Here the Skyline-to-the-Sea Trail branches right to climb up and cross Highway 9, while the more obvious trail (Saratoga Toll Road Trail) continues straight and begins to descend away from the highway.

To the sea!

After crossing the road, the Skyline-to-the-Sea trail closely parallels Highway 9 for the next 1.5 miles, passing junctions on the right for Nutmeg Trail (0.8/2500) and Red Mountain Trail (1.0/2500), followed by a junction with Summit Meadows Trail (1.2/2500) on the left. Summit Meadows Trail crosses

SANTA CRUZ MTNS

Highway 9 and offers a slightly quieter alternate route before rejoining the main trail at Sempervirens Point. Continue on the Skyline-to-the-Sea Trail, walking among coyote brush, blackberry tangles, poison oak, and wood rose in the young mixed-evergreen forest. Soon the first redwoods appear, nice second-growth up to 4 feet in diameter. The trail then encounters a broad dirt road above some large green water tanks—follow the road to cross Highway 9 and reach the expansive vista of Sempervirens Point (1.9/2350'). Looking south, most of the San Lorenzo River drainage can be seen descending toward Santa Cruz and Monterey Bay. West, two prominent ridges define the topography— 2000 foot-high Butano Ridge, closer and almost directly west; and equally tall Bonny Doon Ridge, farther away and southwest. Big Basin and the Waddell Creek drainage are hidden between the two ridges, flowing west to meet the faintly visible Pacific Ocean.

From Sempervirens Point the trail descends south along the low divide between the San Lorenzo River drainage (south) and the Pescadero Creek drainage (north) through thick and shady mixed-evergreen forest. Highway 9 weaves in and out of sight as the trail parallels its route, crossing several small spur roads before reaching the junction with Beckhuis Road (3.5/1800) on the left. Those beginning from Castle Rock State Park join the main route here.

Past Beckhuis Road the trail steadily descends and remains close to and south of Highway 9, crossing several more fire roads en route. Redwoods and buckeye trees appear in damp, shady spots along this section, while a scrubby chaparral community of coyote brush, manzanita, chamise, and sticky monkey flower grows on drier, sunnier west-facing slopes. Before long the trail curves away from Highway 9 to reach Waterman Gap Trail Camp (6.4/1350).

Castle Rock Trailhead to Waterman Gap Trail Camp

Use the description in the backpacking chapter *Castle Rock State Park* to proceed to Castle Rock Trail Camp (2.7/2400). From the Main Camp area of the trail camp, continue on wide Saratoga Gap Trail as it descends and quickly reaches the junction with Frog Flat Trail on the left (3.0/2240). (Those camping at Frog Flat Area can take narrower Frog Flat Trail to reach this junction.) Follow Saratoga Gap Trail as it drops into the moist gully of Craig Springs Creek, one of the many headwaters of the San Lorenzo River. After crossing the flowing stream beneath Douglas-fir and tanoak, the trail curves left and reaches the junction with Travertine Springs Trail (3.4/2100). Bear left onto it. Travertine Springs Trail initially parallels just above Craig Springs Creek, but soon banks right to begin a 2-mile undulating traverse around the upper San Lorenzo headwaters. The broad trail winds along a south-facing, chaparral-clad slope and then makes a steep descent beneath power lines to cross the young San Lorenzo River itself on a wooden bridge (4.4/1680). From here you continue to traverse and pass through chaparral interspersed with an open forest of madrone, tanoak, and young Douglas-fir to reach the trail's namesake, Travertine Springs (5.2/1760). Massive bay trees thrive in this moist spot; the spring is protected by a wooden fence. Human artifacts and ramshackle structures dot the flat, open area and hint at an unknown past. Continuing past the spring, you cross a small wooden bridge and soon encounter the junction with Saratoga Toll Road Trail (5.5/1800).

Turning left on wide Saratoga Toll Road Trail, the hike heads for another headwater stream of the San Lorenzo River, Tin Can Creek. The trail narrows as it heads downward and navigates past a culvert, a dam, and then an old, damaged bridge. It then curves south past Tin Can Creek to reach the junction with Beckhuis Road Trail (6.3/1550). Turn right on Beckhuis Road and make the curvaceous climb to connect with the Skyline-to-the-Sea Trail, reached either via the main road or the cutoff trail that splits left along the way (6.5/1660). Upon reaching the main route (6.7/1800), turn left and proceed as described above to reach Waterman Gap Trail Camp (9.6/1350).

Waterman Gap Trail Camp to Basin Trail Junction

Note that listed mileages in this section correspond to the Skyline-to-the-Sea Trail route continuing from Saratoga Gap. Those who have taken the Castle Rock variation should add 3.2 miles to calculate their total distance traveled.

From Waterman Gap Trail Camp (6.4/1350), the trail narrows and briefly climbs before descending to cross Highway 9 and then Mill Road (6.6/1280). After passing Mill Road, the trail crosses Highway 236 and parallels it briefly on the south side before reaching the junction with Saratoga Toll Road Trail on the left (7.0/1300). From here, the trail again crosses Highway 236 and follows it for several miles as it slowly undulates upward along the San Lorenzo River/Pescadero Creek divide, crossing several private roads en route. Surrounded by private property managed for lumber production, the trail remains within a narrow corridor of state land in a dense, second-growth forest of thin redwoods, Douglas-fir, tanoak, and huckleberry bushes. Again the trail crosses Highway 236 (10.3/1900) and finally curves away from the road; Big Basin Redwoods State Park is only a short distance ahead.

Any questions?

While the park boundary is not marked, the transition is readily apparent as several large, old-growth trees appear in a noticeably older forest. After reaching the junction with East Ridge Trail by trickling Boulder Creek (11.0/1780), you turn uphill, cross Highway 236 one more time (11.1/1820), and then make the final climb out of the San

Lorenzo River watershed to reach paved China Grade Road (11.6/1980). Here the foliage changes abruptly from the damp redwood forest of a shady north-facing slope to the dry chaparral of a sun-exposed, south-facing hillside. The presence of coyote brush, toyon, yerba santa, buck brush, and canyon live oak marks this dramatic ecologic change. Excellent views appear beyond the low-lying vegetation, encompassing the deep Waddell Creek drainage and the still-distant Pacific Ocean to the southwest. Crossing the road, the trail quickly encounters the junction with narrow Basin Trail on the right (11.7/1980). Those headed to Lane Trail Camp for the night should bear right on Basin Trail and refer to the trail description below. Those continuing directly to Big Basin HQ should proceed straight ahead and skip the following section.

Side-trip to Lane Trail Camp

This 6-mile side-trip from the Skyline-to-the-Sea Trail follows Basin Trail to Lane Trail Camp and then returns to the main route via Hollow Tree Trail. Rejoining the Skyline-to-the-Sea Trail 1.8 miles past the Basin Trail junction, this loops adds an extra 4.2 miles and 700 feet of elevation gain/loss to the over-all journey.

From the junction with the Skyline-to-the-Sea Trail (0.0/1960), Basin Trail begins an undulating, gradually rising traverse along the uppermost slopes of the Waddell Creek watershed. After passing several of the many excellent view-points found along this section, the trail enters the shade of dense madrone trees and continues through a more diverse mixed-evergreen forest of Douglas-fir, tanoak, coast live oak, and the occasional redwood. Cresting a small rise, the trail then curves right and enters a region marked in recent years by wildfire. After passing the flame-blackened trunks of gnarled redwoods on a north-facing hillside, the trail returns to the south-facing slopes and a drier world dominated by Knobcone pines. A spindly conifer with namesake cones bursting from everywhere (including on branches and trunks), Knobcone pines survive through a process called serotiny—their cones open only during wildfire. Freshly opened cones populate the burned-out, nutrient-rich soil with a mas-sive influx of seeds, resulting in a region dominated by young trees. As the trail passes through this unusual forest, chaparral such as manzanita and sticky monkey flower can be found intermixed in the dry environment.

Undulating slowly upward the trail next winds through unusual sandstone outcrops dotted with open chaparral and excellent views. Following this rocky and boulder-strewn section, the trail returns to shady north-facing slopes where redwoods instantly reappear. The trail passes three small ephemeral creeks in a forest of tanoak, madrone, and live oak, and then turns abruptly uphill to follow a narrow creek gully to reach a four-way junction (3.1/2280). Hollow Tree Trail—your continuing route—goes left, but Lane Trail Camp is straight ahead, a short 0.1 mile from this junction on a narrow, slightly overgrown trail.

A right turn at the junction takes you to China Grade Road and the start of the Basin Trail Easement, connecting Portola Redwoods and Big Basin Redwoods state parks (described in the backpacking chapter *The Traverse*).

After sleeping like a baby, begin the return descent on Hollow Tree Trail as it winds through thick vegetation regenerating from the recent wildfire. Views are generally obscured by the dense underbrush as the trail contours through the burn zone—blackened young redwoods less than a foot in diameter indicate how recently the area charred. A few old-growth redwood survivors appear intermittently as well, demonstrating their resiliency and resistance to wildfire with burn marks more than 30 feet off the ground. The trail's final view soon opens up, looking down the drainage of Opal Creek and the direction of descent. After crossing the Opal Creek headwaters by a massive redwood tree, the trail ends its contouring traverse by the large metal detritus of Johansen Shingle Mill (built 1927). Massive boilers and large metal pieces can be explored just off the trail near a memorial bench that asks, EVERYBODY HAPPY? Passing beneath young redwood forest, the trail then drops steeply down the narrow creek gully and quickly reaches a short connector trail leading to Middle Ridge Fire Road (4.6/1780). Bearing left, the trail continues its steep descent, makes two creek crossings, and then parallels the flowing stream as it babbles among moss-coated boulders. Crossing yet another small tributary, the trail contours through a lush, lesser burned forest before rejoining the Skyline-to-the Sea Trail (6.0/1270). Bear right and follow the description below.

Basin Trail Junction to Big Basin HQ

From the junction with Basin Trail (11.7/1980), the Skyline-to-the-Sea Trail continues through dense chaparral punctuated by spindly Knobcone pines and the hike's final views. After traversing along the slopes, you then turn downhill on a small ridgeline before curving right to re-enter the lush world of redwood forest. The trail crosses two small headwater trickles of Opal Creek, the first waters of the Waddell Creek drainage, shortly before the junction with Hollow Tree Trail (13.5/1270) and the return route from Lane Trail Camp.

Let the glory begin! For the next 8 miles, the Skyline-to-the-Sea Trail remains entirely within magnificent old-growth redwood forest. After crossing Opal Creek on a wooden walkway, the trail follows the stream as it rushes by huge chain ferns and massive redwoods to reach paved North Escape Road near an informative kiosk (14.0/1060). Cross Opal Creek on the paved bridge, then immediately bear right off the pavement to briefly parallel the road away from the creek. Rejoining the road for a moment before continuing to the right, the trail next reaches the junction with Meteor Trail (14.2/1070). Continuing straight, the route touches the road again where it again crosses Opal Creek on a wide bridge (14.5/1040). While Sequoia Trail continues on the opposite side, the Skyline-to-the-Sea Trail leaves the road and remains on the right side of Opal

Creek. It lines close to the water past the fluted perfection of giant redwood trunks to next reach Maddocks Creek and some interesting history. Here, an interpretive placard tells the story of Maddock, an intrepid early settler who built an entire cabin on this site from a single redwood tree. The soft leaves of hazel bushes appear as the muddy trail continues and quickly crosses Creeping Forest Trail (15.4/970) and Gazos Creek Road (15.5/970), and then reaches the junction with Dool Trail (15.6/960). Named for the third park warden of Big Basin, Dool Trail is the return route for those making the overnight loop trip to Sunset Trail Camp (see below). The Skyline-to-the-Sea Trail continues straight, then reaches the junction for the Big Basin HQ area on the left (15.9/950). To reach Jay Trail Camp, the park headquarters and visitor center, and the goodies for sale at the park general store, turn left here to cross Opal Creek and proceed the short distance to the main complex of buildings along Highway 236. Jay Trail Camp can be found a quarter mile south of park HQ on the north side of the highway.

Big Basin HQ to Berry Creek Falls

From the trailhead parking lot across from the visitor center, take broad Redwood Trail beyond the restrooms and cross Opal Creek to rejoin the Skyline-to-the-Sea Trail at the earlier junction (15.9/950). Bear left and continue toward Berry Creek Falls at the junction with Hammond Connector (16.0/970) and begin a steady climb out of the East Waddell Creek drainage. After several switchbacks, the trail crests into the West Waddell Creek drainage at a junction with Howard King Trail (16.7/1320).

Continuing straight, you pass a connector to Sunset Trail on the right (17.1/1170) as the trail rapidly descends though a spectacular old-growth forest dominated by the thick trunks of mature redwoods—dozens of perfect trees fill the forest view in every direction. Crossing a bridge over Kelly Creek, note the profusion of giant chain ferns that fill the creek bed. As the trail then traverses above the creek, an alternate route splits right to more closely follow the stream's course before rejoining the main trail 0.4 mile later. At the next junction (18.4/530), Timms Creek Trail makes a hair-raising stream-crossing on slippery logs before heading upward along upper West Waddell Creek to connect with Sunset Trail. The canyon gets narrower and rockier as Skyline-to-the-Sea continues downstream, drops to cross West Waddell Creek, briefly climbs to reach a tantalizing view of Berry Creek Falls, and then descends to reach the junction with Berry Creek Falls Trail (19.8/350) at the confluence of the two creeks. This is the turnoff for Sunset Trail Camp and the return loop to headquarters. Even those continuing to the ocean should drop their packs here and make the brief side trip to magical Berry Creek Falls (next section).

Side trip to Berry Creek Falls, Sunset Trail Camp, and the Return Loop to Big Basin HQ

From the creek confluence (0.0/350), Berry Creek Falls Trail immediately leads to a large wooden viewing platform for the waterfall. Unless a recent storm has swollen the waters, Berry Creek Falls are thin and drop in small cascades that mist the lush surrounding greenery. Thimbleberry and sword fern coat the damp ground below; tanoak and redwoods rise above; and 5-finger ferns wave from the surrounding steep, mossy slopes. Passing near the bottom of the water-fall, the trail then climbs steeply above the falls and crosses Berry Creek. The muddy track stays close to the water in a fairy-tale world and soon reaches tumbling Silver Falls. After climbing above Silver Falls on a thrilling vertical section protected with cables near the top, the trail then reaches Golden Falls and its series of distinct cascades pour-ing in waterslide fashion over brilliant orange sandstone. The trail curves right to climb out of the narrow creek canyon and reaches the junction with Sunset Trail (1.0/770). Ocean-bound hikers can turn around here.

Silver Falls

To reach Sunset Trail Camp, bear left and follow the narrow trail as it climbs up steep slopes through a sud-denly drier world of Knobcone pines, manzanita, live oak, and golden chin-quapin to reach Anderson Landing Road in 0.2 mile by a fragrant outhouse. Six sites are available directly across the road (follow the signs), while the remaining four are located 0.1 mile and 70 feet lower, surrounding the large turnout and end of Anderson Landing Road.

To return to Big Basin HQ, follow Sunset Trail as it crosses Berry Creek on a solid wooden bridge before weaving over a small divide separating West Wad-dell and Berry creeks. Fleeting views of both drainages open up before the trail descends to the Timms Creek Trail junction (2.5/780). A long, undulating, and rising traverse from here along Sunset Trail passes the earlier connector trail (4.5/1200), then Middle Ridge Road (4.7/1340), and finally hits Dool Trail immediately before returning to the Skyline-to-the-Sea Trail (5.2/960). Turn

SANTA CRUZ MTNS

right and proceed 0.3 mile to reach the earlier junction for Redwood Trail and Big Basin HQ.

Berry Creek Falls Trail to Waddell Beach

Note: The following backpacking chapter *Inland-from-the-Sea* describes this section in reverse order from Waddell Beach and discusses the area's unique history in greater detail.

From the junction with Berry Creek Falls Trail (19.8/350), the Skyline-to-the-Sea Trail descends to cross rushing West Waddell Creek on a seasonal bridge; those arriving in the winter months may have to ford the creek. A spider paradise, the arcing big leaf maples provide ideal hunting grounds for the insect prey flying up the open creek corridor. Dozens of perfect webs are everywhere, their strands glistening with the moisture of fog and rain. Beyond this point the singletrack trail widens to become the fire road that marks the past limits of logging activity. The forest immediately transforms into denser, younger second-growth as you pass the junction for Howard King Trail (20.1/350) and re-cross the creek to reach a bike rack for those traveling by pedal from the coast.

From here the route follows the wide and mostly level fire road for the remainder of the hike. After crossing the stream again the trail passes a few scattered old-growth trees and momentarily narrows to skirt around a large wash-out before the junction with Henry Creek Trail (20.6/300). The canyon now begins to broaden as members of the approaching coastal scrub community reach inland—ceanothus, sticky monkey flower, coyote brush, coffee berry, blackberry tangles, poison oak, and stinging nettle. Alder, buckeye, and big leaf maple begin to dominate the watercourses as the trail slowly descends to reach the junction with McCrary Ridge Trail (23.0/100). After crossing an arching metal bridge over East Waddell Creek—whose headwaters you followed along Opal Creek 10 miles earlier—the trail reaches Camp Herbert (23.1/100).

Past Camp Herbert, a switchback section avoids a bad section of road and the trail runs along the boundary between parkland and gated private property on the left. Redwoods become increasingly scarce as poison oak explodes in abundance. The hike continues creekside past live oak, bay, and buckeye. On the left, the muddy brown water from feeder creeks passing through private property contrasts markedly with the crystalline streams flowing through undisturbed parkland. A broad flood plain on the right and huge piles of driftwood indicate the power of Waddell Creek at high-water stage. Soon the large, two-headed redwood tree appears that gives Twin Redwoods Trail Camp its name (24.4/60).

Past Twin Redwoods, the Skyline-to-the-Sea Trail quickly encounters a junction on the right leading to Clark Connection Trail and an alternate, hikers-only route to Waddell Creek Ranger Station. To take this narrower, less-traveled trail, bear right to cross Waddell Creek and then turn left (downstream) as

Clark Connection Trail continues up the slopes. The trail climbs briefly to begin a contouring traverse away from the creek past young Douglas-fir and buckeye trees, then crosses several small ephemeral creeks and offers a few intermittent views of the area—including a glimpse of the Pacific Ocean—before descending to reach Waddell Creek Ranger Station.

If remaining on the broad and easier road past this junction, you reach closed Alder Camp on the right (24.6/40) shortly before passing through the hike's final redwood grove. Here, among healthy second-growth trees, a huge and gnarled specimen known as the Eagle Tree was spared the logging ax. Widening as it passes a gated private road on the left, the broad trail crosses Waddell Creek for the final time and passes through a section of private property on a right-of-way—please stay on the road. After curving around a large field of coyote brush, lupine, and wild onion, you pass another private road shortly before reaching Horse Camp and Waddell Creek Ranger Station (25.6/20). The hike's final journey to the beach follows the paved road from the parking area to the unlocked gate by Highway 1. Be watchful as you cross the busy road to reach the sandy expanse of Waddell Beach and journey's end by the sea (26.1/0). Congratulations!

SANTA CRUZ MTNS

PARKS CONTACT INFORMATION

Big Basin Redwoods State Park, 21600 Big Basin Way, Boulder Creek, CA 95006, (831) 338-8860 (recorded message) or (831) 338-8861, www.bigbasin.org, www.parks.ca.gov.

Castle Rock State Park, 15000 Skyline Blvd., Los Gatos, CA 95030, (408) 867-2952, www.parks.ca.gov.

Giving Back

Sempervirens Fund is dedicated to preserving, expanding, and linking parklands in the Santa Cruz Mountains. Drawer BE, Los Altos, CA 94023-4054, (650) 968-4509, www.sempervirens.org.

Inland-from-the-Sea

Coastside Big Basin access and lightly used trail camps

The Park: Big Basin Redwoods State Park

Distances: To Twin Redwoods Trail Camp, 2.4 miles round-trip; To Camp Herbert Trail Camp, 5.0 miles round-trip; To Berry Creek Falls, 11.6 miles round-trip

Total Elevation Gain/Loss: To Twin Redwoods, 200/200; To Camp Herbert, 300/300; To Berry Creek Falls, 500/500

Trip Length: 2 Days

Difficulty: ★★

Best Times: Spring through Fall

Recommended Maps: *Big Basin Redwoods State Park Map, Trail Map of the Santa Cruz Mountains 2;* USGS 7.5-min *Point Año Nuevo, Franklin Point*

After draining old-growth redwood wild, Waddell Creek flows through the broad valley of Rancho del Oso to end its journey at Waddell Beach. Winding alongside it, the Skyline-to-the-Sea Trail provides both hikers and bikers access from the coast to the magnificent waterfalls and old-growth forests of central Big Basin Redwoods State Park. Rich human history and great ecologic diversity are enjoyed along the way.

In 1769, Captain Juan Gaspar de Portolá led a Spanish expedition north from Baja California in search of an overland route to Monterey Bay. Mistakenly passing his intended destination, Portolá continued north into the Santa Cruz Mountains. Portolá and his scurvy-ridden men rested for several days in October 1769 at the mouth of Waddell Creek, where the plentiful seafood and small game allowed them to regain their strength. Rejuvenated, the men dubbed the valley Cañada de la Salud ("Canyon of Health"). A few weeks later, they became the first Europeans to discover San Francisco Bay.

Following the gold rush, the easy costal access and giant

redwoods attracted William Waddell to the area. Under his direction, the area was heavily logged from 1867-1875 and a small town sprang up in the valley to house the forest workers. Waddell was later killed by a grizzly bear. Following this natural retribution, the land was divided into small homesteads populated by hardy folks scrapping a living from the land. Logging continued on a smaller scale until the mid-20th century and several mills operated along the banks of Waddell Creek.

During the early 1900s, construction of the Ocean Shore Railroad began to connect San Francisco and Santa Cruz. A work camp was established at Waddell Beach (1904-1906), but the 1906 earthquake disrupted plans and the railroad never made it so far south. The company shut down its limited San Mateo County operations in 1920 (see the camping chapter *Half Moon Bay State Beach* for more information). Today wind and winter waves occasionally expose remnants of this era near the Waddell Beach parking area.

In 1898, Theodore Hoover first espied the pleasant valley of Waddell Creek and determined to make it his future home. Brother of future president Herbert Hoover, Theodore began acquiring land in 1913 and soon owned roughly 3000

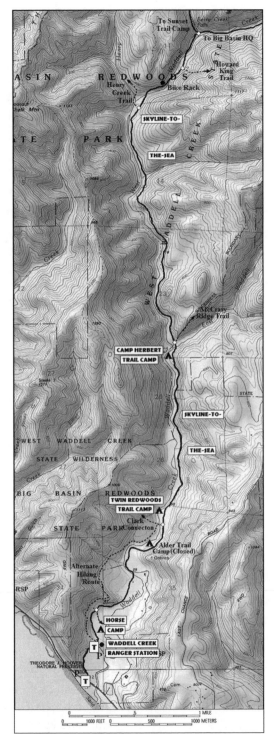

Inland-from-the-Sea

acres of prime real estate. Stretching from Waddell Beach 5 miles inland along the rich bottomlands and adjacent slopes of Waddell Creek to the boundary with Big Basin Redwoods State Park, it was dubbed Rancho del Oso (or "Ranch of the Bear," despite the fact that the last grizzly in the area was killed during the 1880s). In 1975 the family began transferring ownership of most of the ranch to California State Parks, including the land that connects Big Basin Redwoods State Park to the Pacific Ocean. The Hoovers still hold parcels of private property and continue to live here as they have for five generations.

The primary source of historic information for this hike is *Rancho del Oso Trails* by Hulda Hoover McClean. This booklet, along with more detailed information on the history and hiking trails of the Rancho del Oso area, can be obtained at the nearby Rancho del Oso Nature and History Center (open noon–4 P.M. weekends). The posted turn-off from Highway 1 is on the south side of Waddell Creek, a short quarter mile from the Waddell Beach parking area.

Hike Overview

Your journey inland from Waddell Beach on the Skyline-to-the-Sea Trail passes Alder Camp (currently closed) and lightly-used Twin Redwoods and Camp Herbert trail camps en route to Berry Creek Falls and superlative old-growth redwood forest. For most of its length, the hike follows wide, old ranch roads with minimal elevation gain. While the trail is open to bikes for most of its length, the final half mile to Berry Creek Falls is for hikers only—a rack is provided to store bikes while exploring this section on foot. In general, the lesser-traveled Rancho del Oso region provides a delightful contrast to the far busier world found inland around the central Big Basin complex on Highway 236. Close to the coast, conditions are typically cool year-round and fog is common throughout summer. Water is available near the trailhead at Horse Camp. Fishing is prohibited.

The Trail Camps

See the previous *Skyline-to-the-Sea* chapter for descriptions of the trail camps, as well as information on reservations, costs, and regulations. While advance reservations are required for Twin Redwoods and Camp Herbert trail camps, they reputedly seldom fill. Note that the more popular Sunset Trail Camp is also an overnight option on this hike, located 500 feet higher and 1.2 miles beyond Berry Creek Falls (a 14-mile round-trip from the trailhead).

To Reach the Trailhead

Take Highway 1 to Waddell Beach, located 4 miles north of Davenport. Turn inland at the closed (but unlocked) gate found north of Waddell Creek (not the Rancho del Oso Nature and History Center entrance) and follow the road for a half mile to the Waddell Creek Ranger Station and parking lot. Note that this parking area is designated for backpackers only—day-hikers and bikers must leave their vehicles at Waddell Beach. *Public transportation* is available daily to Waddell Beach from the Metro Center in downtown Santa Cruz on Santa Cruz Metro Route 40. For a current schedule call (831) 425-8600 or go online at www.scmtd.com.

Trail Description

From the trailhead by the Waddell Creek Ranger Station parking area (0.0/20), begin on the wide, unpaved road as it passes a hikers-only alternate trail on the left. While hikers may enjoy the narrower alternate trail as it winds along the slopes before rejoining the main route near Alder Camp, the easier bike-accessible route along the broad road is described here. Horse Camp appears quickly on the right, a broad, grassy area with a water bottle-filling spigot designated for overnight equestrian use only—contact park headquarters for more information. Beyond Horse Camp, the trail passes Monterey pine, coast live oak, bay, and Douglas-fir as it curves around a large field of coyote brush, wild onion, and abundant lupine. Passing a private road on the right

(0.3/40), you climb momentarily before descending through a section of private property on a right-of-way—please stay on the road. Note the redwood-sided house on your right across the actively farmed fields. Built in 1913, it was the Hoover family's first home on the property. The trail passes another gated private road on the right (0.8/30) after crossing clear-flowing Waddell Creek and then more closely follows the streamcourse, lined with nice Douglas-firs and buckeye trees.

The road narrows shortly after beginning a 2.5-mile-long section along the park boundary (to your right is private property). After passing some large concrete pieces left over from a fish study conducted on Waddell Creek in the late 1930s, the trail then enters the first redwood grove of the trip. Here, among healthy second-growth

Berry Creek Falls

trees, a huge and gnarled redwood known as the Eagle Tree is one of the few old-growth trees in this area left uncut by William Waddell's logging operations. Closed Alder Camp is just ahead (1.0/40); heavy rains during the 1998 El Niño

SANTA CRUZ MTNS

season flooded Waddell Creek and damaged the camp, leaving massive drift-wood piles. The impact is plainly evident today.

After passing the junction with the hikers-only alternate trail on the left, the trail soon reaches Twin Redwoods Camp (1.2/60). A former Girl Scout summer camp (1920s-1957), the location is named for the large, two-headed redwood tree growing nearby. Poison oak becomes increasingly common from here as you proceed up-canyon. The trail leaves private property behind as it narrows and switchbacks over a large 1955 landslide that buried this section of road; this is some of the most difficult biking of the trip. A short distance later is Camp Herbert (2.5/100), located just below the out-of-sight confluence of East and West Waddell creeks. Those staying overnight at either Twin Redwoods or Camp Herbert should drop their packs and enjoy the excursion to Berry Creek Falls with lightened loads.

Beyond Camp Herbert, the trail crosses East Waddell Creek on an arched metal bridge and reaches Forks Meadows (2.6/100). An open area today dotted with coyote brush, Forks Meadow once was the site of three different mills. Waddell constructed the first in 1867 to process the surrounding timber. At the edge of the meadow, McCrary Ridge Trail splits right.

Continuing on the Skyline-to-the-Sea Trail, the surrounding second-growth forest (note how all the trees are the same height) becomes increasingly dense as the canyon begins to palpably narrow. Plant members of the coastal scrub community—blackberry, ceanothus, coffee berry, sticky monkey flower, stinging nettle, and poison oak—slowly diminish in the increasingly lush environment. The trail parallels West Waddell Creek and winds over several small tributaries, passing the junction with Henry Creek Trail (5.0/300). It then crosses West Waddell Creek on a wooden bridge and reaches the bike rack that marks the end of the bike-accessible section as well as the former boundary between Rancho del Oso and Big Basin (5.3/320).

From here the narrower trail descends to re-cross Waddell Creek, passes the junction with Howard King Trail (5.5/350), and then crosses the creek one last time on a seasonal bridge; those arriving in the winter months may have to ford the creek. The hike then abruptly transforms into a singletrack journey through old-growth redwood forest. The surrounding trees bulge with age and grandeur as the trail quickly reaches the junction with Berry Creek Falls Trail by the confluence of West Waddell and Berry creeks (5.7/350).

The Skyline-to-the-Sea Trail continues straight up West Waddell Creek, reaching park headquarters after 4.0 miles of continuous old-growth forest, but you should bear left on Berry Creek Falls Trail to immediately reach the large wooden viewing platform by the falls (5.8/380). Unless a recent storm has swollen the waters, Berry Creek Falls are thin and drop in small cascades that mist the lush surrounding scenery. While those tired or out of time might consider turning back here, the continuing journey along Berry Creek is highly recommended. For more information on this side-trip along Berry Creek Falls Trail to Sunset Trail Camp, see the description in the preceding chapter *Skyline-to-the-Sea*. After all the fun, return the way you came.

PARK CONTACT INFORMATION

Big Basin Redwoods State Park, 21600 Big Basin Way, Boulder Creek, CA 95006, (831) 338-8860 (recorded message) or (831) 338-8861, www.bigbasin.org, www.parks.ca.gov. Waddell Creek Ranger Station sells maps and books for the area (open noon-4 P.M. weekends year-round).

Giving Back

Sempervirens Fund is dedicated to preserving, expanding, and linking parklands in the Santa Cruz Mountains. Drawer BE, Los Altos, CA 94023-4054, (650) 968-4509, www.sempervirens.org.

The Waddell Creek Association manages the Rancho del Oso Nature and History Center and enriches the park through funding interpretive and research projects. 3600 Highway 1, Davenport, CA 95017, (831) 427-2288.

Portola Redwoods State Park

A distant grove of gargantuan old-growth redwoods

The Park: Portola Redwoods State Park

Distance: 5.0 miles round-trip to trail camp; 12.0 miles round trip to Peters Creek Grove

Total Elevation Gain/Loss: 650/650 to trail camp; 2250/2250 to grove

Trip Length: 2 days

Difficulty: ★★★

Best Times: March-November

Optional Map: *Portola Redwoods State Park Map,* USGS 7.5-min *Mindego Hill*

The cloak of the redwood forest hushes sound, diffuses light, and radiates life. Travel through a dense canopy of regeneration to a shady trail camp, your base for exploring a distant stand of huge old-growth redwoods: the lightly-traveled Peters Creek Grove.

Hike Overview

The journey to Slate Creek Trail Camp winds through a thick redwood forest rejuvenating nicely from recent logging activity. From the camp, a moderately strenuous 7-mile round-trip to Peters Creek Grove rewards with ancient majesty. Nearby Slate Creek also is delightful and makes for good adventuring closer to camp. This trip also makes an excellent excursion from the park's drive-in campground (See the camping chapter *Portola Redwoods State* Park). Expect damp, cool conditions year-round as the forest canopy blocks out most sun and is often infused with fog or rain. While there is no bad time to visit the park, the trail camp is closed December-February.

Slate Creek Trail Camp

Eight sites spread along a broad forested saddle populated with a thick forest of young redwood, Douglas-fir, and tanoak.

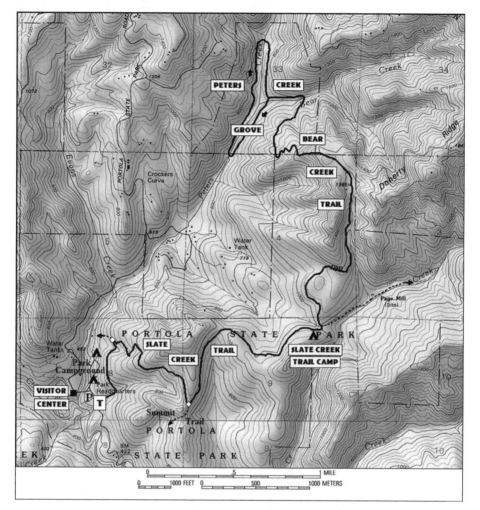

Portola Redwoods State Park

SANTA CRUZ MTNS

While water is not available in camp, perennial Slate Creek can be accessed a third of a mile and a hundred feet down from camp on Slate Creek Trail. Picnic tables and an outhouse are provided, but there are no food lockers to protect your victuals from the ravening raccoons that swarm the area at night—hang your food or it will be gone in the morning.

The trail camp receives moderate use (especially on summer weekends). Except for the busiest summer weekends and holidays, however, it is seldom full. Sites cost $10 per night and can be reserved up to two weeks in advance by contacting the park visitor center at (650) 948-9098. Campfires are prohibited.

To Reach the Trailhead

Take Highway 35 to the turnoff for Alpine Road, located 6 miles north of the Highway 35/9 junction and 7 miles south of the Highway 35/84 junction. Head south on Alpine Road and in 2.5 miles bear left on Price Avenue to continue downward for another 3 miles to the visitor center. Note that the access road is steep and winding, and that RVs and trailers are not recommended. Backpackers will need to register at the visitor center before proceeding to the trailhead, located on the left just past the campground entrance and posted for Slate Creek Trail.

Trail Description

The trail begins on Slate Creek Trail (0.0/430), passing by redwoods, canyon live oak, and the ubiquitous spiny leaves of small tanoak trees and shrubs. You quickly reach the junction with Old Tree Trail (which continues straight on a short and worthwhile side trip)—bear left toward Slate Creek Trail Camp. At the junction, note the large Douglas-fir that toppled in February 2000 due to heart rot, one of the most common forms of death for mature trees. The singletrack trail immediately climbs through still standing Douglas-firs and continues uphill past a spur trail from the campground on the left (0.5/670). Next pass a pleasant bench in the Bolton Memorial Grove before several quick switchbacks lead to a more level traverse punctuated by the appearance of California bay. Continue on Slate Creek Trail as Summit Trail joins from the right (1.3/930), an alternate route back to the park road for the return trip. From here it's a long traverse atop often steep slopes to Slate Creek Trail Camp (2.5/1000) and the junction for Peters Creek on Bear Creek Trail. Slate Creek can be accessed a short distance farther on Slate Creek Trail at a former mill site.

To continue to Peters Creek Grove, bravely pass the caution sign on Bear Creek Trail and begin the STRENUOUS 7-MILE ROUND TRIP HIKE FROM THIS POINT. Winding along Bear Creek, you may notice the decaying automobile among the big leaf maple and hazel by the creek before breaking out into an opening thick with poison oak. A huge, moss-draped coast live oak is on the right past this clearing near the high point of the hike (1450) before the trail passes through thick Douglas-fir and begins the descent into the Peters Creek drainage. A brief view of the valley appears along the ridge beyond a few California buckeye, but the steady drop is mostly uneventful . . . until the redwoods reappear. From the junction at the bottom for the Peters Creek Loop (5.0/740) either direction is good but going left first saves the fattest trees for the very end. The loop twice crosses Peters Creek; it may have to forded following winter storms. The enormous specimens upstream approach 10 feet in diameter and exhibit striking similarity to their even larger cousins, the giant sequoia. They owe their size to the ideal growing conditions and constant water supply found so close to the creek.

PARK CONTACT INFORMATION

Portola Redwoods State Park, 9000 Portola State Park Rd., Box F, La Honda, CA 94020, (650) 948-9098, www.parks.ca.gov. Visitor Center open daily in summer; in the off-season open Friday-Sunday and sporadically the rest of week.

Giving Back

Portola and Castle Rock Foundation publishes maps, brochures, and interpretive materials, and supports interpretive projects at Portola Redwoods and Castle Rock state parks through fundraising efforts. Contact the park for more information.

SANTA CRUZ MTNS

The Traverse

A long-distance epic across the Santa Cruz Mountains, from highlands to the Pacific Ocean, divided into four sections

The Parks: Hidden Villa, Rancho San Antonio Open Space Preserve, Monte Bello Open Space Preserve, Upper Stevens Creek County Park, Long Ridge Open Space Preserve, Portola Redwoods State Park, Pescadero Creek County Park, Big Basin Redwoods State Park

Distance: 39.4 miles one way

Total Elevation Gain/Loss: 6900/7400

Trip Length: 5 days

Difficulty: ★★★★

Best Times: March-November

Recommended Maps: See trail sections below

This five-day backpacking voyage across the Santa Cruz Mountains begins in the foothills above Palo Alto and ends at the Pacific Ocean. Along the way, it tours perennial streams, sweeping vistas, human history, the San Andreas Fault, old-growth redwood forest, misty waterfalls, eight parks, and six trail camps. This mega-hike crosses just one major road on its entire journey (Highway 35). It is a challenge that few have ever completed.

Hike Overview

The Traverse is divided into four sections, each of which can be completed as an individual, point-to-point overnight trip. Combine multiple sections to create a three- to four-day journey, or complete all four sections in one go for the entire five-day Traverse. Each section is described below with directions to trailheads, mileage, elevation, recommended maps, and trail camp and reservation information. Note that the trailhead-to-trailhead distances listed at the beginning of each section are different than the distances between trail camps.

Completing the full Traverse in winter is not possible; Portola Redwood's Slate Creek Trail Camp and drive-in campground are closed December-February. Campfires and dogs are prohibited throughout the hike.

SECTION 1: HIDDEN VILLA TO HIGHWAY 35 VIA BLACK MOUNTAIN TRAIL CAMP

*San Francisco Bay and mountain views,
plus a plunge into the isolated trough
of Stevens Creek and the San Andreas Fault*

The Parks: Hidden Villa, Rancho San Antonio Open Space Preserve, Monte Bello Open Space Preserve, Upper Stevens Creek County Park

Distance: 9.4 miles one way

Total Elevation Gain/Loss: 3500/1750

Trip Length: 2 days

Difficulty: ★★★★

Recommended Maps: *Trail Map of the Southern Peninsula, South Skyline Region Open Space Preserves Map,* USGS 7.5-min *Mindego Hill*

Hike Overview

Section 1 of The Traverse ascends the sheer eastern slopes of the Santa Cruz Mountains to Monte Bello Ridge and a night at Black Mountain Trail Camp. Day two combines a descent into deep Stevens Creek canyon with a steep climb back out to Skyline Ridge and Highway 35. While few people hike up Black Mountain from the east, as your route does, Stevens Creek canyon is popular with mountain bikers. Water is not available between Hidden Villa and Black Mountain Trail Camp. Note that an alternate (and easier) route to Black Mountain Trail Camp is from the main Monte Bello entrance on Page Mill Road (please see the backpacking chapter *Monte Bello Open Space Preserve*).

The Trail Camp

Black Mountain Trail Camp is situated a quarter mile from the summit of Black Mountain at 2700 feet. There are four small sites (maximum four people per site), and one group site for up to 24 people. The cost is $2 per person. The trail camp receives light use year-round. Advance reservations are required and can be made by calling Midpeninsula Regional Open Space District at (650) 691-1200. Water is available. For more information, please see the backpacking chapter *Monte Bello Open Space Preserve*.

To Reach the Trailhead

Take Interstate 280 to the El Monte Ave./Moody Road exit in Los Altos, turn left on Moody Road, and proceed 1.6 miles to the turn-off for Hidden Villa on the left. There is a $5 parking fee. Hidden Villa is closed after dusk, so if you plan on leaving a vehicle overnight, Hidden Villa asks that you contact Visitor Services at (650) 949-9704 to arrange parking. To reach the trailhead, follow the main road and turn left immediately after it crosses Adobe Creek. The trail begins beyond the ranch buildings at road's end.

Hidden Villa and its trails are only open to the public Tuesday-Sunday, from September to May. If beginning your hike on a Monday or during the summer months, use the alternate Rhus Ridge trailhead at adjacent Rancho San Antonio Open Space Preserve. To reach this trailhead, take Interstate 280 to the El Monte Ave./Moody Road exit in Los Altos, turn left on Moody Road, and proceed 0.5 mile to Rhus Ridge Road. Turn left. Rhus Ridge trailhead is on the right in 0.2 mile. Notify the Midpeninsula Regional Open Space District (contact information below) if you plan on leaving your vehicle here overnight.

Trail Description

The walk through Hidden Villa to the trailhead passes farmland once owned by Frank and Josephine Duveneck, who opened an interracial summer camp here in 1945, and an environmental education program in 1970. As they aged, the Duvenecks established a non-profit Trust to manage operations on 1600 donated acres. Today, some 20,000 young students annually attend environmental programs on the organic farm. The Trust also operates a youth hostel (see Appendix C: *Hostels of the Bay Area*), manages a summer camp, rents group facilities, and offers a variety of other fun programs for volunteers, children, and their families.

Agriculture artifacts at Hidden Villa

Just past a large, white barn (built in the 1880s, the oldest structure on Hidden Villa) you reach the unposted trailhead (0.0/580) for Adobe Creek Trail, which heads straight up the shady valley along ephemeral Adobe Creek. Entering a native world of bay and big-leaf maples, the trail quickly crosses a wooden bridge to reach the junction with Bunny Loop Trail (0.1/590). Continue straight on Adobe Creek Trail as it passes a few shady picnic tables and starts a gentle climb. Wood rose, blackberry vines, thimbleberry, scrub oak, hazel bushes, and sword and wood ferns all grow on the steep

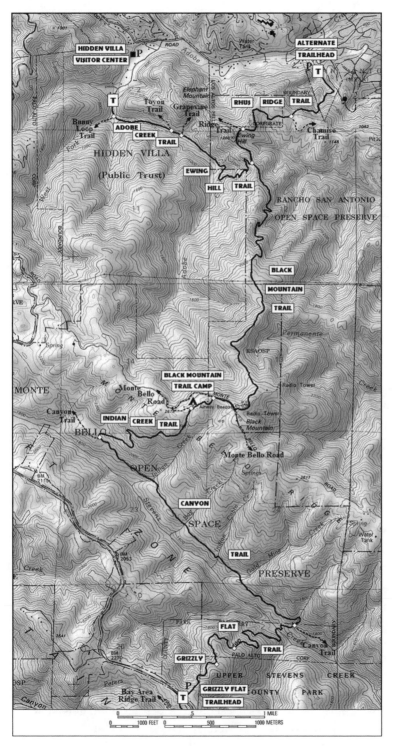

The Traverse: Section 1

surrounding slopes. Crossing the creekbed, the trail next passes Toyon Trail on the left (0.4/710). Remain on Creek Trail to climb briefly and reach the junction for Grapevine and Ewing Hill trails by a distinctive madrone tree (0.5/740).

Proceed straight on Ewing Hill Trail, which soon banks left away from the moist creek and its substantial coast live oaks. As the trail switchbacks upward, it passes through a drier chaparral community of toyon, chamise, sticky monkey flower, manzanita, buckbrush, honeysuckle vines, and the ubiquitous coyote brush. The unsullied Adobe Creek drainage spreads out below as you enter Rancho San Antonio Open Space Preserve. At the ridgetop you're treated to excellent views including Mt. Hamilton (4213′) rising beyond downtown San Jose, and Mission Peak (2517′) to the northeast. The trail crosses over the ridge and momentarily descends to reach the junction with Black Mountain and Rhus Ridge trails (1.5/1230). Those beginning from the alternate Rhus Ridge trailhead join the route here.

If beginning from the alternate Rhus Ridge Trailhead (0.0/480), follow wide Rhus Ridge Trail as it steeply climbs a forested gully to reach the meadows of the Duveneck Windmill Pasture Area and the junction with Chamise Trail (0.6/1100). Named for an old windmill that stood here until 1991, the open landscape is dotted with stalwart oaks and makes for a refreshing rest spot. Once part of the early Mexican land grant of Rancho San Antonio, the fields today provide good views east of bustling Santa Clara Valley and west to the steeply rising slopes of Black Mountain. Remain on Rhus Ridge Trail as it traverses through chaparral before descending into a shady oak forest to reach Black Mountain Trail (1.1/1140). Bear left to join the main route and begin the long Black Mountain Trail ascent.

Singletrack Black Mountain Trail steadily ascends the flanks of its namesake peak, contouring upward through a chaparral community interspersed with coast live oaks. There is a sharp ecological contrast between shadier east-facing slopes (bay, oak, ferns) and more sun-exposed south-facing slopes (chaparral). The trail steadily rises above nearby development, making numerous switchbacks before abruptly transforming into a wide service road used to access the power lines overhead (2.6/1980).

Here the route directly ascends the steep ridgeline, passing beneath two towers on an increasingly rocky and loose trail. The radio towers ahead mark your destination atop Monte Bello Ridge. Mt. Umunhum (3486′) and the southeastern Santa Cruz Mountains are visible as the route briefly crests at 2500 feet, curves around a small knoll above the upper Adobe Creek drainage, and then climbs again to finally reach a gate by the radio tower complex. Drop over the small rise to enter Monte Bello Open Space Preserve and reach Monte Bello Road (4.1/2790). While the antenna-clad summit of Black Mountain is a few hundred yards to the left, turn right on Monte Bello Road and follow signs past Indian Creek Trail to reach Black Mountain Trail Camp (4.5/2700).

After a rejuvenating night, the next day's journey begins on broad Indian Creek Trail (4.5/2730). As you descend, notice the unusually linear nature of the Stevens Creek drainage below. The San Andreas Fault runs directly along the valley bottom; its slow but inexorable movement pulverizes the rocks along its trace, creating a narrow and easily eroded trough through which Stevens Creek flows. Also notice the thick stands of Douglas-fir on the opposite valley slopes. Their presence reflects the increasing amount of precipitation that falls in the central Santa Cruz Mountains, and is a harbinger of ecological changes to come.

The trail passes through open grasslands and chaparral, then through a brief stretch of oak woodlands (watch for hawks and other raptors) before entering a shady canopy of mixed-evergreen forest near valley bottom. Here you reach the junction with wide Canyon Trail (5.5/1970). Bear left (southeast) on Canyon Trail and meander alongside the fault beneath the draping foliage of Douglas-fir and twisting limbs of bay, madrone, big-leaf maple, and canyon live oak.

Canyon Trail slowly descends past a small spring, crosses dribbling Indian Creek, and then contours along the forest margin. Open oak woodlands grow on the flanks of Black Mountain to the left. Although nearby and audible, Stevens Creek is out-of-sight and more than a hundred feet below as it flows through its narrow crease. The first specimens of tanoak and black oak appear shortly before Canyon Trail crosses another trickling creek. The trail then enters Upper Stevens Creek County Park and reaches the junction with Grizzly Flat Trail (7.5/1460).

Bear right on singletrack Grizzly Flat Trail and quickly descend to cross the crystalline waters of Stevens Creek (7.6/1340). A delightful rest stop, the creek harbors small fish, coats glistening stones, and nourishes vibrant streamside plants. Across the stream, Grizzly Flat Trail quickly becomes a wide fire road beneath mixed-evergreen forest. Passing briefly above the flowing creek, the trail then turns right and begins the steep climb to Skyline Ridge. The depth of Stevens Creek canyon is apparent in the unrelenting grade, and Black Mountain is intermittently visible through the trees as the trail ascends past two forks (8.4/1800, 8.9/2110). While all trails rejoin near the top, bearing right at both forks provides a more gradual climb. You reach Skyline Ridge at a small dirt lot beside Highway 35 (9.4/2300).

SANTA CRUZ MTNS

GOVERNING AGENCY/PARK(S) CONTACT INFORMATION

Hidden Villa, 26870 Moody Rd., Los Altos Hills, CA 94022, (650) 949-8650, www.hidenvilla.org, email: info@hiddenvilla.org. Visitor Center open 8:30 A.M.– 5 P.M. Monday-Friday, weekend hours vary depending on volunteer staff.

Midpeninsula Regional Open Space District, 330 Distel Circle, Los Altos, CA 94022-1404, (650) 691-1200, www.openspace.org, email: info@openspace.org. For reservations and trail camp information, call (650) 691-1200.

Giving Back

Those interested in supporting Hidden Villa through volunteer work or financial donations should contact the visitor center (see above) or go online at www.hiddenvilla.org/Assets/canhelp.htm.

For information about volunteer opportunities in Monte Bello Open Space Preserve and other MROSD lands, contact the district at (650) 691-1200, email: volunteer@openspace.org.

SECTION 2: HIGHWAY 35 TO PORTOLA REDWOODS STATE PARK HQ VIA SLATE CREEK TRAIL CAMP

A long, downhill descent into the secluded, redwood-filled canyon of Pescadero Creek

The Park: Long Ridge Open Space Preserve, Portola Redwoods State Park
Distance: 8.4 miles one way
Total Elevation Gain/Loss: 680/2540
Trip Length: 2 days
Difficulty ★★★
Recommended Maps: *Trail Map of the Southern Peninsula, Portola Redwoods State Park Map, Trail Map of the Santa Cruz Mountains 1,* USGS 7.5-min *Mindego Hill, Big Basin*

Hike Overview

Beginning at Grizzly Flat Trailhead on Highway 35, section two of The Traverse winds briefly along the spine of the Santa Cruz Mountains and offers far-reaching views before plummeting west to reach Portola Redwoods State Park.

(side tab) SANTA CRUZ MTNS

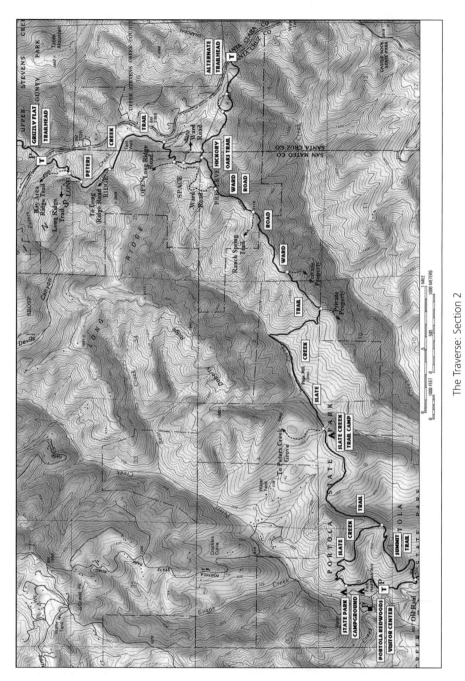

The Traverse: Section 2

🏃 SANTA CRUZ MTNS

After a night at Slate Creek Trail Camp, an easy descent through thick redwood forest deposits you at Pescadero Creek and the Portola Redwoods visitor center. The park offers an excellent drive-in campground; for more information see the camping chapter *Portola Redwoods State Park*.

The Trail Camp

Eight sites are available at Slate Creek Trail Camp in young redwood forest. While water is not available in camp, perennial Slate Creek is 0.3 mile away and can be accessed on the approach. Picnic tables and an outhouse are provided, but no food lockers are available to protect your victuals from ravening raccoons—hang your food or it will be gone in the morning. The trail camp receives moderate use and only fills on the busiest summer weekends and holidays. Sites cost $10 per night and can be reserved up to two weeks in advance by contacting the park visitor center at (650) 948-9098.

To Reach the Trailhead

Take Highway 35 to the Grizzly Flat trailhead, located 3.0 miles north of the Highway 35/9 junction and 3.0 miles south of Alpine Road. An alternate trailhead is located 1.5 miles south of Grizzly Flat on the west side of Highway 35 and reduces the hike by a mile. Note that overnight parking is prohibited along Highway 35; for the alternate trailhead, park in the Charcoal Road area 0.3 mile south of the trailhead or arrange to be dropped off.

Trail Description

The trailhead is located on the west side of Highway 35 directly across from the Grizzly Flat parking lot (0.0/2300). Free maps are often available at the large information board. Begin on Peters Creek Trail and weave through open grass and coyote brush before descending into the shade of a north-facing slope. Wild rose, blackberry, and wood and sword ferns thrive here, joined overhead by bigleaf maple, bay trees, and young Douglas-firs. Beyond another small clearing, the path crosses a minor drainage where white snowberries are visible in the fall and early winter. Poison oak rears its head shortly before the Bay Area Ridge Trail joins from the right (0.3/2150). (For the next 1.3 miles, the hike follows the Ridge Trail route.) Continue straight to cross the Peters Creek bridge and reach the junction with Long Ridge and Peters Creek trails (0.4/2150).

Bear left on Peters Creek Trail as it parallels the alder- and willow-lined creek upstream. In this shady mixed-evergreen forest, the ever-increasing amount of moisture is evidenced by the appearance of sword ferns and ground-hugging wild ginger. You pass an old apple orchard on the left (a few surviving trees still produce fruit each fall), then pass a connector trail on the right to Long Ridge Road (0.9/2200). Here Peters Creek Trail widens and passes through a large tunnel of arcing forest alongside a decaying wooden fence. Stinging nettle appears in abundance as you briefly rejoin Peters Creek before turning away from the stream to quickly reach a closed gate marking the private property of the Jukoji Retreat Center (1.6/2300).

Turn right and head toward Long Ridge Road. After crossing the small dam that encloses the adjacent pond, the trail narrows to singletrack and climbs four switchbacks to reach the junction with Long Ridge and Ward roads (2.1/2480). Some of the best views of the entire hike are approaching. For maximum views, remain on the Bay Area Ridge Trail as it goes left and up Ward Road. It then branches right in a short 0.1 mile to follow a doubletrack trail through open grasslands and sandstone outcrops to the junction with wide Hickory Oaks Trail (2.4/2450). Those beginning from the alternate trailhead join the route here.

If beginning from the alternate trailhead (0.0/2550), cross the well-hidden roadside gate and begin beneath mixed-evergreen forest on a section of the Bay Area Ridge Trail. The trail quickly crests the ridge and bears right beneath a mossy tangle of black and canyon live oaks. Follow the singletrack Bay Area Ridge Trail left as it splits briefly to contour past nice views of the Oil Creek watershed below. After rejoining the broad road, the trail descends to reach the above junction with Hickory Oaks Trail (1.0/2450).

From here you can view the terrain that encompasses the next 10 miles of The Traverse. To the southwest, beyond the deep canyon of Pescadero Creek below, the route climbs up and along Butano Ridge and heads toward out-of-sight Big Basin Redwoods State Park. Slate Creek Trail Camp and a night's rest await on the slopes 1500' below. To the northwest, the deep drainage of San Gregorio Creek is visible. Due south, Highway 9 and the Skyline-to-the-Sea Trail descend the long ridge that extends southwest from Skyline Ridge. Beyond, long Bonny Doon Ridge defines the skyline and western limits of the San Lorenzo River basin.

Follow Hickory Oaks Trail as it leaves the Bay Area Ridge Trail and drops steeply past coast live oaks and buckeyes. The twin drainages of privately-owned Oil Can Creek (left) and Portola's Slate Creek (right) are enjoyed as the route rejoins Ward Road (2.7/2300). Dropping steeply along the ridgeline, the good views continue past the junction with Ranch Spring Trail (3.0/2100) until you reach the boundary of Portola Redwoods State Park (3.1/2000) by a closed gate. Equestrians and bikes are prohibited beyond this point.

Continue the descent through increasing manzanita and coyote brush to enter the thick shade of Douglas-firs, madrone, and coast live oaks. Poison oak is common in this section. After momentarily leveling out, the trail passes the first redwood of the trip on the left and reaches Slate Creek Trail (3.6/1740). Bear right to avoid the clearly marked private property ahead and enjoy the narrowing, duff-covered trail as it undulates through young forest. A steep drop then deposits you at a large metal gate (4.1/1550).

Here Slate Creek Trail branches right off the broad road. Narrowing to singletrack, the path immediately enters the redwood forest—the small, serrated leaves of evergreen huckleberry bushes and large spiny leaves of tanoak are everywhere. Recently logged, this regenerating forest of small redwoods has a thick understory of sword ferns and poison oak. After a long descending traverse, the trail reaches the perennial waters of Slate Creek (4.8/1050). As you approach the creek, watch for the trail cutting steeply left to cross the stream.

Heading now downstream, the route parallels the refreshing waters of Slate Creek and soon reaches the reason for all this second-growth forest—the former site of Page Mill (5.5/930). Surprisingly, a grand old-growth redwood still towers overhead at this spot. From here the trail ascends above the creek to reach the saddle of Slate Creek Trail Camp and a night's R&R (5.8/1000).

(From Slate Creek Trail Camp, a 7-mile round-trip along Bear Creek Trail leads to the remote Peters Creek Grove of large, old-growth redwoods. For more information on this half-day side trip, please see the backpacking chapter *Portola Redwoods State Park*.)

After a recuperative night, continue on Slate Creek Trail as it traverses atop often-steep slopes and through thick forest. Bear right to remain on Slate Creek Trail at the junction with Summit Trail (7.0/930). After descending on several switchbacks, the trail passes a pleasant bench in the Bolton Memorial Grove and then a spur trail leading in from the park campground on the right (7.8/670). Finish the descent at the junction with Old Tree Trail (8.3/430) and turn right to quickly reach the park road (8.4/430). The Portola Redwoods Visitor Center is located down the road to the right, immediately across Pescadero Creek, and marks the end of this section (8.6/400). Backpackers continuing on The Traverse can bear left on Summit Trail to avoid the campground and visitor center and reach the park service road (see following description).

GOVERNING AGENCY/PARK(S) CONTACT INFORMATION

Midpeninsula Regional Open Space District (see above).

Portola Redwoods State Park, 9000 Portola State Park Rd., Box F, La Honda, CA 94020 (650) 948-9098, www.parks.ca.gov. Visitor Center open daily in summer; in the off-season open Fri.-Sun., sporadically the rest of week.

Giving Back

Portola and Castle Rock Foundation publishes maps, brochures, and interpretive materials, and supports interpretive projects at Portola Redwoods and Castle Rock state parks through fundraising efforts. Contact the park for more information.

For information about volunteer opportunities in Long Ridge Open Space Preserve and other MROSD lands, contact the district at (650) 691-1200, email: volunteer@openspace.org.

SECTION 3: PORTOLA REDWOODS STATE PARK TO BIG BASIN REDWOODS HQ VIA LANE TRAIL CAMP

A journey from Portola Redwoods to Big Basin Redwoods State Park via 2000-foot Butano Ridge, with old-growth redwood majesty along Opal Creek

The Park: Portola Redwoods State Park, Pescadero Creek County Park, Big Basin Redwoods State Park

Distance: 11.3 miles one way

Total Elevation Gain/Loss: 2300/1750

Trip Length: 2 days

Difficulty: ★★★

Recommended Maps: *Portola Redwoods State Park Map, Big Basin Redwoods State Park Map, Trail Map of the Santa Cruz Mountains 1,* USGS 7.5-min *Big Basin*

Hike Overview

This third segment of The Traverse steeply ascends Butano Ridge from Portola Redwoods State Park to reach the Basin Trail easement, a 1.5-mile section that passes through private land to reach Lane Trail Camp at the northeastern boundary of Big Basin Redwoods State Park. From camp, the hike descends to join the Skyline-to-the-Sea Trail as it travels along Opal Creek en route to Big Basin HQ. Spectacular and continuous old-growth redwood forest lines the final 2.5 miles.

SANTA CRUZ MTNS

The Trail Camp

Six lightly used sites are available at Lane Trail Camp in a forest of tanoak. Water is not available anywhere near camp and the last reliable source is at Portola Redwoods State Park. Also, wild pigs regularly bulldoze the ground here and many sites have been completely dug up in the recent past. Reservations can be made up to 60 days in advance by calling (831) 338-8861, 10 A.M.–5 P.M. Monday through Saturday. Sites cost $5 per night and there is a $5 non-refundable reservation fee that must be mailed in to secure the site (mail to: 21600 Big Basin Way, Boulder Creek, CA 95006). Overnight fees are paid upon arrival at Big Basin HQ. A maximum of six people are allowed per site. For more information on this and other trail camps in Big Basin, please see the backpacking chapter *Skyline-to-the-Sea*.

To Reach the Trailhead

Take Highway 35 to the turn-off for Alpine Road, located 6 miles north of the Highway 35/9 junction and 7.0 miles south of the Highway 35/84 junction. Head south on Alpine Road and in 2.5 miles bear left on Price Ave. and continue for 3.0 steep and winding miles to the visitor center. Backpackers need to register here before proceeding to the trailhead, located at the end of the park service road beyond the campground. Park staff will advise you on where to leave your vehicle (usually in the lot behind the visitor center).

Trail Description

From the park visitor center (0.0/400), the easiest way to reach the base of Butano Ridge is to follow the paved park service road past the campground. The road undulates through pleasant forest, then passes Slate Creek Trail (0.2/430) and Summit Trail (0.5/470) on the left before reaching a wooden bridge over Pescadero Creek near a cluster of service buildings (0.7/390). Cross the bridge, and after a brief climb you encounter Old Haul Road in Pescadero Creek County Park (0.9/500).

A more scenic route to this point follows Sequoia Loop and Iverson trails from the visitor center to reach the service road immediately below the Old Haul Road junction. Singletrack and precipitous in places, it passes secretive Tiptoe Falls on Fall Creek. At the time of research, however, sections of Iverson Trail were closed indefinitely. Check with park staff before attempting this variation.

Cross Old Haul Road and follow singletrack Portola Trail as it makes two quick switchbacks and climbs parallel to Iverson Creek. The lightly trod tail travels through a deep ravine of trickling water and mossy boulders. Sword and wood ferns thrive beneath spindly, second-growth redwood trees as the trail banks right to gently contour over to the sheer Fall Creek drainage. The route

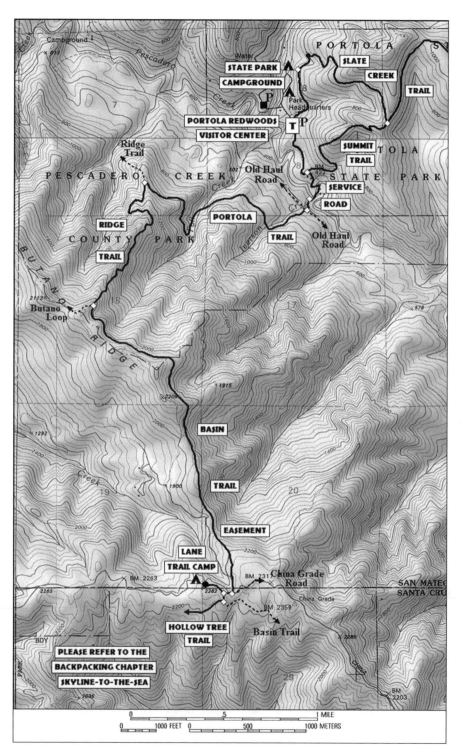

The Traverse: Section 3

then crosses thin Fall Creek, passing fuzzy thimbleberry leaves and five-fingered ferns, and follows the creek briefly before turning sharply right and traversing upward to reach Ridge Trail (2.4/1000). Continue up, up, and away on switch-backing Ridge Trail through continuous forest to reach Basin Trail just below the spine of Butano Ridge (3.7/2020).

Bear left (south) on Basin Trail as it contours steadily along the upper slopes of Butano Ridge and reaches a scenic overlook (4.2/2200) with views into the deep canyon below. (A good sitting bench makes this a pleasant place to rest and enjoy your final views to the east). The trail soon reaches the boundary with the Basin Trail easement (4.4/2200), where redwood stumps and fairy rings tell the tale of logging and redwood regeneration.

For the next 1.5 miles the route passes through private property owned by Redtree Properties. Prominently marked by more than a dozen signs, the ease-ment required 15 years of work and negotiation. Please stay on the trail in this section.

Watch for a still-living chimney tree in the first quarter mile of the ease-ment, easily identified by its girth and the sky peeking through its top. Follow the numerous signs as the trail crosses several private roads along the ridgetop. Shortly before reaching Big Basin, the route climbs steeply to crest at a three-way intersection. Continue across the paved road to quickly reach another large intersection. Across the roads, follow the narrow trail to enter Big Basin Red-woods State Park and reach Hollow Tree Trail (5.9/2280). Lane Trail Camp is found a short distance uphill to the right (northwest).

Following an evocative night's sleep, return to Hollow Tree Trail and follow it down to Opal Creek and the Skyline-to-the-Sea Trail (8.8/1270). In a further 2.5 miles, through old-growth glory, you reach Big Basin HQ (11.3/950). For a detailed description of the trail from Lane Trail Camp to HQ, please see the section *Side-trip to Lane Trail Camp* in the backpacking chapter *Skyline-to-the-Sea*.

GOVERNING AGENCY/PARK(S) CONTACT INFORMATION

Portola Redwoods State Park (see above).

Pescadero Creek County Park, San Mateo County Parks and Recreation Division, 455 County Center, 4th Floor, Redwood City, CA 94063, (650) 363-4020, www.eparks.net.

Big Basin Redwoods State Park, 21600 Big Basin Way, Boulder Creek, CA 95006, (831) 338-8860 (recorded message) or (831) 338-8861, www.bigbasin.org, www.parks.ca.gov.

Giving Back

Portola and Castle Rock Foundation (see above).

Sempervirens Fund is dedicated to preserving, expanding, and linking parklands in the Santa Cruz Mountains. Drawer BE, Los Altos, CA 94023-4054, (650) 968-4509, www.sempervirens.org.

SECTION 4: BIG BASIN HQ TO WADDELL BEACH VIA SKYLINE-TO-THE-SEA TRAIL

Miles and miles of old-growth redwood forest, plus waterfalls, streams, the Pacific Ocean, and the choice of three different trail camps

The Park: Big Basin Redwoods State Park

Distance: 10.3 miles one way

Total Elevation Gain/Loss: 400/1350

Trip Length: 2 days

Difficulty ★★★

Recommended Maps: *Big Basin Redwoods State Park Map, Trail Map of the Santa Cruz Mountains 2,* USGS 7.5-min *Big Basin, Franklin Point, Año Nuevo*

Hike Overview

This final section of The Traverse utilizes the lower Skyline-to-the-Sea Trail on its journey from Big Basin HQ to Waddell Beach. After ascending into the West Waddell Creek drainage, the hike steadily descends through magnificent old-growth forest, passes a fairytale side trip to Sunset Trail Camp and three beautiful waterfalls, and then winds through the broad valley of lower Waddell Creek to reach the Pacific Ocean at Waddell Beach.

The Trail Camps

Three trail camps are available—Sunset, Camp Herbert, and Twin Redwoods. Sunset nicely splits this segment and is more or less equidistant from both Big Basin HQ and Waddell Beach, while Camp Herbert and Twin Red-woods are only a few miles away from journey's end at the Pacific Ocean. Detailed descriptions of these trail camps, along with reservation information, can be found in the backpacking chapter *Skyline-to-the-Sea*.

Trail Description

For a detailed description of this final segment, please see the section *Big Basin HQ to Waddell Beach* in the backpacking chapter *Skyline-to-the-Sea*.

GOVERNING AGENCY/PARK(S) CONTACT INFORMATION

Big Basin Redwoods State Park (see above).

SANTA CRUZ MTNS

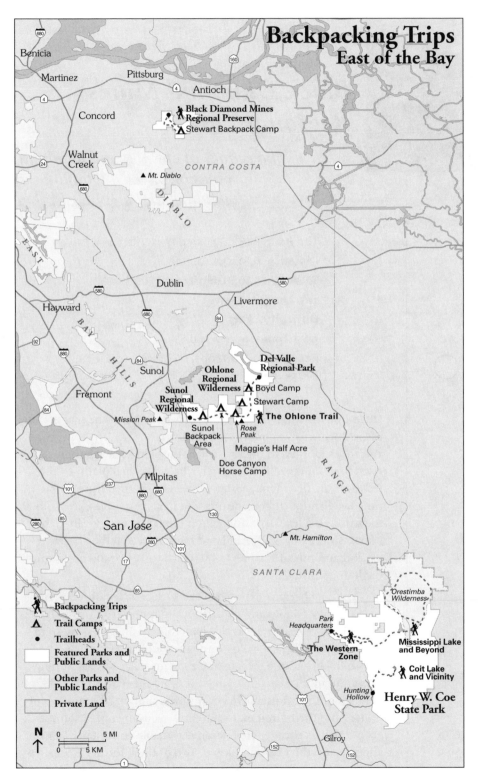

Backpacking Trips
East of the Bay

Benicia

Martinez

Pittsburg

Antioch

Concord

Black Diamond Mines
Regional Preserve
Stewart Backpack Camp

Walnut
Creek

CONTRA COSTA

▲ Mt. Diablo

DIABLO

Dublin

Livermore

Hayward

BAY HILLS

Sunol

Del Valle
Regional Park

Ohlone
Regional
Wilderness

Boyd Camp

Fremont

Sunol
Regional
Wilderness

Stewart Camp

The Ohlone Trail

Mission Peak ▲

Sunol
Backpack
Area

Rose
Peak

Maggie's Half Acre

Doe Canyon
Horse Camp

RANGE

Milpitas

San Jose

Mt. Hamilton

SANTA CLARA

Orestimba
Wilderness

Park
Headquarters

The Western
Zone

Mississippi Lake
and Beyond

Coit Lake
and Vicinity

Hunting
Hollow

Henry W. Coe
State Park

Gilroy

🚶 Backpacking Trips
Λ Trail Camps
● Trailheads
Featured Parks and
Public Lands
Other Parks and
Public Lands
Private Land

N
↑

0   5 MI
0   5 KM

EAST OF THE BAY

Black Diamond Mines Regional Park

*The echoes of eternity and mankind,
plus cows, oaks, wildflowers,
wildlife, and a good old time*

The Park: Black Diamond Mines Regional Park
Distance: 6.8 miles round-trip
Total Elevation Gain/Loss: 1700/1700
Trip Length: 2 days
Difficulty: ★★
Best Times: Spring and Fall
Recommended Maps: *Black Diamond Mines
Regional Park Map,* USGS 7.5-min *Antioch South*

Once upon a time—50 million years or so ago—the marshy edge of California was in today's nearby town of Antioch. Towering volcanoes loomed to the east where the Sierra Nevada range now rises, their flanks rolling down to a broad coastal plain. To the west was the deep blue sea. Creatures and plants forgotten by time lived and died here, flourishing in an equitable climate by the sea. As sea level rose and fell on its eternal cycle of flux, their remains were buried by sand and mud. And coal they became, black diamonds of fortune upon which towns would appear in the human future.

The coal became exposed at the surface as tectonic activity wrinkled Mt. Diablo and its surroundings upward during the past 2-3 million years. Rare was this band of coal and pressing were the energy needs of the blossoming city of San Francisco. The beds quickly became the site of California's largest coal mining operation in the years following the Gold Rush; from the 1860s to the turn of the century, five boomtowns supported hundreds of miners and their families. In the early 1900s the operation was abandoned as cheaper coal became available elsewhere and oil appeared on the fossil fuel scene. Two of these former townsites—

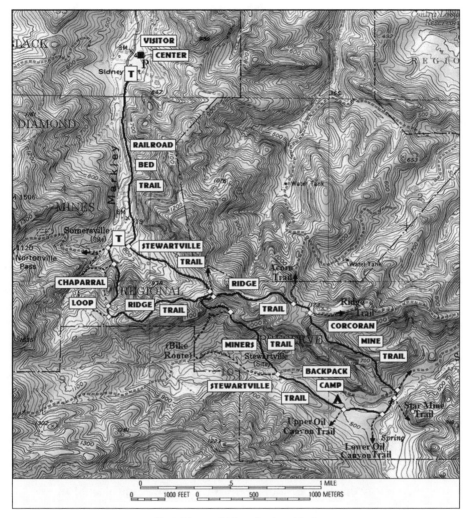

Black Diamond Mines Regional Park

Somersville and Stewartsville—are visited on this hike. If you are interested in a more hands-on exploration of the region's mining history, underground tours of Hazel Atlas Mine are offered on weekends from March through November. Contact the park for more information and a current schedule.

Hike Overview

An easy loop winds along fire roads and singletrack trails through pleasant oak woodlands that are well trampled by cows and seasonally bursting with wildflowers. Despite human use over the years, the ecosystem is surprisingly vibrant and wildlife is commonly seen darting beneath and above the open woodlands. Cows still seem to own the place, however, and it's you—not them—that are fenced in at night.

Bikepacking is an option and most park trails are open for riding. Dogs are allowed and may run unleashed in the backcountry, provided they are under voice control. Epic wildflowers blossom from March through early May, and temperatures generally are warmer than most places in the Bay Area year-round. Avoid the wet months of winter, however: conditions are unpleasantly muddy and the trail camp is closed. Summer heat sears on the many unshaded miles of trail, typically lasting deep into fall.

The Trail Camp

A small, fenced enclosure protects Stewartville Backpack Camp, situated at valley bottom very near the former coal-mining town of Stewartville. Two picnic tables and a few level tent sites are available beneath the shady boughs of buckeye, olive, and walnut trees (the latter two introduced by the miners). While cows roam freely about the area, a sense of isolation from today's world permeates the site. The park also offers Star Mine Group Camp (see Appendix A: *Group Campgrounds of the Bay Area*).

Stewartville Backpack Camp

Reservations are required and can be made by calling the East Bay Regional Park District reservations department at (510) 636-1684, 8:30 A.M.–4 P.M. Monday-Friday. There is $5 per person fee per night, with a maximum of 20 people per site. The camp is not heavily used, but is usually occupied on nice weekends in spring and fall. Potable water is not available at the camp—it is recommended that you bring in all needed water rather than purify the dubious sources nearby. Campfires and alcohol are prohibited, and there is a maximum stay of two nights. Note that arriving campers are required to check in at the visitor center upon arrival.

To Reach the Trailhead

Take the Somersville exit from Highway 4 in Antioch and proceed south on Somersville Road for 2.6 miles to reach park headquarters on the left. Backpackers are required to leave their vehicles in the headquarters parking lot. However, a mile of walking with full packs can be avoided by dropping equipment off at the Stewartville Trailhead a mile farther at road's end.

Trail Description

The following describes the most direct route to the backpack camp, and returns via a different, slightly longer route with scenic views and interesting sites. From the headquarters parking lot (0.0/500), proceed south along Railroad Bed Trail towards the Stewartville Trailhead. The wide Railroad Bed Trail parallels the road, then slowly gains elevation as it follows the old route of the Pittsburg Railroad. Built in the 1860s and operating until the early 1900s, the railroad transported coal 5 miles from the Somersville area to Pittsburg Landing on the Sacramento River for shipment. Bear left at the junction with Stewartville Trail (0.8/800). (If starting your hike from road's end at the backpack drop-off point, continue straight on the paved road for 100 yards and bear left on Stewartville Trail to quickly reach the junction with Railroad Bed Trail.)

Memories of mining days are evident on the opposite valley slopes to the west, where Rose Hill Cemetery houses the remains of local Protestants who succumbed to mine disasters and epidemics. Local flora includes twisting blue oaks laden with large tangles of mistletoe, wispy gray pines with massive cones, and the evergreen leaves of interior live oak. Numerous introduced species of trees also are abundant in this area, including Tree of Heaven, easily identified by its clusters of papery shaker seed pods; California pepper tree, an evergreen with narrow leaves seasonally dangling with small red berries; and eucalyptus.

Continue on wide Stewartville Trail straight past Pittsburgh Mine Trail junction as the path steadily climbs above Markley Canyon to reach the ridgetop and junction with Ridge and Carbondale trails (1.4/1150). Continue straight through the gate to reach a second junction with Ridge Trail on the left (your return route) and bear right to remain on Stewartville Trail. Winding gradually down into the broad valley, the trail shortly reaches the junction with Miners Trail (1.8/980). Bikepackers should continue down Stewartville Trail, while backpackers should take advantage of this singletrack, hikers-only trail. As Miners Trail traverses above the valley alongside manzanita, chamise, toyon, interior and coast live oaks, and gray pines, Mt. Diablo (3849') can be seen looming over the land a scant 6 miles to the southwest. Miners Trail then plummets down to the valley floor and passes above the old entrance to Central Mine, in operation for nearly 40 years during the late 19th century. At valley bottom (2.5/550), proceed across the stream gully to return to Stewartville Trail and bear left to reach the backpack camp (3.0/500).

Above Stewart Valley

After a pleasant night, continue on Stewartville Trail past three intersections on the right—for Upper and Lower Oil Canyon trails and Star Mine Trail—to reach the junction with Corcoran Mine Trail (3.3/460). Bear left and begin climbing wide Corcoran Mine Trail past sandstone outcrops, large manzanita bushes, and gray pines. Blue oaks begin to dominate and views get ever nicer as the route climbs to the junction with Ridge Trail (4.1/1100). As the route continues left on Ridge Trail and passes a junction on the right for Acorn Trail (4.2/1140), far-reaching views to the northeast reveal the broad fan of the Delta and confluence of the mighty Sacramento and San Joaquin rivers, while views southwest are dominated by the massif of Mt. Diablo.

Returning to the earlier junctions with Stewartville Trail (4.7/1150), a different—and interesting—return route can be taken by remaining on Ridge Trail as it continues west. Oaks disappear as Ridge Trail passes through a chaparral community of chamise and manzanita joined for the first time by Coulter pines, a less-common tree here at the northern limits of its range. Producing the largest cones of any conifer, it can be identified by its erect, single-trunk character and long needles in bundles of three. A maze of trails winds through the area—bear right at the junction with Chaparral Loop (5.4/1130) and remain right at all junctions for the most direct route down to Stewartville Trailhead (5.8/760). Along the way you pass numerous artifacts from mining days, including the entrance to Hazel Atlas Mine (see above). Return to the headquarters parking lot on Railroad Bed Trail (6.8/500).

PARK CONTACT INFORMATION

Black Diamond Mines Regional Park, 5175 Somersville Road, Antioch, CA 94509, (925) 757-2620, www.ebparks.org/parks/black.htm. The visitor center is open 8 A.M.–4:30 P.M. daily, year-round.

Giving Back

The Regional Parks Foundation supports and funds the acquisition, development, and stewardship of parklands in the East Bay Regional Park District through private contributions. Box 21074, Crestmont Station, Oakland, CA 94620, (510) 544-2200, www.regparksfdn.org.

Those interested in *volunteering* for Black Diamond Mines Regional Park—or any other unit of the East Bay Regional Park District—should contact the district's volunteer coordinator for more information, (510) 544-2515, email: volunteers@ebparks.org.

The Ohlone Trail

Oak woodlands, spring wildflowers, rolling ridges, high peaks, distant views, the deepest wild in the East Bay Regional Park District

The Parks: Sunol Regional Wilderness, Ohlone Regional Wilderness, Del Valle Regional Park

Distance: 19.5 miles one-way

Total Elevation Gain/Loss: 6500/6150

Trip Length: 3-4 days

Difficulty: ★★★★

Best Times: Spring and Fall

Recommended Maps: Ohlone Wilderness Regional Trail Permit and Map, EBRPD *Sunol Regional Wilderness* and *Del Valle Regional Park* Maps; USGS 7.5-min *La Costa Valley,* and *Mendenhall Springs*

For Alternate Out-and-Back Overnight Trips:
Sunol Backpack Area from Sunol Trailhead:
8.0 miles round-trip, 2600/2600, ★★★
Boyd Camp from Del Valle Trailhead:
4.6 miles round-trip, 1600/1600, ★★★
Stewart's Camp from Del Valle Trailhead:
14.0 miles round-trip, 3800/3800, ★★★

Stretching nearly 20 miles through the most remote land in the entire East Bay Regional Park District, the Ohlone Trail is a point-to-point journey remarkable for its isolation, beauty, and strenuous hiking. The adventure connects Sunol Regional Wilderness with Del Valle Regional Park via Ohlone Regional Wilderness, a hidden, high-elevation wonderland accessible only by trail. The proximity of such a lightly-traveled hike to civilization is exceptional.

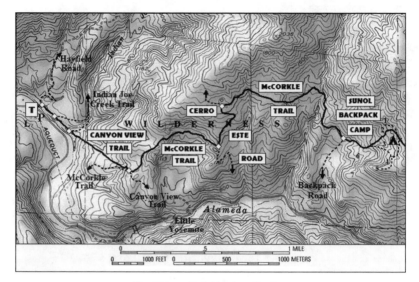

The Ohlone Trail: Western Section

Hike Overview

Strenuous and constant elevation change across hilly terrain defines the entire measure of the Ohlone Trail. A minimum of three days is recommended to complete it; four leisurely days is delightful. A car shuttle or pre-arranged pick-up is required at trail's end. While hiking the entire trail in two days is possible, it allows little time for relaxation and enjoyment. Better two-day trips are possible by hiking out-and-back to the closest trail camps from the respective trailheads.

While the Ohlone Trail can be completed in either direction, the trip is described from west to east, Sunol to Del Valle, in the direction of more gradual elevation gain (beginning at Del Valle necessitates a 2500-foot climb with full packs in the first 5 miles, a burning introduction to the adventure). A permit ($4) is required to use the Ohlone Trail and is available at Sunol and Del Valle parks, or through the EBRPD reservation office (see below). An extremely useful map and detailed information about the hike is included with the permit.

The hills here are surprisingly lofty for the Bay Area and more than 7 miles of trail travel above 3000 feet, making weather conditions highly variable. The heat of summer sun on miles of unshaded trail can be oppressive, while the cold heights—and possibility of snow—make winter less appealing. Spring is prime-time for this hike as wildflowers explode in one of the Bay Area's most dazzling and diverse displays. Wildflowers are extraordinary from March through May and dozens of different species can be seen along the trail, including lupine, fiddlenecks, California poppies, western hound's tongue, brodeia, baby blue eyes, witch hazel, shooting stars, buttercups, scarlet pimpernel, Chinese houses, and California gilia. The Sunol Visitor Center provides displays and handouts on the common flora and fauna encountered in the area. Note that spring reaches the higher elevations on this hike several weeks later than at lower elevations. While wildflowers peak and trees leaf out below 1000 feet in Sunol and Del Valle during the last week of March and first week of April, the higher elevations don't experience full spring glory until middle to late April.

The Trail Camps

Backcountry camping is limited to five trail camps, each of which provides outhouses and potable water (except in the driest of conditions). From west to east they are Sunol Backpack Area, Doe Canyon Horse Camp, Maggie's Half Acre, Stewart's Camp, and Boyd Camp. Each is described in detail below. *Reservations* are required to use the trail camps and can be made by calling the EBRPD reservation office at (510) 636-1684, 8:30 A.M.–4 P.M. Monday-Friday. While advance reservations are strongly recommended, it is

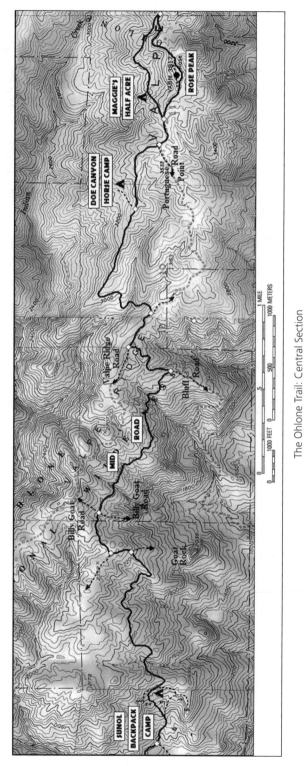

The Ohlone Trail: Central Section

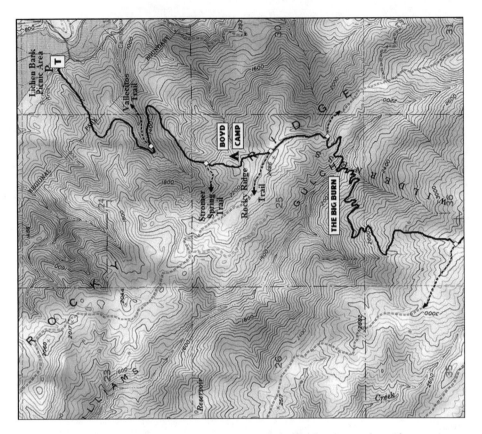

possible to make last-minute arrangements at the parks themselves if space is available. Trail camps cost $5 per person per night, and there is a one-time reservation fee of $6. Reservations are for specific sites—the information below will help you request an ideal location. Trail camp permits and information will be mailed to you and each person must also carry an Ohlone Trail permit (see above). Despite the heat, summer weekends are the busiest and most trail camps are full. Outside of these times, space is usually available. Fires, alcohol, dogs, and bicycles are prohibited on the Ohlone Trail.

For the first night—or for a pleasant two-day out-and-back adventure—Sunol Backpack Area is the recommended destination. Only 4 miles from the trailhead, a night at Sunol allows a later start (providing ample time to shuttle vehicles) as well as the opportunity to fully enjoy a spectacular location. The other options for the first night—Maggie's Half Acre and Doe Canyon Horse Camp—are a strenuous 10-mile hike from the trailhead and require an early start. For those completing the hike in three days, Stewart's Camp is recommended for the second night, located in an idyllic valley 10 miles from Sunol and a 6-mile plummeting descent from trail's end in Del Valle. For a four-day trip, any combination of overnights at Maggie's Half Acre, Stewart's Camp,

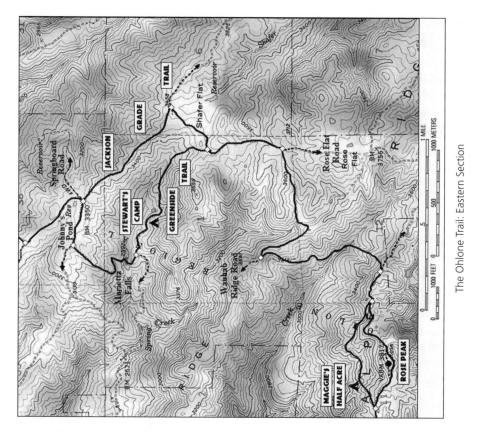

The Ohlone Trail: Eastern Section

or Boyd Camp after a first night at Sunol Backpack Area allow ample time to relax, explore, and fully enjoy the Ohlone Trail experience.

Sunol Backpack Camp offers seven sites scattered across 500 vertical feet on a steep hillside fenced to keep out roaming cattle. Privacy is excellent, views outstanding, and each individually named site unique. Site 1 (Sycamore), capacity 5, shades beneath sycamores near the top of the hill. Site 2 (Stars Rest), capacity 30, the largest site, is on top of the hill, and has great views but limited shade except for the picnic table. Site 3 (Hawk's Rest), capacity 5, is small and shady with sweet rock outcrops and views. It's also closest to water, but only has one good tent site. Site 4 (Eagles Eyrie), capacity 10, has limited shade, spectacular views, and is close to water. Site 5 (Sky Camp), capacity 5, is very isolated and shady beneath blue oaks, and has epic views. Site 6 (Cathedral Camp), capacity 10, is very shady near the bottom of the hill, has no views, and is far from water. Site 7 (Oak View), capacity 5, is very isolated near the bottom of the hill and has some shade beneath twisting blue oaks. It has good views but no picnic table, and is farthest from water.

Doe Canyon Horse Camp provides two sites designed for use by equestrian groups, but backpackers are permitted to camp here if space is available. The

EAST OF THE BAY

trail camp is located at an elevation of 3300 feet and consists of two large clearings situated amid low-lying brush. An outhouse, water, hitching posts, and limited views are nearby.

Maggie's Half Acre provides three sites at an elevation of 3480 feet on the upper flanks of Rose Peak (3817'), making this the highest designated campsite in the Bay Area. Despite its lofty location, views are obscured by a dense surrounding forest of live oaks, gray pine, bay, and some very gnarly black oaks. Sites 1 and 3 shelter away from the trail in shady worlds beneath ancient oaks and have a capacity of 4-6 people. Site 2 is larger, located by the path and water, and accommodates up to 14 people. City lights peek through the shady canopy at night.

Stewart's Camp shelters at 3160 feet, offers only one site, and is located on the shady edge of a vast open valley populated almost exclusively by massive black oaks. The small site is located near the water and outhouse, and is surrounded by a denser forest of live oaks, bay, and buckeyes. Space is limited, but up to 24 people are permitted to camp in the site.

Boyd Camp hides at an elevation of 2200 feet on moderately forested slopes of blue oak, black oak, and gray pine. The camp is only 2 miles from the Del Valle trailhead, but access requires a heart-pumping climb of 1300 vertical feet and the area is consequently lightly trafficked. There are two sites, both nicely removed from the trail and, unfortunately, the water; the only source is a year-round spring located almost a half mile and 300 vertical feet below camp. Site 1 is smaller and shelters beneath shady blue oaks adjacent to an unusually nice buckeye tree. Site 2 is on the edge of a small grassy clearing with less shade but much more space.

To Reach the Sunol Trailhead

Take Interstate 680 east of Fremont to the Calaveras Road exit and proceed south on Calaveras Road for 4.3 miles to Geary Road. Turn left on Geary Road, reaching the entrance kiosk in 1.8 miles. The trailhead is located across Geary Road from the Ohlone Trail sign-in panel, approximately 100 yards past the visitor center.

To Reach the Del Valle Trailhead

Take the North Livermore Avenue exit from Interstate 580. Head south and proceed through town (North Livermore Avenue becomes South Livermore Avenue). About 1.5 miles outside town, turn right at Mines Road, go about 3.5 miles, and continue straight on Del Valle Road as Mines Road turns left. The park entrance is about 3.5 miles ahead. Past the entrance station continue on Del Valle Road for 0.8 mile, cross the bridge, and turn right to the Lichen Bark Picnic Area and Ohlone Trail Parking Area.

To Reach the Sunol Trailhead
from Del Valle Trailhead

After dropping off a shuttle vehicle, return to central Livermore and turn left onto 1st Street. Proceed 0.6 mile on 1st Street to Holmes Road and turn left. In 2 miles, bear right on Vallecitos Road/Highway 84 and continue for another 6.5 miles to Interstate 680. Go underneath the freeway, turn left on Paloma Road, pass back beneath 680 and go straight at the next stop onto Calaveras Road. Continue as above.

Trail Description

Note that the Ohlone Trail is a route comprised of many different trails. Many junctions—but not all—will be posted and indicate the correct direction for the Ohlone Trail. Most are numbered to correspond with the Ohlone Trail permit and map. The trail passes through numerous gates—leave them as you find them. Water sources are generally scarce, with the only sure supplies available at the trail camps. Be sure and fill up at the trailhead before you start since the first available water is not until Sunol Backpack Camp.

After registering at the Ohlone Trail sign-in board, begin the adventure across Geary Road at the wooden bridge over Alameda Creek. Alameda Creek is the largest watershed in the East Bay, draining more than 700 square miles, and its deep valleys are your regular companions during the first half of the trip. The mottled, smooth gray trunks and twisting branches of California sycamores line the creek and appear throughout the Ohlone Trail in damp stream gullies, providing excellent shade. With their broad leaves, sycamore trees can lose up to fifty gallons of water per day and grow only where such large volumes of water are available. Also keep an eye out for poison oak and stinging nettle, ubiquitous and unfriendly companions on this hike.

Across the bridge, bear right on the wide path and continue straight on Canyon View Trail as it passes junctions on the left for Hayfield Road (0.1/410), Indian Joe Nature Trail (0.2/410), and Indian Joe Creek Trail (0.3/410). Canyon View Trail soon climbs away from the creek and into a drier environment populated primarily by blue oaks, the most drought-tolerant of all oaks. Easily recognized, its leaves are shallowly lobed with smooth margins. After passing though one of numerous cattle gates to come, Canyon View Trail reaches a four-way intersection with McCorkle Trail (0.8/700). Go left on McCorkle Trail. Cows are still permitted to graze along much of the Ohlone Trail and are commonly seen in this area.

The now overgrown trail climbs steadily up the ridgeline before turning east to traverse through chaparral. The low-lying and shrubby chaparral community flourishes in arid environments and appears throughout the hike. Common members include coyote brush, toyon, sticky monkey flower, bracken fern, coffee berry, and plenty of poison oak. Valley oak, another frequent tree on this hike, also begins to appear along this section, identified by its 2- to 4-inch deeply lobed leaves. After passing beneath some huge coast live oaks, the trail then reaches the junction with wide Cerro Este Road (1.7/1180). Bear left on Cerro Este Road, make the steady uphill climb to the next junction with McCorkle Trail (2.1/1430), and bear right on singletrack McCorkle Trail. Traversing steadily across open slopes, the trail offers outstanding views of Mission Peak to the west, and to the south the Calaveras Reservoir, the upper Alameda Creek watershed, and more distant peaks of the Diablo Range. After making a steep, switchbacking drop into the "W" Tree Rock Scramble, the trail continues its traverse to reach the junction with Backpack Road (3.4/1150) and the gated edge of Sunol Backpack Camp.

After passing through the gate, the trail climbs steeply up the hillside. An almost indiscernible use path splits right just past the gate and lead to sites 6-7. About halfway up the hillside, the main trail makes an unsigned fork. Bear right to reach sites 3-5, or continue straight ahead to find sites 1-2 near the top of the hill. The one water source is located right above site 3. Interesting serpentine outcrops protrude from the hillside here, easily identified by the waxy green color found on unweathered surfaces.

After a delightful night, the next day begins with a climb to the top of the hill where a gate marks the edge of Sunol Regional Wilderness. For the next 2 miles the trail passes through land leased from the San Francisco Water District—hikers are requested to stay on the trail during this section. Undulating

Backpacking Sunol

EAST OF THE BAY

through open serpentine grasslands dotted with rock outcrops and fabulous spring wildflower displays, the open trail provides far-reaching views as it traverses along the upper slopes of the Alameda Creek drainage. The trail winds above Goat Rock, a distinctive promontory composed of erosion-resistant red chert, and then turns uphill. Bear left at the first unposted junction with Goat Rock Road (5.3/2170) and right at the second junction (5.5/2320) to continue westward on Mid Road.

Shortly thereafter you pass through another gate and enter Ohlone Regional Wilderness just before reaching the four-way junction with Billy Goat Road (5.8/2390). The route continues straight on Mid Road and begins a rising traverse slowly toward the ridgeline above. The cities of the South Bay begin to appear in the southern distance, while intermittent views of distant South San Francisco can be spotted to the northwest. The trail turns left at the junction with Bluff Road (7.1/2650), and then climbs to the ridgeline and junction with Valpe Ridge Road (7.4/2840). Go right on Valpe Ridge Road, through another gate, and proceed along the airy slopes. As the trail banks left at the junction with Portuguese Point Road (7.7/2920), it leaves the upper Alameda Creek watershed for the first time and drops into the headwaters of Indian Creek, a separate drainage that rejoins Alameda Creek near Interstate 680.

After crossing South Fork Indian Creek, the trail resumes its climb and soon passes above 3000 feet for the first time. Views north begin to appear and the massif of Mt. Diablo (3849′) is easily spotted more than 25 miles distant. At this higher elevation, black oak also begins to appear for the first time. A common denizen of higher elevations around the state, black oak is relatively uncommon in the Bay Area and found only at higher elevations in the Diablo Range and Santa Cruz Mountains. It is easily identified by the large, lobed leaves, and leaf points ending in a pointy bristle. In spring its new leaves emerge a brilliant red before turning green. The wispy, multi-trunked forms of gray pine become more common as well, and the evergreen leaves of live oaks start to appear. Thankfully, poison oak diminishes considerably at these higher elevations.

A short side-trip 200 feet downhill at the junction for Doe Canyon Horse Camp (8.9/3380) leads to the large clearing, water source, and outhouse by the campsites. Continuing, the trail reaches another junction with Portuguese Point Road (9.3/3540) after passing through a gate held shut with a loop of barbed wire. Continue straight to quickly reach the spur trail on the left for the campsites at Maggie's Half Acre (9.5/3590), located a quarter mile down the forested north slopes of Rose Peak.

While the trail to Maggie's Half Acre traverses around to rejoin the main trail 0.6 mile past the campsites, this bypasses the summit of Rose Peak (3817′). A side-trip not to be missed, Rose Peak is only 32 feet lower than Mt. Diablo, is the highest point on the hike, and offers extraordinary 360-degree views. On a good day, the vista stretches from San Francisco to the Sierra Nevada and is highlighted on the Ohlone Trail permit and map. A large plastic cylinder protects a summit register for personal notes, contributions, and reflections. To reach Rose Peak, continue on the Ohlone Trail past the trail camp junction and make the short detour to the top from the main trail as it skirts around just below the summit.

Continuing past Rose Peak, you pass the opposite junction for Maggie's Half Acre (10.2/3590) and then briefly parallel the fenced park boundary where a private road splits right (10.5/3590). Curving left, the trail begins its northern journey to Del Valle after 10 miles of westward progression.

After plummeting more than 400 feet to cross shady North Fork Indian Creek, the trail then climbs the more open opposite slopes. Look down the Indian Creek drainage to spot the small, rounded forms of Coyote Hills, visible on the edge of the Bay, marking the location where Alameda Creek ends its journey in Bay waters. After passing a junction for Wauhab Ridge Road (11.5/3490) on the left, the route cuts back to attain the ridgetop and then dips down into the head of Box Canyon. Passing a small cattle pond, the trail climbs along the park boundary, turns left at the junction with Rose Flat Road (12.4/3640), and then gently undulates north to reach the junction with Greenside Trail (12.9/3490).

To reach Stewart's Camp from here, turn left and descend 0.6 mile on Greenside Trail to the outhouse, water source, and campsite. Those staying overnight here can rejoin the Ohlone Trail by continuing on Greenside Trail and

Sweet Sunol

bearing right on Springboard Road to reach Johnny's Pond. From the Greenside Trail junction, the Ohlone Trail continues straight across the open meadows of Shafer Flat to reach the junction with Jackson Grade Trail (13.3/3460) and heads left (northwest) along the ridgeline that hems in the beautiful valley of upper La Costa Creek. Gigantic blue and black oaks punctuate open fields flourishing with wildflowers and the steep, inviting landscape is easy to explore in all directions. Stewart's Camp (3160′) sits in the bottom of the valley on the west side of La Costa Creek.

Reaching Johnny's Pond at a four-way intersection with Springboard Road (14.0/3350), the time has come to stop and relax. With distant views reaching north to Mt. Tamalpais, the Golden Gate, and Mt. Diablo, plus a nearby waterfall to explore, this is no time to rush. Murietta Falls (2990′) is located along Greenside Trail, a half-mile west of Stewart's Camp and a mile from Johnny's Pond via Springboard Road and Greenside Trail. Dropping 60 feet in a thin rivulet on a rocky cliff face, the waterfall is seldom more than a thin trickle. More interesting are the rocky outcrops and exciting scramble required to access the falls. To find Murietta Falls, follow the use paths downstream where Greenside Trail crosses La Costa Creek.

From Johnny's Pond, the Ohlone Trail continues straight on Jackson Grade Trail and offers ever vaster views of San Francisco and Sutro Tower, the East Bay Hills, Mission Peak, and north to your final destination, Lake Del Valle. Enjoy these final high-elevation views, for once you turn right at the junction for The Big Burn (14.6/3300) the plummeting descent to trail's end begins.

Dropping immediately, the broad trail soon narrows to singletrack and poison oak once again rears its ugly leaves. On this north-facing slope, shaded from sun's rays, the vegetation is dense, blocks the view, and encroaches on the trail in many places. Wild cucumber, maidenhair ferns, and gooseberry join bay, black oak, and thick poison oak on this shady section. Dropping endlessly on numerous switchbacks, the trail loses 1400 feet of elevation in only 1.7 miles before finally reaching the bottom of Williams Gulch (16.3/1890). Here you pass beneath sycamores and alders while crossing the ephemeral creek. The trail gradually widens to become a broad path as it switchbacks steeply out of Williams Gulch and passes through open fields of blue oak with intermittent views north to Mt. Diablo. It reaches the Rocky Ridge Trail junction (17.0/2380) at the end of the hike's final sustained climb.

Continuing straight, you resume the steep drop to quickly reach the outhouse and campsites of Boyd Camp (17.2/2240) in a shrubbier forest of blue oak, gray pine, coyote brush, toyon, and coffee berry. From Boyd Camp the trail takes a direct, knee-jarring line straight down, passing the junction for water at Stromer Spring Trail (17.6/1940) just before coast live oak reappear and the trail passes through another gate. Manzanita appears for the first time on the hike and coyote brush becomes increasingly common on the continuing descent.

Take the time to record your passing in the logbook where the trail reaches the Ohlone Trail sign-in panel by the junction with Vallecitos Trail (18.5/1190). Vallecitos Trail heads right down a creek gully toward the campground, while the Ohlone Trail continues straight on a steadily descending traverse to finally reach trail's end at Lichen Bark Picnic Area (19.5/750). Good work!

PARKS CONTACT INFORMATION

East Bay Regional Park District, 2950 Peralta Oaks Court, Box 5381, Oakland, CA 94605-0318, (510) 562-PARK, www.ebparks.org.

Sunol Regional Wilderness, 1895 Geary Rd., Sunol, CA 94516, (925) 862-2244 or (925) 862-2601, www.ebparks.org/parks/sunol.htm.

Del Valle Regional Park, 7000 Del Valle Rd., Livermore, CA 94550, (925) 373-0332, www.ebparks.org/parks/delval.htm.

Giving Back

The Regional Parks Foundation supports and funds the acquisition, development, and stewardship of parklands in the East Bay Regional Park District through private contributions. Box 21074, Crestmont Station, Oakland, CA 94620, (510) 544-2200, www.regparksfdn.org.

Alameda Creek Alliance is a community watershed group dedicated to preserving and restoring the natural ecosystems of the Alameda Creek drainage basin. Box 192, Sunol, CA 94516, (510) 845-4675, www.alamedacreek.com.

Those interested in *volunteering* for the parks along the Ohlone Trail—or any other unit of the East Bay Regional Park District—should contact the district's volunteer coordinator for more information, (510) 544-2515, email: volunteers@ebparks.org.

EAST OF THE BAY

Henry W. Coe State Park

*The Bay Area's wildest, deepest,
and most strenuous backcountry*

Located in the heart of the Diablo Range, vast Henry W. Coe
State Park features soaring ridges, steep canyons, gurgling creeks,
thriving oaks, abundant wildlife, radiant spring wildflowers, and
the immortal words etched on the monument to Henry W. Coe—
MAY THESE QUIET HILLS BRING PEACE TO THE SOULS OF THOSE WHO
ARE SEEKING.

Encompassing more than 85,000 acres, Henry Coe is the
largest state park in Northern California. Hidden from development by its rugged topography, the park offers more than 400
miles of trails and provides endless opportunities for isolation.
Unrestricted backcountry camping is permitted in the park's
farther regions, making it the only Bay Area location where
camping is allowed outside of designated trail camps. Despite
all this, the park is lightly visited and few ever trek into the backcountry. There are good reasons, however, for this absence of
crowds.

The park's endless succession of deep valleys hemmed by
steep ridges makes for extremely strenuous hiking. Most backpacking trips require several thousand feet of elevation change
on often challenging trails, and good fitness is required for any
overnight trip. From late May through the first rains of winter,
water is scarce in the park; a few perennial sources remain in the
western regions, but most backcountry sources disappear by June.
Longer backpacking trips are generally not recommended in
summer or fall due to baking temperatures (often in the 90s),
plus miles of unshaded trail and little to no water.

The three featured trips described below are excellent examples of the park's backpacking opportunities. Countless other
adventures await personal discovery on your own.

BACKPACKING IN HENRY COE: AN OVERVIEW

The park is divided into 12 backcountry zones. In the popular Western Zone, near the main park entrance, camping is restricted to 19 designated trail camps. In the rest of the park, backcountry camping is unrestricted—you may bed down anywhere you like. (Please minimize your impact by adhering to the guidelines outlined in the chapter *Safety, Gear, and the Wilderness Ethic.*) A backcountry permit is required and must be obtained the day of your departure. All trail camp and backcountry permits are first-come, first-serve—no reservations are accepted—and there is a fee of $2 per night per person. Quotas for each zone are seldom met, and securing a backcountry permit is rarely an issue. If your trip begins at the main park entrance, obtain your permits from the visitor center. In the southern region, permits are available from a self-service station (occasionally staffed on weekends) at Hunting Hollow.

Three main trailheads access the Henry Coe backcountry. The main entrance is located on the park's northwestern edge and is the most popular (two of the featured trips begin here). The park visitor center and headquarters are found here. A drive-up campground is nearby (see the camping chapter *Henry W. Coe State Park*) and potable water is available. On the park's southwestern border, Hunting Hollow and Coyote Creek trailheads are located less than 2 miles apart and offer few amenities beyond pit toilets. They are popular with equestrians and mountain bikers, yet are seldom used by hikers. The featured trip to Coit Lake & Vicinity begins at Coyote Creek Trailhead.

It is strongly recommended that you purchase the *Henry W. Coe State Park Trail and Camping Map* to complement the maps in this book. It covers the entire park and all its trails and is available at the park visitor center, or can be ordered by sending a check payable to the Pine Ridge Association for $5 (paper map) or $6.50 (plastic). Mail to: Map Request, Box 846, Morgan Hill, CA 95038.

Park Information/Visitor Center

Located in a reconstructed ranch building at the main park entrance, the Henry Coe visitor center houses an excellent bookstore, sells state park maps and all USGS quads for the area, and offers extensive literature about the park's natural history. Open spring and summer 7 A.M.–8 P.M. Friday-Sunday, sporadically on other days and during fall and winter. Box 846, Morgan Hill, CA 95038, (408) 779-2728. The park's web site, www.coepark.org, also contains comprehensive information.

To Reach the Main Park Entrance and Visitor Center

Take Highway 101 to Morgan Hill and exit on East Dunne Ave. Head east and follow East Dunne Ave. for 11 miles to the visitor center parking lot at road's end. After leaving the residential area of Morgan Hill, the road narrows to a twisting, exciting ascent. (Directions to the Hunting Hollow and Coyote Creek trailheads are provided in the Coit Lake & Vicinity description below.)

Crowds, Facilities, and the Best Times to Go

Fewer than 100,000 people visit Henry Coe annually, a pleasant contrast to the millions that visit the popular parks of the North Bay. Spring's wildflowers and fall's golden hues attract the most visitors, especially on weekends, while summer's baking heat and winter's wet chill reduce visitation to a minimum.

Backcountry camping in Henry Coe is primitive. A few trail camps in the Western Zone provide outhouses, but water is obtained from nearby springs or streams and few picnic tables or other amenities are provided. (Descriptions of each Western Zone trail camp can be found online at www.coepark.org/sites-backpacking.html; photographs of the trail camps are available at the park visitor center.) In the deeper backcountry, a few established sites and amenities can be found by Coit and Mississippi lakes; otherwise the camping is completely undeveloped.

Backcountry excursions are highly dependent on water, making winter and spring most viable. Winter comes with its own headaches, however: surprisingly heavy rains, occasional snow, muddy trails, and cool temperatures. The spring months, especially April, are optimal; the wildflowers are exceptionally vibrant, and warm, sunny days are common. By the end of May, summer is in full swing and backcountry water sources usually have dried up.

EAST OF THE BAY

Wood Duck Pond above Pacheco Creek

Fishing

The park is dotted with artificial lakes, constructed by ranchers for their thirsty cattle. The reservoirs provide excellent angling opportunities for large-mouth bass, black crappie, and green sunfish. The featured trips below visit several of these lakes, including the two largest: Mississippi and Coit. Fishing is permitted year-round; a valid California fishing license is required. Plastic worms and lures reportedly work well.

Bikepacking

A large number of trails in Henry Coe are old ranch roads open to bicycles, but mountain biking in the park is a burly undertaking. Most trails are steep, rough, and extremely strenuous. Add weight on your back and it's even more challenging. Numerous trail camps and backcountry spots are accessible by pedal, including both Coit and Mississippi lakes. Note, however, that the featured trips below are for foot travel only and bikepackers must take alternate routes not described here.

Rules and Regulations

Backcountry camping is by permit only. *Maximum Group Size:* 8. *Dogs and wood fires* prohibited. *Camp stoves* permitted, except in times of extreme wildfire risk. *Bikes* are allowed on all former ranch roads in the park, prohibited in Orestimba Wilderness.

THE NATURAL HISTORY OF HENRY COE: A BRIEF SURVEY

A series of long, high ridges defines the topography of Henry W. Coe State Park. Most trend in a north-south direction and trap moisture from east-moving storms. Each successive ridge to the east receives less precipitation, creating a marked precipitation gradient across the park. The park's western regions receive twice as much annual rain (25-30″) as those in the east (10-20″), a pattern that greatly affects the park's ecosystems.

The main park entrance area is located atop 2500-foot Pine Ridge on the western edge of the park. This long ridge receives enough moisture to support a diverse oak woodland ecosystem (valley, black, and coast live oaks are common), which is joined by both gray pine and, oddly, tall Ponderosa pine. Ponderosas are common throughout the Sierra Nevada foothills, but are found in only one other place in the Bay Area (Henry Cowell Redwoods State Park). On the eastern

Wild pig gone bad

flanks of Pine Ridge, bay trees, madrone, buckeye, and a variety of ferns flourish on shady slopes. Pockets of chaparral appear on exposed hillsides, but are uncommon. Along the many forks of Coyote Creek below Pine Ridge grow California sycamores, drawing suste-nance from the streambeds. Look for these water-loving trees at moist creek-sides throughout the park. Poison oak is ubiquitous along Pine Ridge and throughout the park—be watchful!

Above the Coyote Creek drainage

Blue, Willow, and Rockhouse ridges rise progressively east of Pine Ridge, followed by the tall ridgeline of Bear Mountain (2604′). These define the drier eastern margins of the Coyote Creek watershed and are cloaked with chapar-ral. Oak woodland grows near valley bottoms, with hardy blue oak and gray pine appearing in greatest abundance and surrounded by a wide variety of shrubs and wildflowers. In the chaparral, chamise and buckbrush predominate and provide little shade for hikers on long ridgetop traverses. This pattern repeats itself in the southern regions of the park, where Mahoney, Wasno, Wil-low, and Pacheco ridges define the topography.

Beyond Bear Mountain, in the northeast region of the park, the topography changes. Instead of a series of long ridges, singular Robinson Mountain (2656′) dominates 23,300-acre Orestimba Wilderness. Three creeks—Red, Robinson, and Orestimba—ring the massif. Flowing through broad valleys, they provide habitat for a wide but low-lying corridor of blue oak savanna. Large gray pines and creekside sycamores join this hardiest of oak species below the thick chap-arral of higher elevations.

Temperature inversions are common in Henry Coe's deep valleys in winter and spring, with cooler air masses settling at lower elevations. This is particu-larly evident in spring as higher valley slopes are already green with new leaves and flowers, while trees along the valley bottoms lag several weeks behind.

Birdlife is abundant in the park (137 species have been identified), and among the most audible are introduced wild turkeys that strut the woodlands searching for females in spring. You may frequently hear them gobbling in the trees. Male turkeys can be surprising aggressive—use caution. Large golden

EAST OF THE BAY

eagles, red-tailed hawks, and acorn woodpeckers are just a few of the other species that call the park home.

Mammals such as bobcats and mountain lions are common, preying on the park's numerous deer and small rodents. Non-native wild pigs also are abundant. These large, black, hairy creatures search for food by rooting the ground with their snouts; their "pig tracks" are common throughout the park. They have poor eyesight and usually are quickly scared off.

THE WESTERN ZONE

Deep canyons, nice views, and a year-round swimming hole

Distance: 12.1 miles round-trip
Total Elevation Gain/Loss: 2500/2500
Hiking Time: 2 days
Difficulty: 3 stars
Maps: *Henry W. Coe State Park Trail and Camping Map,* USGS 7.5-min *Mt. Sizer, Mississippi Creek*

The convoluted drainage of Coyote Creek surrounds Pine Ridge. A mosaic of streams flowing through shady canyons, the watershed can be accessed via several steep trails from the main park entrance area. This journey tours some of the best features of the Western Zone: Pine Ridge, three different trail camps, two forks of Coyote Creek, and the perennial swimming waters of China Hole. Unlike most trips in Henry Coe, this adventure can be tackled in any season due to the presence of year-round water.

Hike Overview

Beginning at the main park entrance, the hike travels along Pine Ridge before plummeting more than a thousand feet to reach China Hole Trail Camp by Coyote Creek. After winding through The Narrows, a thin gap carved by the East Fork, the hike reaches Los Cruzeros Trail Camp. Returning toward Pine Ridge on Poverty Flat Road, the route winds over the open hillsides of Jackass Peak, passes Middle Fork Coyote Creek and Poverty Flat Trail Camp, and climbs steeply back up Pine Ridge. The journey may be reduced by more than 2 miles via a connector trail between Poverty Flat and China Hole on Creekside Trail, an option that skips both the Narrows and Los Cruzeros Trail Camp.

The Trail Camps

The three trail camps featured below are among the most popular in the park. Given their proximity to the main entrance, they occasionally fill on busy weekends. Therefore, your overnight options may be limited depending on season. While the featured hike is contained to the Western Zone, Blue Ridge Zone—and its unrestricted camping—can be readily accessed a short distance upstream from Los Cruzeros Trail Camp.

Los Cruzeros Trail Camp is located at the midpoint of the hike, neatly dividing the trip into two equal segments. Three well-spaced sites are available near East Fork Coyote Creek. Los Cruzeros is not the best summer destination; the sites offer minimal shade and the adjacent section of creek usually dries up by June.

China Hole Trail Camp features one site near a small sandy beach on the banks of Coyote Creek. Located 100 feet downstream from its namesake swimming hole, the small camp has access to year-round water and large rocks ideal for sunbathing.

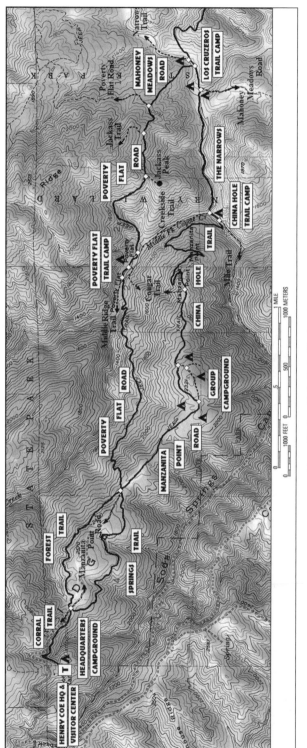

Henry W. Coe State Park: Western Zone

The creek can turn somewhat green in late summer and fall—a filter is recommended. This is not the most secluded place to camp; China Hole is a popular destination, especially on weekends.

Poverty Flat Trail Camp features five sites along the banks of Middle Fork Coyote Creek. Several sites have picnic tables, and there is a centrally located outhouse. Poverty Flat is shaded during the hot summer months; water is often available from the creek through July and some upstream pools typically remain into fall.

Trail Description

Los Cruzeros Trail Camp

The route begins across the road from the visitor center on singletrack Corral Trail (0.0/2650). After crossing a small bridge, the trail contours into a lush world of black oak, bay trees, buckeye, snowberry bushes, and coast live oak. It then winds above precipitous slopes before encountering the first big-berry manzanita of the trip. Dozens of manzanita varieties exist, but few approach the massive size of these specimens; their twisting, blood-red trunks are almost treelike in girth. Chamise, toyon, and honeysuckle vines—common members of the park's chaparral community—appear alongside.

Soon after breaking into open hillsides graced with large valley oak, the trail reaches a six-way junction at Manzanita Point Road (0.6/2510). Cross the wide road, grab an interpretive brochure from the post, and continue on Forest Trail. (Adjacent Springs Trail and Manzanita Point Road both reconnect in a mile and are alternate routes for the return journey.) Forest Trail has numbered markers (which correspond to descriptions on the free brochure) that highlight many of the park's common trees and shrubs. After contouring through this shady educational world, the trail rejoins Manzanita Point Road (1.8/2330) at its junction with Springs Trail and Poverty Flat Road.

Bear left on wide Manzanita Point Road as it undulates along the ridgetop past valley oak and ponderosa pine. The road then passes the pleasant Manzanita Group Camps (see the camping chapter *Henry W. Coe* for more information on these sites) before reaching China Hole and Madrone Spring trails just past sites 6 and 7 (2.6/2260). Turn left on China Hole Trail to begin the descent.

China Hole Trail initially contours below the last group sites (a spur trail splits right to site 9), passing some final ponderosa pines that give way to black oak, madrone, and blue oak. Soon the trail steeply dives through a corridor of massive big-berry manzanita (this unusual forest of skeletal fingers gives Manzanita Point its name) and later a zone burned by prescribed fire (a posted sign tells the story). Here manzanita diminishes, and thick chamise and buckbrush thrive on the regenerating hillside. The low-lying vegetation offers good views below of the Coyote Creek watershed and its multiple drainages. California sage and sticky monkey flower appear in the chaparral mix as the trail next encounters Manzanita Point and the junction with Cougar Trail (3.7/1910).

Continue straight on China Hole Trail to begin a series of long, descending switchbacks (note the marked ecological difference between the sun-exposed southern slopes of chaparral and shadier north slopes of oak woodland) to canyon bottom and the junction with Mile Trail (5.2/1150). To reach China Hole Trail Camp, bear left (upstream) to cross the creek and then quickly switchback roughly 30 feet above the water. Bear left on the obvious use trail and descend to the pleasant site.

To continue the journey from the junction with Mile Trail, proceed a short distance upstream. In summer and fall this stream is the only reliable water source on the hike, so fill your bottles. It's also a great swimming hole. After a refreshing dip continue upstream to quickly reach the confluence of Coyote Creek's Middle Fork (left) and East Fork (right). China Hole and Poverty Flat trail camps are connected via Creekside Trail along the Middle Fork, a shorter return option. To reach Los Cruzeros Trail Camp and complete the full Western Zone loop, bear right up the East Fork and enter the lush world of The Narrows.

While there is no officially maintained trail through The Narrows, the use path is generally obvious and closely parallels the creek. This route requires crossing the stream in several places, and, depending on season and flow, this can be a rock-hop or knee-deep ford. In times of heavy rains The Narrows may become impassable—use caution.

Profuse spring wildflowers color the ground beneath bay trees, willows, alders, and sycamores in this canyon environment, and soon you reach wide Mahoney Meadows Road and the first site of Los Cruzeros Trail Camp near the confluence of East Fork Coyote and Kelly creeks (6.2/1230). Bear left on Mahoney Meadows Road to by-pass the second site (upstream and out of sight from the road on a curve of East Fork Coyote Creek) and reach the third site at the northern Mahoney Meadows Road creek crossing. If these are full, unrestricted camping is available a quarter mile upstream from Mahoney Meadows Road, beyond the boundary of Blue Ridge Zone.

The junction with Willow Ridge Trail (6.3/1230) is located upstream on the right, just past the third site. Those continuing on to Mississippi Lake should skip ahead to the next hike description (*Mississippi Lake and Beyond*).

Otherwise, to head back toward Pine Ridge, follow wide Mahoney Meadows Road north as it rock-hops the creek and climbs steeply through open woodland of blue oak and gray pine. Turn left at the junction with broad Poverty Flat Road (6.8/1620) and remain on Poverty Flat Road as it ascends to reach Jackass Trail (7.0/1790) before gently descending to a saddle below Jackass Peak (1784').

From here, a short side-trip leads to the level summit and its near-360° views. Several forks of Coyote Creek are visible below.

Poverty Flat Road plummets past this point to reach Middle Fork Coyote Creek and Creekside Trail (8.2/1150), which arrives from China Hole (see above). The vegetation is lush once again; black oak and bay trees thrive, and the wide streambed of sycamores is a pleasant backdrop to Poverty Flat Trail Camp. Poverty Flat's five sites are spread along the stream close to the road: site 5 by the Creekside Trail junction; sites 3 and 4 by the outhouse and junction with Cougar Trail (8.3/1160); site 2 by the creek crossing; and site 1 just upstream from the Middle Ridge Trail junction (8.5/1240).

To continue, remain on Poverty Flat Road as it begins a steady thousand-foot ascent along the flanks of Pine Ridge. (It is also possible to return via Manzanita Point and China Hole Trail by following Cougar Trail south from Poverty Flat. This singletrack variation adds a mile to the journey.) Poverty Flat Road contours gently and sometimes ascends steeply for short, strenuous sections through a lush environment marked by the presence black oak, buckeye, madrones, and spring wildflowers. An intense switchbacking climb at the end finally deposits you back on top of Pine Ridge at the earlier junction with Manzanita Point Road (10.2/2330).

From here you can return on a different route by following Springs Trail as it travels along the margin of open oak woodland and past several dribbling springs to reach Corral Trail (11.5/2510) and the final section back to the visitor center (12.1/2650).

MISSISSIPPI LAKE AND BEYOND: THE ORESTIMBA WILDERNESS

The most remote wilderness in the Bay Area

Distance: 24 miles round-trip to Mississippi Lake; 50+ miles round-trip to Orestimba Wilderness

Total Elevation Gain/Loss: 6000/6000 to Mississippi Lake, 9500/9500 to Orestimba Wilderness

Hiking Time: 3-4 days to Mississippi Lake; 5 days to 2 weeks for Orestimba Wilderness

Difficulty: ★★★★★

Maps: *Henry W. Coe State Park Trail and Camping Map,* USGS 7.5-min *Mt. Sizer, Mississippi Creek, Mustang Peak, Wilcox Ridge, Mt. Stakes*

To reach vast and remote Orestimba Wilderness requires hiking more than 15 miles across some of the Bay Area's most rugged terrain. It's another 15 arduous miles back out. In between, stay as long as you possibly can in this seldom-visited wilderness area. It's an epic.

En route, in the middle of the park, is Mississippi Lake. At nearly a mile long, it's the largest lake in Henry Coe and home to a sizeable population of large-mouth bass. The surrounding blue oak woodland and a developed lakeshore site make this haven a worthwhile trip in its own right.

Hike Overview

The first part of the trip follows the route outlined in The Western Zone above, descending Pine Ridge to China Hole and continuing through The Narrows to Los Cruzeros Trail Camp at the base of Willow Ridge. After climbing Willow Ridge and traveling its roller-coaster ridgeline, the hike reaches Mississippi Lake. Beyond the lake, you drop into the Orestimba Creek watershed and embark on a 20-mile loop around Robinson Mountain in Orestimba Wilderness. The most straightforward return option is to retrace your steps, but other routes are available—ask park staff about utilizing County Line and Bear Mountain roads.

While the crystalline creeks in Orestimba Wilderness flow throughout winter and spring, they usually dry up by the end of May. Check with park staff about water availability if you are planning a late-spring excursion.

A journey into Orestimba Wilderness requires excellent fitness, considerable self-reliance, and good map-reading and route-finding skills. Trails are often overgrown, unsigned, and/or indistinct; bushwhacking is occasionally necessary. Know what you're doing and be prepared for the unexpected.

Camping Information

This backpacking trip visits the Western, Interior, Mississippi, and Orestimba Wilderness zones. Beyond the Western Zone, camping is permitted anywhere. Please respect the land and leave no trace of your passage. Recommended trail camps in the Western Zone (your approach route) for the first night are Los Cruzeros and Willow Ridge (described below). In the event that these trail camps are full, Blue Ridge Zone (and its unrestricted camping) can be readily accessed a short distance upstream from Los Cruzeros. Small Mississippi Zone surrounds its namesake lake and the trail camp here occasionally fills on busy weekends. While it is possible to reach Mississippi Lake in one day, it is an arduous 12-mile hike and not recommended. Good campsites are abundant throughout Orestimba Wilderness.

Trail Description

For the first part of this hike, please refer to the description in *The Western Zone* above and proceed to Los Cruzeros Trail Camp (6.2/1230). Before leaving

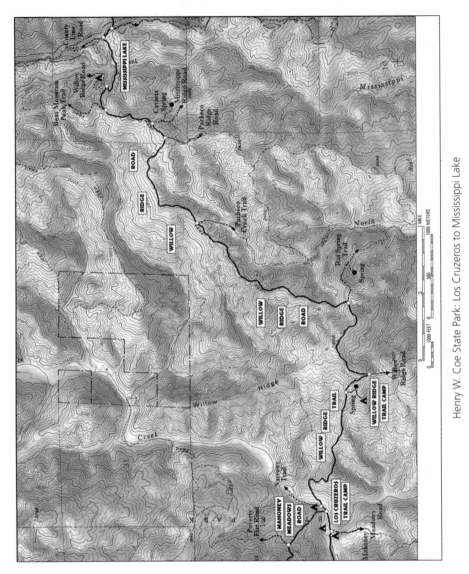

Henry W. Coe State Park: Los Cruzeros to Mississippi Lake

camp, fill your water bottles at adjacent Coyote Creek, the last reliable source for the next 6 miles. Then continue on singletrack Willow Ridge Trail, located on the right just past the northern Mahoney Meadows Road creek crossing. After momentarily dropping to the creekbed, Willow Ridge Trail begins a climbing traverse up the ridge. Black oak soon appears as the trail winds along the oak woodland/chaparral margin and then descends briefly on a shadier north slope marked by bay trees and coffee berry. Climbing again, the route obtains the ridgeline and begins a more direct ascent. Broken-down barbed wire fence appears in places, relics of the land's ranching days.

The trail then climbs relentlessly along the ridgeline, alternating between black-oak shade and scratchy chaparral. Near the top is a junction on the right for Willow Ridge Trail Camp (7.5/2190). The camp is located a short 0.2 mile down this thin trail past Willow Ridge Spring. Here blue oak, gray pine, and coast live oak provide shade for several grassy clearings with excellent views of ridges to the west. Overall it's a good site, but nearby Willow Ridge Spring is unreliable—bring sufficient water if staying the night.

Beyond the trail camp and back on the main route, the top of Willow Ridge is soon attained (7.8/2400); turn left onto Willow Ridge Road. For the next 4 miles, the route follows the dry and exposed ridgeline as it endlessly undulates through chamise-dominated chaparral. Marking the divide between the Coyote Creek and Pacheco Creek watersheds, the ridge provides far-reaching views. From the junction with Eagle Pines Trail (8.2/2610), vast stretches of the park spread out below. East Fork Coyote Creek flows through a linear valley to the north, the massif of Bear Mountain and its ridges is visible northeast, and Willow Ridge Road can be seen snaking northeast toward hidden Mississippi Lake. Continue hiking on Willow Ridge Road as you drop steeply to reach Rat Spring Trail on the right (8.6/2450). (Rat Spring is located on a spur trail 0.3 mile down Rat Spring Trail; it varies in volume and quality depending on season.)

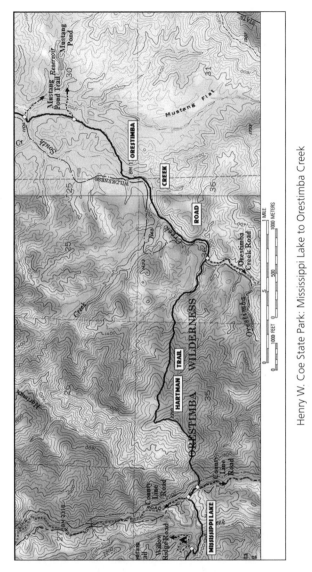

Henry W. Coe State Park: Mississippi Lake to Orestimba Creek

EAST OF THE BAY

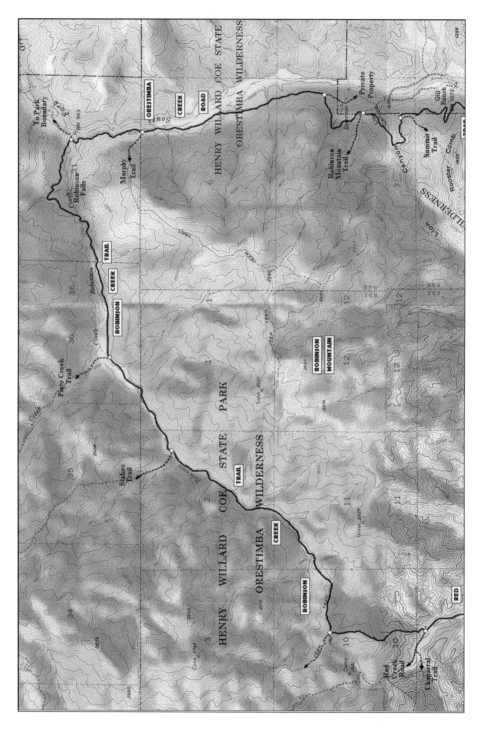

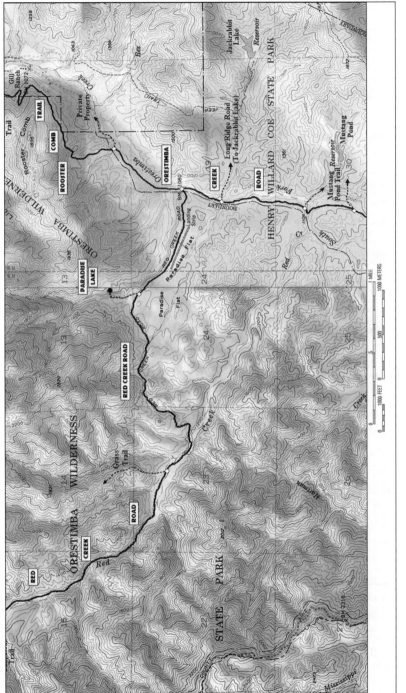

Henry W. Coe State Park: Orestimba Wilderness

Shortly beyond Rat Spring Trail, a 3-4' diameter metal wrecking ball (a strange relic . . .) sits rusting by the trail. Wild cucumber vines, yerba santa, abundant poison oak, coyote brush, buckbrush, and manzanita add variety to the chaparral, joined by the occasional coast live oak, blue oak, and bay tree. The young trees provide a few shady patches for rest; they also serve as evidence of the wildfires that regularly sweep through the chaparral communities. Based on the size of the trees, the area has likely burned in the past 20-30 years.

The roller coaster grinds onward as you pass several trails joining from the right—Pacheco Creek Trail (10.3/2250), Pacheco Ridge Road (11.2/2470), and Mississippi Ridge Road (11.4/2400). Another potential water source, Caviata Spring, is located 0.2 mile down Mississippi Ridge Road (be sure to bear left at the fork, see map). Beyond this point the route finally descends to the lake, passing Bear Mountain Peak Trail on the left (11.8/2250) before reaching the junction with Mississippi Lake Dam Road (12.0/2150). To reach the nearby established picnic site (tables and shade), bear left to remain on Willow Ridge Road; the site is located 0.2 mile ahead by the lakeshore. To continue toward Orestimba Wilderness, turn right and descend to the southern lakeshore on the dam road.

Surrounded by thriving oak woodland, Mississippi Lake is an oasis in an otherwise dry landscape. Turtles, rabbits, birds, and other wildlife are abundant. The 0.7-mile-long lake can be circumnavigated (a 3-mile loop) in search of campsites and fishing spots. Good sites are scattered throughout, but lakeshore access is often difficult due to thick shrubbery and poison oak. Outhouses are located near the dam and at the lake's northern end. The bass fishing is excellent.

After filling up water bottles (the lake is your only source for the next 2.5 miles), follow well-graded Mississippi Dam Road past the lake's southern shore to reach County Line Road (12.5/2180) and turn right to quickly find posted Hartman Trail on the left (12.6/2210). County Line Road marks the watershed divide between Pacheco Creek, which ultimately flows west into the Bay, and Orestimba Creek, which heads east into the Central Valley. The road also travels the border between Santa Clara and Stanislaus counties, and defines the western boundary of Orestimba Wilderness.

Hartman Trail is not maintained. Thin, sometimes indistinct, and over-grown, it immediately drops through oaks and chaparral to reach a small saddle before climbing to the top of a promontory (2210') with good views northeast. Robinson Mountain (2656') and Orestimba Wilderness are clearly visible, and the rocky outcrop of Rooster Comb can be spotted on Robinson's eastern flanks.

From the promontory, the trail curves briefly north before cutting right and dropping steeply through a dense chamise corridor. The route re-enters full oak woodland as the trail reaches a barbed wire fence above a small gully at 1400 feet. The path becomes increasingly indistinct here—go left across the gully to regain the small ridge and then watch for a path branching right back into the small drainage. The trail completely peters out at this point; keep following the drainage downwards to reach Orestimba Creek Road (14.7/1170).

Campsites are abundant in the broad, delightful valley of Orestimba Creek. One good overnight option is Kingbird Pond, tucked away 1.2 miles south of Hartman Trail; follow Orestimba Creek Road south for 0.7 mile and bear left on Kingbird Pond Trail. If not stopping for the night, continue north (downstream) on Orestimba Creek Road as it winds along the broad creekbed through vibrant blue oak woodland.

The level hiking here is pleasant compared to the strenuous route in. Also, you can eschew the wide road and travel directly along the banks of Orestimba Creek, a pleasant cross-country route. A mile north of Hartman Trail, the road deviates slightly from the creek. Opt for the off-trail streamside route, unless you're interested in exploring Mustang Pond. Accessed via half-mile Mustang Pond Trail, the small lake can be reached from Orestimba Creek Road at a southern junction (16.2/1210) and a northern junction (16.6/1170). Immediately upstream from the northern junction, Red Creek joins Orestimba Creek and a few uncommon juniper trees grow in the streambed. After crossing the creek by the northern junction for Mustang Pond, the winding road leaves and then returns to the creek before reaching Long Ridge Road on the right (17.3/1100). (Long Ridge Road leads to another pond, Jackrabbit Lake, 1.6 miles

Outdoor reflection

to the east. If side-tripping, be sure to bear left at the fork 1.2 miles out. The lake covers 6 acres in spring but diminishes in summer and fall.)

A short 0.3 mile beyond Long Ridge Road you pass Red Creek Road on the left (17.6/1070)—your return route. (Paradise Flat is a short distance west along lower Red Creek Road and makes an idyllic picnic or camping spot.) The loop around Robinson Mountain begins at this point, as Orestimba Creek Road continues downstream to reach Rooster Comb Trail on the left (18.2/1060). Orestimba Creek Road continues through private property, so you must follow singletrack Rooster Comb Trail to stay inside the park.

Rooster Comb Trail becomes overgrown and indistinct in places, but begins climbing through open blue oak woodland to steadily traverse the slopes above Gill Ranch. As you round the eastern corner of Rooster Comb, the trail becomes rockier. Chaparral now predominates—chamise, sticky monkey flower, scrub oak, and poison oak are common. A pair of switchbacks then descends, but as of 2002, this section of trail was heavily overgrown and disappeared abruptly into thick scrub oak. If you have difficulty finding or entirely lose the trail, contour around the slopes and descend slightly to rejoin the path.

After passing the posted trail to Rooster Comb Summit on the left (20.0/1250), Rooster Comb Trail descends into Lion Canyon and switchbacks near the bottom to cross an ephemeral trickle. Leaving the narrow canyon, the trail continues north and traverses the slopes above the park boundary. It then passes faint Robinson Mountain Trail on the left (20.8/1150) and winds above the property fence and a small reservoir before descending to rejoin Orestimba Creek Road (21.3/1050).

North of Gill Ranch, the level valley of Orestimba Creek reaches nearly a quarter mile in width. Orestimba Creek Road travels along the valley's western margin and offers easier walking, but the off-trail route along the stream is more dramatic. Here enormous California sycamores line the rocky streambed, their roots feeding into the water like giant hoses. Blue oak woodland lines either side of the valley as do a few outlying valley oak. The Robinson Creek drainage is apparent ahead, tracing from the west. Bear left on Robinson Creek Trail beyond the confluence of Orestimba and Robinson creeks (23.2/940) and head west below Robinson Mountain's northern flanks. Anglers may continue 0.7 mile downstream from the confluence along Orestimba Creek to reach the park's northeastern boundary. While trout reportedly are present along this section of creek, you may have to fish for a long, long time to find one.

Robinson Trail is a wide, grassy road that initially climbs above hidden Robinson Creek. The trail cuts deeply into the hillside to traverse around a small tributary; secretive Robinson Falls is located immediately upstream from this tributary's confluence with Robinson Creek. While it is possible to come within earshot by descending off-trail past the tributary, large rock outcrops and steep slopes preclude reaching Robinson Creek Trail itself. The falls may be best reached by dropping down before you reach the tributary or by traveling directly along Robinson Creek above its confluence with Orestimba Creek.

Robinson Trail abruptly drops to reach Robinson Creek in a narrow riparian canyon, flush with buckeyes, poison oak, and gray pines. After crossing the small creek, the trail fades into grass, re-crosses the creek several more times, and then suddenly enters an open field studded with huge sycamores and good campsites. Shortly past this meadow, Pinto Creek and Trail join Robinson Creek from the north in a Sierra-esque conifer landscape of large gray pines (25.2/1180). A scrambling side-trip up overgrown Pinto Creek rewards with a secluded swimming hole.

Beyond Pinto Creek, Robinson Creek Trail becomes more apparent and the canyon gradually narrows. After crossing a tributary as large as the main creek, the trail becomes only intermittently visible— stay close to the creek as the canyon continues to narrow and level ground disappears. Conditions are quite dry as surrounding chamise encroaches on an increasingly thin strip of blue oaks. As the ever-narrowing canyon bends west, the trail turns up a wash gully on the south slopes. Traversing upward, the obvious road soon attains the ridgeline divide between Robinson and Red creeks (27.6/1580). Good views appear once again as the Red Creek valley opens up below.

Hidden Pinto Creek

After savoring the view, bear right along the ridgeline on an overgrown and unnamed, but easy-to-follow, road to the top of the nearby knoll (1767'). Two roads join here—bear left to begin the steep ridgeline descent into the valley. The trail passes a small pond shortly before reaching Red Creek Road (28.8/1270).

Red Creek Road marks the final leg of the Robinson Mountain loop. The long spine of Bear Mountain (2604') rises southwest above the valley and defines the high ridge margin of the Red Creek watershed. Your route heads downstream (south) along Red Creek, where the wide trail passes through a narrow valley continually lined with blue oaks and, in spring, with round, tufted flowers of purple Owl's clover. The valley widens noticeably as the route passes Grass Trail on the left (30.5/1210) and then bends north to wind over low-lying foothills. After a steady but gradual ascent the road descends to a small tributary and enters Paradise Flat.

Site of an old landing strip, aptly named Paradise Flat is a massive field of blue oak savanna more than a mile long. Grass and spring wildflowers flourish in this idyllic landscape, which makes an ideal final stop on the circuit around Robinson Mountain. Shady campsites are everywhere and seasonal water is

EAST OF THE BAY

often available from the two small creeks that border the area to the north and south. Red Creek Road travels along the flat's northern edge, reaching the junction for Paradise Lake shortly after curving back eastward (32.2/1250).

Paradise Lake is located a short 0.3 mile from Red Creek Road and abuts the rocky southern flanks of Robinson Mountain. The snags protruding from the lake belie its man-made nature but the setting is pleasant and the scenery excellent. Back on Red Creek Road, you soon return to Orestimba Creek Road to complete the loop around Robinson Mountain (33.1/1170). From here, the long journey home begins. The most direct route retraces your route for 11.4 miles past Mississippi Lake to Los Cruzeros Trail Camp via Orestimba Creek Road, Hartman Trail, and Willow Ridge Road and Trail. The state park map reveals several alternative routes back to Los Cruzeros, but they all require more effort. From Los Cruzeros several alternate routes are possible to the main park entrance (see *The Western Zone* above). When finally back at the trailhead and Henry Coe visitor center (51.4/2650), take time to celebrate.

SOUTHERN HENRY COE: COIT LAKE AND VICINITY

*Lakes, tantalizing views, and a hidden waterfall
in Coe's vast southern backcountry*

Distance: 12.4 miles round-trip to Coit Lake, plus 3-6 miles of side-trips
Total Elevation Gain/Loss: 3800/3800
Hiking Time: 2-4 days
Difficulty: ★★★
Maps: *Henry W. Coe State Park Trail and Camping Map,* USGS 7.5-min *Gilroy Hot Springs*

The rising bulwark of Wasno Ridge guards the approach to Henry Coe's southern backcountry. Rising more than 1500 feet above the southern trailheads, the ridge separates the main stem of Coyote Creek from its inland headwaters and is a heart-pumping obstacle that keeps hiking traffic to a minimum. East of Wasno Ridge, Willow Ridge rises 500 feet above small Kelly Lake and marks the divide between the Coyote Creek and Pacheco Creek watersheds. Coit Lake, the second largest in the park, nestles on the other side and provides an ideal base camp for further exploration. Several small ponds, seldom-trod creek valleys, a maze of trails, and hidden Pacheco Falls await discovery.

Hike Overview

Beginning from Coyote Creek trailhead on Coe's southwestern edge, this trip steeply ascends Wasno Ridge on singletrack Anza and Jackson trails before

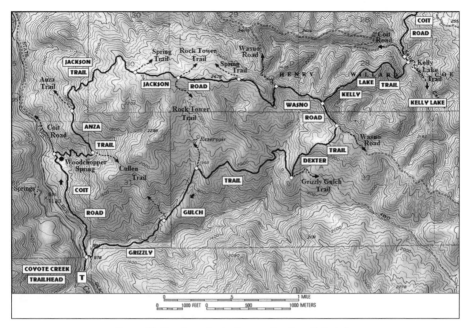

Henry W. Coe State Park: Coyote Creek to Kelly Lake

following old ranch roads past Kelly Lake and over Willow Ridge to Coit Lake. The way back follows Dexter and Grizzly Gulch trails for a more gradual descent down Wasno Ridge. While this journey makes for an excellent overnight trip, the effort and scenery merit at least one extra day for exploration.

Water is readily available in season from Coyote Creek at the trailhead, and from several springs and ponds en route (a filter is highly recommended). The hike can be completed year-round (Kelly and Coit lakes provide reliable water sources), but the baking heat, shadeless slopes, and increasingly funky water make this a less attractive option in summer and fall.

Camping Information

This hike travels through (in order) the Mahoney, Kelly, Coit, and Grizzly Gulch backcountry zones. The required backcountry permit can be obtained from a self-service station at nearby Hunting Hollow Trailhead (see directions below). Camping is unrestricted in this region of the park. A few established sites and outhouses can be found around Coit and Kelly lakes, otherwise all camping is primitive. Camping is prohibited within a half mile of the trailhead; Woodchopper Spring (described below) is a mile from the trailhead and provides the closest, best option. For those arriving late in the day, nearby Coyote Creek County Park has a drive-in campground (see the camping chapter *Coyote Creek County Park*).

EAST OF THE BAY

To Reach Coyote Creek Trailhead

Take the Leavesley Road exit from Highway 101 in Gilroy and follow Leavesley Road 1.8 miles east to New Ave. Turn left and follow New Ave. 0.6 mile to Roop Road and turn right. At this point Roop Road becomes Gilroy Hot Springs Road and reaches Coyote Creek County Park on the left in 3.0 miles. Continue 3.0 more miles past the park entrance to reach Hunting Hollow trailhead on the right and stop to obtain your backcountry permit. The station is occasion-

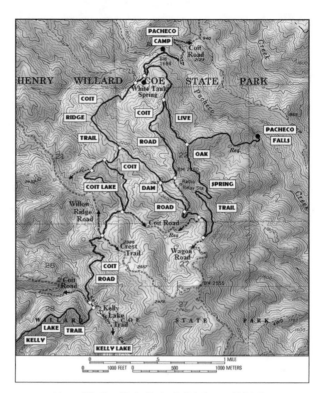

Henry W. Coe State Park: Coit Lake and Vicinity

ally staffed on weekends. Coyote Creek trailhead is located 1.7 miles farther at a bridge marking the farthest public access permitted on Gilroy Hot Springs Rd. While it is possible to park overnight here, several cases of vandalism and theft have been reported. The park recommends leaving your vehicle at safer Hunting Hollow Trailhead. To conserve energy, consider dropping your gear at Coyote Creek before walking back along the road from Hunting Hollow.

Trail Description

From Coyote Creek Trailhead (0.0/940), begin down wide Coit Road. The hike initially parallels the creek and quickly meets Grizzly Gulch Trail (your return route), which joins from the right (0.1/960). Continue on Coit Road to begin a slow climb that soon passes a fenced cattle-loading enclosure from recent ranching days. Large, big-berry manzanita appear shortly before the trail crests and descends briefly past valley oak and a giant rusting water tank to reach Anza Trail on the right (1.0/1090). At the junction, an interpretive sign highlights the 1775-1776 Spanish expedition, led by Juan Bautista de Anza, that attempted (and failed) to find a route through this convoluted region. The Spaniards dubbed this area "Sierra del Chasco" ("Mountains of Deception"); they would be the last Europeans to visit the area for nearly a hundred years.

Woodchopper Spring and its water faucet are located by the trail junction and provide a dependable source for much of the year (check with park staff in late summer and fall). Several shady campsites are also nearby. Turning uphill on Anza Trail, you pass beneath bay trees and coast live oak as the shady single-track path switchbacks steadily upward to reach Cullen Trail on the right (1.6/1440). Bear left to remain on Anza Trail and traverse open slopes flush with spring wildflowers and good views. At the junction with Jackson Trail (1.9/1560), turn right to head toward Kelly Lake.

Jackson Trail is steep and sustained, and views expand on the ascent. Looking north, Pine Ridge and the main park entrance area are visible 6 miles away—tall and distinctive ponderosa pines can be identified on clear days. Beyond, Lick Observatory can be spotted atop Mt. Hamilton (4213′). As the trail attains the Wasno ridgeline, views reach as far south as Fremont Peak (3171′) east of Monterey Bay, and beyond to the Santa Lucia Range of Big Sur. Just beyond two small ponds, the trail reaches the junction for seasonally dribbling Elderberry Spring (3.3/2360).

Jackson Trail now widens to become Jackson Road as it hugs the ridgeline. Shortly before attaining the ridge's highest point (2676′), the route passes a four-way junction for Rock Tower Trail (3.7/2520). Continue climbing on Jackson Road over this high point and then begin a slow descent past hidden Spring Trail on the left (4.2/2630). Then bank sharply left to reach Wasno Road (4.7/2420). Turn right and briefly follow the road to Kelly Lake Trail on the left (4.9/2420).

Kelly Lake Trail first undulates through pleasant blue oak woodland studded with gray pines, but then the plummet begins. Black oak, coast live oak, bay, buckeye, and huge manzanita populate the shady slopes. Kelly Lake remains hidden from view until the very end, where the trail deposits you on the dam enclosing the northern shore.

Narrow Kelly Lake is enclosed by steep and brushy slopes, discouraging lakeshore camping and access. Take the trail to the dam's north end. For better camping options, turn right on Kelly Lake Trail, which parallels the eastern lakeshore; a good camping area can be found above the lake's south end in the upper Kelly Creek drainage. Additional camping options are downstream near Kelly Creek below the dam, and there

The folds of the Diablo Range

are a few small clearings tucked in the brush near the lakeshore. To continue on the main journey to Coit Lake, however, bear left at the northern end of the dam and then turn right on Coit Road by the pre-fab outhouse (5.9/1880).

Wide Coit Road initially climbs through a lush environment of varied oaks, bay trees, and buckeye before traversing across more open slopes. Views of the Kelly Creek drainage below and Wasno Ridge above appear as the hillside becomes increasingly cloaked with chaparral. You crest southern Willow Ridge between Kelly and Coit lakes; this is the divide between the Coyote Creek and Pacheco Creek watersheds. A four-way junction with Willow Ridge Road is met here (6.7/2240)—continue straight on Coit Road. The trail then descends through young oaks rivaled in size by adjacent manzanita to reach the reedy southern shore of Coit Lake (7.0/2080).

Coit Lake is ringed by easy trails. An established campsite and outhouse are located on the southwest shore; a few good sites (and another outhouse) are located by the dam on the lake's northern edge; and a grassy area resides near the fenced enclosure at Coit Lake Horse Camp on the eastern shore. A mix of blue oak, gray pine, coast live oak, manzanita, chamise, and coyote brush surround the lake, joined by abundant poison oak. While shore access is easier here than at Kelly Lake, there are only a few spots wide enough for good fishing; try the area around the dam for your chance at the lake's numerous bass and crappie. Drinking water can usually be drawn from the outflow near the dam. Otherwise the lake is the only source.

There are numerous other campsites and secret spots within a few miles of Coit Lake. Hoover Lake is 2.5 miles north along Willow Ridge Road. Also, the drainage below Coit Lake Dam makes for fun off-trail exploration through open woodlands. But the recommended adventure is to Pacheco Creek and its

Pacheco Creek Canyon

Gray pine and sycamore

seldom-visited waterfall, a 6-mile loop from Coit Lake with close to 2000 feet elevation gain/loss. Additionally, those looking to spend the night deeper in the park should consider camping near small Wood Duck Pond, located less than a half mile above the falls.

To reach the falls, proceed to Live Oak Spring Trail either via Coit Dam Road and then Coit Road from the north end of the lake, or via Coit Road from the south end of the lake. Live Oak Spring Trail splits and then rejoins as it traverses the slopes above Pacheco Creek canyon—take the lower option or risk missing the falls turnoff. Watch for the unmarked trail on the right to the falls, located just south of where Live Oak Spring Trail rejoins itself near two collapsed oak trees. The trail passes Wood Duck Pond as it descends a small ridgeline en route to the shady gorge below the falls. Roughly 200 feet above the creek, a spur trail splits left to reach vertical views into the rock chasm below.

The broad valley of Pacheco Creek above the falls also makes for idyllic camping and exploration. From Coit Lake's north end, follow Coit Dam Road and then Coit Ridge Trail past aptly named White Tank Spring to Coit Road and Pacheco Camp. From Coit Lake's south end, follow Coit Road all the way to Pacheco Camp. It's a 2-4 mile round-trip depending on route.

After savoring Coit Lake & Vicinity for as long as possible, you may be tempted to vary your return route to Kelly Lake Trail based on several alternate routes noted on the state park map. However, the most direct option is to retrace your steps on Coit Road to Kelly Lake Trail to its earlier junction with

EAST OF THE BAY

Wasno Road (9.1/2420). From there, the shortest route home descends into Grizzly Gulch to the south. Bear left on Wasno Road to quickly reach Dexter Trail on the right (9.3/2420).

Descend on Dexter Trail through open blue oak woodlands and beyond a diminutive pond on the left. Then drop steeply past increasing bay trees and coast live oak to reach the unsigned junction with Grizzly Gulch Trail (9.9/1940). Turn right on Grizzly Gulch Trail and traverse a moist creek gully and then contour shady slopes. At Rock Tower Trail on the right (10.9/1740), you may take a short half-mile detour 250 feet uphill to reach another small pond ringed by impressive oaks.

Back on Grizzly Gulch Trail, the route begins a more direct descent above a narrow creek gully. Valley oak, buckeye, and madrone soon appear, indicative of the moist riparian environment. A few hundred feet from the bottom you pass the posted junction for indistinct Cullen Trail on the right (11.4/1270). Grizzly Gulch Trail descends into an increasingly lush world and soon reaches canyon bottom and crosses Grizzly Gulch Creek. Sycamores, ferns, and black oak appear as the trail ascends and contours the slopes above the creek. It then passes Spike Jones Trail on the left (12.1/1060) and returns to Coit Road (12.3/960). Turn left to return to Coyote Creek trailhead (12.4/940).

Giving Back

The Pine Ridge Association assists park staff in designing interpretive materials and presenting educational programs to the public. It offers a volunteer training program. Membership is $15 and has many benefits. Box 846, Morgan Hill, CA 95038, (408) 779-2728, www.coepark.org.

Appendices

Monterey Pine above Kirby Cove,
Marin Headlands

Group Campgrounds of the Bay Area

A variety of campsites designated specifically for large groups are available throughout the Bay Area. Of the more than 30 group camping locations, nearly 20 are in parks with family campgrounds and thus described in great detail earlier in the book—these 20 are only listed here. The remaining parks not previously mentioned are briefly described below. As regulations and reservation systems vary by park district, information is arranged by governing agency rather than region. Unless otherwise mentioned, all sites provide restrooms, fire pits, picnic tables, and water.

State Parks

Nearly all Bay Area state parks that offer family campgrounds provide at least one group site that may be used by groups of any kind. Youth groups (under 18 years of age) must be accompanied by at least 1 adult for every 15 youths. Maximum length of stay is 7 nights. As with family campsites, reservations are made through Reserve America at (800) 444-PARK or online at www.reserveamerica.com.

The following state parks offer group sites:

Samuel P. Taylor State Park, 2 sites.

Mt. Tamalpais State Park, 2 sites.

Bothe–Napa Valley State Park, 1 site.

Sugarloaf Ridge State Park, 1 site.

Half Moon Bay State Beach, 1 site.

Portola Redwoods State Park, 4 sites.

Big Basin Redwoods State Park, 4 sites.

Mt. Diablo State Park, 4 sites.

Golden Gate National Recreation Area

The National Park Service provides two sites at Rob Hill Group Camp in the Presidio. Located in a grove of eucalyptus, the sites offer nearby views of Baker Beach. Groups of any kind may use the sites. Open April-Oct. Both sites minimum 30 and maximum 50 people. Maximum 4 vehicles per site. $50/night. Call (415) 561-5444 for reservations.

Midpeninsula Regional Open Space District

MPROSD offers one group site at Black Mountain Backpack Camp. See the backpacking chapter *Monte Bello Open Space Preserve* for more information.

San Mateo County Parks

With the exception of Memorial County Park, all group campgrounds in the San Mateo County Park District are limited to use by non-profit youth groups only. Reservations can be made up to a year in advance by calling the park district reservation office at (650) 363-4021, TDD (650) 268-7807. Many sites are fully booked far in advance. Prices do not include a $4/vehicle entry fee. Detailed information, including pictures of the different sites, is available at www.eparks.net.

The following San Mateo County Parks offer group sites:

Memorial County Park, 2 sites usable by any group, 6 youth group sites.

San Bruno Mountain State and County Park, 1 youth group site, maximum 50 people; $1.50/child/night, minimum $50; located in coastal scrub and eucalyptus trees.

Junipero Serra County Park, 2 youth group sites, Oak Cove and Iris Point, maximum 25 people per site; $1.50/child/night; located behind the cities of Millbrae and San Bruno; good views throughout the park.

San Pedro Valley County Park, 1 youth group site, maximum 15 people; $1.50/child/night; located in the shade of willows below Montara Mountain; campfires not permitted.

Huddart County Park, 3 youth group sites, maximum 50 people per site; $100; located in shady redwood and mixed-evergreen forest east of Skyline Ridge on Kings Mountain Road.

Sam McDonald County Park, 3 youth group sites, maximum 50 people per site; $1.50/child/night; located in redwood forest west of Skyline Ridge on Pescadero Road; see the backpacking chapter *Pescadero Creek County Park* for additional information about the area.

APPENDIX A

Santa Clara County Parks

With the exception of Mt. Madonna County Park, all group campgrounds in the Santa Clara County Park District are limited to use by non-profit youth groups only. All youth group sites cost $30/night for the first night, and $10 each additional night. For reservations, call the district reservations office at (408) 355-2201 9 A.M.–4 P.M. Monday-Friday. There is a $6 reservation fee and maximum stay of 7 nights.

The following Santa Clara County Parks offer group campgrounds:

Sanborn County Park, 1 youth group site.

Uvas Canyon County Park, 1 youth group site.

Mt. Madonna County Park, 2 group sites, 3 youth group sites.

Joseph D. Grant County Park, 3 youth group sites.

Ed R. Levin County Park, 1 youth group site, maximum 200 people; located in the western foothills of the Diablo Range east of Milpitas; limited shade, lots of facilities.

East Bay Regional Park District

With nearly 30 group campgrounds, the East Bay Regional Park District offers the greatest number of group sites of any governing agency in the Bay Area. The sites are available for use by groups of any type, but groups not affiliated with a non-profit organization must provide a $250 deposit. Reservations can be made for the entire year beginning the first Monday in November for Alameda and Contra Costa county residents, and the first Monday in February for residents of other counties. Reservations can be made no later than 14 days in advance. To make reservations, call the district reservations office using the number appropriate for your area: Oakland area and locations outside the East Bay (510) 636-1684 or (510) 562-2267; Contra Costa County (925) 676-0192; Livermore area (925) 373-0144; Hayward area (510) 538-6470, TDD (510) 633-0460. The reservations office is open 8 A.M.–6 P.M. Monday-Thursday, 8 A.M.–4:30 P.M. Friday, April–Labor Day; winter hours: 8:30 A.M.–4:30 P.M. Monday-Friday. Prices range from $35 to $225 depending on group size, group type, and county of residence. Note that winter rains may close some of the sites.

The following East Bay Regional Parks offer group campgrounds:

Anthony Chabot Regional Park, 7 sites.

Del Valle Regional Park, 6 sites (4 are hike-in only).

Sunol Regional Wilderness, 5 sites.

Briones Regional Park, 3 sites. Maud Whalen Camp, maximum 75 people and 3 vehicles/site, located 1 mile from park entrance and main parking area.

Wee-Ta-Chi Camp, maximum 100 people and 4 vehicles/site, located 1.5 miles from park entrance and main parking area. Also Homestead Valley, maximum 500 people. Sites are located in open oak woodlands and grasslands.

Black Diamond Mines Regional Park, 1 site. Star Hill Group Camp, located in a grassland and oak woodland community, no water provided. Maximum 40 people and 8 vehicles. See the backpacking chapter *Black Diamond Mines Regional Park* for more information on the area.

Tilden Regional Park, 3 sites. Wildcat View, maximum 75 people and 2 vehicles/site, 0.3 mile from parking lot. New Woodland, maximum 50 people and 2 vehicles/site, 0.3 mile from parking lot. Both are located in the Tilden Nature Area in the Berkeley hills, 0.3 mile from the main parking area, accessible via public transportation, administered by Wildcat Canyon Regional Park. Gillespie Camp, maximum 75 people and 8 vehicles. Located at the southern end of the park on South Park Drive.

Redwood Regional Park, 1 site, Girls Camp, hike-in only during winter months. Located in a large grassy clearing 0.5 mile from Skyline Gate parking area on Skyline Blvd., maximum 75 people and 2 vehicles/site. The only camping near redwoods in the East Bay.

Las Trampas Regional Park, 1 site, Corral Camp. Located west of Danville in a secluded canyon, popular with equestrian groups, maximum 50 people and 2 vehicles/site, 0.25 mile from main parking area.

Garin Regional Park, 1 site, Arroyo Flat. Located in a secluded valley just east of Hayward, accessible by public transportation. maximum 75 people and 2 vehicles/site, 0.1 mile from main parking area.

Coyote Hills Regional Park, 1 site, Dairy Glen. Located by the San Francisco Bay near the east side of the Dumbarton Bridge (Hwy. 84), maximum 200 people and 2 vehicles/site, 0.3 mile from parking area.

Going Farther: Overnight Outdoor Adventures in the Greater Bay Area

Just beyond the Bay Area await many more destinations perfect for overnight outdoor adventure. Parks in Sonoma County and the Sacramento–San Joaquin Delta are within a two-hour drive for residents of the North Bay, San Francisco, and East Bay. Parks in Santa Cruz County can be reached within two hours from the East Bay, South Bay, and San Francisco.

SONOMA COUNTY AND VICINITY

Sonoma Coast State Beach

Stretching more than eight miles from Bodega Bay to the mouth of the Russian River, Sonoma Coast State Beach includes four different and distinct campgrounds within its boundaries. Here on the rural Sonoma Coast, ready beach access in the midst of rugged coastal scenery banishes the Bay Area to a world of distant memory. Highway 1 or Highway 116—choose your twisting road of preference for access. There are plenty of great outdoor destinations to explore in the area. Reservations can be made for two of the campgrounds—Bodega Dunes and Wright's Beach—up to seven months in advance by calling (800) 444-7275 or going online at www.reserveamerica.com. For more information: Sonoma Coast State Beach, 3095 Highway 1, Bodega Bay, CA 94923, (707) 875-3483.

Bodega Dunes Campground, located in a vast field of sand dunes by the longest beach on the Sonoma Coast. Access via Highway 1 north of Bodega Bay. Amenities: 98 developed sites; hike/bike sites; hot showers; dump station; plentiful beach; hiking in the dunes and headlands; surfing. Monarch butterflies cluster here in the winter, and seasonal whale watching is popular from Bodega Head. Lightly used campground. $12/night.

Wright's Beach, located three miles south of Highway 116 and the Russian River on Highway 1. Amenities: 30 tightly spaced sites located adjacent to the beach; Popular RV campground; en route camping allowed for self-contained vehicles; interesting geology at nearby Shell Beach. Many sites are reserved 6-7 months in advance. Sites 1-8 are closest to beach. $12/night.

Pomo Canyon and Willow Creek Environmental Sites, located away from the coast and two miles apart on Willow Creek Road just south of the Russian River. Amenities: primitive first-come, first-serve walk-in sites; pit toilets. Pets not allowed, no RV camping in the parking lot. Pomo Canyon: 20 sites, water. Willow Creek: 11 sites, no water, river access. $7/night.

Sonoma County Park District

Sonoma County manages its own set of small parks in the greater North Bay region, several of which offer camping facilities. Sites are usually better suited for self-contained vehicles, but tent camping is possible. Camping reservations can be made beginning the first Monday in November for the entire following calendar year by calling (707) 565-CAMP (-2267), 10 A.M.–3 P.M. Monday-Friday. Reservations must be made at least 10 days in advance, up to two sites may be reserved by an individual, and there is a $7 reservation fee for each site reserved. A small number of sites in each campground are not open to reservations and held as first-come, first-serve. For more information: Sonoma County Regional Parks Department, 2300 County Center Drive, Suite 120A, Santa Rosa, CA 95403, (707) 565-2041, www.sonoma-county.org/parks.

Spring Lake Regional Park, located west of Santa Rosa less than 4 miles from downtown on Newanga Avenue. Amenities: 29 closely spaced sites near the shore of 72-acre Spring Lake; 2 handicapped sites; boat launch and boat rental; visitor center; showers; fishing; swimming lagoon with lifeguard; ready access to the popular mountain biking trails of bordering Annadel State Park. $16/night. 1 group site, maximum 100 people, $50-200. For more information: 5390 Montgomery Dr., Santa Rosa, CA 95405, (707) 539-8092.

Doran Regional Park, located on the large spit enclosing Bodega Bay to the south on Doran Park Road. Amenities: 128 tightly packaged sites popular with RVs next to 2 miles of beach in an unusual location; 9 tent-only sites; 3 handicapped-accessible sites; showers; dump station; nearby boat launch. $16/night. 1 group site, maximum 50 people, $50-100.

Westside Regional Park, located on the west side of Bodega harbor adjacent to the boat launch. Popular with anglers. Amenities: 47 sites for self-contained vehicles only—*no tent camping;* showers. $16/night. For more information call (707) 875-3540.

Stillwater Cove Regional Park, located 16 miles north of Jenner on Highway 1. Amenities: 20 sites with nearby coastal access to a small lagoon popular with divers, anglers, and small boaters; 1 hike/bike site; 210-acre park with short hiking trails; hot showers; launch facility; dump station. $16/night. For more information call (707) 847-3245.

Other Destinations

Fort Ross Reef Campground, located 10 miles north of the Russian River on Highway 1 and 2 miles south of Fort Ross State Historic Park. Amenities: 21 first-come, first-serve sites hidden in a small coastal valley; fascinating nearby Russian history and re-created fort; for the adventurous, there are five miles of seldom-traveled wild coastline to the south. $10/night. Narrow, twisting access road—vehicles longer than 17 feet not permitted. For more information: Fort Ross Reef Campground, 19005 Highway 1, Jenner, CA 95450, (707) 847-3708 or -3286.

Skyline Wilderness Park, located on Immola Avenue just outside the city of Napa on a scenic hillside overlooking the valley. A public park on private land run by a local citizens group. Amenities: excellent spring wildflowers; wild back-country trails; disc golf course; and native plant garden. RV camping year-round in a large gravel lot. Tent camping permitted in the summer months, exact times vary year to year. For more information: 2201 Immola Ave., Napa, CA 94559, (707) 252-0481.

Napa County Fairgrounds, located on Oak Street in Calistoga, just north of the Highway 29/128 junction. Amenities: 46 paved RV sites in a large parking lot, full hookups and dump station available, adjacent lawn for tent camping, showers, convenient access to Calistoga attractions. Not wilderness. To the north, scenic Highway 29 twists seven miles up the flanks of Mount St. Helena to reach Robert Louis Stevenson State Park and its seldom-trod trails. Fairgrounds open year-round for camping, for reservations call (707) 942-5111. $22/night, $25/night with sewer hookups. For more information: 1435 Oak St., Calistoga, CA 94515, (707) 942-5111.

Lake Solano County Park, located on Highway 128 east of Lake Berryesa by scenic Putah Creek in the Coast Range foothills. Amenities: shady sites; beautiful spring wildflowers in surrounding oak woodlands; swimming; boating; fishing; showers; and dump station. 90 sites total, 40 RV sites with full hook-ups. In summer, $15/night, $18/night with hook-ups; winter $8/night. For reservations, call 1-800-939-PARK. For more information: 8685 Pleasant Valley Road, Winters, CA 95664, 1-800-939-PARK.

THE SACRAMENTO–SAN JOAQUIN DELTA

Brannan Island State Recreation Area, located 10 miles northeast of Antioch on Highway 160 by the southern shores of the Sacramento River. Large campground in the flat waterways maze of the Sacramento-San Joaquin confluence. Amenities: shady sites; swimming; boat ramp; fishing; windsurfing; visitor center, river wildlife; showers; and dump station. Over 140 sites total, including 32 berthing slips for boat-in camping and 8 walk-in sites. 6 group camps, maximum 30 people. Popular in summer. For more information: 17645 Highway 160, Rio Vista, CA 94571, (916) 777-6671.

Sandy Beach County Park, located a mile south of the Highway 12 bridge (3 miles north of Brannan Island State Recreation Area) on the northern banks of the Sacramento River. Delta world. Amenities: swimming; boat ramp; fishing; showers; full hook-ups; and dump station. 42 sites total. $12/night, $15/night with full hook-ups. For more information: 2333 Beach Drive, Rio Vista, CA 94571, (707) 274-2097.

SANTA CRUZ COUNTY AND VICINITY

Santa Cruz County State Beaches

Lining the shore of northern Monterey Bay, four state beaches provide developed campgrounds, ready beach access, and easy accessibility to Highway 1 and surrounding amenities. Reservations can be made up to seven months in advance by calling (800) 444-7275 or going online at www.reserveamerica.com. From north to south, the four state beach campgrounds are:

New Brighton State Beach, located just east of Santa Cruz adjacent to Highway 1 in Capitola. Closed for renovations until 2004. Amenities: 112 developed campsites on a bluff overlooking northern Monterey Bay; hike/bike site; interpretive nature trails; showers; dump station. $12/night. Very popular in the summer—reserve well in advance. For more information: New Brighton State Beach, 1500 Park Avenue, Capitola, CA 95010, (831) 464-6329.

Seacliff State Beach, located adjacent to New Brighton, access via State Park Drive from Highway 1. Amenities: 26 very popular beachfront RV sites with full hook-ups, *no tent camping.* Fully reserved seven months in advance. Nearby fishing pier and concrete ship. $18/night. For more information: Sea Cliff State Beach, 201 State park Dr., Aptos, CA 95001, (831) 685-6500.

Manresa State Beach, located west of Watsonville, access from Highway 1 just south of Aptos via San Andreas Road. Amenities: 63 walk-in sites; plenty of ocean and sand. $12/night. Park closed from December to mid-March. Least crowded of the state beach campgrounds but reservations are recommended summer weekends. For more information: 205 Manresa Beach Rd., La Selva, CA 95076, (831) 761-1795.

Sunset State Beach, located west of Watsonville, 16 miles south of Santa Cruz. Access from Highway 1 via Mar Monte, San Andreas Road south, and Sunset Beach Road. Amenities: 90 developed campsites sheltered from wind by pines and sand dunes; showers; 7 miles of beach. $12/night. One group site (maximum 50 people), $75. Reserve well in advance for summer weekends. For more information: 201 Sunset Beach Rd., Watsonville, CA 95076, (831) 763-7063.

Other Destinations

The Forest of Nisene Marks State Park, located east of Santa Cruz and 4 miles inland from Aptos on Aptos Creek Road, protects more than 10,000 acres of redwood forest regenerating from intensive logging in the late 19th and early 20th centuries. Bordering the San Andreas Fault, the park's topography is rugged and riddled with faults—the epicenter of the 1989 Loma Prieta quake was within park boundaries. West Ridge Trail Camp is located in the heart of the park and offers the opportunity for overnight trips into the redwood backcountry. Depending on route, the hike is a minimum 10-mile round-trip with roughly 2000 feet of elevation gain. The camp also can be reached by bike, a 14-mile round-trip journey on Aptos Creek Fire Road. Water is not provided at camp. No campfires. 6 sites. For more information and trail camp reservations call (831) 763-7062.

Fremont Peak State Park, located atop a prominent mountain with incredible views of the entire Monterey Bay. Access via Highway 156 in San Juan Bautista on San Juan Canyon Road (Hwy. G1). Small park with twisting access road, no vehicles over 25 feet permitted. Amenities: 19 first-come, first-serve sites and 6 reservable sites, $7. One group site, Bill Flat, maximum 100 people, $50. Adjacent to astronomical observatory with regular summer programs. For more information: Fremont Peak State Park, 221 Garden Rd., Monterey, CA 93940, (831) 623-4255. Observatory schedule and information: (831) 623-2465, www.fpoa.net.

Laguna Seca Regional Park, located just 8 miles east of Monterey on the north side of Highway 68. Located near all the attractions of the Monterey area and adjacent to a world-class auto and motorcycle raceway. Not wilderness. RV hook-ups, tent camping. For reservations call (888) 588-CAMP or (831) 755-4899. For more information: Monterey County Park District, Box 5279, Salinas, CA 93915-5279, (888) 588-2267, www.co.monterey.ca.us/parks.

AND GOING EVER FARTHER . . .

Recommended Destinations Approximately
2-3 Hours from Most of the Bay Area

North: The Sonoma and Mendocino Coast—Salt Point, Van Damme, Russian Gulch, MacKerricher, and Manchester State Parks, and Gualala Point County Park campgrounds; Lake Sonoma drive-in and boat-in camping; Clear Lake State Park campground; Cache Creek BLM Corridor backpack from

Highway 29; Snow Mountain Wilderness in Mendocino National Forest; Colusa Sacramento River SRA campground and nearby wildlife refuges. . . .

South: Pinnacles National Monument's wildflowers, epic geology, and private campground; The Big Sur coast—Andrew Molera, Pfeiffer-Big Sur, and Limekiln state parks and campgrounds; endless backpacking deep in the Santa Lucia Mountains within 160,000-acre Ventana Wilderness; campgrounds on Nacimiento Road. . . .

Almost Camping: Hostels of the Bay Area

Tucked away in beautiful locations, seven hostels provide affordable accommodations in the midst of the Bay Area outdoors. Hostels provide a roof overhead, kitchen facilities, shared bunkrooms, hot showers, hiking trails winding from the front door, and a social atmosphere filled with international voices. Consider it luxury camping with a traveler's twist.

You'll need a car to reach most hostels, and bring a sleeping bag or sheets and blankets to comfort the bare mattresses provided. Most hostels close down completely during the day—all guests must vacate the premises and no check-in possible. Alcohol, smoking, and dogs are prohibited. With the exception of West Point Inn, all hostels are part of the Hostelling International (HI) network; membership ($25) saves you $3/night at most hostels, as well as other benefits. Learn more about HI and the hostels of the Bay Area at www.norcalhostels.org.

THE NORTH BAY

Marin Headlands Hostel, located in two turn-of-the-century buildings in former Fort Barry in the heart of the Marin Headlands. Offers front-door access to the trails and attractions of the Headlands, easy striking distance to San Francisco, and immaculate facilities in a charming building. For driving directions and more information about the area see the camping chapter *The Marin Headlands.* 104 beds, 5 private rooms. Dorm beds $15/night, private rooms $45. Towels ($.50) and sheets ($1) available for rent. Open year-round but closed 10 A.M.–3:30 P.M. daily. A small daily chore is requested of all guests. Reservations necessary weekends year-round and weekdays in summer. For more information: Fort Barry, Building 941, Sausalito, CA 94965-2607,

(415) 331-2777, www.headlandshostel.homestead.com, email: marinhdl@nor-calhostels.org.

West Point Inn, located on the flanks of Mt. Tamalpais in the last remaining structures of the Mount Tamalpais and Muir Woods Railroad (1896-1930). A hike-in backcountry lodge rather than hostel, a stay here requires walking 2 miles from the parking lot at Pantoll Ranger Station. Epic views over the Bay Area and front-door access to hiking and biking trails. It's rustic: shared bathrooms, no electricity, and guests need to bring sleeping bag, food, and lighting. A fully-equipped communal kitchen is available. 7 private rooms in the main lodge and 5 private cabins perched on the adjacent hillside. $30/night for adults, $15/night under 18. Open Tuesday-Saturday year-round. Closed Sunday and Monday nights. For general information call (415) 388-9955 11 A.M.–7 P.M. Tuesday-Friday; 24-hour reservation line: (415) 646-0702.

Point Reyes Hostel, located just off Limantour Road on the northern edge of Philip Burton Wilderness (see the backpacking chapter *Point Reyes National Seashore* for more information on the area). Surrounded by rolling hills, the isolated hostel sits square in the middle of the area burned by the 1995 Vision fire (it was saved only by burying the entire building in fire-retardant foam) and is less than 2 miles from the long, sandy stretch of Limantour Beach. An excellent layover or starting/ending point for hiking and backpacking trips into the wilderness. 40 beds in four dorm rooms. One family room for those with children 5 or younger. $14/night. Towels ($1) and sheets ($1) available for rent.

View from West Point Inn

Open year-round but closed 10 A.M.–4:30 P.M. daily. A small daily chore is required of all guests. Reservations necessary weekends year-round and weekdays in summer. For more information: Box 247, Point Reyes Station, CA 94956, (415) 663-8811.

THE PACIFIC COAST

Point Montara Lighthouse Hostel, located in historic structures surrounding the quaintly beautiful Point Montara Lighthouse (est. 1875) on Highway 1, 25 miles south of San Francisco and 7 miles north of Half Moon Bay. Accessible via *public transportation* on SamTrans Bus 294 from the Hillsdale CalTrain station (for more info: (800) 660-4287, www.samtrans.com). Great ocean views and good tidepools await along 4 miles of protected coast at nearby James Fitzgerald Marine Reserve. Also, numerous hiking trails wind up adjacent Montara Mountain. 45 total beds in 4 bunkhouses, 5 private rooms. Dorm beds: HI members $15/night, non-members $18/night. Private rooms: HI members $45/night, non-members $51/night. Open year-round. Closed 10 A.M.–4:30 P.M. daily. Reservations necessary weekends year-round and weekdays April-September. Private rooms are booked up far in advance. For more information: Box 737, Montara, CA 94037-9999, (650) 728-7177, email: himontara@norcalhostels.org.

Pigeon Point Lighthouse Hostel, located on an isolated rocky point just off Highway 1, 20 miles south of Half Moon Bay and 27 miles north of Santa Cruz. Housed in historic Coast Guard buildings below 115-foot Pigeon Point Lighthouse and on top of 35-foot cliffs pounded by the Pacific Ocean. The hostel is remote, scenic, and unique. While no parkland surrounds the hostel, Butano and Año Nuevo state parks are nearby, state beaches line Highway 1, and most of the Santa Cruz Mountains are readily accessible for a day trip. 53 beds, 4 private rooms for 2-3 people, family room for those with small children. A hot tub is available for guest use. Dorm beds: HI members $15/night, non-members $18/night. Private rooms: HI members $45/night, non-members $51/night. Towels ($.50) and sheets ($1) available for rent. Open year-round. Closed 10 A.M.–4:30 P.M. daily. Reservations necessary weekends year-round and weekdays in summer. Private rooms are booked up four months in advance. For more information: 210 Pigeon Point Rd., Pesacdero, CA 94060, (650) 879-0633.

THE SANTA CRUZ MOUNTAINS

Sanborn Hostel, located in Sanborn County Park on the eastern slope of the Santa Cruz Mountains. Housed in a large building of logs and sandstone built in 1908 as the summer cabin for the 1st Superior Court judge of Santa Clara

County. The hostel is enveloped by redwood forest and offers heart-pumping hikes in the surrounding park. See the camping chapter *Sanborn County Park* for directions and park information. 39 dorm beds. HI members $10/night, non-members $12/night. Towels ($.25) and sheets ($.50) available for rent. Open year-round. Closed 9 A.M.–5 P.M. daily. Reservations recommended weekends year-round and weekdays in spring, late summer, and fall. For more information: 15808 Sanborn Rd., Saratoga, CA 95070, (408) 741-0166, www.sanbornparkhostel.org.

Hidden Villa Hostel, located in a secluded, 1600-acre non-profit educational farm and wilderness preserve in the eastern foothills of the Santa Cruz Mountains above Los Altos Hills. The first youth hostel opened west of the Hudson River (1937), this is a relaxed destination with heated bathroom floors amid a working organic farm and has nearby uphill hiking trails leading toward the summit of Black Mountain and views of the South Bay. See the backpacking chapter *The Traverse* for driving directions and more hiking information. 34 beds spread among a main bunkhouse, plus several small, adjacent cabins, including two private cabins for two people. Dorm beds: HI members $15/night, non-members $18/night. Private cabins: $30 for one person, $36 for two; non-members $41. Also available is Josephine's Retreat, a separate and secluded rental cabin for two tucked on the valley slopes, $125/night weekends, $45/night weekdays. Hostel open September-May. Closed 11 A.M.–4 P.M. daily. Popular with school groups, reservations always recommended. For more information: 26870 Moody Road, Los Altos Hills, CA 94022, (650) 949-8648, www.hiddenvilla.org, email: hostel@hiddenvilla.org.

APPENDIX D

Private Campgrounds and RV Parks of the Bay Area

If public campgrounds are full, or you have an RV, here are your options. These private enterprises run for profit and not "wilderness experience." They offer a range of facilities. With more amenities, prices are higher ($20/night and up); expect to pay more than park campgrounds. Tent camping opportunities will be specifically mentioned, otherwise sites are for RVs only. Contact private campgrounds directly for current prices and information.

THE NORTH BAY

Marin County

　　Marin RV Park, 2140 Redwood Hwy., Greenbrae, CA 94904, 1-888-461-5199. Just south of San Rafael. *Tent camping* on gravel. 89 sites with full hook-ups.

　　Olema Ranch Campground, 10155 Hwy. 1, Box #175, Olema, CA 94950, (800) 655-CAMP (2267). 31 sites with full hook-ups. 58 sites with partial hook-ups. 175 tent sites. *Tent camping* $20/night. Only option for Point Reyes area if nearby parks are full.

　　Novato RV Park, 1530 Armstrong Ave., Novato, CA 94945, 1-800-733-6787, www.novatorvpark.com. 69 sites with full hook-ups.

　　Petaluma KOA, 20 Rainsville Rd., Petaluma, CA 94952, 1-800-992-2267, email: sfkoa@aol.com. 112 sites with full hook-ups, 62 sites with partial hook-ups. 108 tent sites. *Tent camping* $30/night.

Olema Ranch Campground

The Sonoma Coast

Bodega Bay RV Park, 2000 Highway 1, Bodega Bay, CA 94923, www.bodegabayrvpark.com, 72 total sites, 49 with full hook-ups.

Porto Bodega Marina, 1500 Bay Flat Road, Bodega bay, CA 94923, (707) 875-2354, 58 total sites, 41 with full hook-ups.

The Russian River Region (East to West)

Mirabel Trailer Park and Campground, 7600 River Road, Forestville, CA 95436, (707) 887-2383. *Tent camping.* 116 RV/tent sites.

River Bend Campground, 11820 River Road, Forestville, CA 95436, (707) 887-7662, reservations 1-800-877-0816. *Tent camping.* 23 tent-only sites, 44 RV-only sites.

Schoolhouse Canyon Campground, 12600 River Road, Guerneville, CA 95446, (707) 869-2311. *Tent camping.* 39 RV/tent sites.

The Willows, 15905 River Rd., Guerneville, CA 95446, 1-800-953-2828, www.willowsrussianriver.com. *Tent camping* $18/night.

Riens Sandy Beach, 22900 Sylvan Way, Monte Rio, CA 95462, (707) 865-2102. *Tent camping.* 4 RV/tent sites, 11 RV-only sites.

Casini Family Ranch Campground, 22855 Moscow Road, Duncan Mills, CA 95430, (707) 865-2255, reservations 1-800-451-8400. *Tent camping.* 225 total sites. Full hook-ups available.

Lake Berryesa and Points East

Pleasure Cove Resort, 6100 Highway 128, Napa, CA 94558, (707) 966-2172, www.vacanet.com/pleasure.htm. *Tent camping.* Electrical hook-ups available.

Steele Park Resort, 1605 Steele Canyon Road, Napa, CA 94558, (707) 966-2123, reservations 1-800-522-2123, www.steelepark.com. *Tent camping.* 48 RV/tent sites. Full hook-ups available.

Spanish Flat Resort, 4290 Knoxville Road, Napa, CA 94558, (707) 966-7700, www.spanishflatresort.com. *Tent camping.* 120 RV/tent sites.

Lake Berryesa Marina Resort, 5800 Knoxville Road, Napa, CA 94558, (707) 966-2161, www.lakebarryessa.com. *Tent camping.* 50 RV sites with full hook-ups.

Rancho Monticello Resort, 6590 Knoxville Road, Napa, CA 94558, (707) 966- 2188, www.ranchomonticelloresort.com. *Tent camping.* 50 RV/tent sites, full hook-ups available.

Putah Creek Park, 7600 Knoxville Road, Napa, CA 94558, (707) 966-2116, reservations (707) 966-0794. *Tent camping.* 200 tent-only sites, 55 RV-only sites. Full hook-ups available.

Gandy Dancer RV Park, 4933 Midway Road, Vacaville, CA 95688, (707) 446-7679. 51 sites with full hook-ups.

Neil's Vineyard RV Park, 4985 Midway Road, Vacaville, CA 95688, (707) 447-8797, www.neilsvineyard.com. Full hook-ups available.

Tradewinds RV Park, 239 Lincoln Rd. West, Vallejo, CA 94590, (707) 643-4000. 78 sites with full hook-ups.

SAN FRANCISCO, SANTA CRUZ MOUNTAINS, AND SURROUNDING PENINSULA (NORTH TO SOUTH)

Candlestick RV Park, 650 Gilman Ave., San Francisco, CA 94124, 1-800-888-CAMP. 120 sites with full hook-ups. Closest to San Francisco.

Onterra San Francisco RV Park (formerly *Pacific Park RV Resort*), 700 Palmetto Ave., Pacifica, CA 94044, (650) 355-7093, www.sanfranciscorv.com. 257 sites with full hook-ups.

Pillar Point RV Park, 4000 Cabrillo Highway, (650) 712-9277. 74 sites, including 50 with full hook-ups.

Pelican Point RV Park, 1001 Miramontes Rd., Half Moon Bay, CA 94019, (650) 726-9100. 75 sites with full hook-ups.

Costanoa Coastal Lodge & Camp, 2001 Rossi Rd. at Hwy. 1, Pescadero, CA 94060, (800) 738-7477, www.costanoa.com, email: info@costanoa.com. *Tent camping* $30/night. Luxury cabins, RV sites, and tent sites.

Trailer Villa RV Park, 3401 E. Bayshore Rd., Redwood City, CA 94063, (800) 366-7880. 90 sites with full hook-ups.

Saratoga Springs, 22801 Big Basin Way, Saratoga, CA 95070, (408) 867-9999. *Tent camping* $25/night. 28 sites with full hook-ups, 23 tent sites.

Carbonero Creek RV Park, 917 Disc Dr., Scotts Valley, CA 95066, (800) 546-1288. *Tent camping.* 102 sites with full hook-ups, 8 sites with partial hook-ups.

Smithwoods Resort, 4770 Highway 9, Felton, CA 95018, (831) 335-4321. 80 sites with full hook-ups.

Cotillion Gardens RV Park, 300 Old Big Trees Rd., Felton, CA 95018, (831) 335-7669. *Tent camping.* 80 sites, 59 with full hook-ups, 19 with partial hook-ups.

Santa Vida RV Park and Campground, 1611 Branciforte Dr., Santa Cruz, CA 95065, (831) 425-1945. *Tent camping.* 43 sites with full hook-ups, 4 sites with partial hook-ups.

EAST OF THE BAY

The East Bay and Delta Regions

Audiss RV Park, 5828 El Dorado Ave., El Cerrito, CA 94530, (510) 525-3435. 28 sites with full hook-ups.

Trailer Haven, 2399 East 14th St., San Leandro, CA 94577, (510) 357-3235. 39 sites with full hook-ups.

Delta Marina RV Park, 100 Marina Drive, Rio Vista, CA 94571, (707) 374-2315. 24 sites with full hook-ups.

Duck Island RV Park, 16814 Highway 160, Rio Vista, CA 94571, (916) 777-6663, reservations 1-800-825-3898. 21 sites.

Eddo's Harbor and RV Park, 19530 Sherman Island/E. Levee Road, Rio Vista, CA 94571, (925) 757-5314, www.eddosresort.com. *Tent camping.* 12 tent sites, 44 RV-only sites with full hook-ups.

Delta Marina RV Resort, 100 Marina Drive, Rio Vista, CA 94571, (707) 374-2315. 25 sites with full hook-ups.

The South Bay

Parkway Lakes RV Park, 100 Ogier Ave., Morgan Hill, CA 95037, (408) 779-0244. 104 sites. Full hook-ups available.

Uvas Pines RV Park, 13210 Uvas Rd., Morgan Hill, CA 95037, (408) 779-3417. 40 sites with full hook-ups.

Maple Leaf RV Park, 15200 Monterey Rd., Morgan Hill, CA 95037, (800) 797-1818. 270 sites with full hook-ups.

Oak Dell Park, 12790 Watsonville Rd., Morgan Hill, CA 95037, (408) 779-7779. 57 sites with full hook-ups.

Selected Sources and Recommended Reading

ATLASES

Benchmark California Road &Recreation Atlas. 2nd ed. Benchmark Maps, 2000.

Northern California Atlas & Gazetter. 4th ed. Yarmouth, ME: DeLorme, 1998.

REGIONAL MAPS (INDIVIDUAL PARK MAPS REFERENCED IN TEXT)

—————, *Peninsula Parklands Map.* 3rd edition. Palo Alto, CA: The Trail Center, 2000.

—————, *Santa Cruz Mountains Trail Maps 1&2.* Los Altos, CA: Sempervirens Fund, 1999.

—————, *Trail Map of the Central Peninsula.* Palo Alto, CA: The Trail Center, 2001.

—————, *Trail Map of the Southern Peninsula.* Palo Alto, CA: The Trail Center, 1996.

Olmsted, Gerald. *A Rambler's Guide to the Trails of the East Bay Hills: Central Section.* 3rd ed. Berkeley, CA: The Olmsted & Bros. Map Co., 1995.

Olmsted, Gerald. *A Rambler's Guide to the Trails of the East Bay Hills: Northern Section.* 3rd ed. Berkeley, CA: The Olmsted & Bros. Map Co., 1995.

Olmsted, Gerald. *A Rambler's Guide to the Trails of Mt. Tamalpais and the Marin Headlands.* 8th ed. Berkeley, CA: The Olmsted & Bros. Map Co., 1998.

FLORA AND FAUNA

Evarts, John, and Marjorie Popper, editors. *Coast Redwood: A Natural and Cultural History.* Los Olivos, CA: Cachuma Press, 2001.

Fisher, Chris and Joseph Morlan. *Birds of San Francisco and the Bay Area.* Redmond, WA: Lone Pine Publishing, 1996.

Johnson, Sharon G., Pamela C. Muick, Bruce M. Pavlik, and Marjorie Popper. *Oaks of California.* Los Olivos, CA: Cachuma Press, 1991.

Johnston, Verna R. *California Forests and Woodlands.* Berkeley, CA: University of California Press, 1994.

Keator, Glenn, Ruth M. Heady, and Valerie R. Winemiller. *Pacific Coast Fern Finder.* Berkeley, CA: Nature Study Guild, 1981.

Lanner, Ronald M. *Conifers of California.* Los Olivos, CA: Cachuma Press, 1999.

Lederer, Roger. *Pacific Coast Bird Finder.* Berkeley, CA: Nature Study Guild, 1977.

Little, Elbert L. *National Audubon Society Field Guide to North American Trees, Western Region.* New York: Alfred A. Knopf, 1998.

Lyons, Kathleen, and Mary Beth Cooney-Lazaneo, *Plants of the Coast Redwood Region.* Boulder Creek, CA: Looking Press, 1988.

McMinn, Howard, and Evelyn Maino. *An Illustrated Manual of Pacific Coast Trees.* 2nd ed. Berkeley, CA: University of California Press, 1981.

Peterson, Roger Tory. *Western Birds.* New York: Houghton Mifflin, 1990.

Spellenberg, Richard. *National Audubon Society Field Guide to North American Wildflowers, Western Region.* New York: Alfred A. Knopf, 1998.

Sims, Lee. *Shrubs of Henry W. Coe State Park.* 2nd ed. Morgan Hill, CA: Pine Ridge Association, 1997.

Stuart, John, and John Sawyer. *Trees and Shrubs of California.* Berkeley, CA: University of California Press, 2001.

Watts, Phoebe. *Redwood Region Flower Finder.* Berkeley, CA: Nature Study Guild, 1979.

Watts, Tom. *Pacific Coast Tree Finder.* Berkeley, CA: Nature Study Guild, 1973.

GEOLOGY

Alt, David D., and Donald W. Hyndman. *Roadside Geology of Northern California.* 2nd ed. Missoula, MT: Mountain Press Publishing Company, 2000.

Galloway, Alan J. *Geology of the Point Reyes Peninsula.* Bulletin 202, California Division of Mines and Geology, 1977.

Harden, Deborah R. *California Geology.* New Jersey: Prentice-Hall, 1998.

Konigsmark, Ted. *Geologic Trips: San Francisco and the Bay Area.* GeoPress, 1998.

McPhee, John. *Assembling California.* New York: Farrar, Straus and Giroux, 1993.

USGS. *Geologic Map of California.* 1:750,000. 1977.

Wahrhaftig, Clyde. *A Streetcar to Subduction and Other Plate Tectonic Trips by Public Transport in San Francisco.* Revised ed. Washington, D.C.: American Geophysical Union, 1984.

REGIONAL INFORMATION

————, *California Coastal Resource Guide.* California Coastal Commission and Berkeley, CA: University of California Press, 1987.

————, *California Coastal Access Guide.* 4th ed. California Coastal Commission and Berkeley, CA: University of California Press, 1991.

————, *Golden Gate National Recreation Area Guide to the Parks.* San Francisco, CA: Golden Gate National Parks Association, 1995.

Arnot, Phil. *Point Reyes: Secret Places and Magic Moments.* San Carlos, CA: Wide World Publishing/Tetra, 1992.

Briggs, Winslow. *The Trails of Henry W. Coe State Park: Coe Ranch Section.* Morgan Hill, CA: Pine Ridge Association, 2000.

Browning, Peter, editor. *The Discovery of San Francisco Bay: The Portola Expedition of 1769-1770.* Lafayette, CA: Great West Books, 1992.

Cassady, Stephen. *Spanning the Gate.* Santa Rosa, CA: Squarebooks, 1986.

Dunham, Tacy. *Marin Headlands Trail Guide.* Novato, CA: Cottonwood Press, 1989.

Evens, Jules. *The Natural History of the Point Reyes Peninsula.* Point Reyes National Seashore Association, 1993.

Gilliam, Harold and Ann Lawrence. *Marin Headlands: Portals of Time.* San Francisco, CA: Golden Gate National Park Association, 1993.

Lorentzen, Bob, and Richard Nichols. *Hiking the California Coastal Trail: Volume 1.* Mendocino, CA: Bored Feet Publications, 1998.

Lowry, Alexander, and Denzil Verardo. *Big Basin.* Los Altos, CA: Sempervirens Fund, 1973.

Margolin, Malcolm. *The East Bay Out.* Revised ed. Berkeley, CA: Heyday Books, 1988.

Margolin, Malcolm. *The Ohlone Way: Indian Life in the San Francisco-Monterey Bay Area.* Berkeley, CA: Heyday Books, 1978.

Paddison, Joshua. *A World Transformed—Firsthand Accounts of California Before the Gold Rush.* Berkeley, CA: Heyday Books, 1999.

Rusmore, Jean. *The Bay Area Ridge Trail: Ridgetop Adventures Above San Francisco Bay.* Berkeley, CA: Wilderness Press, 1995.

Rusmore, Jean, Betsy Crowder, and Frances Spangle. *South Bay Trails: Outdoor Adventures in & Around Santa Clara Valley.* 3rd ed. Berkeley, CA: Wilderness Press, 2001.

Rusmore, Jean, Betsy Crowder, and Frances Spangle. *Peninsula Trails: Outdoor Adventures on the San Francisco Peninsula.* 3rd ed. Berkeley, CA: Wilderness Press, 1997.

Sprout, Jerry & Janine. *Golden Gate Trailblazer.* Markleeville, CA: Diamond Valley Company, 2001.

Taber, Tom. *The Santa Cruz Mountains Trail Book.* 8th ed. San Mateo, CA: The Oak Valley Press, 1998.

Vanderwerf, Barbara. *The Coastside Trail Guidebook.* El Granada, CA: Gum Tree Lane Books, 1995.

Weintraub, David. *East Bay Trails: Outdoor Adventures in Alameda and Contra Costa County.* Berkeley, CA: Wilderness Press, 1998.

Weintraub, David. *North Bay Trails: Outdoor Adventures in Marin, Napa, and Sonoma Counties.* Berkeley, CA: Wilderness Press, 1999.

Weintraub, David. *Monterey Bay Trails: Outdoor Adventures in Monterey, Santa Cruz, and San Benito Counties.* Berkeley, CA: Wilderness Press, 2001.

White, Peter. *The Farallon Islands, Sentinels of the Golden Gate.* San Francisco, CA: Scottwall Associates, 1995.

Whitnah, Dorothy L. *Point Reyes.* 3rd ed. Berkeley, CA: Wilderness Press, 1997.

Yaryan, Willie, and Denzil & Jennie Verardo. *The Sempervirens Story: A Century of Preserving California's Ancient Redwood Forest.* Los Altos, CA: Sempervirens Fund, 2000.

APPENDIX E

Index

INDEX

INDEX

INDEX OF MAPS

Overview Maps

Campground Maps

Topographic Backpacking Maps

Wilderness Press covers the San Francisco Bay Area

Peninsula Trails
Outdoor Adventures on the San Francisco Peninsula

The only guide that covers all the parks and open spaces from San Bruno Mountain to Saratoga Gap. Includes the vitally useful "Trails for all Seasons and Reasons," so you can choose just the right trail.

ISBN 0-89997-197-0

South Bay Trails
Outdoor Adventures in & around Santa Clara Valley

Explore Silicon Valley's 125,000 acres of public open space, from San Jose to the Santa Cruz Mountains. Over 100 routes and 568 miles of trails in the southern San Francisco Bay Area are described.

ISBN 0-89997-284-5

East Bay Trails
Outdoor Adventures in Alameda & Contra Costa Counties

53 hikes in 31 parks in the East Bay parklands offer respite and recreation, from the Carquinez Strait to the Ohlone Wilderness, San Francisco Bay to Mt. Diablo.

ISBN 0-89997-213-6

North Bay Trails
Outdoor Adventures in Marin, Napa, & Sonoma Counties

Includes perennial favorites such as Mt. Tamalpais and Point Reyes plus lesser known gems in mountains, meadows and coastlines just north of San Francisco Bay.

ISBN 0-89997-236-5

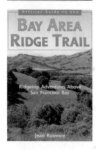

Bay Area Ridge Trail
Ridgetop Adventures Above San Francisco Bay

This official guide covers the 230 completed miles of the planned 425-mile recreation trail encircling the San Francisco Bay. Includes trailhead access, on-the-trail directions, side trips, facilities, and maps.

ISBN 0-89997-280-2

For ordering information, contact your local bookseller or Wilderness Press, www.wildernesspress.com